Policies and Practices in Evening Colleges, 1971

by

The Research Committee of the
Association of University Evening Colleges

William A. Hoppe

Editor and Research Director

The Scarecrow Press, Inc.
Metuchen, N. J.   1972

ISBN 0-8108-0452-2

Library of Congress Catalog Card Number 71-175929

Table of Contents

3

4

5

6

PART X: STUDENT RECRUITMENT

INDIVIDUAL COLLEGES AND SCHOOLS
RESPONDING TO SURVEY

*indicates AUEC member institutions

9

10

Preface

This survey of "Policies and Practices in Various
Evening Colleges and Divisions of Colleges and Universities
in the United States" was made by the Research Committee
of the Association of University Evening Colleges in the
interest of evening divisions and colleges throughout the
United States.

Questionnaires were sent to community colleges,
senior colleges and universities throughout the United States
and Canada--including the entire membership of the Association of University Evening Colleges and additional colleges
and universities. A total of 146 institutions responded including the following:

State Universities	47	Church-Related Institutions	22
State Colleges	16	Private Colleges	14
Community Colleges	17	Private Universities	23
Private Institutions	7	Total	146

As Chairman of the 1970-71 Research Committee, I
wish to thank each evening division director and evening college Dean who responded to our questionnaire; without this
cooperation this study would not have been possible. Three
new sections have been added to the 1969 study published by
Scarecrow Press: 1) Organizational Structure, 2) Educational
Television Programs, 3) Non-Credit Programs. These are
Parts Six, Seven and Eight of the present work. In addition,
a number of additional educational institutions are included in
this study.

The study is intended to assist those institutions that
are planning to organize an evening division, or a division
of continuing education by using this publication as a refer-
ence--it includes admission policies, fees, faculty and faculty
recruitment, scheduling, organizational structures, non-
credit programs, etc., found in community colleges, senior
colleges and universities of various sizes. The study should

13

also be of interest to institutions planning to broaden their programs for adults in the evening division.

I wish to thank also the members of the AUEC Research Committee for the advice and assistance in completing the study. The members of the Executive Committee of AUEC, including our President, Dr. Joseph P. Goddard, should receive credit for their wholehearted support in approving this research. Finally, we wish to acknowledge the grant which was awarded by the Research Committee of the University of South Alabama to support this study.

Conclusions

This study includes ten general parts: I. Admission Policies; II. Terminology; III. Fees; IV. Faculty and Faculty Recruitment; V. Scheduling and Research; VI. Organizational Structure; VII. Educational Television Programs; IX. General Policies; and X. Student Recruitment.

I. ADMISSION POLICIES

The results show that most institutions have flexible admission policies for adults to allow them to take credit courses as part-time degree students of "special" or non-degree students. A large percent of the institutions allow adults to register up to the day of registration or within a week of registration--many allow adults to register after classes have begun.

a. 93 institutions (71%) have no deadline for applications or allow adults to register within one week of the date of registration.

b. 121 institutions (89%) allow adults to register for credit courses without submitting a transcript including 18% provisional registration. In most instances, students are tentatively classified as "special" or "non-degree" students who must be matriculated as degree students after completing a certain number of hours with satisfactory grades.

c. Approximately 90% of the institutions will allow an adult to register as a "special" or "non-degree" student--and students may take from 8 hours to an indefinite number of hours before being required to matriculate as degree students.

d. 69 institutions (70%) require a high school transcript or GED (some stipulating age) for admission as a "special" or "non-degree" student. 24 institutions (11%) admit students as "special" students if they have "sufficient background to pass the course" or else list "no specific requirements" for entrance.

15

e.   55 institutions (37%) require only high school graduation (no specific grade point average) or GED for admission as a regular degree student.   28 institutions (20%) require high school graduation with satisfactory grades or a certain grade point average.

f.   75 institutions (53%) allow students to register for credit courses by mail.

g.   94 institutions (71%) allow students to enter the institution as degree students without being required to take a standard examination such as the ACT or CEEB.

h.   38 institutions (35%) offer special degree programs for adults--37 additional institutions are considering offering special degree programs in the near future.

i.   In 57 institutions the Director or Dean of the Evening Division or College together with the Faculty Admissions Committee formulates the admission policies.   In some instances (particularly in smaller institutions), the Director or Dean performs this task.

j.   116 institutions (96%) allow day and evening students to enroll in the same classes.   In 27 of these institutions, special permission is necessary.

k.   85 institutions (60%) do not schedule an orientation program for evening students; 31 institutions do have orientation programs for evening students--usually just before or during registration or the first week of classes.

l.   23 institutions have an Evening Advisory Committee.

II.   TERMINOLOGY

49 titles are used to designate the division, school or college which serves the academic needs of adults attending evening classes.

III.   FEES

52 institutions charge lower fees for evening students; 62 institutions charge the same fees.   In some instances, the basic tuition is the same, but evening students are not

16

charged health fees, activity fees, etc. Refunds are on a percentage basis on a sliding scale for each week's attendance.

IV. FACULTY AND FACULTY RECRUITMENT

a. Most institutions have no fixed policies regarding the percentage of full-time faculty that teach evening classes. However, only 17 institutions (14%) have less than 25% full-time faculty teaching evening classes, and 24 institutions (20%) have 85 to 100% full-time faculty teaching evening classes.

b. The Dean or Director of the Evening Division or College is responsible for hiring full-time faculty members for teaching evening classes in 48 institutions (37%); 26 institutions (19%) delegate this responsibility to department chairmen in some instances.

c. 77 institutions (78%) reported that the Dean or Director could reject a faculty member assigned to teach evening classes. However, in only 52 institutions (37%) of those reporting, the Dean or Director can employ full or part-time faculty members to teach evening classes if the department chairman refuses to staff these classes.

d. 29% of the institutions answering this question employ full-time faculty members who teach exclusively in the evening.

e. Salary ranges for part-time faculty start at approximately $100 per quarter hour (or $300 for a 3-hour course) and extend to $550 per quarter hour (or $1650 for a 3-hour course) depending upon the resources of the institution, the qualifications of the instructor, etc.

f. Only 33 schools report that faculty meetings are held for evening faculty members--60 institutions do not schedule any faculty meetings in the evening.

g. 89 institutions (69%) allow faculty members to teach credit and/or non-credit courses as an overload for additional salary. In 36 of these institutions, overloads are restricted to one 3-hour course per term.

h. In some institutions, a very small percentage of the budget is spent for recruitment purposes. This ranges up to 10-12% in two or three isolated cases.

17

V. SCHEDULING

a. The Director or Dean of the Evening Division, School or College is responsible for the evening class schedule in 108 institutions (84%) of the total institutions reporting; in 43 institutions (or 21%), the department chairman submits an evening class schedule for approval by the Dean or Director. Consideration is given to student needs, faculty availability, space limitations, past class enrollments and budget limitations in making out the evening class schedule.

b. Research: it was gratifying to learn that some schools encourage research in adult education with the students and faculty in their institutions. Some research was reported in 35 colleges and universities.

c. 85 schools reported that evening classes compared favorably with day classes in terms of quality--some schools stated that, in their opinion, some evening classes were superior to day classes.

d. Part-time students are eligible for the Dean's list by completing a certain number of hours with a grade-point average ranging from 3.00 to 3.50 in 75 institutions.

e. The minimum number of students required to constitute a class ranged from 3 to 25 students. 54 institutions (45%) require a minimum of ten students; 38 institutions (34%) require 12 to 15 students, and 27 institutions (23%) require 3 to 9 students.

VI. ORGANIZATIONAL STRUCTURE

a. The size of the administrative staff in various institutions ranges from 1 to 55. It is interesting to discover that institutions with approximately the same size student body have administrative staffs that vary considerably, i. e. , two institutions reported administrative staffs of 10 members. One of these institutions has an evening enrollment of 1205 and the other institution 2211. However, one institution--the one with the smaller enrollment--offers non-credit programs, conferences and institutes, and educational TV courses supervised by the Dean and the Assistant Dean of Continuing Education--with the registration handled by the Evening College staff. The institution with the larger enrollment in evening classes offers no educational TV courses and very few non-credit courses. Another institution with

18

an administrative staff of 10, holds extension courses off-campus which requires a Director of Extension, and also has a Law Enforcement Institute with a Director who is responsible to the Dean of the College of Continuing Education. In some of the smaller institutions, one Director does all the scheduling, counseling, directs the non-credit programs and, in one instance, collects all the fees.

b. 13 out of 18 institutions that are branches of the state university system have administrative autonomy; only 7 out of 15 such institutions report that they have academic autonomy.

VII. EDUCATIONAL TELEVISION PROGRAMS

a. 44 institutions (32%) offer courses on Educational and/or commercial TV. In 31 of these institutions, students earn residence credit that may be applied on a degree. In 7 institutions, extension credit may be earned.

b. 17 institutions offer non-credit TV courses.

c. In 11 institutions that offer TV courses, the department or division or the instructor supervises the Education TV course offered.

d. Some institutions use either full-time or part-time instructors for TV courses: however, 21 institutions use both full-time and part-time instructors.

e. In 14 institutions, faculty members receive extra remuneration for teaching a course on educational TV; in 14 institutions, the faculty load is reduced.

f. In 14 colleges or universities, the admissions office and/or registrar handles registration for TV courses; in 9 institutions, the Office of the Division of Continuing Education handles the registration.

g. 25 institutions use standard procedures for registration; 10 institutions use mail registration for TV courses.

h. 19 institutions depend upon fees for paying the expenses of a TV course; other institutions either set aside an amount in their budget for educational TV courses or obtain a grant or special appropriation to finance TV programs.

i. Educational TV courses are scheduled at varied hours: in the early morning, in the middle or late afternoon, or in the evening.

VIII. NON-CREDIT COURSES

a. 111 institutions (77%) offer non-credit courses--99 in business; 88 in Arts and Sciences; 51 in Education; 52 in Engineering, and 47 in various other areas such as Law, Community Development.

b. 47 institutions have a budget for non-credit programs and 34 institutions have no budget allotment for this program. 93 institutions--with or without a budget--expect the non-credit courses to pay for themselves.

c. Faculty salaries for teaching a non-credit course range from $100 to $1500--depending upon the resources of the institution, the qualifications of the instructor, and/or the type and length of the course

d. 82 institutions offer conferences and institutes as part of their non-credit programs. Some colleges and universities offer as many as 250 to 300 conferences each year. Clinicians receive from $25 to $100 per day--again this depends upon the resources of the institution as well as the qualifications of the clinicians, travel expenses, etc.

IX. GENERAL

a. It was interesting to learn that 29 colleges and universities reported that credit and/or non-credit courses were being offered by their division or college in "storefront" locations off-campus for economically-deprived populations. Some of these programs are listed under the heading "Innovative Practices."

b. Students do participate in discussions regarding the academic program in 61 colleges and universities. In most cases (55 institutions) students are members of various college or university committees - academic affairs, curriculum, Senate, etc. In 14 institutions, students are contacted through questionnaires, surveys and personal conferences.

c. Some of the innovative practices used at 47 colleges and universities are exciting: the use of appointed or elected "ombudsmen" to whom a student can anonymously bring complaints or problems; student participation in Model City programs, special programs to assist the economically and educationally disadvantaged students - such as "Pride," or the off-campus course offered at Bakersfield College "Parent Education in the Ghetto."

    d. 67 institutions (58%) reported that their Evening Division or College is receiving adequate support; 77 institutions (66%) stated that their administration in their institutions recognized the need and importance of the adult education program.

X. STUDENT RECRUITMENT

    a. 100% of the institutions reporting use the newspaper extensively for publicity purposes; 98 institutions (71%) use programs and spot announcements on the radio, and 66 institutions use the medium of television for publicity purposes.

    b. 89 institutions reported that special brochures and/or contacts were prepared for industry and 72 institutions publicized their programs through personal contacts with civic clubs and other civic organizations.

Summary of the Survey

I. ADMISSION POLICIES

1. Do you have a deadline for application for admission to evening classes 93 vs. 50?
  yes   no

2. If so, what is the deadline?

One month 12   University of Windsor (Aug. 15), Brooklyn College of the City University of New York, University of Toronto (Aug. 15), Queensborough Community College, St. Joseph's College, University of Arkansas (Aug. 22), University of Toledo, Iona College, Suffolk University, Upsala College, Manatee Junior College (degree students), PMC Colleges.

1 to 3 mos. 10   New York University (June 1), The University of New Mexico, The University of Denver, University of Bridgeport, Sir George Williams University, Millard Fillmore College, Prince George's Community College, University of Washington, University of South Florida, Old Dominion College.

One week 9   LaSalle College, University of New Hampshire, Rollins College, Baylor University, St. Mary's Dominican College, St. Peter's College, Community College of Baltimore, Bradley University, Hofstra University.

Two weeks 8   Dutchess Community College, Drexel University, Iowa State University (10 days), Towson State College, San Diego Evening College, University of Tennessee at Chattanooga, Bryant College, Thomas More College.

Three weeks	5	County College of Morris, University of Southern Mississippi, University of Georgia, DeKalb College, Washburn University of Topeka.
4 to 6 mos.	5	The American University, Utica College-Syracuse University, Ohio State University, Nassau Community College, Springfield College.
No deadline (Some through late registration period)	83	Aurora College, American International College, Bakersfield College, Boston College, University of Cincinnati, University of California (Berkeley)-University Extension, University of Detroit (A & S, Bus. Adm.), Drake University, Drury College, East Carolina University, Fairleigh Dickinson University, George Washington University, Georgia Southern College, University of Hawaii, Harvard University-Extension, Idaho State University, Indiana Central College, Johns Hopkins University, Joint University Center-MSU/UT, University of Kentucky, Louisiana State University (Baton Rouge), Louisiana State University (New Orleans), University of Louisville, Loyola University (Chicago), Loyola University (New Orleans), University of Maine, Marietta College (Ohio), Manhattan Community College, Manatee Junior College, Miami-Dade Junior College, Miami University (Ohio), University of Minnesota, Mississippi State College for Women, University of Missouri, Memphis State University, Modesto Junior College, Mohawk Valley Community College, Northeastern University, University of Nebraska, North Carolina State University, University of North Carolina, Northern Illinois University, Northern Virginia Junior College, The New School, Orange County Community College, University of Oregon, The Pennsylvania State University, Pensacola Junior College, Post Junior College, Philadelphia College of Textiles, C. W. Post College, Pratt Institute, Purdue

23

University (Calumet Campus), Queensborough Community College, Rider College, Roanoke College, University of Rochester, Rochester Institute of Technology, Rockford College, Rockhurst College, Roosevelt University, Russel Sage College, Seminole Junior College, St. Louis University, Southwestern Michigan College, Springfield College, University of South Carolina, University of Southern Mississippi, Sacred Heart University, South Texas Junior College, St. Francis College, St. Joseph's College, University of Tampa, Temple University, University of Tennessee (Knoxville), University of Tennessee (Nashville), Texas Christian University, Trenton State College, Union College, University of Utah, Utah State University, Wayne State University, Western New England College, The University of West Florida, Utica College-Syracuse University, Washington University, Virginia Commonwealth University, College of William & Mary, Xavier University, University of Oklahoma.

3. May a student register for credit courses before transcripts are submitted?

97	27	25
yes	no	provisionally

4. May a student take a certain amount of work for credit as a non-matriculating student?

115	10	2
yes	no	provisionally

If so, how many hours may be taken?

10 - 20 <u>41</u>   University of South Carolina, Northern Illinois University, County College of Morris, University of West Florida, University of Oregon, Marietta College (Ohio), Louisiana State University (New Orleans), University of Detroit, Vir-

ginia Commonwealth University, University of Denver, The American University (12 hrs-grad), University of Southern Mississippi, Utah State University, Post Junior College, University of Rochester, Mohawk Valley Community College, Aurora College, Russell Sage College, Union College, Bryant College, Prince George's Community College (9), University of Miami (Ohio), Manatee Junior College, Rider College, Memphis State University, Manhattan Community College, Pratt Institute, Purdue University (Calumet Campus), DeKalb College, Rochester Institute of Technology, University of Tampa, College of William & Mary, American International College, Nassau Community College, University of Louisville, Miami University (Ohio), University of South Florida (grad), Georgia Southern College, Washburn University of Topeka, University of Nebraska-Omaha, Old Dominion College.

21 - 30 15 Centenary College of Louisiana, Drake University, Roanoke College (21), Roosevelt University, University of New Mexico, University of New Hampshire, University of Bridgeport, Indiana Central College, Suffolk University, University of Maine, Bradley University, Springfield College, C. W. Post College, Towson State College, PMC Colleges.

31 - 60 13 The American University (undergrad), Northeastern University, The Pennsylvania State University (of last 60 hrs.), The University of Georgia, Philadelphia College of Textiles, Temple University, Washington University (St. Louis), East Carolina University, Northern Virginia Community College, St. Peter's College, University of Utah, Western New England College, University of South Florida.

61 - 95 5 Drury College, University of Tennessee (Nashville), Joint University

25

Other	8	Center (MSU/UT), Utica College-Syracuse University, The University of Tennessee (Knoxville). Eight hours of work - must have a degree (LaSalle College); six courses for credit before matriculating (Univ. of Windsor); non-degree students must complete each course satisfactorily (Drexel University); two courses a semester - no limit (North Carolina State University); six hours (Xavier University); two courses - 8 hrs. - (Boston University); non-matriculated students may take 9 hrs. in the summer only (Louisiana State University - Baton Rouge).
Unlimited Hours	34	Dutchess Community College, George Washington University, Trenton State College, University of Kentucky, Idaho State University, Sacred Heart College, Bakersfield College, University of California-Berkeley, Orange County Community College, Iowa State University, Brooklyn College of the City University of New York, University of Nebraska, St. Joseph's College, University of Arkansas, St. Mary's Dominican College, Ohio State University, City College of New York, University of Minnesota, Upsala College, St. Louis University, Boston College, University of Maryland, Texas Christian University, Thomas More College, Loyola University (Chicago), University of Washington, Wichita State University, Wayne State University, Baldwin-Wallace College, Northwestern University, Fairleigh Dickinson University, Harvard University-Extension, Johns Hopkins University (16 for deg. student), Ohio State University.

5. What are the admission requirements for:

A. Non-matriculating or "special" students?

    (1) High school graduation, GED, and/or entrance examinations   <u>47</u>

Centenary College of Louisiana, County College of Morris, Marietta College (Ohio), Drake University, University of Detroit, Virginia Commonwealth University, George Washington University, Trenton State College, University of Southern Mississippi, Idaho State University, Sacred Heart University, Utah State University, University of Bridgeport, The Pennsylvania State University, Orange County Community College, Utica College-Syracuse University, Washington University (St. Louis), St. Joseph's College, East Carolina University, Suffolk University, Union College, Bryant College, Ohio State University, University of Cincinnati, University of Maine, Upsala College, Memphis State University, Manhattan Community College, University of Maryland, Thomas More College, Loyola University (New Orleans), The New School, Boston University, Loyola University (Chicago), Community College of Baltimore, Wichita State University, University of Tampa, Jefferson State Junior College, American International College, Nassau Community College, Hofstra University, Manatee Junior College, Fairleigh Dickinson University, Springfield College, C. W. Post College, Temple University (School of Bus. Adm.), University of Nebraska-Omaha, Ohio State University, Rockford College.

(2)   High school graduation, GED (some schools required % score) and, if applicable, a college transcript.   <u>4</u>

Northern Illinois University, Roanoke College, Brooklyn College of City University of New York, Old Dominion College.

(3)   Sufficient background to pass the course.   <u>17</u>

University of Denver (21 years.), Post Junior College, Mohawk Valley Community College, Northeastern University, Philadelphia College of Textiles, University of Missouri (21 yrs.), University of Nebraska, Aurora College, Russell Sage College, St. Mary's Dominican College (non-credit), Pratt Institute, Texas Christian University, Purdue University (Calumet Campus), Rochester Institute of Technology, Western New England

27

College, Community College of Baltimore (mature individual), Rochester Institute of Technology.

(4) 18 years - high school graduation   <u>5</u>
Bakersfield College (plus ability to profit), University of New Hampshire, Prince George's Community College, Miami-Dade Junior College, San Diego Evening College.

(5) 19 years - high school graduation   <u>1</u>
University of New Mexico

(6) 21 years and/or high school graduation   <u>10</u>
University of Tennessee (not working for degree), North Carolina State University (must not have been suspended within last three years), Joint University Center (MSU/UT), University of Utah (good standing), University of Tennessee at Chattanooga (plus experience), Mississippi State College for Women, East Tennessee State University, University of Tennessee at Knoxville, Northwestern University, Rider College (or G. I.).

(7) High school graduation, GED, or mature person with special needs   <u>2</u>
Rollins College, Xavier University (21 yrs.)

(8) Satisfactory high school record (some schools require specific GPA) and evidence of preparation   <u>2</u>
St. Peter's College, University of South Florida

(9) Statement of good standing from former institution   <u>7</u>
Drury College, Louisiana State University (New Orleans), The American University (21 yrs.), University of Arkansas, College of William & Mary, Louisiana State University (Baton Rouge), Washburn University of Topeka (or out of college one year).

(10) High school certificate (specific units specified)   <u>1</u>
The Johns Hopkins University

(11) Students with a B. A. or B. S. degree   <u>3</u>
LaSalle College, Drexel University, Baldwin-Wallace College

(12) No specific requirements   <u>7</u>
University of Minnesota, Modesto Junior College, Rockhurst College, Wayne State University, Southwestern Michigan College, Seminole Junior College, Towson State College

(13)   Other special requirements
       Satisfactory SAT scores (University of South
       Carolina, Indiana Central College, Upsala
       College); students must be 21 yrs. of age
       and out of Grade 13 for two years or Grade
       12 for three years (University of Windsor);
       2. 0 average for transfer students-upper 1/2
       of class, ACT, SAT or entrance examina-
       tion and high school diploma (Roosevelt Uni-
       versity); non-degree students must be eli-
       gible for credit at the time of their enroll-
       ment (University of Kentucky); high school
       graduation, 21 years of age and marked de-
       gree of maturity, CEEB or SAT score of
       750 or above (16 acceptable high school
       units except for mature adults) - (Univer-
       sity of Georgia); have a degree or a demon-
       strated need for the course (Millard Fill-
       more College); high school certificate and
       SCAT scores (City College of New York);
       (Bradley University); same as day students -
       SAT and/or entrance examinations (Univer-
       sity of Washington); 23 years of age or
       special recommendation (Georgia Southern
       College); "special" students must be 24 years
       of age or older for admission (Miami Uni-
       versity - Ohio); attendance, $5. 00 applica-
       tion fee and registration for classes (North-
       ern Virginia Community College).

B.   Degree students?

     (1)   High school graduation or GED and/or entrance
           examinations   56
           Dutchess Community College, Roanoke Col-
           lege, George Washington University, Trenton
           State College, University of Southern Mis-
           sissippi, South Texas Junior College, Idaho
           State University, Bakersfield College, Sacred
           Heart University, Post Junior College, Uni-
           versity of Rochester (and college transcripts),
           University of Bridgeport, The Pennsylvania
           State University, Rollins College, University
           of Nebraska, Washington University (St.
           Louis), University of Arkansas, East Caro-
           lina University, Aurora College (and college
           transcripts), Russell Sage College, Millard
           Fillmore College, Suffolk University, North-

29

ern Virginia Community College, Bryant
College, St. Mary's Dominican College,
Ohio State University, Pensacola Junior Col-
lege, St. Peter's College, Miami-Dade Jun-
ior College, Seminole Junior College, Uni-
versity of Maryland, Manhattan Community
College, Rockhurst College, Pratt Institute,
Thomas More College, Loyola University
(New Orleans), The New School, Boston Uni-
versity, Loyola University (Chicago), Com-
munity College of Baltimore, Rochester
Institute of Technology, Southwestern Michi-
gan College, Mississippi State College for
Women, Wichita State University, Baldwin-
Wallace College, Jefferson State Junior Col-
lege, Hofstra University, Miami University
(Ohio), Fairleigh Dickinson University, C. W.
Post College, San Diego Evening College,
Rockford College, Ohio State University,
PMC Colleges.

(2) High school graduate (satisfactory grades or
certain GPA), ACT, CEEB, or SAT (Minimum
scores)   25

University of South Carolina, The University
of Tennessee (Knoxville), Rider College,
Bradley University, Tulane University,
Nassau Community College, Washburn Uni-
versity of Topeka, Springfield College,
Centenary College of Louisiana, University
of Oregon, Virginia Commonwealth Univer-
sity, The American University, The Uni-
versity of Kentucky, Utah State University,
University of Tennessee (Nashville), Joint
University Center (MSU/UT), University of
Hawaii, Utica College-Syracuse University,
University of Toledo, Iona College, Prince
George's Community College, St. Peter's
College, Upsala College, East Tennessee
State University, University of Nebraska-
Omaha.

(3) High school graduation, 15-16 units (some
specify), and satisfactory scores on ACT,
CEEB, SAT   3

St. Louis University, College of William
and Mary, Old Dominion College

(4) High school graduation with specific course requirements and/or units or GPA   6

Philadelphia College of Textiles, St. Joseph's

College, St. Francis College, Western New England College, American International College, The Johns Hopkins University.

(5) High school graduation or college transcripts, minimum score on ACT, CEEB, or SAT examinations   6

Drexel University, Indiana Central College, Brooklyn College of City University of New York, Memphis State University, DeKalb College, University of Tampa.

(6) No admission requirements   1

University of Minnesota

(7) Same as day students   8

University of South Carolina, Drake University, University of New Hampshire, Sir George Williams University, University of Tennessee at Chattanooga, Texas Christian University, University of Washington, Louisiana State University (Baton Rouge).

(8) Upper 1/2 of class or upper 1/2 of national average on SAT   8

Northern Illinois University, Iowa State University, Baylor University, Roosevelt University, Purdue University (Calumet Campus), Xavier University, University of Louisville, University of Oklahoma.

(9) Grade 13 with 60% on seven papers   1

University of Windsor

(10) High school graduation with a "C" average 2

University of Detroit, University of New Mexico.

(11) Other requirements   24

Eligible to return to previous college (Drury College); admission requirements vary according to degree program and/or with various schools (New York University - Wayne State University); six (or less) evening courses (Marietta College - Ohio), high school diploma and a predicted grade point average of 1. 6 based upon the CEEB examination (North Carolina State University), SUNY Admission Examination is required plus high school diploma and recommendation (Orange County Community College); 21 years of age and otherwise qualified by previous study and experience to pass the course (University of Denver), New York State Regents Scholarship examination is re-

quired and used as a basis for admission
(Mohawk Valley Community College); regular
students must satisfactorily complete forty
quarter hours with an average of 2. 0 or
better and have evidence of high school graduation (Northeastern University); above average high school record, CEEB score of 950
or predicted grade point average of 2. 0 (16
acceptable high school units), (University of
Georgia); in the University of California Extension, no degrees are granted, and students do not matriculate in the University.
Most students already have degrees, and are
interested only in continuing education (University of Calif. at Berkeley-Univ. Ext.),
a high school certificate - must rank in the
upper 2/3 of the graduating class (University of Missouri); a high school diploma and
completion of 8 - 10 credits as a "special"
student satisfactorily.   (Union College); high
school graduation and SCAT scores (City
College of New York) (Boston College); 21
years of age and high school diploma - must
have not been dismissed from another university (University of Utah); meet University
requirements or complete thirty hours selected by the academic unit (University of
Maine); 18 yrs. or older and must be able
to benefit by instruction (Modesto Junior
College); other colleges and universities
have other special admission policies for
degree students.

C.   Are students who are rejected as day students advised to apply for evening classes?

Yes 27 Are they automatically accepted? Yes 15
No 65   No 12

6.   Do you use mail registration? 76 If so, what procedure is used?

(1)   Part-time students are mailed sufficient scheduling and registration forms with information for processing - on a first-come, first-
served basis (County College of Morris).

(2)   Registration by mail is used for off-campus
courses offered through Continuing Educa-

tion. The student may mail in his resignation materials with fees before a particular deadline each quarter (University of West Florida).

(3)   Continuing Education students may obtain registration materials at the first class meeting or at other centers or regional offices. All cards contained in the registration packet are to be completed and mailed with a check to the Division of Continuing Education (University of Oregon).

(4)   The student clips the section from the brochure requesting materials for registration by mail. If the course is approved, materials are sent and the student is registered by returning them completed with a check for tuition (University of Windsor).

(5)   Pre-printed forms are mailed and returned to a central registration location as a form of mail registration (George Washington University).

(6)   Mail registration for summer session only was conducted for the first time in 1970. Summer session schedule with the application form was included in a Sunday supplement to two metropolitan newspapers. Registration forms and confirmation of enrollment were handled by subsequent correspondence (The American University).

(7)   The application is included in the catalog; when it is received, the applicant is cleared for admission by the admissions and records office. The class schedule and registration materials are mailed back to the student who doesn't need to come to the campus until the first day of classes (North Carolina State University).

(8)   Each bulletin has an application which may be mailed up to two weeks prior to the first class. After that time, registration must be in person (Post Junior College).

(9)   Packets are mailed to former students and are received by the students early in August. Packets must be returned no later than a specified date in late August. This system is most effective (Northeastern University).

(10) a) Two weeks before "in person" registration: write, telephone, or visit to get forms

b) One week before "in person" registration: forms must be in office (Joint University Center) (MSU/UT)

(11) Mail registration is held for two weeks and starts two-three weeks prior to in-person registration (Utica College-Syracuse University).

(12) Mail registration is employed and is successful, with 60% of our students using mail registration. A month is designated (ending two weeks or so before "regular" registration) for mail registration. Students may pick up (or be mailed) registration "packets" which include a four-part form, a data identification card, library card, return envelope and class schedule. To pre-register, a student must include his advisor's approved roster card. After new students are accepted and have a scheduling interview, they are permitted to pre-register (St. Joseph's College).

(13) Mail registration forms are printed in the evening brochure. The office staff completes the registration forms and 50% of the tuition is required at the time of registration. (Aurora College)

(14) Registration by mail is optional; if used, students complete the following information on cards provided: 1) an application for admission or enrollment form; 2) a request to register for graduate credit form - if a graduate student; 3) a sectional registration card. This is to be returned to the Division of Continuing Education with payment of the registration fee that is applicable (University of Arkansas).

(15) Students receive a pre-printed registration form, self-addressed envelope, and a copy of both the credit course offerings and the non-credit course offerings for the next quarter. Students enter the department name, course number, section number, hours credit, and hour and days for which they desire to register on the registration form and return the form to the University together with a check or money order. The student then receives a class card for each course in which he is enrolled and a receipt for payment of fees. The class card is the stu-

dent's admission to class. Parking permits are not purchased by mail (University of Tennessee - Knoxville).

7. What are the retention policies (probation & suspension) for your undergraduate evening students?

A. Regular students

Grade point average of "C"	52
No retention policy	8
Same as for day students	13
Varies according to the school, college or program	2
Certain GPA according to the number of hours the student has taken or year enrolled (Limited examples are listed below)	60

-1. 0 after 30 hours; 1. 50 after 60 hours; 1. 75 after 90 hours (LaSalle College)

-Undergraduates - 2. 0; graduates - 3. 0; twelve semester hours below "B" or six semester hours below "C" for undergraduates constitute academic dismissal (Northern Illinois University)

-Grade point average of less than 1. 8 - probation (Dutchess Community College)

-"C" to "C+" average required - there is no probation - if grade point average falls below "C" the student is suspended for one year (Roanoke College)

-No probation status for students in the division. 1. 6 for 25-35 hrs. ; 1. 8 for 36-65 hrs. ; 2. 0 for 66 hrs. or more (Trenton State College)

-1. 75 for non-degree students after completing 12 hours; 2. 0 average required for degree students - below the required average results in probation; dismissal at the discretion of the Director (University of Detroit)

-Students failing 2/5 are placed on probation (Sir George Williams University)

-A student is placed on probation when he becomes 12 grade points deficient. A student is suspended if the grade point deficiency is increased during probation. (Baylor University)

-Any failure to meet course requirements incurs the penalty of refused registration in the faculty.

A student whose attendance at lectures or labs or whose work is deemed by the council to be unsatisfactory, may have the registration cancelled at any time by the council. A mature student on probation must obtain standing on the initial attempt on at least three of his first five subjects in order to have his probationary status removed. If a student fails more than two of his first five subjects, he will not be allowed to re-register in any degree course (University of Toronto).

-First quarter freshmen must achieve a grade point average of 1. 5, second and third quarters, 1. 75, fourth and subsequent quarters, 2. 0 (University of Utah).

-Degree students are suspended after 72 hours with less than 1. 5; there is no policy on special students (Miami-Dade Junior College).

-1. 5 after the first semester of freshman year; 1. 7 after the second semester of the freshman year; 2. 0 thereafter (St. Mary's Dominican).

-Students must maintain a 1. 5 for 18 credits; 1. 7 for 30 credits; 1. 9 for 60 credits; 2. 0 is required to graduate (St. Joseph's College).

-Students may be continued on probation one time, and if a 1. 8 GPA for a sophomore or a 2. 0 average is not obtained, a student is dropped (St. Francis College).

-Degree students with a grade point average of 1. 5 are placed on probation and suspended the next term if the grade point average is not 1. 7 (Seminole Jr. College).

-There is an annual review of each student's record and an interview with each whose record is unsatisfactory. Evening students drop out if they are not doing satisfactory work, making probation unnecessary (American International College) (PMC Colleges).

B. Non-degree or "special" students

No specific policy	41
Same as for degree students	68
No regulations but limitation on hours that can be taken	5
Record is reviewed - individually	6
Satisfactory performance in work taken	2

36

8. Do you require ACT or CEEB examinations for adults in the Evening Division?

$$\frac{12}{\text{ACT}} \qquad \frac{20}{\text{CEEB}} \qquad \frac{9}{\text{yes}} \qquad \frac{94}{\text{no}}$$

Are other tests required?

$$\frac{35}{\text{yes}} \qquad \frac{54}{\text{no}}$$

List of other tests used:

(1) Roosevelt University Entrance Examination (Roosevelt University)

(2) SCAT Test (The American University) (City College of N. Y.)

(3) Placement tests in Math and English (Roanoke College) (Northeastern University) (University of Missouri) (DeKalb College) (University of North Carolina) (Queensborough Community College) (Jefferson State Jr. College) (Modesto Junior College)

(4) The SAT and an achievement test (Prince George's Community College)

(5) The Adult College Aptitude Test is required for all degree students and is used for placement and advisement (Baldwin-Wallace College)

(6) Placement tests in Reading and English (Nassau Community College)

(7) The SCAT is required for matriculated students for admission and for placement tests in English and Math (Manatee Junior College)

(8) The SAT or Ohio Test for degree students (Rider College)

(9) The School of Humanities requires Purdue Modern Language Placement Exam (Purdue University - Calumet Campus)

(10) Department evening tests are used in some areas (Pratt Institute)

(11) TOEFL examination is used for advisement (University of Hawaii)

9. Do you offer a special degree program for adults?

$$\frac{40}{\text{yes}} \qquad \frac{70}{\text{no}}$$

37

Schools Offering Special Degree Programs

	Degree(s)	Enrollment	School
1.	Associate Degree	2084 f. t. 2211 p. t.	County College of Morris
2.	Bachelor of Science Degree	42 f. t. 1163 p. t.	Drury College
3.	Bachelor of Arts in Liberal Arts and Bachelor of Arts in Bus. Adm.	519 p. t.	Marietta College (Ohio)
4.	Bachelor of General Studies	500	Roosevelt University
5.	Assoc. in Arts (Eve. degree for adults)	181	New York University
	Assoc. in Applied Science (Business)	132	New York University
	Assoc. in Applied Science in Early Childhood Education & Social Work (Day program with some sections for adults	60	New York University
6.	Bachelor of Business Administration	70	University of Detroit
7.	BGS, BSGS, BSG and CS, BSO, BSEH	2000	George Washington University
	(Undergrad), MSA (graduate)	4500	George Washington University
8.	Bachelor of Science in General Studies		The American University
	Bachelor of Science and Master of Science in Administra-		

38

	Degree(s)	Enrollment	School
	tion of Justice		The American University
9.	Associate in Arts Degree	307	Sacred Heart University
10.	Bachelor of Science in General Studies	1314	University of Rochester
	Master of Science in General Studies	1379	University of Rochester
11.	Associate Degree in Applied Business	87	University of New Hampshire
12.	Associate in Science	-	Northeastern University
	Bachelor of Science	-	Northeastern University
13.	Associate in Science; Associate in Finance Master of Art	397	Indiana Central College
14.	A Small College Degree Program	290	Brooklyn College of the City University of New York
	A Special Baccalaureate Program for Adults	196	
15.	Bachelor of Technology; Bachelor of Science in Systems and Data Processing and Industrial Management and Urban Affairs	43 p. t. 3505 f. t.	Washington University (St. Louis)
16.	Bachelor of Arts in Industrial Mgt.	-	Aurora College
17.	Bachelor of Business Administration in "Life Experience"	643	St. Francis College

	Degree(s)	Enrollment	School
18.	Bachelor of General Studies	130 f. t. 770 p. t.	Rollins College
19.	Bachelor of Science in General Studies	1492	Suffolk University
20.	Certificate in Transportation and Traffic Management and in Law Enforcement	50	Bryant College
21.	Certification in Corrections	36	St. Mary's Dominican College
22.	ASBA and DSBA - Major in Transportation and Traffic Management	30-40	Bryant College
23.	Bachelor of Science	3000+	University of Cincinnati
24.	Bachelor of Science, Bachelor of Arts	23 f. t. 429 p. t.	Upsala College Upsala College
25.	Bachelor of Arts (General Studies)	12,000	University of Md.
26.	Bachelor of Arts in Administration Bachelor of Science in Business Adm.	1331 f. t. -	Rockhurst College Rockhurst College
27.	Bachelor of Arts degree	-	Texas Christian Univ.
28.	Associate of Arts degree Two special sequences in Bachelor's program in Sociology: Corrections and Child Welfare	145 f. t. 811 p. t.	Thomas More College Thomas More College

	Degree(s)	Enrollment	School
29.	Bachelor of Arts	650	Loyola Univ. (New Orleans)
30.	Bachelor of Science in Bus. Adm.	197 f. t. 800 p. t.	Xavier University
31.	Bachelor of Liberal Studies; Bachelor of Urban Affairs, Master of Liberal Studies, Master of Urban Affairs	Total eve. enroll- ment: 172 f. t. 3700 p. t.	Boston University
32.	Associate in Arts	150	Rochester Institute of Technology
33.	Bachelor of Science in General Studies Bachelor of Science in Law Enforcement	1381	Louisiana State Univ. (Baton Rouge)
34.	Bachelor of Arts in Extension Studies	5000	Harvard University (Un. Ext.)
35.	Bachelor of Arts in Liberal Studies	2591	Rider College
36.	Bachelor of Science Master of Business Administration	755 f. t. 1682 p. t. 127 f. t. 763 p. t.	Temple University Temple University
37.	Bachelor of Arts, Bachelor of Com- merce	93 f. t. 1851 p. t.	University of Rich- mond
38.	Associate in Arts	946	Thomas More College
39.	Bachelor of Inde- pendent Studies	-	Univ. of South Florida
40.	1) Certificate in Arts & Sciences	3753 undergraduate	

Degree(s)	Enrollment	School
(any of 11 areas);	1727 graduate	
Advanced Study		
in Education; Ad-		
vanced Study in		
Liberal Arts,		
General Business,		
Accounting or		
Management; 2)		
Bachelor of Sci-		
ence in Arts and		
Sciences (any of		
11 areas); Nursing,		
Business (three areas),		
Education, Engineer-		
ing (any area); 3)		
Master of Liberal		
Arts, Master of		
Education, Master		
of Science in Nu-		
merical Science,		
Master of Science	The Johns Hopkins	
with Education Major	University	

41. Bachelor of General
    Studies   6958 f. t.   University of Ne-
         6227 p. t.   braska-Omaha

42. Bachelor of Liberal   University of Okla-
    Studies   1014 f. t.   homa
    Master of Liberal
    Studies
    Master of Arts in
    Government and   University of Okla-
    Economics   1622 p. t.   homa

43. Master of Business
    Administration   1340 f. t.   PMC Colleges
         1189 p. t.

Distribution Requirements for Special Degrees

School and Degree(s)	Distribution Requirements
1. County College of	1. Data Processing Technology-
Morris Associate	Humanities-6 hours, Social
Degree	Sciences-6 hours; Business-

School and Degree(s)	Distribution Requirements

6 hours; Math and Science-6 hours; Data Processing Courses-33 hours; electives-8 hours; Total hours-65.

2. Law Enforcement-Humanities-12 hours; Social Science-21 hours; Math and Science-10 hours; Law Enforcement-18 hours; Electives-6 hours; Total hours-67.

3. Biological/Medical Lab. Technology-Humanities-9 hours; Social Science-6 hours; Math and Science-6 hours; Biol. -Chem. courses-44 hours; electives-5 hours; Total hours-70.

4. Electronics Technology-Humanities-9 hours; Social Science-3 hours; Math and Science-22 hours; Electronics-30 hours; Flectives-5 hours; Total hours-69.

2. Drury College Bachelor of Science Degree

12 hours in each of three divisions 1) Arts-Humanities, 2) Social Sciences, 3) Science-Math; a minimum of 18; a maximum of 30 hours in the major; Total hours-124.

3. New York University AAS (Public Service); Associate in Arts; Associate in Applied Science; Associate in Science

Areas of concentration; Liberal Arts, Business, Pre-Physical Therapy, Teacher Aides, Social Work Assistants, Pre-Respiratory Therapy. In each program, a minimum of 52-64 hours to a maximum of 64 are stipulated, required courses.

4. Marietta College (Ohio) Bachelor of Arts (Liberal Arts; Bus. Adm.)

48 semester hours in first elected division; 12 semester hours in each of the two remaining divisions. A total of

School and Degree(s)	Distribution Requirements
	120 hours required for a degree. The area of concentration with the credit requirements are 18 hours in any department. The evening program differs from the day program in that there is a "general area of concentration" rather than a major.
5. University of Detroit (Bus. Adm.) Bachelor of Bus. Adm.	Areas of concentration: Management, Marketing, Finance or Accounting. 40% non-business courses, and 20% float between liberal arts and business. Total hours-120. (AACSB standards).
6. George Washington University Bachelor of General Studies	Undergraduate: Communications-12 hours; Humanities-12 hours; Natural Sciences-6-8 hours; Math-9 hours; Social Science-12 hours; Business and Economics-15-18 hours; electives-4 hours; Concentration-33 hours; related electives-27 hours; Total hours, 120.
Bachelor of Science in General Cartography	Area of Concentration: 60 hours (Cartography, Geodesy)
Bachelor of Science in Oceanography	Area of Concentration: 60 hours (Oceanography)
Bachelor of Science in Environmental Health	Area of Concentration: 25 hours (Environmental Health)
Master of Science in Administration	Core requirements: 18; area of Concentration-12-18; electives-0-6; Total hours-36.
7. Roosevelt University Bachelor of General Studies	Degree program is divided into four sections: The Pro-Seminar, the required courses in the area of concentration, the BGS Seminars in the Humanities; the Social Sciences, and

School and Degree(s)	Distribution Requirements
	the Natural Sciences, and the Supervised Internship in Community Service.
8. Sacred Heart University Associate in Arts	Areas of Concentration: Business-64 hours; Accounting-64 hours; Liberal Studies-64 hours.
9. University of Rochester Bachelor of Science in General Studies	English composition, one literature course, two additional Humanities courses, three courses in Social Sciences, two courses in Natural Sciences; 56 hrs. required in the area of Concentration: Social Studies, Humanities or Natural Sciences. Total hours-128.
Master of Science in General Studies	Students may major in: Applied Math, Chem. Eng. , Materials Science, Mech. and Aerospace Sciences, Optics, and Statistics. Varied distribution requirements depending upon major area. Total hours-30.
10. University of New Hampshire	50%-technical; 25%-general education; 25% elective. Total hrs. -64, with concentration of 10 courses in ABM and two courses in Communications.
11. Northeastern University Associate in Science Bachelor of Science	Bachelor of Science requires 174 hrs. to complete.
12. Indiana Central College Associate in Science; Associate in Finance	Liberal Arts-13 hrs. ; subject area-55 hrs. ; Total hrs. -72. Other degree program: Liberal Arts-20 hrs. Subject area-8

School and Degree(s)	Distribution Requirements

hrs. and Research-4 hrs.
Total hrs. -32.

13. Rollins College
    Bachelor of
    General Studies

English-6 hrs.; Humanities-12
hrs.; Soc. Sci. -12 hrs.; Math
and/or Science-12 hrs.; Major
area-30 hrs.; electives-48 hrs.
Total hrs. -120. Areas of concentration: Humanities, Soc.
Sci., Math/Sci., Prep for
Teaching, Business, Criminal
Justice-30 hrs.

14. Brooklyn College
    of the City Uni-
    versity of New
    York
    Small College
    Degree Program
    Special Bacca-
    laureate Program
    for Adults

Areas of concentration: Afro-
American, Anthropology, Art,
Biology, Chemistry, Classics,
Economics, Education, English,
Geology, Health Education,
History, Home Economics, In-
formation Science, Integrated
Science, Judaic Studies, Math,
Modern Language, Music, Phi-
losophy, Physics, Political Sci-
ence, Psychology, Puerto Rican
Studies, Social Studies, Soci-
ology, Speech & Theater

15. Washington Uni-
    versity (St. Louis)
    Bachelor of Tech-
    nology
    Bachelor of Sci-
    ence in Systems
    & Data Process-
    ing
    Industrial Manage-
    ment & Urban
    Affairs

Composition and Rhetoric-6 hrs.;
Humanities-12 hrs. Soc. Sci. -
12 hrs.; Math/Science-12 hrs.;
Arts & Sciences electives-12
hrs.; Major area-36-60 hrs.
Total hours-120. Areas of
concentration: Accounting,
Business Administration, Eco-
nomics. Distribution require-
ments: Chemistry, English,
History, Industrial Management,
Sociology, Systems and Data
Processing

16. Aurora College
    Bachelor of

Humanities-9 hrs.; Social and

School and Degree(s)	Distribution Requirements

Arts in Industrial Management | Behavior Sciences-9 hrs.; Bible and Religion-6 hrs.; Physical Education-4 hrs.; Language or alternative-15 hrs.; Natural Science and Math-9 hrs.

17. St. Francis College

Bachelor of Business Administration in "life experience" | B. B. A. - Management, Marketing and Accounting

Associate in Science in Administration-Computer Science, Bus. Adm. | A. A. S. - Computer Science and Business Administration

Associate in Arts | A. A. - Liberal Arts & Pre-Teaching

18. Suffolk University

Bachelor of Science in General Studies | Humanities-12 hrs.; Soc. Sci. - 12 hrs.; Biology and Physical Science-14 hrs.; English-12 hrs.; History-6 hrs.; Language-12 hrs.; Total hrs. -122. Area of concentration: Humanities-42 hrs.; Social Science-42 hrs.; Science-42 hrs.

19. Bryant College

Associate in Science in Business Administration

Bachelor of Science in Bus. Adm. | Areas of concentration: Accounting, Transportation, Economics, Marketing and General. Concentration in Accounting, Transportation and General requires 120 hrs. Concentration in Management, Economics and Marketing requires 123 hrs.

Master of Business Administration | Foundation courses-18 hrs.; Advanced courses-30 hrs.

School and Degree(s)	Distribution Requirements

20. St. Mary's Dominican College
Certificate in Corrections — Students take courses in Psychology, Social Welfare and Sociology; Total hours-67

21. Rockhurst College
Associate in Business Administration — Required hours-80
Bachelor of Science in Bus. Adm. — Required hours-128

22. Upsala College
Bachelor of Arts
Bachelor of Science — Courses include: English, Natural Science, Social Science, Humanities and 12 courses in the area of concentration. Foreign language is required for the B. A. ; one course in Math for the B. S. degree. Areas of concentration: Natural Science, Social Science, Humanities and Business. Total hours-128.

23. University of Maryland
Bachelor of Arts in General Studies — English-9 hrs. ; History-6 hrs. ; Social Science-7 hrs. ; Math-3 hrs. ; Humanities-3 hrs. ; Speech-3 hrs. ; Language or Economics and Accounting-12 hrs. ; primary concentration-24 hrs. ; electives-23 hrs. ; Total hours-120-122.

24. Texas Christian University
Bachelor of Arts — Divisional concentration in Humanities, Natural Sciences (incl. Math), or Social Science

25. Thomas More College
Associate in Arts — Programs in Accountancy, Arts,

School and Degree(s)	Distribution Requirements

Business Administration, Chemical Technology, Computer Science, Economics, English, History, Philosophy, Psychology and Sociology. Distribution requirements: English-6; Philosophy-6; Theology-6; Math-6; Soc. Sci. -3-6.

Two special sequences in Bachelor of Arts program in Sociology; Correction and Child Welfare

English-12 hrs.; Fine Arts-4 hrs.; Language-6-9 hrs.; Philosophy-12 hrs.; Theology-12 hrs.; Math-6 hrs.; Natural Science-8 hrs.; Soc. Sci. -9 hrs. plus requirements in area of concentration.

26. Loyola University (New Orleans)
    Bachelor of Arts

Degree offered in the following areas: Soc. Studies, Liberal Studies, Commercial Science, and Police Science. Distribution requirements: English-12 hrs.; Math-6 hrs.; Speech-3 hrs.; History-6 hrs.; Science-18 hrs.; Field of Concentration-21 hrs. with some variation. Total hours-128.

27. Xavier University
    Arts & Sciences

Distribution requirements: M/L-10 hrs.; Sciences-6-8 hrs.; Management-6 hrs.; Humanities-12 hrs.; Social Sciences-15 hrs.; Theology-12 hrs.; Philosophy-15 hrs.; major area of concentration-30-36 hrs. Total hours-120.

    Business

Same requirements except no language, and a business core of 27 hrs.

28. Boston University
    Bachelor of Liberal Studies
    Bachelor of Ur-

Undergraduate degrees: fourteen courses - two English; four Humanities; four in Social

School and Degree(s)	Distribution Requirements
ban Affairs Master of Liberal Studies Master of Urban Affairs	Sciences; four in Sciences. Graduate degrees: MLS - three-year long seminars in Humanities, Science and Social Sciences. Total hrs. for completion of undergraduate-128 hrs. (32 courses) and 40 hrs. (10 courses) for graduate.

29. Rochester Institute of Technology
    Associate in Arts
    Bachelor of Science — 25% Math and Science; 25% General Education; 50% Professional Courses

30. Louisiana State University (Baton Rouge)
    Bachelor of Science in General Studies
    Bachelor of Science in Law Enforcement — 46 hrs. in one area of Humanities, Soc. Sci. or Natural Sciences. Student must have 18 hrs. in each of the other two areas. Remaining hrs. are electives. Total hours-128.

31. Northwestern University
    Bachelor of Philosophy
    Bachelor of Science in General Education — Ph. B. requires 12 hrs. in a language. No language is required for the B. S. in General Education - no lab science.

32. University of South Florida
    Bachelor of Independent Studies — The curriculum is divided into four parts: Humanities, Natural Sciences, Social Sciences, Inter-area Studies. Each of the four areas is comprised of two major phases of work - guided independent study and an area seminar.

33. University of
    Nebraska-Omaha
       Bachelor of Inde-   Core areas: English-6 hrs. ;
       pendent Studies   Soc. Sci. -12 hrs. ; Natural Sci-
                                ences-Math-9 hrs. ; Humanities-
                                12 hrs. ; area of concentration-
                                30 hrs. ; First minor-12;
                                Second minor-12; Electives-
                                32 hrs. ; Total hrs. -125.
                                Students may choose an
                                area of concentration from 29
                                different areas in Arts & Sci-
                                ences, Business, Engineering,
                                Law Enforcement and Correc-
                                tions, Urban Studies, Recrea-
                                tion Leadership, Physical Edu-
                                cation, Home Economics and
                                Physical Education.

34. Harvard Univer-
    sity (Univ. Ext.)
       Bachelor of Arts   16 courses required (including
       in Extension   60 upper-level credit) with the
       Studies   following areas of concentra-
                                tion: Humanities, Natural Sci-
                                ences, Social Sciences; distri-
                                bution: candidates will - what-
                                ever their areas of concentra-
                                tion - pass at least one full
                                course in each of three areas
                                (Humanities, Natural Sciences
                                or the Social Sciences).

35. Rider College
       Bachelor of Arts   Core requirements - 68 hrs. :
       in Liberal Studies   18 hrs. in one area, 12 hrs.
                                in each of two other areas plus
                                electives. Total hours - 128.
       Bach. of Sci. in   Core requirements: 68 hrs. ;
       Bus. Adm.   professional courses, 60 hrs.
       Secr. Sci. or Chem. Total hours - 128.
       Six Assoc. in Arts   64 hrs. required to complete
       degree program   the degree.

36. The Johns Hopkins Univ.

19 different de-
grees offered plus
certificate pro-
grams
1) Certificate in
Arts & Sciences

Sample program listed:
Courses in Humanities, Social
Sciences, and Science - Electives in 14-20 hrs. - Total
hrs. - 60.

2) B. S. in Arts
and Sciences (any
of 11 areas)

Humanities-22 hrs.; Soc. Sci. -
12 hrs.; Science-6-12 hrs.;
Major area-40 to 58 hrs.; plus
electives.   Total hours - 120.

3) Bachelor of
Science in Nurs-
ing

Humanities - 16 hrs.; Soc.
Sci. -18 to 20 hrs.; Science -
6-12 hrs.; Professional
Courses - 38 hrs. plus electives.   Total hours - 120.

4) Master of
Liberal Arts

Three-year courses must be
taken in seminars in History of
Ideas - 18 credits; two other
year courses or equivalent in
Advanced Courses in Liberal
Arts.   A minimum of one
year's study or equivalent (30
credits) must be completed in
evening college and/or summer
session within five years.

5) Other degrees:
B. S. in Business;
B. S. in a major
in Education; M. S.
in Education; B. S.
in Engineering (any
area); M. S. in Ap-
plied Physics; M. S.
in Numerical Sci-
ence

37. Temple University
Bachelor of Sci-
ence

At least 40% required in Liberal Arts; no lab requirements
in the evening

School and Degree(s)	Distribution Requirements
Master of Bus. Adm. (administered by a separate graduate division)	30 hours above prerequisites required.

38. University of Richmond

Bachelor of Arts	Field of concentration 42-48 hrs. (English, Economics or History); 60 hrs. in Liberal Arts: English-12; Math-6; Science-8; History-6; electives plus courses in major areas
Bachelor of Commerce	18 hrs. in Accounting, Banking, Economics, Finance, Management, Marketing, Personnel, Total hours - 124.
Master of Commerce	Total hours - 36.
Master of Humanities	Total hours - 36

10. Are you considering offering a special degree program for adults in the near future?

38	60
yes	no

1. Univ. of South Carolina
2. New York Univ.
3. Univ. of Oregon
4. Marietta Coll. -Ohio
5. Drake University
6. The American Univ. (additional)
7. Utah State Univ.
8. Joint Univ. Center (MSU/UT)
9. Orange County Community College
10. Rollins College
11. Iowa State Univ.
12. Indiana Central Coll.
13. Baylor University
14. Brooklyn Coll. of City Univ. N. Y.
15. Queensborough Community College
16. University of Missouri
17. Utica College-Syracuse Univ.
18. The New School
19. University of Washington
20. University of Nebraska
21. University of Arkansas
22. University of Hawaii
23. Iona College
24. The Univ. of New Mexico
25. Millard Fillmore College
26. Suffolk University (Grad)
27. St. Mary's Dominican College

28. Univ. of Minnesota
29. Univ. of North Caro-
    lina
30. Univ. of Richmond
31. Pensacola Junior
    College
32. St. Peter's College

33. University of Maine
34. Memphis State University
35. University of Maryland
36. Xavier University (addi-
    tional)
37. Western New England Coll.
38. PMC Colleges

11. What are the admission requirements for the special degree program(s)?

   (1) Same as for regular degree students (Aurora
        College) (Sacred Heart Academy) (Rider
        College) (Northeastern University) (The Amer-
        ican University)
   (2) A 2.0 GPA, acceptable scores on admissions
        tests (Drury College)
   (3) Requirements vary according to degree - the
        basic core requirements for admission to
        special degree programs is high school grad-
        uation. Some adults are admitted on the
        basis of the adult admission tests and others
        on SAT scores. In some cases, they are
        admitted provisionally subject to the earning
        of an equivalency diploma within one calendar
        year (New York University)
   (4) The Deans of the concerned colleges or schools
        in conjunction with the University Admissions
        Office formulate the admission policies
        (George Washington University)
   (5) Different requirements for each area of con-
        centration (Roosevelt University)
   (6) The Director of Graduate Studies formulates the
        admission policies for the Master of Science
        degree program in General Studies (Univer-
        sity of Rochester)
   (7) High school graduation or the equivalency (Uni-
        versity of New Hampshire) (Washington Uni-
        versity)
   (8) College graduation, GRE scores and recommen-
        dations (Indiana Central College)
   (9) A high school diploma (Suffolk University)
  (10) Fifteen acceptable high school units, advanced
        college standing, or by examination (Loyola
        University-New Orleans)
  (11) High school diploma and two years of high
        school algebra for undergraduate degree; for

graduates - a college degree with a 3. 0 GPA on a 4. 0 base, and A. T. G. S. B. examinations. (Bryant College)

(12) For undergraduates: graduation in the upper 50% of the high school class or successful previous college work; graduates: a mid-B average in the latter half of degree plus appropriate specific prerequisites (The Johns Hopkins University)

(13) Functional adult status, a minimum of 58 applicable credits; a "C" average on academic amnesty as a returning adult - (University of Nebraska-Omaha)

12. Who formulates admission policies for evening students at your institution?

A. Regular degree students

(1) Faculty Admissions Committee (generally includes Director or Dean of the Evening Division or College) 57

(2) President's or Dean's Council 6

(3) Dean and/or Director of Admissions Office 17

(4) Evening Division or College Committee or Board and/or Director 14

(5) Administration and Directors 12

(6) Faculty of the College or School 7

(7) Dean of the College 3

(8) Board of Higher Regents 1

Other

(1) The Director of Continuing Education (County College of Morris)

(2) The State Board of Higher Education (University of Oregon) (Jefferson State Junior College)

(3) The Board of Supervisors of the University (Louisiana State University)

(4) The Board of Trustees (Dutchess Community College) (Purdue University-Calumet Campus)

(5) Dean, Director of Admissions and Director of Continuing Education (Roanoke College)

(6) The Deans of the various colleges involved (Virginia Commonwealth College) (George Washington University)

(7) The Senate formulates the admission policies

for evening students (University of California at Berkeley - Ext. Div.) (University of Windsor) (University of Rochester) (University of Tennessee at Knoxville) (University of Utah) (Rollins College) (Boston College)

(8) The Dean of Instruction (Trenton State College)

(9) The Provost-Continuing Education along with the administration and admissions committee are responsible for admissions policies (Utah State University)

(10) The Dean of Pupil Personnel formulates the admission policies (Bakersfield College)

(11) The academic departments formulate the admission requirements for evening students (The Pennsylvania State University)

(12) Admissions Office for the University of Tennessee in Knoxville (Joint University Center-MSU/UT)

(13) Dean of the Evening College is totally responsible for admission policies (Xavier University)

(14) The faculty and the Board of Trustees (Seminole Junior College)

(15) Board of Higher Education for the City University of New York (Brooklyn College of the City University of New York)

(16) The Extension Division and the various colleges formulate the admission policies (University of Nebraska) (Wayne State University)

(17) The Director of Special Programs (Union College)

(18) Admission policies are set by the State of Ohio (University of Cincinnati)

(19) The Registrar and the Dean of Special Education formulate the admission policies for evening students (Manatee Junior College)

(20) The Administrative Board for University Extension (Harvard University-Univ. Ext.)

(21) Dean of Educational Services with University Council & Graduate Council (Miami University-Ohio)

B. Non-degree or "Special" students

(1) Same committee/individual/board as for degree students   49

(2) Admissions Office or Registrar   4

(3) Evening College Dean or Director   7

(4) Administration or Directors   3

(5) Division, School or College of General Studies
      (or Cont. Ed.)   3
(6) Admission Committee   3
(7) The Dean of Instruction   3

Other

(1) The Director of Special Programs (Union Col-
     lege)
(2) The administration and faculty (University of
     Washington)

C. Special degree programs for adults (if different re-
    quirements for admission)

(1) Faculty Committee   7
(2) Admissions Officer   2
(3) Administrative council with the Director
     of Admissions   6

Other

(1) The Director of Continuing Education (County
     College of Morris)
(2) State Board of Higher Education (University of
     Oregon)
(3) The Dean, with the consent of the faculty Senate
     (University of Rochester)
(4) The Executive Committee of the Division of
     Continuing Education (Univ. of New Hamp-
     shire)
(5) The Director of Admissions and Dean (Suffolk
     University)

13. To what extent may day and evening students enroll in
the same class?

(1) No restrictions 85   (2) Special permission
     necessary 33   (3) Not permitted 6

Other

(1) There is a minimum cross-registration between
     part-time and full-time students (County Col-
     lege of Morris) (University of California at
     Berkeley-Univ. Ext.)
(2) Enrollment of day and evening students is limited
     only by facilities and expedience (Marietta

57

College) (Millard Fillmore College)

(3) Students may enroll in day and evening classes whenever there is room (The American University) (University of Kentucky) (Sir George Williams University)

(4) Day students are admitted to evening classes if they have irreconcilable conflicts in the day program or if their numbers are needed to enlarge the evening classes (Bakersfield College) (Post Junior College)

(5) Day and evening students may enroll in the same classes on a 50%-50% basis (Fairleigh Dickinson University)

(6) Whenever necessary for reasons of conflict in schedule or because a course is offered in one division and not in the other (University of Rochester)

(7) No more than one-third of an evening class can be day students (University of New Hampshire)

(8) Currently an experiment is being made on one campus - allowing day students into certain sections of our part-time program (Northeastern University)

(9) Day students are allowed to register for evening classes up to 10% of the evening registration (Utica College-Syracuse University)

In your opinion, what are the advantages and/or disadvantages of the combined class with day and evening students?

Advantages

(1) Working students are able to carry a full academic load (University of South Carolina)

(2) It gives a broader perspective and more incentive for both day and evening students to work harder (Centenary College of Louisiana)

(3) The advantages of the combination are the sharing of expenses and intermingling of mature and immature students (University of Oregon) (Bakersfield College)

(4) Our experience has been that adults plus full-time students make a good combination (University of Detroit)

(5) Combined day/evening classes create a learning experience of more breadth for the student (George Washington University)

(6) The advantage to a combined class is that the educational needs of the adult student can be better served if he is given the flexibility of enrolling in either day and/or evening classes (The American University) (University of Missouri)

(7) An unlimited enrollment of day/evening students is encouraged due to the small enrollment in some classes so that students can find a better selection of courses (Utah State University)

(8) It helps improve the diversity of the class (Sacred Heart University)

(9) The process of exchange seems to work very well - day students become aware of differences in people who attend part-time (Maturity, experience, professional training) and evening students are stimulated and interested by contacts with full-time undergraduates (University of Rochester)

(10) The advantage to a day/evening combination is that evening students, older, more practical and experienced, can tie theory and practice together - older ideas on new meaning (University of New Hampshire)

(11) The combined class gives more flexibility to meet student needs; the "cross-fertilization" factor is advantageous (University of Georgia)

(12) Day/evening combination classes are very limited, but it is felt that there are various advantages such as the stimulation of the older by the younger students, fostering relevance by exposure of the day student to the non-cloistered evening student and a general narrowing of the generation gap (University of California-Berkeley)

(13) In the opinion of the University College, there are two advantages: 1) to insure potential small evening classes materializing, and, 2) department chairmen take a greater interest in the evening program (East Carolina University)

(14) The advantages of the combined classes are life styles, attitudes, age and experience mix (Russell Sage College)

(15) The advantages of this is flexibility for students; better utilization of faculty and a healthier educational climate for all (Wichita State University)

59

Disadvantages

(1) Regular day students sometimes take evening classes and thereby displace evening students (The American University)

(2) "We sometimes have pressure to take more students in the evening classes than can be accommodated. " (University of Missouri)

(3) A disadvantage is the generation gap (Millard Fillmore College)

(4) Class grading curve is sometimes unfair to evening students and some intimidation exists where classes are out of balance (Baldwin-Wallace College)

(5) With a high percentage of young students in a mixed class, adults do not respond freely in class (Jefferson State Junior College)

(6) The diversity of background of students (Tulane University)

(7) Day students gripe "adults are too eager beavers", "adults gripe that younger student is 'hep' and test-wise" - too much competition (Manatee Junior College)

14. Do you have an orientation program for evening students?

32	85
yes	no

When is it held?

Before registration	12
First week of classes	2
On registration day	4
Beginning of the semester (qtr)	9
During the semester (qtr)	5
In August	1

15. Additional comments on admission

(1) We are considering organization of an Admission Advisory Committee (University of South Carolina)

(2) Non-high school graduates may be allowed to register for credit courses with prior approval of the Director of Continuing Education Division (County College of Morris)

(3) Evening Division Advisory Committee suggests development and liaison (University of Oregon)

(4) "We do demand rather close counseling in the selection of each subject, insuring that it helps to fulfill degree requirements" (University of Windsor)

(5) Special non-degree enrollment is not encouraged (University of Denver)

(6) The college graduate who does not meet academic standards for direct admission to a graduate program may apply for admission to a Graduate Certificate Program administered by the College of Continuing Education. If he completes the Certificate Program with a satisfactory grade point average, he may be considered for admission to a graduate degree program (The American University)

(7) A study is being made on admission standards for minority groups holding positions in Head Start, WIN, CAP, etc. (Utah State University)

(8) An individual pre- and post-admissions counseling is provided along with orientation information through a newsletter (University of Georgia)

(9) We have an Evening College faculty and three standing committees: 1) Committee on Policy and By-Laws, 2) Curriculum Committee, and 3) Committee on Academic Advisement. Our faculty has just approved a new admissions policy which must be approved by the Board of Curators. One feature of the policy provides that applicants over 21 years of age, veterans, etc., who may not qualify for admission as regular students may be admitted by virtue of a special preparation or attainments as special students. This feature of the admissions policy was in part the outgrowth of a study conducted by the Evening College relating to the academic performance of adults (University of Missouri)

(10) Admissions are limited to students living in a 50-mile radius of the campus (Millard Fillmore College)

(11) An orientation course which evening students may take (1 sem. hr. credit) is offered, but it is not required for graduation (Pensacola Junior College)

(12) We have what is known as an open admission policy which results in an attrition no greater

than the restrictive admissions of the day programs. However, many students at night take several courses before they decide on matriculation which would invalidate this claim (Rochester Institute of Technology)

II. TERMINOLOGY

1. Title of Division, School or College:

A. Fvening Division   20

LaSalle College, University of South Carolina (in Gen. Studies), Northern Illinois University (in College of Cont. Ed.), Centenary College of Louisiana, Louisiana State University-New Orleans, University of Detroit (of the Arts & Sciences College), University of Bridgeport, Indiana Central College, Sir George Williams University, Baylor University, Russell Sage College, Suffolk University, Bryant College, Prince George's Community College, Rockhurst College, Loyola University-New Orleans, Western New England College, Northwestern University, Fairleigh Dickinson University, PMC Colleges.

B. Evening College   18

Drury College (in the Cont. Ed. Div.), Virginia Commonwealth University (Summer School), Drexel University, South Texas Junior College, Philadelphia College of Textiles, University of Missouri, St. Joseph's College, Pensacola Junior College, University of Cincinnati, Texas Christian University, Xavier University, Bradley University, American International College, Manatee Junior College, The Johns Hopkins University, University of North Carolina, San Diego Evening College, Rockford College.

C. University College   10

Drake University (Center for Cont. Ed.), Northeastern University, East Carolina University (Div. of Cont. Ed.), University of Maryland, Loyola University-Chicago, Tulane University, Hofstra University, University of Louisville, Louisiana State University, (Baton Rouge), The University of Richmond.

D. Division of Continuing Education   30

County College of Morris, The University of West Florida, University of Oregon, The University of

New Mexico, Idaho State University, North Carolina State University, Bakersfield College, University of Southern Mississippi, Sacred Heart University, Post Junior College, University of New Hampshire, Mohawk Valley Community College, The Pennsylvania State University, Orange County Community College, Utica College-Syracuse University, University of Arkansas, Millard Fillmore College, University of Tennessee-Chattanooga, St. Mary's Dominican College, Ohio State University, University of Utah (Dept. of Evening Classes), University of Maine, Community College of Baltimore, Southwestern Michigan College, Wichita State University, Mississippi State College of Women, Jefferson State Junior College, University of Tennessee-Knoxville, Springfield College, Old Dominion College, Ohio State University.

E. College or School of Continuing Education 9
Northern Illinois University, New York University, Roosevelt University, The American University, University of Hawaii (and Community Service), Washington University-St. Louis, Rochester Institute of Technology, East Tennessee State University

F. Other Titles
(1) College or School of General Studies - University of South Carolina, Brooklyn College of the City University of New York, City College of New York, George Washington University
(2) Evening School - Marietta College-Ohio
(3) Office of Continuing Education - Dutchess Community College, University of Denver, University of Tampa
(4) Evening Program and Continuing Education - Roanoke College, Manhattan Community College
(5) Evening College of Business Administration - University of Detroit
(6) Division of Extension or University Extension - University of Windsor, Utah State University, University of California at Berkeley, Iowa State University, University of Toronto, Harvard University
(7) University School of Liberal and Applied Studies - University of Rochester
(8) Nashville Campus of University of Tennessee - University of Tennessee-Nashville
(9) Center for Continuing Education - University of

63

Georgia, University of South Florida
(10) Joint University Center - Memphis State Univ. /
University of Tennessee-Memphis
(11) Central Florida School for Continuing Studies -
Rollins College
(12) Evening and General Studies Division - Queensborough Community College
(13) Department of Evening and Special Classes -
University of Minnesota
(14) Evening Session - St. Francis College, St.
Peter's College
(15) Division of Adult Continuing Education - University of Toledo
(16) Evening Program - Aurora College, Modesto
Junior College, DeKalb College
(17) Division of Business Administration - Iona College
(18) Division of Special Programs - Union College,
C.W. Post College, (and Adult Ed.)
(19) Continuing Adult Education and Community Services - Northern Virginia Community College
(20) Department of Evening and Special Classes -
University of Minnesota
(21) Division of Special Programs - Miami-Dade
Junior College
(22) Division of General Studies - Upsala College
(23) Division of Continuing Studies - Memphis State
University
(24) Metropolitan College - St. Louis University,
Boston University
(25) Division of Evening Studies - Seminole Junior
College
(26) Division of Building Science and Division of
Continuing Education - Pratt Institute
(27) Evening and Saturday Division - Thomas More
College
(28) Evening Classes (no separate division) - Purdue
University-Calumet Campus, University of
Washington
(29) Division of Social Research - The New School
(30) Division of Urban Extension - Wayne State University
(31) Division of Educational Services - Baldwin-
Wallace College
(32) School or College of Continuing Studies - College
of William & Mary, University of Nebraska-
Omaha
(33) Evening and Extension Division - Nassau Com-

64

munity College

(34) Residence Credit Center - Miami University-Ohio
(35) Department of Evening Studies - Georgia Southern College
(36) School of Business Administration - Temple University
(37) Evening College and Summer Programs - Towson State College
(38) Division of Public Services - University of Oklahoma

2. How would you define the meaning of the term as used in your institution?

A. Evening Division

(1) Regular collegiate degree - oriented programs offered in the evening (LaSalle College)
(2) Created to meet the cultural and professional needs of men and women who are employed during the day (University of South Carolina)
(3) An extension of the college day into the evening (Centenary College of Louisiana)
(4) A Division serving the part-time evening students on campus (Northern Illinois University)
(5) The administrative unit which keeps the student's academic records-evening students (Louisiana State University-New Orleans)
(6) A Division of the University primarily concerned with a series of credit and non-credit courses, conferences and institutes, and, in addition, it actually encompasses all phases of part-time study done by adults (University of Bridgeport)
(7) Includes all classes scheduled after 6 p. m. and on Saturday mornings (Sir George Williams University)
(8) A Division to include the University College plus Continuing Education (Baylor University)
(9) The Division responsible for adult education, degree and non-credit special courses, evenings and Saturdays on and off-campus (Bryant College)
(10) It's a college with the sun-set (Western New England College)
(11) Each of five day divisions is academically responsible for it's own evening program which

is identical to the day programs leading to degrees (Northwestern University)

B. Evening College

(1) A program for adults 18 years of age or older not in full-time school; for individuals who cannot pursue an educational program in the regular session of the college; the program will provide leadership in the cultural and intellectual life of the surrounding community (Drury College)

(2) A separate administration, operating much as a second shift would do in industry (Virginia Commonwealth University)

(3) The Evening College is completely autonomous under a program of studies offered after 6 p. m. (Drexel University)

(4) Day classes offered as night classes (South Texas Junior College) (Indiana Central College)

(5) The Evening College offers courses, credit and non-credit, for both matriculated and non-matriculated students in the evening for students who are unable to attend day classes. Students can "set their own pace" as far as load is concerned. (Philadelphia College of Textiles)

(6) Although 85% descriptive, it is a misnomer; afternoon, Saturday morning and summer day and evening sessions are directed through this division (St. Joseph's College)

(7) College in the evening. This is a pure extension of the day school, although entrance requirements are less stringent. No physical education is required of evening students. (Pensacola Junior College)

(8) A college that offers its own Associate and Bachelor's degrees, controls its own faculty and has identical status as other campus colleges (University of Cincinnati)

(9) An extension of the college facilities into the evening hours in order to make university education available to those unable to attend classes in the day and especially to fix responsibility for seeing that the needs of adults are met (Texas Christian University)

(10) An accredited four-year college granting Bache-

lor and Associate degrees, but also offering special non-credit courses for adults (Xavier University)

(11) Evening College of the Division of Continuing Education (Manatee Junior College)

(12) A program for part-time higher education for adults (The Johns Hopkins University)

(13) Evening College (a part of the College of Arts and Sciences administered by an official of the Extension Division) defined: A general (two-year) program for adult students (University of North Carolina)

C. University College

(1) University College is one of nine colleges which offer evening and extension classes. The Center of Continuing Education develops programs with business, industry, and community service, as well as other groups of a non-credit nature (Drake University)

(2) University College covers part-time undergraduate offerings in business, liberal arts, law enforcement, and Allied Health Sciences (Northeastern University)

(3) A University program to provide specialized services for adult students (East Carolina University)

(4) Three-credit divisions operating in Maryland, and three-credit divisions overseas plus a Conference and Institute Division, and a Residential Center of Adult Education; defined: A service-oriented administrative unit facilitating the continuing education responsibilities of the University which also grants degrees. University College serves as the State Agency for Community Services and Continuing Education (Title I of Higher Education Act) (University of Maryland)

(5) Full-time college for students seeking a General Studies Degree or a Degree in Law Enforcement (Louisiana State University-Baton Rouge)

(6) The part-time, degree-granting division which offers classes in the late afternoon. evening, and on Saturday (Loyola University-Chicago)

(7) University College derives its name from the fact that it offers courses selected from the various fields of the Arts and Sciences, and

67

Business Administration as represented in various colleges and schools of the University (Tulane University)

    (8)   College of the University offering programs and courses for adults (Hofstra University)

    (9)   Encompasses all Continuing Education programs (University of Louisville)

   (10)   University College is a University within a University (not a college) as it is oriented toward a community (University of Richmond)

D.   Division of Continuing Education (Limited examples)

    (1)   Continuing Education basically represents the opportunity for adults to earn their undergraduate degree on a part-time basis. It also includes non-credit institutes, conferences, workshops, and extension courses (Springfield College)

    (2)   Educational opportunities offered by the University beyond those offered in articulated day school programs (Millard Fillmore College)

    (3)   A Division with the responsibility for coordinating evening classes, administering off-campus classes, and directing the program of institutes, seminars and non-credit courses (University of Tennessee-Chattanooga)

    (4)   In addition to special students who are formerly enrolled, the division is involved in all non-credit courses offered throughout the University, including cooperative extension, conferences, short courses, seminars, etc. (Ohio State University)

    (5)   Department of Conferences and Evening School under the Dean of Continuing Education (University of Tennessee-Knoxville)

    (6)   The function of Continuing Education at the University of West Florida is to administer off-campus credit courses and both on and off-campus non-credit programs. (The University of West Florida)

    (7)   Includes non-degree students, off-campus centers and programs, extension courses, correspondence courses, non-credit courses, conferences and seminars (University of New Mexico)

    (8)   The administrative unit responsible for all credit and non-credit programs over and above those

administered by day deans of the University (University of Southern Mississippi)

(9) All forms of University Extension and adult education except agricultural extension (The Pennsylvania State University)

(10) Credit and non-credit courses offered after 4:30 p. m. (on and off campus) and special interest courses (Orange County Community College)

(11) Although most people in the college consider this to be just an evening program, we have tried to view it in a broader sense as any type of program (credit or non-credit) offered to adults on a part-time basis. "We see it as encompassing both courses and seminars and institutes offered either during the day or in the evening. We try to think of it in the sense of a program which attempts to provide and encourage life-long learning for a wide variety of people and achieved through a variety of means. " (Utica College-Syracuse University)

(12) Any program not part of the day program except when NSF grants are involved - also includes day programs in the summer session (Rochester Institute of Technology)

(13) A Division through which educational services of the University are extended to individuals and groups other than day students - includes both credit and non-credit programs. (East Tennessee State University)

E. Other terminology defined:

(1) Evening School - A program of credit courses offered in the evening, primarily to serve adult communities (Marietta College-Ohio)

(2) Evening Program and Continuing Education - This office takes care of evening classes; the Continuing Education program was added to take care of non-credit activities (Roanoke College)

(3) Evening College of Business and Administration - One of the co-equal colleges of the University with an independent budget, curriculum, etc. with a Dean (University of Detroit)

(4) Division of Field Services - The title in no way reflects the function of the division, and a

title change is forthcoming (Trenton State College)

(5) Division of Extension - An extension of the day program to those unable to attend regular day classes (University of Windsor)

(6) College or School of General Studies - The College is concerned with all off-campus part-time educational programs (George Washington University)

(7) University School of Liberal and Applied Studies - It is essentially the evening counterpart of the College of Arts & Sciences. It combines with the professional schools to comprise the evening session (University of Rochester)

(8) Nashville campus of the University of Tennessee - "We operate as an autonomous unit of the University. " (University of Tennessee - Nashville)

(9) Center for Continuing Education - A Program for credit and non-credit courses, institutes, conferences, seminars and other educational services designed to meet the unique needs of adults who wish to continue their education (University of Georgia)

(10) University Extension - The Continuing Education and public service arm of the University (University of California at Berkeley - Univ. Ext.)

(11) Joint University Center MSU/UT - This joint center grew out of a former extension center. "We offer only evening classes (except on Saturdays in the morning) - no degree. " The Division receives equal support from Memphis State University and the Univ. of Tennessee

(12) Central Florida School of Continuing Studies - A college program primarily for adults who wish to continue their education (Rollins College)

(13) Evening and General Studies Division - A division of the college with the following areas of responsibilities: evening session, adult continuing education programs, community service program, extension program, basic educational skills training program and an Urban Center (when developed) (Queensborough Community College)

(14) Extension courses and conferences - Adult education implies "Quantitative educational ex-

periences as vital a part of continuing education, i.e., learning new skills, up-dating old
ones, new techniques, etc. Qualitative educational experiences are the second part of
any Continuing Education definition; i.e.,
personal development, growth and maturity.
This can involve both positive and negative
influences on us as individual members of
society." (Iowa State University)

(15) Division of Adult Continuing Education - The
Division operates as part of the year-round
service of the University providing degree
work through various colleges, as well as instruction through groups interested in non-
credit programs (University of Toledo)

(16) Evening program - The Evening Program is not
a separate college; it is part of the total program and of immediate concern to the Dean;
it supplements and strengthens the day curriculum (Aurora College)

(17) Division of Special Programs - Any education
program scheduled evenings, weekends, and
off-campus for persons beyond what was formerly regarded as "normal" school age (Miami-
Dade Junior College)

(18) Division of Continuing Studies - A Division offering functions to service the needs of students who do not choose to make college work
a full-time objective (Memphis State University)

(19) Metropolitan College offers continuing, non-
degree education for adults (St. Louis University) Offers part-time evening education
and degree credit (Boston University)

(20) Evening College of Arts and Sciences and Business (Boston College)

(21) Division of Building Science and Division of
Continuing Education - Both schools are within the School of Continuing Education and
Professional Studies - the terms apply to
formal credit programs for adults and non-
credit professional programs unrestricted as
to age or background (Pratt Institute)

(22) A Division of Social Research - "Covers all
non-degree courses, includes certificate programs (day and evening) (The New School)

(23) Division of Urban Extension - The extension
programs of the University to an Urban Set-

ting (Wayne State University)

(24) Evening and Extension Division - The administrative unit of the college which initiates, guides, facilitates and provides leadership in a many-faceted program for those persons not regularly enrolled as day students on the campus (Nassau Community College)

(25) Residence Credit Center - Any part-time program in the late afternoon or evening (Miami University-Ohio)

(26) Center for Continuing Education - Coordination of off-campus credit courses, non-credit activities, community services and special adult degree programs (University of South Florida)

(27) Evening School - Borrows faculty, courses, and subject specialists (department chairmen) but "we have our own management, quality control and we consider ourselves a vital and unique part of our college and the future of our national intelligence" (Rider College)

(28) School of Business Administration - The Division of the School of Business Administration which administers the evening undergraduate program in Business Administration (Temple University)

3. How would you define Continuing Education? (Limited examples)

(1) Formal or informal, credit or non-credit offerings designed to meet the educational needs of individuals over their entire life span (University of South Carolina)

(2) Continuing Education includes courses, conferences, self-study, seminars, lectures, educational television; it is a process and not a teaching method (Joint University Center-MSU/UT)

(3) Continuing education is primarily for adults who wish to continue study usually after a period of interruption (Rollins College)

(4) Continuing Education is life-long education for adult students. It may be credit, non-credit, short courses or conferences and institutes (East Carolina University)

(5) Continuing Education tends to mean non-credit courses, conferences, institutes, etc., especially for people who already have one or

more college degrees, particularly professional ones (New York University)

(6) Continuing Education is a series of learning situations aimed at solving problems recognized
by the learner as needing solutions. This
includes both formal and informal experiences
moving a person from where he is in the
direction of some desired goal (Drake University)

(7) Continuing Education is a life-long project -
either for credit or non-credit, either formal
or informal (Louisiana State University-New
Orleans)

(8) Educational opportunities for area residents
whose daily responsibilities prevent them
from attending the college's day division as
full-time students and who seek to complete
initial higher educational objectives, up-date
skills and techniques and to seek cultural enrichment (Dutchess Community College)

(9) Study by adults, either credit or non-credit, in
the late afternoon, the evening, and on Saturday mornings (Virginia Commonwealth University)

(10) Continuing Education provides an educational
program, and associated student services.

(11) That work which is undertaken during adult life
and may include credit or non-credit courses
and study towards an undergraduate and/or
graduate degree (Trenton State College)

(12) Continuing Education used at the University of
Denver implies non-credit courses or programs. It is defined as educational opportunities offered for anyone whose chief occupation or role in life is no longer that of a
full-time student. This definition applies to
both credit and non-credit programs (University of Denver)

(13) Continuing Education represents the 10% of a
person's time needed to keep up personally,
socially and professionally with the world today (Union College)

(14) A never-ending process with no necessary relationship to degrees held. Credit courses
are an integral part of continuing education
(St. Mary's Dominican College)

(15) Services to help a person who needs more knowledge during his lifetime than he can obtain in

73

normal high school and college. With rapidly
advancing technology in all fields, continuing
education is of greater importance than any
other previous period in history.

(16) Any education (credit, non-credit, vocational,
technical, etc.) that adds to existing education (Pensacola Junior College)

(17) Both credit and non-credit courses given to
persons who have completed their formal education (Seminole Junior College)

(18) Continuing Education may be formal or informal.
It may involve credit or non-credit, but in
any event it serves the student by providing
him with information, knowledge, or cultural
values which enhance his ability to earn a
living, his zeal for living, or his role in
society (Purdue University-Calumet Campus)

III. FEES

1. Is there a fee differential between day and evening
classes?

$\frac{53}{\text{yes}}$ $\frac{65}{\text{no}}$

2. If so, what is the justification?

(1) Day students have services and facilities not
available to evening students (Post Junior
College) (University of Rochester)

(2) Part-time students are mobile, and the fee is
priced accordingly (University of Detroit)

(3) The off-campus locations do not use the campus
facilities (George Washington University)

(4) Adult clientele is less affluent (Marietta College-
Ohio)

(5) The fee differential is due to the lack of sufficient legislative appropriations (University
of Hawaii)

(6) The fee for evening college is lower to compete
with several evening community colleges
(Rockhurst College)

(7) Evening students pay less than 1/2 the tuition
of day students (Northeastern University)

(8) There is a fee differential between day and
evening classes - the basic tuition for ex-

tension classes is $5 per term, plus registration, conferences, and laboratory fees. (Harvard University - Univ. Ext.)

(9) The part-time program is not entitled to most of the extra curricular benefits and activities, and the cost of instruction is less (Northeastern University)

(10) Evening students do not pay an application fee, college commons fees, health service fee, new student fee, or change of registration fee (Aurora College)

Examples of Comparative Day and Evening Tuition

Part-time Day	Part-time Evening	School
$1600 (f. t. day)	$38 per sem. hr.	LaSalle College
Off-campus courses are $3 per qtr. hr. more than on-campus crs.		Univ. of West Fla.
$60 per sem. hr.	$35 per sem. hr.	Marietta Coll. -Ohio
$25 (f. t.)	$3 college fee	Dutchess Comm. Coll.
$211 for 3hr. crs.	$100 for 3-hr. crs.	Roanoke College
$55 per cr. hr.	$42 per cr. hr.	Univ. of Detroit
$68 per hr. (plus center fee)	$50 per hr.	Geo. Washington Univ.
$175 per term (f. t.)	$20 per cr.; grad. st. -$25	Trenton State College
$45 per qtr. plus institute fee of $30, $50 or $70 depending on credit carried or qtr. of study	$25 per qtr. plus annual institute fee of $35	Drexel Univ.
$55 per cr.	$42 per cr.	Univ. of Detroit
---	No fees charged evening students	Bakersfield College Univ. of Bridgeport
$120 per crs.	$100 per crs.	Univ. of New Hampshire
$50 per/sem hr.	$22 per/sem hr.	Loyola Univ. -New Orleans
$50 per/hr.	$38 per/hr.	Rider College
$80 per/sem hr.	$30 per/sem. hr.	Johns Hopkins Univ.
Students in the regular day program pay approx. twice the fee of students in the part-time evening		Northeastern Univ.

Part-time Day	Part-time Evening	School
$200 plus $20 activity fee (f. t.)	$17 per /cr. hr.	Orange Cty. Comm. College
$2400 per yr. (f. t. day)	$25 per /sem. hr.	Rollins College
$9 per /cr.	$20 per /cr.	Univ. of Hawaii
$14 plus $5. 25 for fees	$17 per /cr. hr.	Univ. of Nebraska
$80 per /sem. hr.	$40 per /sem. hr.	Washington Univ. (St. Louis)
$50 per /cr.	$35 per /cr.	St. Joseph's College
$270 per /course	$117 per /course	Union College
$45 per /sem. hr.	$16. 67 per /sem. hr.	Bryant College
$40 per /cr. hr.	$25 per /cr. hr.	Rockford College

3. What are your refund policies?

(1)	Percentage refund within first week only	4
(2)	Percentage refund within two weeks	14
(3)	Percentage refund within three weeks	10
(4)	Percentage refund within four weeks	10
(5)	Percentage refund within five weeks	14
(6)	Percentage refund within six weeks	5
(7)	Percentage refund within seven weeks	1
(8)	Percentage refund within nine weeks	1
(9)	Percentage refund within 1/3 or 1/2 of term	2
(10)	No refund after classes begin	4
(11)	"Same as for day students"	7
(12)	Within 10 days	4
(13)	Percentage basis - sliding scale	37

Examples of Refund Policies (Partial Listing)

(1) First week - 90%; second week - 80%; third week - 70%; fourth week - 60%; fifth week - 50%; sixth week - 40%; seventh week - 30%; none thereafter (LaSalle College) (University of Rochester)

(2) Students have ten days to drop all courses with a full refund (Northern Illinois University)

(3) If a student withdraws within a week after the first class he will receive a 50% refund (Centenary College of Louisiana; County Col-

lege of Morris)

(4) Full refund after the first meeting of the class; no refund after the sixth meeting (Drury College)

(5) There is no refund of 1/3 down payment; refund on a decreasing percentage basis is made up to six weeks, and no refund is made after that time (Marietta College-Ohio)

(6) Refunds are based on a diminishing scale of 90% for the first week to 0% after five weeks (Drake University)

(7) A refund for reduction of hours carried is made if the drop occurs before the date specified to add courses for credit (Louisiana State University-New Orleans)

(8) 80% - first week of classes; no refund after that time (Roanoke College)

(9) Prior to beginning of classes 100% refund; within two weeks (due to illness) - 50%; no refund after second week (Virginia Commonwealth University)

(10) One-half tuition can be refunded first two weeks of class, and nothing thereafter (University of New Hampshire),

(11) Refund policy of 50% by course, and 50% if student withdraws during first 50% of total class hours (The Pennsylvania State University)

(12) 70% - first week; 50% - second week; none thereafter (Philadelphia College of Textiles)

(13) 25% refunds are made if drops within the first two weeks of classes; no refunds are made thereafter (Sir George Williams University)

(14) Refunds are made on the basis of one-half of tuition from one day of class to mid-semester (University of Kentucky)

(15) There are no refunds for students who drop one or more courses but remain in school (Bakersfield College)

(16) 75% refund - first week; 37 1/2% refund - second week (of 10 week sessions) (University of Hawaii)

(17) Full refund before the end of the first week - after that no refund (St. Francis College)

(18) Within 1st week of semester - 80%; 1 to 3 weeks - 60%; 3 to 5 weeks - 40%; none thereafter (St. Mary's Dominican College)

(19) No refund is given unless a class is cancelled (Modesto Junior College) (University of Rich-

mond) (The Johns Hopkins University)
(20) Mail registrant who withdraws prior to regular
registration receives a full refund minus
$5.00 processing fee; withdrawal prior to
deadline (second week) 75% refund (College of
William & Mary)

IV.   FACULTY AND FACULTY RECRUITMENT

1.   Do you have a policy regarding the percentage of faculty
for evening classes that are full-time faculty members?

26	86
yes	no

Approximately what percentage are full-time?

17	26	33	21	25
0 - 24%	25 - 40%	45 - 60%	61 - 84%	85 - 100%

2.   Recruitment

A.   Who has the final authority for hiring full and/or
part-time faculty members for evening classes in
your institution?

Full-time		Part-time	
Dean and/or Director	49	Dean and/or Director	11
President or Chancellor	9	Same as f. t. faculty	11
V. P. for Acad. Affairs	5	Dean of College(s)	15
Department Chairmen	26	Department Chairmen	2
Both Chmn. and Dean/Dir.	20	Both Chmn. and Dean/	
Dean(s) of Day College	16	Dir.	17
Asst. Dean of Div. /Coll.	1	County Personnel Dir.	
Comm. on faculty apps.	2	for Board of Ed.	1
Dean of Instr. or V. P.	5		
Bd. of Trustees or Governor	3		
Dir. of Cont. Ed.	1		
Dean of Special Ed.	1		
Univ. Ext. Dean	2		
Dir. of Div. of Bus. Ad.	1		
County Personnel Dir.	1		

B.   Can you as Director or Dean of the Evening Division
or College, reject a faculty member who has been

78

assigned to teach evening classes?

$$\frac{78}{\text{yes}} \quad \frac{21}{\text{no}}$$

C. Do you employ full-time faculty members who teach exclusively in the evening?

$$\frac{38}{\text{yes}} \quad \frac{88}{\text{no}}$$

Schools Employing Full-Time Faculty Members in the Evening

1. LaSalle College
2. Univ. of South Carolina
3. County College of Morris
4. Drury College
5. New York University
6. Drake University
7. University of Detroit
8. Utah State University
9. Univ. of So. Mississippi
10. Univ. of Tenn. -Nashville
11. Univ. of Georgia (Waycross Center)
12. Joint Univ. Center - MSU/UT
13. Bklyn. Coll. of City U. of N. Y.
14. Queensborough Comm. College
15. Northeastern Univ.
16. Univ. of Missouri
17. St. Joseph's College
18. East Carolina University
19. Prince George's Comm. College
20. City College of New York
21. University of Minnesota
22. St. Peter's College
23. University of Utah
24. University of Richmond
25. University of Maryland
26. Texas Christian University
27. Loyola Univ. - New Orleans
28. Rochester Institute of Technology
29. Jefferson State Junior Coll.
30. Miami University - Ohio
31. C. W. Post College
32. San Diego Evening College
33. Rockford College
34. University of Oklahoma

D. What is the salary range for part-time faculty? What salary do you pay for overloads?

Municipal or State Colleges and Universities

Institution	Salary, Part-time	Salary, Overloads
1. Univ. of South Carolina	$600-$1000 per/course	$600-$1000 per/course
2. New York University	$450-$1000 per/course	$450-$1000 per/course
3. Univ. of West Florida	$750-$1250 per/course	9% of instructor's base salary per/course
4. Virginia Commonwealth Univ.	$705 per/3-hr. course (f.t.) $235 per/cr. hr. (p.t.) ($20 extra for 3/hr cr. course meeting two times per week; $60 extra for grad. instr.)	No overloads permitted
5. University of Windsor	1/6 base salary for the rank is paid (p.t. or f.t.)	1/6 of base salary for the rank is paid (p.t. or f.t.)
6. University of Kentucky	---	Based on course level: 100-411 level - $220/cr. 400-500 level - $240/cr. 600-800 level - $260/cr.
7. Idaho State University	$170-$185 per/sem. hr.	Overloads permitted - no salary listed
8. North Carolina State Univ.	Salary determined and paid for through departments	Extra Compensation restricted to 20% of 9 mos. salary - paid through departments
9. Utah State University	$140-$180 per/qtr. hr.	Overloads permitted - no salary listed

80

Institutions	Salary, Part-time $1000-$2000 per/course	Salary, Overloads $1100-Instructor; $1400-Asst. Prof. $1700-Assoc. Prof.; $2000-Prof.
10. Univ. of New Hampshire		
11. Trenton State College	$205 per/sem. hr.	$205 per/sem. hr.
12. City College of New York	$16-$26 per/contact hr.	$16-$26 per/contact hr.
13. Univ. of Minnesota	$207-$319 per/cr. hr.	$207-$319 per/cr. hr.
14. Univ. of Cincinnati	$135-$200 per/qtr. hr.	$200-$270 per/qtr. hr.
15. University of Utah	$120-$239 per/cr. hr.	1/63 times annual salary per/cr. hr. with maximum of $239 per/cr. hr.
16. University of Maine	$720-$900 per/3-hr. crse.	1/12 of faculty member's salary with maximum of $1250 for 3/hr. course
17. University of Maryland	Salary range for 3/hr. class $710-Instr.; $875-Assoc. Prof.; $785-Asst. Prof.; $975-Prof.	$710-Instr.; $875-Assoc. Prof.; $785-Asst. Prof.; $975-Prof.
18. Purdue Univ.-Calumet Campus (Grad)	$150-$210 per/wkly. contact hr. $120-$130 per/wkly. lab hr. $200-$285 per/wkly. contact hr.	Overload salary is based upon 1) faculty salary, 2) contact hrs., 3) numerical index value to the level of the proposed course
19. Pennsylvania State Univ.	$200-$240 per/cr.	$240 per/cr.
20. Univ. of Tenn.-Chattanooga	$480-$675 per/3-hr. crse.	$275-$300 per/sem. hr.
21. Bklyn. Coll. of City Univ. of N.Y.	---	$240-$390 per/cr. hr. $450-$720 per/3/cr. crse.
22. DeKalb College	$450 per/crse.-M.A. to $750 per/crse. Ph.D. plus 3 yrs. experience $16-$20 per/contact hr.	
23. Univ. of Washington	$16-$20 per/contact hr.	$16-$20 per contact hr. or $600 per 3/cr. lecture crse.

Institutions	Salary, Part-time	Salary, Overloads
24. Wichita State University	$135 per/cr. hr.	No overloads permitted
25. Wayne State University	$10-$25 per/contact hr.	$525-Instr.; $690-Assoc. Prof.; $525-Asst. Prof.; $750-Prof.
26. College of William & Mary	$675-$825 per/3 hr. crse.	$780-$825 per/3 hr. crse.
27. East Tenn. State Univ.	$150-$170 per/qtr. hr.	$100-$210 per/qtr. hr.
28. Univ. of Tenn.-Knoxville	$166.66-$200 per/cr. hr.	$166.66-$200 per/cr. hr.
29. Miami University	$170-$310 per/cr. hr.	$170-$310 per/cr. hr.
30. Georgia Southern College	$600 per/crse.	$600 per/crse.
31. Washburn Univ. of Topeka	$160 per/hr.	$160 per/hr.
32. Univ. of No. Carolina	$900-$1600 per/crse.	No overloads permitted
33. Joint Univ. Center-MSU/UT	$450 per/30 hrs. class instr.	$450 per/30 hrs. class instr.
34. University of Hawaii	$260 per/cr. - Instr. $490 per/cr. - Professor	$260 per/cr. - Instr. $490 per/cr. - Professor
35. University of Toronto	56 faculty "cross-appointed"	$1675 per/crse. - Lect. $2100/ per crse. Asst. Prof., $2530 per/crse.; Assoc. Prof.-$3650 per/crse.; Professor
36. University of Missouri	W/A & S-$3000 for 25% f.t. most are shared 50/50 with a dept. in faculty of A & S $720 per/3 hr. crse. - Instr. $770 per/3 hr. crse. - Instr. B, $1105 per/3 hr. crse. - Assoc. Prof. $1210 per/3 hr. crse. - Professor	Instructors may teach one over-load class per year - faculty in rank teach evening classes as part of regular load.
37. University of Nebraska	No part-time faculty	$850 per/3 sem. hr. crse. Amt. received cannot exceed 20% of annual salary.
38. University of Toledo	$10-$25 per/hr.	$750-$100 per/crse.

Institutions	Salary, Part-time	Salary, Overloads
39. East Carolina University	$10-$20 per/contact hr.	$10-$20 per/contact hr.
40. Memphis State University	$480-$960 per/crse.	$480-$960 per/crse.
41. University of Oregon	$590 per/3 sem. hr. crse.	$150-$250 sem. hr.
42. Univ. of Nebraska-Omaha	$165 per/cr. hr.	$165 per/cr. hr.
	$600-$800 per/3 hr. crse.	3% of contract salary for each 1 hr. teaching load
43. Ohio State University	$190 per/contact hr. M.A.; A.B.D. (all but dissertation) $230 per/contact hr. Doctoral equivalent	$220 per/contact - Instr.; $230 per/contact - Asst. Prof.; $245 per/contact - Assoc. Prof.; $260 per/contact hr. - Prof.
44. Towson State College	$604 per/3-cr. hr. - Instr. $683 per/3-cr. hr. - Asst. Prof. $761 per/3-cr. hr. - Assoc. Prof. $840 per/3-cr. hr. - Professor	No overloads permitted
45. San Diego Evening Coll.	Step I $156 per/hr.; Step II $162 per/hr; Step III $169 per/hr.; Step IV $176 per/hr.	
46. University of Oklahoma	No part-time faculty	$125 per cr. hr. to equivalent of regular salary
47. Univ. of Calif. at Berkeley	$15-$18 per/cl. hr.	---
48. Univ. of Georgia	$550 per/5 qtr. hr. crse.	$550 per/b qtr. hr. crse.
49. Millard Fillmore College	$870 per/3 sm. hr. crse. Inst.-$1050; Asst. Prof.-$1350; Assoc. Prof.-$1800; Prof.	No overloads permitted
50. Univ. of So. Mississippi	$350 for undergraduate crse.; $400 for graduate crse. (4 hrs.)	No overloads permitted

Institutions	Salary, Part-time $400-$600 per/crse.	Salary, Overloads $400-$600 per/crse.
51. Univ. of Tenn. -Nashville		

Private and Church-Related Institutions

Institutions	Salary, Part-time $400-$600 per/crse.	Salary, Overloads $400-$600 per/crse.
1. LaSalle College	$650-$1344 per/3 cr. hr.	No overloads permitted
2. Drury College	$112-$250 per/sem. hr.	$144-$250 per/sem. hr.
3. Marietta College-Ohio	$700-$950 per/crse.	$700-$950 per/crse.
4. Drake University	$600-$750 per/3 hr. crse.	No overloads permitted
5. Roanoke College	$233 per/cr. hr.	$233 per/cr. hr.
6. Univ. of Detroit-Eve. Coll.	$250 per/cr. hr.	No overloads permitted
7. George Washington Univ.	$700-$1000 per/3 sem. crse.	$700-$1000 per/3 sem. hr. crse.
8. Roosevelt University	$600 per/crse.	No overloads permitted
9. University of Denver	$100-$1000 per/crse.	No overloads permitted
10. Drexel University	$30-$66 per/3 hr. eve.	No overloads permitted
11. The American University	$715 per/3 hr. crse. - lect. $950 per/3 hr. crse. - Adj. Profs.	$950 per/3 hr. crse. -off campus Some departments - no over-loads
12. Univ. of Detroit-McNichols	$250 per/cr.	$300 per/cr.
13. Sacred Heart University	$540-$600 per/3 hr. crse.	$540-$600 per/3 hr. crse.
14. University of Rochester	$1060 per/crse. - Instr., $1120 Asst Prof., Assoc. Prof., $1200 per/crse	$1060 per/crse.-Instr., $1120 per/crse.-Asst Prof.-$1160 per/crse.; Assoc. Prof.-$1200 per/crse.; Professors
15. Northeastern University	$15-$22.50 per/hr.	$15-$22.50 per/hr.
16. Univ. of Bridgeport	$170-$225 per/crse.	$150-$180 per/crse.
17. Indiana Central College	$120-$184 per/cr. hr.	$190 per/cr. hr.

	Institutions	Salary, Part-time	Salary, Overloads
18.	Rollins College	$700-$750 per/crse.	$1000 per/crse.
19.	Sir George Williams Univ.	$1000 per/2-hr. crse, $1200 per/3-hr. crse., $1650 per/4-hr. crse.	No overloads permitted
20.	Utica Coll.-Syracuse Univ.	$570-$780 per/3-hr. crse.	$225 per/cr. hr. Instr. to $300 per/cr. hr. Full Professors
21.	Washington Univ.-St. Louis	$185-$285 per/unit	Amount received cannot exceed 20% of a faculty member's regular pay
22.	St. Joseph's College	$720-$1070 per/3-hr. crse.	$720-$1070 per/3-hr. crse.
23.	Aurora College	$8-$20 per/class hr.	No overloads permitted
24.	Iona College	$210-$300 per/cr. hr.	No overloads permitted
25.	Suffolk University	$700 per/3-sem. hr. crse.	No overloads permitted
26.	Union College	$250 per/cr., $300-$400 per/cr. Graduate Faculty	$250 per/cr., $300-$400 per/cr. Graduate Faculty
27.	Bryant College	$725 per/3-hr. crse.	$725 per/3-hr. crse.
28.	St. Mary's Dominican Coll.	$175 per/sem. hr.	Paid by sem. hr.
29.	St. Peter's College	$165-$290 per/cr. hr. based on rank	$165-$290 per/cr. hr. based on rank
30.	Upsala College	$210 per/contact hr. Instr. & Asst. Prof.; $275 per/contact hr. - Assoc. & Full Professors	$275 per/contact hr. - Assoc./Full Prof.
31.	Boston College	$52. 50 per/evening	$52. 50 per/evening
32.	Rockhurst College	$17, $22, or $35 per/one 90-min. session	$17, $22, or $35 per/one 90-min. session
33.	Pratt Institute	$250-$400 based on contact hrs.	$250-$400 based on contact hrs.
34.	Texas/Christian Univ.	$400-$750 per/crse.	No overloads permitted

	Institutions	Salary, Part-time	Salary, Overloads
35.	Thomas More College	$160 per/sem. hr. -A. B., $175 per/sem. hr. -M. A., $185 per/ sem. hr. -Ph. D.	Asst. Prof., $190 per/sem. hr. - Assoc. Prof., $195 per/sem. hr. -Professors
36.	Phila. Coll. of Textiles and Science	$180-$250 per/cr.	$200-$250 per/cr. or $550-$750 per/crse.
37.	Loyola Univ. -New Orleans	$500 per/3-sem. hr. crse.	$500 per/3-sem. hr. crse.
38.	Xavier University	$500-$1500 per/crse.	No overloads permitted
39.	The New School	$500-$550 per/3 hr. crse.	$500-$550 per/3 hr. crse.
40.	Metropolitan Coll. -Boston University	$160-$240 per/cr. hr.	10% of base salary per crse.
41.	Loyola Univ. -Chicago	$500-$650 per/3 hr. crse.	No overloads permitted
42.	Bradley University	$200 per/sem. hr.	No overloads permitted
43.	Rochester Inst. of Tech.	$249-$306 per/contact hr. -B. S. $309-$363 per/contact hr. -M. S. $366-$429 per/contact hr. -Ph. D.	$249-$306 per/contact hr. -B. S. $309-$363 per/contact hr. -M. S. $366-$429 per/contact hr. -Ph. D.
44.	University of Tampa	$500 per/3 hr. crse. -M. A., $600 per/3 hr. crse. -Ph. D.	$500 per/3 hr. crse. -M. A., $600 per/3 hr. crse. -Ph. D.
45.	Baldwin-Wallace College	$155-$229 per/contact hr.	$155-$229 per/contact hr.
46.	American International Coll.	$600-$775 per/3 hr. crse.	$600-$775 per/3 hr. crse.
47.	Tulane University	$500-$725 per/crse.	$700-$975 per/crse.
48.	Univ. of Louisville	$215-$305 per/cr. hr.	$215-$305 per/cr. hr.
49.	Northwestern University	$550-$800 per/2 sem. hr. crse.	$650-$800 per/2 sem. hr. crse.
50.	Hofstra University	$200 per/cr. hr. -$275 per/cr. hr.	$200-$275 per/cr. hr.
51.	Fairleigh Dickinson Univ.	$8-$12 per/hr.	No overloads permitted
52.	Springfield College	$607-$847 per/class	$607-$847 per/class
53.	C. W. Post College	$175-$375 per/credit	$225-$375 per/credit

86

Institutions	Salary, Part-time	Salary, Overloads
54. Rider College	$200 per/sem. hr.-Instr. $225 per/sem. hr.-Asst. Prof., $240 per/sem. hr.-Assoc. Prof., $260 per/sem. hr.-Professor	$200 per/sem. hr.-Instr., $225 per/sem. hr.-Asst. Prof., $240 per/sem. hr.-Assoc. Prof., $260 per/sem hr.-Prof.
55. The Johns Hopkins Univ.	$225 per/sem. hr. up-depending upon qualifications of instr.	Depends on qualifications of instructor
56. Temple University	$300-$600 per/sem. hr.	No overloads permitted
57. University of Richmond	$700-$775 per/crse.	$500 per/crse.
58. Centenary Coll. of Louisiana	$300-$750 per/sem. hr.	No overloads permitted
59. PMC Colleges	$600-$900 per/crse. per sem.	$170-$245 per/cr. hr.
60. Russell Sage College	$300-$350 per/cr. hr.	$300-$350 per/cr. hr.

Private and State Community (Junior) Colleges

Institutions	Salary, Part-time	Salary, Overloads
1. County College of Morris	$180-$270 per/cr. hr.	$190-$270 per/cr. hr.
2. South Texas Junior Coll.	$480-$510 per/cr. hr.	$510 per/crse.
3. Bakersfield College	$8.83 per/class hr.	1/1000 of base salary; none less than $8.83 per/class hr.
4. Post Junior College	$225 per/sem. hr.-Instr., $250 per/sem. hr.-Asst. Prof. $275 per/sem. hr.-Assoc. Prof., $300 per/sem. hr.-Professors	Evening classes usually taught as part of normal load; if not the salary is the same as for part-time.
5. Queensborough Comm. Coll.	$240-$371 per/sem. hr.	$240-$371 per/sem. hr.

Institutions	Salary, Part-time	Salary, Overloads
6. No. Virginia Comm. Coll.	$100-$200 per/qtr. hr.	$100-$200 per/qtr. hr.
7. Prince George's Comm. College	$200 per/contact hr. -M A., $225 per/contact hr. -M A. plus 15-30; $250 per/contact hr. -M A. plus 60, $275 per/contact hr. -Ph. D.	$200 per/contact hr. -M A., $225 per/contact hr. -M A. plus 15-30; $250 per/contact hr. -M A. plus 60, $275 per/contact hr. -Ph. D.
8. Pensacola Junior College	$10 per/sem. hr. -B.A., $12.50 per/sem. hr. -M.A., $15 per/sem. hr. -Ph. D.	$10 per/sem. hr. -B.A., $12.50 per/sem. hr. -M.A., $15 per/sem. hr. -Ph. D.
9. Modesto Junior College	$6.50-$13 per/hr.	No overloads permitted
10. Manhattan Comm. Coll.	$16-$25 per/hr.	$16-$25 per/hr.
11. Comm. Coll. of Baltimore	$200-$250 per/cr. hr.	No overloads permitted
12. Southwestern Michigan Coll.	$175 per/cr. hr.	$175 per/cr. hr.
13. Jefferson State Junior Coll.	$400 per/crse. -B.A. $450 per/crse. -M.A., $500 per/crse-M.A. plus 30 hrs., $550 per/crse-Ph.D.	No overloads permitted
14. Manatee Junior College	$600-$700 per/3 sem. hr. crse.	$600-$700 per/3 sem. hr. crse.
15. Central Comm. State Coll.	$250-$300 per/sem. hr.	No overloads permitted
16. Dutchess Comm. College	$220-$270 per/cr. hr.	$220-$270 per/cr. hr.
17. Miami-Dade Junior Coll.	$550-$750 per/3 hr. crse.	3/4 of one-month's salary for overload
18. Orange County Comm. Coll.	$240-$345 per/cr. hr.	$240-$345 per/cr. hr.
19. Suffolk Community College	$200-$250 per/sem. hr.	$200-$250 per/sem. hr.

E. Can you as Evening Director (or Dean) engage an instructor without the consent of the department head if this person refuses to staff these classes?

$\dfrac{53}{\text{yes}}$ $\dfrac{38}{\text{no}}$

F. Do you hold regular faculty meetings with your evening faculty?

$\dfrac{33}{\text{yes}}$ $\dfrac{60}{\text{no}}$

If so, when are they held?

Before classes begin	$\underline{2}$	Once each semester or	
First week of classes	$\underline{2}$	quarter	$\underline{21}$
		Once a year	$\underline{10}$

Other

(1) Four times a year (plus called meetings) (New York University) (The American University)
(2) In the evening (Dutchess Community College)
(3) Periodically (Roosevelt University)
(4) Faculty meetings are attended by both day and evening faculty (The American University)
(5) Faculty meetings are held the second week of the quarter (University of Southern Mississippi)
(6) Faculty meetings are held on Friday and Sunday afternoons (University of Bridgeport)
(7) Once a month (University of Tennessee-Nashville)
(8) Irregular meetings only are held for evening faculty (The Pennsylvania State University)
(9) In the late afternoons (University of Toronto)
(10) Faculty meetings are held weekly (Modesto Junior College)
(11) Faculty meetings are held twice quarterly (Jefferson State Junior College)
(12) Faculty meetings are held twice a month (University of Richmond)

G. What are your policies regarding regular faculty members teaching credit or non-credit courses or participating in conferences, etc., as an overload?

$\underline{\hspace{1cm}39\hspace{1cm}}$	$\underline{\hspace{0.5cm}57\hspace{0.5cm}}$	$\underline{\hspace{0.5cm}33\hspace{0.5cm}}$
none permitted	permitted	restricted

Amount of Overload Permitted

(1) Limit of 3 (or 4) sem. (qtr.) hrs. (or one class) per sem. (qtr.)   36

(2) Limit of 6-9 hrs. per year beyond normal schedule   5

(3) Two nights a week (6 sem. hrs.) in the evening division   2

(4) Consent of Academic Dean or Department Head   2

(5) Amount received cannot exceed 20% regular salary   6

(6) Six hours of credit may be taught as an overload each year   2

(7) A maximum of eight hours permitted for overloads per term   1

(8) An overload class allowed each year   1

(9) Restricted to 15 hrs. per quarter   1

H. Is there a budget allotment for recruitment in your budget?

<u>30</u>   <u>32</u>
yes   no

If so, what % of the budget?

Less than 1% . .7	5% 5
2-2 1/2% 4	7 1/2% . . .1
3-4% 2	10% 2
	12 to 20% . .2

V. SCHEDULING

1. Are you, as Dean or Director, responsible for the evening class schedule in your institution?

Yes <u>110</u>   No <u>33</u>

2. If not, who is responsible?

Registrar	3	Day Dean(s)	9
Department Heads	7	Dir. Adult Ed. Div.	1
Dean of A & S	2	Univ. Ext. Dean	1
Univ. Admin.	4	Head, Class Programs	1
Dean of Spec. Ed.	1	Assoc./Asst. Dean,	
Assoc. Dean Ed. Serv.	1	Eve. Div.	2
		V. P., Acad. Affairs	1

3. What is the procedure for compiling the evening class schedule in your college or university?

(1) Department heads (or schools) submit evening class schedule for approval by the Dean or Director who makes revisions. 43

(2) The schedule is based upon the needs of the students and the requirements of the curricula. 8

(3) The Registrar requests schedule, submits tentative schedule to the Evening Division or College for approval. 4

(4) The evening class schedule is planned by the Director(s) or Dean or College and then is submitted to departments for staffing and possible suggestions or revisions. 7

(5) Courses are scheduled in cycles over the years to enable students to meet degree requirements - the schedule is revised only when necessary. 3

(6) Past schedules are carefully checked to see what courses materialized and what courses are needed to meet the curricula requirements and student needs. 5

(7) The departments send their evening class schedule to the Registrar. This office compiles the schedule and mails catalogs. 2

Additional Procedures

(1) The program administrator or department head turns in "room cards" requesting appropriate space for classes. After approval of the Curriculum Committee, the recommendations are submitted to the Chancellor and Board of Trustees for formal approval. (New York University)

(2) The schedule is compiled according to availability of instructors and off-campus sites. (University of West Florida)

(3) According to the Director "We try to avoid difficult combinations, and keep courses and their pre-requisites on the same evening." (University of Windsor)

(4) Compiling the evening class schedule involves a procedure of coordinating with the field education officer and the University with the CGS staff. (George Washington University)

(5) Required courses are offered on a pre-deter-
mined schedule regardless of the number of
students enrolled. (Drexel University)

(6) Day/evening classes are included on the same
schedule. (The American University)

(7) The schedule is compiled from surveys, demand,
and course sequences. (Idaho State University)

(8) Courses required for all programs are offered
each year and summer - other or special
curricular requirements every two years and
summer. (Post Junior College)

(9) The University Extension Dean is responsible
for scheduling evening classes, but schedules
are compiled by department heads and programmers in the various extension academic
departments. (University of California -
Berkeley - Univ. Ext.)

(10) Class schedules are compiled on the basis of
regular rotation, and special needs. (Indiana
Central College)

(11) The Associate Dean of Continuing Education
recommends off-campus and non-credit
courses. (Orange County Community College)

(12) Student surveys, past schedules, past student
responses, course sequences, instructor a-
vailability, and facilities are all taken into
consideration when preparing the class schedule. (Rollins College)

(13) The Program Director makes tentative schedules, negotiates with departments for staff -
courses are added by request or need. (University of Hawaii)

(14) The schedule is compiled by the estimated need
based on experience. Schedules are announced six years in advance. (University
of Toronto)

(15) The evening class schedule is compiled by each
of 22 field offices for an overall total of more
than 200 class locations. (Pennsylvania State
University)

(16) The Director of University Evening Classes on-
campus, Off-Campus Center Directors, and
Extension Coordinators are responsible for
class schedules for on and off-campus locations. Students are polled to determine needs,
staff availability is determined and current
student profiles are reviewed along with prior
quarter offerings before compiling the evening

class schedule which takes into account projected needs of students. (University of
Georgia)

(17) The evening class schedule is coordinated by the
Coordinator and department chairmen prior to
the Dean of Instruction's approval. (Seminole
Junior College)

(18) The Directors coordinate classes, then a consolidated list is sent to departments with requests for staff. (University of Maryland)

(19) Information is compiled from the various departments for all parts of the schedule, both
day and evening. This information is assembled and many of the requirements are
put together by the Assistant Dean for Academic Affairs in cooperation with the Assistant Director for Administration who is in
charge of space use and the Assistant Dean
for Evening Administration (Calumet Campus).
(Purdue University)

(20) Students tentatively select classes for next year
in March. The results dictate next year's
schedule. (Western New England College)

4. Do you as Dean or Director have the authority to revise
or make additions to the evening class schedule?

$\frac{92}{\text{yes}}$ $\frac{12}{\text{no}}$ $\frac{3}{\text{with consultation}}$

5. Are your three-hour classes scheduled on one night 49
two nights 35 or both 46 ?

6. Research

The Research Committee of AUEC is interested in any research projects in adult education which have been completed, or are in progress, or planned for the near future.
Do you have any research projects completed or in progress
at your institution?

$\frac{26}{\text{yes}}$ $\frac{80}{\text{no}}$

School   Topic
(1) New York University   "A History of the Division of
                           General Education, N. Y. Uni-

School	Topic

versity, 1934-1959, Ed. D. thesis - Anna Freidus.
"Patterns of Educational Use of a Televised Public Destroyer" sponsored by the University Council on Education for Public Responsibility. Study Director, Harry N. Miller
"New York University's Harlem Seminars" - a narrative account of a Title I project under the direction of Harry L. Miller.
"Survey on University Adult Education in the Metropolitan Area of New York" - a study made possible by a grant from the Fund for the Advancement of Education, The Ford Foundation under the direction of Mrs. Caroline Ellwood.
"An Evaluation of the MIND Adult Education Center of West 114th'St. in Harlem" - an evaluation of a novel attempt at prevocational basic education for residents of 114th St. between 7th and 8th Ave. by MIND, Inc., a subsidiary of Corn Products Corp.

(2) Marietta College(Ohio)

A summary of course offerings and enrollments for the past ten years.

(3) University of Denver

The Office of Continuing Education of the University of Denver plans to cooperate with other schools in the Denver area on a project sponsored by the Adult Education Council of Metropolitan Denver which obtains information on enrollment trends.

(4) The American University

Various projects are underway through the Labor Studies Center-Title I projects and a Research in Educational Technology

School	Topic
	is planned.
(5) Utah State University	A study has just been completed entitled, "Utah State University Educational Services on the Uintah and Ouvay Indian Reservations." (historical)
(6) C. W. Post Junior College	In progress - Performance Objectives in Business Administration Curriculum.
(7) Mohawk Valley Community College	A study of Part-time Adult Students in a Community College.
(8) Northeastern University	A doctoral student is currently conducting a research project on Student Activities.
(9) University of Tennessee-Nashville	Research in progress relating to the characteristics of evening school students.
(10) The Pennsylvania State University	A sizeable number of research projects are underway through an applied research unit operating under Continuing Education.
(11) Joint University Center - MSU/UT	Doctoral dissertations: concerns how evening administrators select courses.
(12) Orange County Community College	Five-year Predictions of Continuing Education Programs at Orange County Community College.
(13) University of Missouri	a) Predictors of Academic Success Among Evening College Students b) Financial Needs Analysis of Evening Students c) Personal Data Relating to Evening Students d) Students Who Lift the Evening College - Employment

95

School	Topic
	Status of Evening Students.
(14) St. Joseph's College	A study has been made of the academic progress of evening students of the first through the fifth quintile in high school - of students admitted in 1963-65.
(15) University of Arkansas	Director's dissertation: "An Analysis of the Role and Scope of General Extension Services of the University of Arkansas Division of Continuing Education."
(16) St. Mary's Dominican College	A study of a Bachelor of Liberal Studies Program.
(17) Mississippi State College for Women	A research project "Continuing Education for Women" is in progress.
(18) East Tennessee State University	A study is planned to compare day and evening classes, procedures and results.
(19) Nassau Community College	A research project has been completed on the "Cooperative Opportunity in Public Education (COPE)"
(20) Miami University-Ohio	Some research projects in adult education have been completed or are in progress.
(21) Temple University	"A comparative study of Day and Evening Undergraduates in Temple University," a dissertation by John S. Schultz - completed.
(22) University of Nebraska-Omaha	A Comparison of the Academic Performance of Students who have earned degree credit through CLEP General Examination Battery vs. those who have not - in cooperation with

7. How do you compare your day and evening classes in terms of quality?

85	21	8	2
equal	evening equal or better	more variability	day classes superior

8. Are your part-time students (evening) eligible for the Dean's List?

76	53
yes	no

School	Hrs. Req. Dean's List	Min. Grade Point Avg.
LaSalle College	30	3. 40
Univ. of South Carolina	12	3. 50
Drury College	8	3. 30
Dutchess Comm. College	12	3. 20
Univ. of Detroit (Bus. &Adm)	6	3. 00
Virginia Commonwealth Univ.	Same as day	Same as day
George Washington Univ.	12 (Columbian Coll. stud. must have honors in at least 60% of 15 hrs. course wk.)	3. 50
Roosevelt University	15	
Drexel University	6 1/2	3. 50
Univ. of Detroit (A & S)	9	3. 00
South Texas Jr. College	9	3. 50
Idaho State University	12	3. 33
Univ. of So. Mississippi	15	3. 25
Post Junior College	12	3. 00
Univ. of Rochester	8	3. 50
Mohawk Valley Comm. Coll.	12	3. 00
Northeastern University	18	3. 00
Univ. of Georgia (Honor's List)	10	3. 40
Phila. College of Textiles	6	3. 50 (1st honors)
		3. 30 (2nd honors)
Indiana Central College	15	10. 50
Rollins College	(at time of graduation)	3. 50

School	Hrs. Req. Dean's List	Min. Grade Point Avg.
B'klyn. Coll., City U. of N. Y.	30	3. 30
Sir George Williams Univ.	30	3. 00
Queensborough Comm. Coll.	15	3. 00
Univ. of Missouri	9	3. 20
Utica Coll. -Syracuse Univ.	6	3. 20
St. Joseph's Coll. (Eve. Div. List)	Soph. level or above	3. 00
St. Francis College	8	3. 00
Aurora College	9	3. 50
Iona College	--	3. 40
Russell Sage College	6	3. 00
Millard Fillmore College	8	3. 00
Suffolk University	9	3. 00
Union College	--	3. 00
Ohio State University	12	3. 25
City College of New York	32	3. 20
St. Peter's College	18	3. 50
Univ. of Cincinnati	6	3. 50
University of Maine	12	3. 00
Memphis State Univ.	15	3. 40
Seminole Junior College	6	3. 00
Modesto Junior College	30 units	3. 20
Manhattan Comm. College	12	3. 30
Boston College	9	82%
University of Maryland	15	3. 50
Pratt Institute	8	3. 00
Thomas More College	8	3. 50
Purdue Univ. -Calumet Campus	12	3. 00
Loyola Univ. -New Orleans	9	3. 00
DeKalb College	10	4. 00
Xavier Univ. (Eve. Coll. List)	6	3. 25
Metropolitan Univ. -Boston University	2 crses. each sem.	3. 30
Loyola Univ. -Chicago	After 20 hrs.	3. 20
Univ. of Washington	Varies	Varies
Rochester Inst. of Tech.	12	3. 20
Wichita State University	12	3. 25
Western New England Coll.	18	3. 00
Baldwin-Wallace College	14	3. 50
East Tennessee State Univ.	14	3. 50
Univ. of Tenn. -Knoxville	12	3. 00
Tulane University	4 units	3. 40
Nassau Comm. Coll.	12 during the year	3. 25
Univ. of Louisville	7	3. 00

School	Hrs. Req. Dean's List	Min. Grade Point Avg.
Louisiana St. Univ. -Baton Rouge	--	3. 50
Miami Univ. -Ohio	9	3. 00
Manatee Junior College	12	3. 00
Georgia Southern College	Full load equiv.	--
Washburn Univ. of Topeka	12	--
C. W. Post College	12	3. 50
Rider College	8	3. 00
Univ. of Nebraska-Omaha	12	3. 50
Old Dominion College	18	3. 50

9. What is the minimum number of students required to constitute a class?

Ten or more students	55	12 - 15 students	38
3 - 9 students	27	28 - 1 ratio	1

Is an instructor's salary reduced if he teaches a class below minimum size?

21	76
yes	no

Remarks:

1. Faculty are paid $100 per student. (American University)
2. An instructor's compensation is reduced below the break-even point. (Sacred Heart University)
3. Faculty receive 80% of their regular salary. (Post Junior College)
4. An instructor is paid on a per-student basis. (University of New Hampshire)
5. If a class of ten students is permitted, and travel and other direct costs amount to $75, the instructor will have to agree to teach the class for $475 (i. e. , $550 less $75). (University of Georgia)
6. 85% of tuition received will go to the faculty member. (Indiana Central College)
7. Regular faculty receive tuition collected when teaching less than fifteen students; part-time faculty receive compensation reduced by 1/2 each student's tuition under fifteen. (Rollins College)
8. In rare cases, a teacher is paid all tuition receipts less 10%. (University of Hawaii)
9. Instructors teaching less than twelve students are

paid a salary pro-rated with class size. (University of Nebraska)

10. The salary is adjusted according to payment of fees. (Russell Sage College)

11. If tuition does not pay instructor's salary, a conference is held with the instructor beforehand and determination is made regarding salary. (St. Mary's Dominican College) (University of Nebraska-Omaha) (Rockford College) (San Diego Evening College)

VI   ORGANIZATIONAL STRUCTURE

1. What is the size of the administrative staff in your evening division or college?

   A. Institutions with an evening enrollment of 5000 or over [see B. for 1000-4999; C. for less than 1000]:

School	Evening Enrollment	No. of Staff Members	Size of Teaching Staff Full-Time	Part-Time
The Pennsylvania State University	122,000	100	55	5100

1) Director 2) Associate Directors (all categories) 3) Assistant Dean 4) Assistant Directors 5) Director of Non-Credit Programs 6) Director of Conferences & Institutes 7) Business Manager for the evening 8) A large variety of other positions

University of Minnesota	35,000	8	-	1000

1) Director of Evening Classes 2) through 8) Seven additional staff members

New York University	-	55	138	826

1) Dean of Continuing Education - responsible for the overall policy, administrative responsibilities and Chairman of the Faculty; 2) Vice-Dean - The Dean's "Alter Ego" is responsible for day-by-day

School	Evening Enrollment	No. of Staff Members	Size of Teaching Staff Full-Time	Part-Time

administrative and budget control; 3) through 5) three Associate Deans - of Business and Industry (non-credit), Division of Continuing Education (non-credit), Director of Association in Arts Degree Program for Adults; 6) Assistant Dean and Director of American Language Institute (non-credit); 7) Assistant Dean and Director of Community Services (non-credit); 8) Assistant Dean and Director of Special Events and Public Information; 9) through 16) Eight Directors - College Preparatory Program and Foreign Language Program (non-credit), Center for Safety (non-credit, undergraduate and graduate), Reading Institute (non-credit), Opportunities Program, Associate in Applied Sciences-Business (credit), Institute on Federal Taxation, Town Hall, Associate of Applied Science (public service) and Associate in Science (credit); 17) through 29) Twelve Assistant or Associate Directors; 30) Director of Admissions; 31) Registrar; 32) Recorder

School	Evening Enrollment	No. of Staff Members	Full-Time	Part-Time
George Washington University	24,000	30	-	410

1) Dean - responsible for overall operation of the College of General Studies; 2) Assistant Dean - operates as Director of Credit Programs and assumes role of Dean in his absence; 3) Directors (several) - responsible for a significant segment of the operation as presently organized; 4) Assistant Directors (several) - assist the Directors in operations.

University of South Florida
17,000+ overall

1) Dean - responsible for the overall administrative supervision of Continuing Education; 2) through 3) Two Directors - BIS Adult Degree Program and Off-campus; 4) Assistant Director - assists Dean and Coordinator of Off-campus credit courses and non-credit courses.

University of Maine   21,000   13   76   64

1) Director - overall administrative responsibility for the Division of Continuing Education; 2) Assistant Director - does programming and advising; 3) Director of Adult Education Center - directs programs on five campuses; 4) Director of Conferences and Institutes; 5) Director of Counseling - counsels students and formulates policies and procedures in the area; 6) through 13) eight additional staff members

University of California
(Extension Division)   40,000 per yr.   -   -   280

1) Dean - overall administrative responsibility; 2) Assistant Deans - general administrative responsibilities with emphasis on academic matters, fiscal matters; 3) Evening Registrar - responsible for student enrollment, collection of fees, and recording of grades.

Northeastern University
    12,500   13   150   450

1) Dean - overall administrative responsibility for University College; 2) through 5) four Assistant Deans - program directors.

University of Maryland
    12,000   22   28   550

1) Dean - responsible for stateside and overseas programs; 2) through 3) Assistant Deans - academic affairs and overseas programs; 4) Chancellor - overall administrative responsibility; 5) through 7) three Directors; 8) through 10) three Assistant Directors; 11) Director of Adult Education Center;

103

12) Director of Conferences and Institutes; 13) Registrar-responsible for all University College state-side registration; 14) Business Manager – finance and budget; 15) through 22) eight additional staff members.

School	Evening Enrollment	No. of Staff Members	Size of Teaching Staff Full-Time	Part-Time
Bradley University	5000 overall 1000	2	350	–

1) Dean of Evening College – overall administrative responsibility for the Evening College, Summer School, Conferences, Continuing Education and Alumni Education; 2) Assistant Dean – assists the Dean in administering the programs for the Evening College.

The New School	10,000	4	–	500

1) Dean – responsible for all academic and fiscal matters; 2) Assistant Dean – works under the supervising Dean; 3) Director of Admissions; 4) Registrar.

Brooklyn College of the City University of New York	10,000	73	60	500

1) Director (and Assoc. Dean of the Faculty) – responsible for the overall administration of the School including baccalaureate program, higher educational opportunities for non-matriculated students and for disadvantaged groups, for recommending faculty and other administrative officers for appointment to the staff, budget; 2) Associate Director – Deputy of the Director and acts for him in his absence, direction of the Small College Program.

104

University of Cincinnati

7661 credit
2000 non-cr.   10   423

1) Dean - responsible for overall policy of the Evening College including liaison with top university administration and other colleges; 2) Assistant Dean - responsible for non-credit programs of the Evening College; 3) through 4) two Associate Deans - operational aspects of the College, student counseling; 5) through 10) six Assistants to the Dean - three responsible for operational aspects of the College, two counselors, and one in charge of public relations.

Modesto Junior College

9000   4   -

1) Dean - administratively responsible for the evening program, organizes, develops and administers all phases of the educational program so that adults in the community may continue their educational activities. Works closely with the Dean of Instruction and the Curriculum Committee in the development of the curriculum, procures and orients instructional staff, prepares class schedules, provides counseling services for adults, prepares and administers budget, evaluates curricula, etc.; 2) Assistant Dean - serves as assistant to the Dean, director of the summer session, acts as Principal of Modesto Evening High School, makes arrangements for adult education forums, etc.; 3) Coordinator of Special Programs - provides programs in Adult Basic Education, Citizenship Training, Programs for the Physically Handicapped, Teacher Aids, etc., initiates surveys and makes community assessments to determine needs, provides counseling, advising and testing services as necessary, etc.; 4) Coordinator of Vocational Projects - assists the Dean of Instruction in staff responsibilities for various special projects.

University of Oregon

9000   4   50-60

School	Evening Enrollment	No. of Staff Members	Size of Teaching Staff	
			Full-Time	Part-Time

1) Director - overall responsibility and supervision of the Division of Continuing Education; 2) through 4) three Assistants.

School	Evening Enrollment	No. of Staff Members	Full-Time	Part-Time
Virginia Commonwealth University	4500	15	180	235

1) Dean of Continuing Education - administrator responsible for the program; 2) Director of the Evening College and Summer Sessions; 3) through 7) five Assistant Directors - assist the Director in the various programs; 8) one secretary to the Evening College.

School	Evening Enrollment	No. of Staff Members	Full-Time	Part-Time
Fairleigh Dickinson University	9000	5	-	900

1) Dean - responsibility for all-university and supervision; 2) Assistant to the Dean, acts as "deputy" for the Division; 3) Director - in charge of the evening division on one campus (there are four campuses; 4) through 5) two additional staff members.

School	Evening Enrollment	No. of Staff Members	Full-Time	Part-Time
The American University	3134 Fall '70 5367 Non-degree	28	19	170

1) Dean - responsible for the overall operation of the College; 2) through 5) four Assistant Deans - program development, off-campus and special programs, institutes and management programs; 6) through 14) ten Directors; 15) through 23) nine Assistant Directors; 24) through 27) four Admission members - advisement staff - admission and registration functions for non-degree students are per-

formed primarily by academic advisors and representatives of Center for Administration of Justice, English, Language Institute, Pride, Coordinator of Off-campus programs).

Miami-Dade Junior College
8100   -   3   200-300

1) Director - responsible for the Special Programs Division including the evening division, week-end college, off-campus centers, non-credit programs; 2) through 3) two additional staff members.

The Johns Hopkins University
7500   -   8   321

1) Dean - overall responsibility for the operation of the Evening College, academic and administrative leadership, planning programs, outside and faculty relations, budget, executive operations within the University; 2) Associate Deans - responsible for day-to-day operations particularly the direction of graduate programs, program planning, advising students, faculty and staff, recruitment of faculty, general operation of this program and the admission of graduate students; 3) through 6) Directors of Major Divisions - plans the program and staff within the particular division, new programs within the division and advise students and faculty; 7) Registrar - a particular section of the registrar's office is devoted to the Evening College work; 8) Administrative Assistants - general administrative duties within the Evening College.

University of Nebraska
6000   2   82   28

1) Director; 2) Assistant Director - responsibility of supervising evening classes together with three other areas of responsibility.

107

School	Evening Enrollment	No. of Staff Members	Size of Teaching Staff Full-Time	Part-Time
Nassau Community College	7256	8	-	600

1) Dean - Dean of Instruction for the Evening and Extension Division; 2) Assistant Dean - responsible for the part-time; 3) through 4) two Directors of Special Programs; 5) through 8) one administrative officer - three administrative assistants - in charge of Independent Study and assistants to the Assistant Dean.

School	Evening Enrollment	No. of Staff Members	Size of Teaching Staff Full-Time	Part-Time
Memphis State University	6000+	5 (plus 6 clerical)	700	Number varies

1) Director - chief administrator of personnel, program administration and budget; 2) Assistant Director - serves as extension director and administers several budgets within the division; 3) Director of Non-Credit Programs - prepares literature, hires teachers and administers registration; 4) Director of Conferences and Institutes; 5) Director of Extension - organizes classes, hires teachers, registers students, etc.

School	Evening Enrollment	No. of Staff Members	Size of Teaching Staff Full-Time	Part-Time
University of Utah	5000-6000	17 (plus 9 p. t.)	6	494

1) Dean - overall administrative responsibility for the Division of Continuing Education; 2) Associate Dean; 3) Director of Adult Education; 4) Director of Non-Credit Programs; 5) Director of Conferences and Institutes; 6) Registrar (evening); 7) Business Manager; 8) through 17) ten additional full-

time staff members; 18) through 26) nine part-time staff members.

University of Toronto
5734   18   250   56

1) Director - responsibility for both credit and non-credit areas, summer and winter programs; 2) Assistant executive committee member of those faculty councils participating in part-time programs; 2) Assistant Directors - responsible for credit programs, planning, liaison with faculty, hiring teaching staff, etc.; 3) Course Coordinator - creates, develops, evaluates and administers non-credit programs.

Northern Virginia Community College
5510   4   -   -

1) through 2) two Directors - one on each campus responsible for evening classes and Saturday morning classes and all community services and non-credit offerings; 3) through 4) two Assistant Directors.

Manhattan Community College
5600   5   -   173

1) Dean - administrative responsibility for the Evening and Continuing Education programs and development of community service programs; 2) through 5) four additional administrative officers.

Millard Fillmore College
5100   10   150   150

1) Dean - overall responsibility for the Division of Continuing Education; 2) through 10) nine additional staff members who "all do something of everything and coordinate our efforts to keep all oper-

ations functioning smoothly."

School	Evening Enrollment	No. of Staff Members	Size of Teaching Staff Full-Time	Part-Time
Harvard University (University Extension)	5000	2	All part-time	
University of Washington	5017	6	-	177
Joint University Center Memphis State/UT	5000	4	-	65

1) Director - overall administrative responsibility; 2) Assistant Director.

1) Director - responsible for the administration of all credit classes after 5:30 p.m. which are offered by the University; 2) five additional staff members - non-credit courses are under the Director of Continuing Studies - Short Courses and Conferences are under the Director of Extension Services.

1) Director - overall supervision, recruiting of teachers, selection of courses for adult education division (non-degree college credit), budget preparation; 2) Assistant Director - recruits teachers, supervises publicity and mailing lists, supervises librarian, supervises admission, etc.; 3) Associate Director - directs non-credit programs, conferences and institutes, organizes and creates programs, recruits and supervises teachers, prepares publicity; 4) Assistant Business Manager - supervises cashier and bookstore manager, liaison with building manager, purchasing.

Queensborough Community College

5200	38	18	395

1) Associate Dean - coordinates schedules and room assignments, develops off-campus educational centers, assists in developing new courses, general supervision of evening centers, assists in student counseling, registration procedures, etc.; 2) Coordinator of Adult Education - develops and supervises non-credit adult education programs, institutes, conferences, etc.; 3) Director of Admissions; 4) Registrar - student record maintenance, registration, etc.; 5) Business Manager; 6) Assistant to the Dean - liaison to off-campus educational extension centers, completes reports, coordinates schedule of courses and registration guide, general supervision of evening division; attends meetings as directed.

Trenton State College

5200+	8	145	207

1) Director - overall responsibility; 2) through 5) four Assistant Directors; 6) through 8) three Counselors.

Pensacola Junior College

2000 credit	9	181	20
1000 enrichment			
2000 vocational			

1) Director - responsible for overall administration of the Evening College; 2) Assistant Director - assumes the Director's task in his absence, is responsible for the evening non-credit programs, seminars, etc.; 3) Registrar - evening registration; 4) Business Manager - routine business affairs in the evening; 5) through 6) two Counselors.

B. Institutions with an evening enrollment of 1000 to 4999.

School	Evening Enrollment	No. of Staff Members	Size of Teaching Staff	
			Full-Time	Part-Time
St. Joseph's College	4800	23	11	191

1) Dean - overall responsibility for administration of Evening College; 2) Assistant Dean; 3) Executive Vice-President - oversees the evening operation, curriculum, and faculty; 4) Director of Academic Advising - advises students and is in charge of admissions; 5) Registrar; 6) Director of Student Affairs - part-time coordinator with extra-curriculars, academic advising; 7) Cashier - reports to the Evening Dean, but, works with the College Treasurer in charge of accounts receivable.

| Pratt Institute | 4500 | 3 | - | 30 |

1) Dean - academic and administrative director of the school; 2) Director - academic and administrative director of academic programs; 3) Director of Non-Credit Programs.

| Drexel University | 4379 | 22 | 14 | 285 |

1) Dean; 2) through 20) nineteen additional staff members.

| Bakersfield College | 4770 | 2 | - | 210 |

(1 f.t and 1 p.t.)

1) Dean; 2) Associate Dean

Washington University
(St. Louis)   4363   21   63   224

1) Dean - responsible for the development and implementation of policies regarding the administration of the School of Continuing Education; 2) Assistant Dean and Director - implementation of policies regarding the credit and non-credit programs in University College; 3) Director of Summer School & Assistant Dean - plans and executes summer courses for both day and evening divisions; 4) Director of Residential Adult Education Center - overall upkeep of facility, staff and food service, schedules conferences and short courses; 5) Director of Conferences and Institutes - on and off-campus; 6) Director of Admissions and Adult Counseling Service; 7) Business Manager - maintains official financial records.

Towson State College
                      4226   4   170   85

1) Dean; 2) Associate Director - responsible for general administration and finance; 3) through 4) two academic coordinators - responsible for student advising and various other duties.

C. W. Post College   4500   4   -   -

1) Director - Adult Education and Special Programs and Director of Adult Studies with responsibility for student services plus catalysts in program development; 2) Assistant Director - serves staff support functions; 3) through 4) two counselors. NOTE: A separate Division of Continuing Education and Summer Session is staffed with two administrators.

City College of New York
                      4200   30   45   288

School	Evening Enrollment	No. of Staff Members	Size of Teaching Staff Full-Time	Part-Time

1) Dean; 2) Associate Dean - responsible for the summer session; 3) Assistant Dean - refunds, student resignations, etc.; 4) Associate Registrar; 5) Business Manager (evening); 6) through 30) Administrative Assistants, Office and Secretarial Assistants.

School	Evening Enrollment	No. of Staff Members	Full-Time	Part-Time
University of Toledo	4000	5	15	25

1) Dean - Adult and Continuing Education; 2) Assistant Dean; 3) three additional administrators.

| Orange County Community College | 3812 | 4 | - | 259 |

1) Dean - establishes policies, aims and objectives; 2) Associate Dean - executes policy and objectives as relate to non-credit, community services and off-campus courses; 3) Coordinator of Special Projects - establishes conferences, seminars, etc. and supervises independent study; 4) Coordinator - Women's Programs - establishes courses (credit and non-credit) for women and supervises funded programs for the disadvantaged.

| Northern Illinois University | 3700 | 10 | - | 344 (total faculty) |

1) Dean - administrative head of the College of Continuing Education; 2) Director of Adult Education; 3) Director of Conferences and Institutes; 4) Director of Extension - responsible for off-campus courses; 5) Director of Industrial and Business Services; 6) Director of Law Enforcement Institute.

| Purdue University Calumet Campus | 3305 | 3 1/2 | 150 | 100 |

1) Dean and Director - overall management of the Calumet Campus both day and evening; 2) Assistant Dean for Evening Administration - responsible for development of all related services needed by part-time students and Continuing Education programs; 3) Coordinator of Continuing Education - responsible for the development and coordination of all programs - both credit and non-credit - that are not scheduled on our regular academic calendar; 4) Coordinator of Supervision Programs - (1/2 time) - responsible for the development and coordination of non-credit offerings oriented toward industrial supervision and management.

Mohawk Valley Community College
2800-3400   6   -   200

1) Dean; 2) Assistant Dean; 3) through 4) two assistant Directors; 5) through 6) two Counselors.

Northwestern University
3208   3   -   150

1) Dean - responsible for the entire evening program; 2) Assistant Dean - admissions, counseling, publications, etc.; 3) Registrar - responsible for academic records of part-time evening students.

Metropolitan College 3575
Boston University   14   232   189

1) Dean; 2) through 3) two Assistant Deans - one in charge of student affairs and administration and the other in charge of Academic Affairs; 4) through 14) eleven additional staff members.

Miami University-Ohio
3400   7   -

School	Evening Enrollment	No. of Staff Members	Size of Teaching Staff Full-Time	Part-Time

1) Dean – overall administrative responsibility for the Residence Credit Centers; 2) Associate Dean; 3) Director; 4) Assistant Director; 5) Director of Admissions; 6) Registrar; 7) Business Manager.

School	Evening Enrollment	No. of Staff Members	Full-Time	Part-Time
LaSalle College	3148	3	83	129 part-time

1) Dean; 2) Director of Admissions; 3) Registrar.

| Wichita State University | 3200 | 7 | – | 10 part-time (non-credit) |

1) Director – overall administrative responsibility for the Division of Continuing Education; 2) Director of Non-credit Programs; 3) Counsellor; 4) Coordinator of Special Programs.

| Roosevelt University | 3000 | 8 | | |

1) Dean – chief administrator of the College of Continuing Education; 2) Associate Dean; 3) Assistant Dean; 4) Director of the Reading Institute; 5) Director of the Upward Bound Project; 6) administrative secretary; 7) two additional secretaries responsible to the Reading Institute and Upward Bound Project.

| University of Hawaii | 3500 (plus 15,000 attending various activities) | 32 | – | 160 |

1) Dean – general responsibility and liaison with the University Administration; 2) Associate Dean – fiscal officer and personnel manager; 3) Assistant Dean – responsible for services, advising and

administration; 4) through 8) five Directors - Courses and Curricula, Special and Professional Programs, Community Services Center for Governmental Development, Center for Labor-Management Training; 9) through 12) three Directors - Non-Credit Programs, Evening Credit Programs, Teachers Credit Programs; 13) through 16) three Counselors; 17) eighteen coordinators, 21 secretarial clerks and other civil service staff.

University of Denver 2922   1

1) Coordinator of Continuing Education - directs and administers the entire non-credit program.

University of Rochester
2693   72 (p.t.)   -   133

1) Dean; 2) Associate Dean; 3) Director - also Dean of University School and Director of the Summer and Evening Session; 4) Assistant Director; 5) Registrar; 6) Director of Graduate Studies (part-time); 7) Public Relations - special assignment of University School.

Rider College 2591   6   81   96

1) Dean - full responsibility of all phases of the Evening School; 2) Associate Dean - Director of Guidance and chief of all records; 3) Assistant to the Dean; 4) Director of Off-Campus Centers - responsible for programs at two centers and also is VA coordinator; 5) Director of Student Services - in charge of evening student senate, newspaper and all extra-curricular activities; 6) Director of Special Programs - Director of the Law Enforcement Program and other special programs.

University of Tennessee-Knoxville
2715   8   372   88

School	Evening Enrollment	No. of Staff Members	Size of Teaching Staff Full-Time	Part-Time

1) Dean; 2) through 5) four Assistant Directors - administer off-campus programs, programming of evening courses, student records and non-credit programs; 6) Director of Conferences and Institutes; 7) through 8) two coordinators - Director of Conferences and Institutes and short term non-credit offerings; 9) Cashier; 10) Project Director - heads the Head Start supplementary training - funded program.

| Suffolk University | 1495 (plus 885 evening law students) | 1 | 56 | 53 |

1) Associate Dean - responsibilities include the development and supervision of the evening program, advising, preparation of advertising and promotional material, development of curriculum, preparation of course schedules, directing the summer session, and teaching one course.

| Tulane University | 2002 | 9 | 70 | 94 |

1) Dean; 2) Assistant Dean - responsible for non-credit programs; 3) Director of Conferences and Institutes; 4) through 5) two Assistants to the Dean - office management, student counseling, bulletins, schedules, and faculty appointments; 6) three secretaries; 7) one record secretary.

| Community College of Baltimore | 2600 | 4 | - | - |

1) Dean - overall responsibility for the Evening Division (responsible to the President); 2) Assistant Dean; 3) Director of Summer Sessions; 4) Director of Off-campus Centers - Director of Non-Credit Programs and Conferences and Institutes of all in a separate Division - the Division of Community Services.

118

University of Missouri

2383   9   81   79

1) Dean - plans instructional program, budget, etc.; 2) Associate Dean - assists in the instructional programing, publications and mailing, research and assists with advisement; 3) Assistant Dean - responsible for advising, transcript evaluation, student records, class schedules and student organizations; 4) Counselor; 5) through 6) part-time Assistant Counselors.

Drake University   2500   17   80   75

1) Dean - overall responsibility for the University College; 2) through 3) two Assistant Deans; 4) through 5) two Directors - coordinating and programming; 6) through 7) two Coordinators - handle Urban Affairs and Employment Security Training; 8) through 10) three Directors - admission, counseling and placement of evening students; 11) seven secretaries.

Dutchess Community College
2364   4

1) Dean - responsible for developing and operating the Office of Continuing Education and summer school and for providing adequate programs to meet the needs of part-time students; 2) through 3) two Assistant Deans; 4) Director of Admissions and Registrar who are shared with the day school.

University of New Hampshire
2000   6   -   100

1) Director; 2) through 6) five Assistant Directors - responsible for credit courses, summer session,

119

short courses, conferences and certificate programs.

School	Evening Enrollment	No. of Staff Members	Size of Teaching Staff Full-Time	Part-Time
Russell Sage College	2000	6	-	135

1) Dean; 2) Associate Dean - Director of Summer session, catalog preparation, advisement, etc., 3) through 6) four additional staff members.

University of Tennessee-Nashville	2500	15	50	94

1) Chancellor - overall responsibility for the Administration of the Nashville Center; 2) Vice-Chancellor; 3) Associate to the Chancellor; 4) Assistant Vice-Chancellor; 5) Director; 6) Assistant Director in charge of Student Services; 7) Director of Conferences and Institutes; 8) Registrar; 9) Business Manager.

Loyola University - Chicago	2534	4	93	70

1) Dean (administrative) - overall responsibility for University College; 2) Assistant Dean; 3) through 4) two additional staff members.

East Tennessee State University	2500	4 (10 clerks)	14	33

1) Dean - administratively responsible for the School of Continuing Education; 2) Director - responsible for the operation of Kingsport University Center; 3) Assistant Director; 4) Director of Non-Credit Programs.

University of Louisville
2300   15   157   123

1) Dean - supervises all aspects of the University College program; 2) Assistant Dean - plays an advisory role in policy and supervision of faculty relations, students and administrative institutions within the University; 3) Director of Audio-Visual Program; 4) Director of Upward Bound Program; 5) Director of Non-Credit Courses; 6) through 15) additional staff members.

Hofstra University   2000   5 f.t./8 p.t.   238   225

1) Dean - general supervision of University College (adult branch of the University), graduate program and summer session; 2) Associate Dean responsible for evening undergraduate students; 3) Associate Dean responsible for attending key meetings, etc.; 4) Assistant to the Dean - counsels adults attending days, coordinates Liberal Arts in Extension, plans and coordinates the non-credit liberal arts programs; 5) Director of Non-Credit Programs; 6) through 8) three part-time coordinators; 9) Coordinator and extension programs; 10) through 13) four part-time advisors; 14) Admissions Office (evening); 15) Registrar (evening).

County College of Morris
2211   10   31   76

1) Associate Dean - responsible for administering the Continuing Education Division; 2) Director - responsible for day-to-day operations; 3) Counselor - Evaluator.

School	Evening Enrollment	No. of Staff Members	Size of Teaching Staff Full-Time	Part-Time
University of Richmond	1944	3 (plus larger staff day/eve. comb.)	28	108

1) Dean - overall operation and directs administration of 350 students in Day Division; 2) through 3) two Associate Deans - in charge of the evening programs and non-credit institutes for Business and Community Development with Management, Urban and Research Centers; 3) Director of Admission (day/evening); 4) Registrar and Director of Admission (day/evening).

Jefferson State Jr. College	1800	4	24	48

1) Director of the Division of Continuing Education; 2) Director of Extension; 3) Registrar (evening); 4) Director of Student Services.

DeKalb College	1770	1	43	55

1) Dean of the College; 2) Associate Dean for the Evening - responsible for the entire evening academic and non-credit courses; 3) Director of Adult Education Center.

Temple University	1700	2	122	51

1) Dean - overall responsibility for the School of Business Administration; 2) Associate Dean.

The University of Tennessee - Chattanooga
1597   3   73   21

1) Director - coordinator of evening programs; 2) through 3) two additional staff members.

Union College   1500   8   -   60

1) Director - administers duties of the registrar, advisors, development, finance, advertising, publications, scheduling, faculty relations, institutes, public relations, community services; 2) through 8) seven additional staff members.

University of Southern Mississippi
1500   15   21   150

1) Dean; 2) through 4) three Directors; 5) Director of Adult Education; 6) Director of Non-Credit Programs; 7) Director of Conferences and Institutes; 8) Director of Extension.

Utica College - Syracuse University
1400   3   55   55

1) Director; 2) Assistant Director - all phases of credit programs; 3) Counselor.

Bryant College   1430   5   35   38

1) Dean - works with department chairmen on faculty and with the curriculum committee on courses and degree content, counsels evening students and reviews records for graduation; 2) Director; 3) Evening Division Counselor; 4) through 5) two additional staff members.

School	Evening Enrollment	No. of Staff Members	Size of Teaching Staff	
			Full-Time	Part-Time
Rockhurst College	1331	3	19	59

1) Director; 2) Registrar; 3) Secretary

Texas Christian University	1500	4	-	200

1) Dean; 2) Assistant Dean; 3) Director of Special Courses; 4) Director of Civic Affairs.

Xavier University	1400	2 1/2 plus 3 f. t. clerical	100-120	60-80

1) Dean - totally responsible for the administration of the Evening College and summer school, teaches one graduate course per semester, and is a member of 15 university-wide committees; 2) Assistant Dean - teaches 1/2 time, responsible for summer session, and assists the Dean; 3) Equivalent of one full-time Counselor; 4) through 6) three full-time secretaries.

Indiana Central College	1257	7	-	71

1) Dean - responsible for faculty, staff, schedule and budget; 2) Director of Student Services; 3) Director of Non-Credit Programs.

Baylor University	1233	4	Staff for 100-120 classes	

1) Dean; 2) Assistant Dean; 3) through 4) two additional assistants.

| Drury College | 1205 | 10 | 20 | 70 |

1) Dean - overall supervision of the Evening College; 2) Associate Dean; 3) Director of Non-Credit Programs; 4) Director of Conferences and Institutes; 5) Director of Extension - coordinates off-campus residence center, orders all books and handles veteran affairs; 6) Registrar; 7) Assistant Registrar.

University of South Carolina

| | 1200 | 10 | 4 | 74 |

1) Dean; 2) Assistant Dean; 3) Director of Non-Credit Programs; 4) Director of Conferences and Institutes.

Louisiana State University-New Orleans

| | 1200 | 2 | 97 |

1) Director - chief administrator of the Evening Division; 2) Counselor.

University of Detroit

| | 1174 | 6 | 7 | 63 |

1) Academic Dean; 2) through 3) two Assistant Deans; 4) through 5) two staff members.

University of Kentucky

| | 1350 | 2 | - | 75-90 |

School	Evening Enrollment	No. of Staff Members	Size of Teaching Staff Full-Time	Part-Time
Boston College	1076	2	-	80

1) Director - responsible for preparing course offerings, counseling, registration of students, financial responsibility; 2) Secretary - assists the Director.

1) Dean; 2) Counselor - role of coordinator of student services, student organizations, plans orientation, etc.

Washburn University of Topeka	1000	9	-	100

1) Director; 2) Assistant Director - administers evening college and Forley AFB program; 3) through 9) additional staff members.

College of William & Mary	1085	4 1 1/2 clerical		

1) Dean - responsible for the entire continuing education program at the policy level; 2) Associate Dean - responsible for directing operation of the Evening College and Division of Extension; 3) Assistant Directors - work in the field; 4) Director of Summer Session.

Idaho State University	1000	1		

1) Director - responsible for 1000 students per semester plus an additional 1000 students off-campus, scheduling, and overall administration.

Rollins College   1000   6   -   100

1) Director - supervises program, directs administrative staff, formulates program, contacts in-structors, advises and counsels students, prepares budget, serves on college committees; 2) through 6) five administrative assistants.

Manatee Junior College
     1000 plus 600   3   27
      senior citizens

1) Dean; 2) Assistant Dean; 3) Coordinator of Manatee Junior College Senior Citizens Program - plans programs for senior citizens which are attended by over 1000 students over 65 years of age.

Baldwin Wallace College
     1000   1 1/2   65   40

1) Director - directs evening session, summer session, special programs, etc.; 2) Administrative Assistant (part-time); 3) two counselors for 8 per cent of time.

American International College
     1075   11   116

1) Dean - all inclusive except for services provided by the registrar's office; the Dean is responsible for the non-credit programs; 2) through 11) ten additional staff members.

School	Evening Enrollment	No. of Staff Members	Size of Teaching Staff Full-Time	Part-Time
Thomas More College	956 cr. 774 non-cr.	2 full-time 1 one-half time	19	63

1) Dean - supervises credit programs and course offerings as well as academic standards, etc.; 2) Assistant to the Dean; 3) Director of Conferences and Institutes - development of special interest groups (LEEP), supervision of details for conduct of institutes and special programs.

School	Evening Enrollment	No. of Staff Members	Size of Teaching Staff Full-Time	Part-Time
PMC Colleges	1147	2	20	52

1) Dean; 2) Assistant Dean - scheduling, classrooms, publicity and promotion, etc.

C. Institutions with an evening enrollment of less than 1000:

School	Evening Enrollment	No. of Staff Members	Size of Teaching Staff Full-Time	Part-Time
Centenary College of Louisiana	197	1	15	15

1) Director - recruits students, plans curriculum offerings each semester, hires and fires faculty, counsels students, plans degree programs, plans and directs non-credit offerings, acts as Registrar, maintains transcripts, collects fees, makes reports, etc.

School	Evening Enrollment	No. of Staff Members	Size of Teaching Staff Full-Time
University of West Florida	715	3	81 (total faculty)

1) Director - administers off-campus credit programs, non-credit programs; 2) Director of Adult Education; 3) Director of Non-Credit programs - administers in-service training programs 1/2 time and teaches 1/2 time.

Roanoke College   240   18   12
(164 in special courses)

1) Director - directs evening program and continuing education.

Utah State University 500   13   1   100

1) Vice-President - designated as Director of Cooperative Extension and is responsible for the total program; 2) Assistant Directors - eleven in all; 3) Director of Non-Credit Programs.

Sacred Heart University
306   2   46

1) Director; 2) Assistant Director.

Post Junior College 119   2   23   8

1) Director in charge of advertising, admission counseling, scheduling, hiring of faculty, supervision, seminars, curriculum coordination with day school, etc.; 2) Secretary - acts as assistant.

University of Georgia
480   62   25-30 credit
(1035 off-campus)   10-15 non-credit

| | | | Size of Teaching Staff | |
School	Evening Enrollment	No. of Staff Members	Full-Time	Part-Time

1) Vice-President for Services - overall responsibility; 2) Director of Center for Continuing Education; 3) through 5) three Associate Directors of the Center; 6) through 7) two Directors of Adult Education; 8) Coordinator of Off-campus Non-Credit Programs; 9) Assistant Director for Conferences and Institutes; 10) Assistant Director for Extension; 11) Director of University Evening Classes; 12) Assistant Director for Inter-Institutional Program; 13) Assistant Director for Program Development and Evaluation; 14) Coordinator of Governmental Training; 15) Supervisor of Independent Study; some staff members are joint-staffed with other units of the University.

School	Evening Enrollment	No. of Staff Members	Full-Time	Part-Time
Philadelphia College of Textiles	950	2		89

1) Dean; 2) Assistant Dean; 3) three secretaries.

| Aurora College | 350 | 3 | 16 | 35 |

1) Director; 2) two Assistants.

| Iona College | 856 | 1 | 5 | 7 |

1) Director - coordinates the program for the division after consultation with Deans and department heads.

| East Carolina University | 820 | 5 | 11 | 26 |

130

1) Dean - overall responsibility for University College; 2) Associate Dean; 3) through 5) Program Directors.

Ohio State University 777   9   Day faculty teach in the evenings

1) Assistant Vice-President - Director of Continuing Education activities; 2) through 4) three Associate Directors - in charge of Industrial Relations, in charge of Conferences and facilities; in charge of Urban Extension program; 5) Field Representative; 6) Facilities Coordinator.

Seminole Junior College
664   2   29   34

1) Director - overall administrative responsibility for Division of Evening Studies; 2) one additional staff member.

St. Mary's Dominican College
275 credit   2   20-30
65 non-cr.

1) Director; 2) Assistant Director.

Georgia Southern College
255   2   15

1) Dean - responsible for administering the program in the Department of Evening Studies; 2) one other staff member.

131

School	Evening Enrollment	No. of Staff Members	Size of Teaching Staff	
			Full-Time	Part-Time
Mississippi State College for Women	322	2	-	8

1) Director of Continuing Education - supervises instruction and employs faculty; 2) Dean - policy-making and final decisions--approves faculty; 3) Registrar; 4) Business Manager.

School	Evening Enrollment	No. of Staff Members	Full-Time	Part-Time
University of Tampa	400	1	-	35

1) Director - responsible for all administration and direction of Adult Education - non-credit programs, conferences, institutes and extension.

School	Evening Enrollment	No. of Staff Members	Full-Time	Part-Time
Southwestern Michigan College	400	1	-	26

1) Director - administers the Continuing Education programs including the following specific assignments, participates in the formation of Academic and Administrative policy, plans and directs the Continuing Education Program through consultation with department heads and Deans of A & S and Applied Sciences, works with individuals and advisory committees to develop non-credit vocational and special interest courses, works with business and industry and labor in the development of apprentice programs, organizes speaker's bureau and publishes an appropriate brochure for this service, schedules extension courses at appropriate locations, recruits and evaluates faculty, etc.

School	Evening Enrollment	No. of Staff Members	Full-Time	Part-Time
Springfield College	400	5	40	20

1) Director; 2) Assistant Director; 3) through 5) three other staff members.

University of North Carolina

650   6   –   34

1) Director; 2) Assistant to the Director; 3) Advisor; 4) Registrar; 5) Administrative secretary; 6) one additional staff member.

Rockford Evening College

879   5 1/2   20   30

1) Dean - full responsibility for administration of the program; 2) through 5) four other staff members.

VL   (Cont'd.)

2. In your estimation, what size administrative staff is required for administering an evening credit program or a non-credit program with various enrollment?

    Note: The size staff will be determined largely on the responsibilities delegated to the particular division or college, and the variety of programs - credit and non-credit, extension, TV, etc.

| | Credit Program Only | | | | | | | | Administering, Organizing and Supervising Non-Credit Courses, Conferences, Institutes | | | | | | |
| | Staff Members | | | | | | | | Staff Members | | | | | | |
Enrollment	1	2	3	4	5-6	7-10	12-15		1	2	3	4	5-6	7-10	15
300	13	7	3	1		1			12	4			2		
500	11	7	3	3	2				14	2	3	1	1	1	
800	7	5	5	5	2				8	7	2	2	2	1	
1000	4	6	7	6	2	1			4	8	3	1	2	1	
2000	1	5	6	5	8	4	2		2	5	7	2	2	3	
5000	1	1	3	5	8	8	1		1	3	5	4	4	2	2

3. If your institution is a branch of the state university system, do you have:

A. Administrative Autonomy?

$\dfrac{13}{\text{yes}}$ $\dfrac{5}{\text{no}}$

(
(1) Mohawk Valley Community College
(2) Pennsylvania State University
(3) Orange County Community College
(4) University of Nebraska - Omaha
(5) Millard Fillmore College
(6) University of Tennessee-Chattanooga
(7) Manhattan Community College

(1) North Carolina State University
(2) University of New Hampshire
(3) Joint University Center MSU/UT
(4) East Tennessee State University
(5) Miami University - Ohio

134

(8) University of Maryland
(9) Nassau Community College
(10) University of Louisville
(11) Louisiana State University-Baton Rouge
(12) University of Richmond
(13) University of Oklahoma

B. Academic Autonomy?

$$\frac{7}{\text{yes}} \qquad \frac{9}{\text{no}}$$

(1) Mohawk Valley Community College
(2) Orange County Community College
(3) Manhattan Community College
(4) Nassau Community College
(5) University of Louisville
(6) University of Richmond
(7) University of Nebraska-Omaha

(1) North Carolina State University
(2) University of New Hampshire
(3) Pennsylvania State University
(4) Joint University Center MSU/UT
(5) East Tennessee State University
(6) University of Nebraska
(7) Louisiana State University-Baton Rouge
(8) Miami University - Ohio
(9) University of Oklahoma

VII. EDUCATIONAL TELEVISION PROGRAMS

1. Do you offer courses by means of educational television?

$$\frac{45}{\text{yes}} \qquad \frac{96}{\text{no}}$$

2. If so, do students earn residence credit?

$$\frac{32}{\text{yes}} \qquad \frac{7}{\text{no}}$$

135

or extension credit?

3. Will their credits count toward a degree?

$$\frac{7}{\text{yes}} \quad \frac{9}{\text{no}}$$

$$\frac{32}{\text{yes}} \quad \frac{3}{\text{no}}$$

SCHOOLS OFFERING COURSES BY MEANS OF EDUCATIONAL TELEVISION

Name of School	Types of Courses	Residence Credit	Extension Credit	Degree Credit	Grad.	Undergrad.
(1) University of South Carolina	Credit/Non-Credit	Yes	No	Yes	Yes	Yes
(2) Drury College	Credit	Yes	No	Yes	-	-
(3) New York University	Credit-Wash. Sq. 2 Non-cr. crs. per sem.	Yes	No	-	-	-
(4) University of Oregon	Credit/Non-credit	No	Yes	-	-	-
(5) Drake University	Sunrise Semester (credit) (non-credit)	No	Yes	-	-	Yes
(6) Dutchess Community College	offered by State Univ. of N.Y. supervised by SUNY	-	-	Yes	-	Yes
(7) The University of Detroit	Education courses	Yes	-	Yes	-	-
(8) Virginia Commonwealth Univ.	Two credit courses	Yes	-	Yes	-	-
(9) University of Denver	Credit	Yes	-	Yes	No	Yes
(10) North Carolina State Univ.	Non-Credit	No	No	No	No	No
(11) Utah State University	Credit	Yes	-	No	-	-
(12) Univ. of New Hampshire	Credit	Yes	-	Yes	-	-
(13) Pennsylvania State Univ.	Grad/Undergrad.	No	Yes	Yes	Yes	Yes
(14) University of Georgia	Non-credit	No	No	No	No	No
(15) Univ. of Calif.-Berkeley	Credit	No	Yes	Possible	No	No
(16) Orange Cty. Comm. College	Non-credit	No	No	No	No	No

Name of School	Types of Courses	Residence Credit	Extension Credit	Degree Credit	Grad.	Undergrad.
(17) Iowa State University	Undergrad/Grad.	Yes	Yes	Yes	Yes	Yes
(18) St. Francis College	Credit	Yes	No	Yes	-	Yes
(19) University of Toledo	Non-credit	No	No	No	No	No
(20) Union College	Credit	Yes	No	Yes	Yes	Yes
(21) Northern Va. Comm. Coll.	Credit	Yes	No	Yes	No	Yes
(22) University of Minnesota	Credit	Yes	No	Yes	Yes	Yes
(23) Pensacola Jr. College	Credit	Yes	No	Yes	No	Yes
(24) University of Utah	Credit/Non-Credit	Yes	No	Yes	Yes	Yes
(25) University of Maine	Credit/Non-Credit	Yes	No	Yes	No	Yes
(26) Memphis State University	Credit	Yes	No	Yes	-	Yes
(27) St. Louis University	Non-credit	No	No	No	No	No
(28) Modesto Jr. College	Non-credit	No	No	No	No	No
(29) University of Maryland	Mathematics	Yes	-	Yes	No	Yes
(30) Texas Christian University	Credit	Yes	No	Yes	Yes	Yes
(31) Xavier University	Methods courses in Education	Yes	No	Yes	-	Yes
(32) Comm. Coll. of Baltimore	Credit	Yes	No	Yes	No	Yes
(33) Univ. of Washington	Non-credit	No	No	No	No	No
(34) Rochester Inst. of Techn.	Credit/Non-Credit	Yes	No	Yes	No	Yes
(35) Wayne State University	Credit	Yes	Yes	Yes	Yes	Yes
(36) College of Wm. & Mary	Credit	No	Yes	Yes	Yes	Yes
(37) Nassau Comm. College	Credit	Yes	No	Yes	No	Yes
(38) Miami University-Ohio	Credit	Yes	No	Yes	No	Yes
(39) Georgia Southern College	Credit/Non-Credit	Yes	No	Yes	No	Yes
(40) Washburn Univ. of Topeka	Credit/Non-Credit	Yes	No	Yes	No	Yes
(41) Harvard Univ.-Univ. Ext.	Non-credit	No	Yes	Yes	No	Yes

Name of School	Types of Courses	Residence Credit	Extension Credit	Degree Credit	Grad.	Undergrad.
42) Univ. of Nebraska-Omaha	Credit	Yes	No	Yes	No	Yes
43) San Diego Evening College	Credit/Non-Credit	Yes	No	Yes	No	Yes
44) Towson State College	Credit	Yes	No	Yes	No	Yes
45) University of Oklahoma	Credit	Yes	No	Yes	No	Yes

4. Who supervises your educational television courses:

(1) The department, division and/or instructor offering the course   <u>12</u>

Institutions - University of South Carolina, Pennsylvania State University, University of California-Berkeley, Iowa State University, Pensacola Jr. College, University of Maryland, Community College of Baltimore, Nassau Community College, Georgia Southern College, Washburn University of Topeka, Rochester Institute of Technology, University of Oklahoma.

(2) The College of Education   <u>2</u>

Institutions - Virginia Commonwealth University (A & S), Xavier University

(3) The Dean or Director   <u>5</u>

Institutions - Drury College, Union College, St. Louis University, University of Utah, Towson State College

(4) Commercial or ETV Station Personnel   <u>2</u>

Institutions - Drake University, North Carolina State University

(5) State University of New York   <u>1</u>

Institution - Dutchess Community College

(6) Oregon Educational Broadcasting Company   <u>1</u>

Institution - University of Oregon

(7) Mass Communications   <u>2</u>

Institutions - University of Denver, University of Georgia

139

(8) The New IM LS (Instr. Media) and/or Library Sciences & related — 2
Institutions - Utah State University, Orange County Comm. College
(9) The Director of Instructional Services of the New Hampshire Network — 1
Institution - University of New Hampshire
(10) Specialists in the field of Educational Television — 1
Institution - St. Francis College
(11) Administrative Board — 1
Institution - Harvard University
(12) Director of Radio TV Department (Speech) — 1
Institution - Miami University-Ohio
(13) Program Supervisor — 1
Institution - Modesto Junior College
(14) Television Coordinator and/or Manager of Telecourses — 3
Institutions - University of Washington, Wayne State University, San Diego Evening College
(15) The Division of Continuing Education — 2
Institutions - University of Maine, College of Wm. & Mary
(16) Assistant Dean for Academic Programs — 1
Institution - University of Nebraska - Omaha

5. How do you handle the educational television courses for teachers?

(1) Teachers may enroll if the course is required for state certification, or for general interest. (University of South Carolina)
(2) Part-time faculty teach under the School District contracts. (University of Oregon)
(3) The Director of the Division of Education supervises the TV courses. (Univ. of Detroit)
(4) Educational TV courses are held for elementary teachers immediately after their classes are over.

(5) Teachers may enroll for "certificate" credits in the Extension Division prior to formal admission to a higher degree program. (Wayne State University)

(6) TV courses are offered for teachers through the School of Education and the faculty of Arts and Sciences - it is administered by the School of Continuing Studies. (College of William & Mary)

(7) Courses for teachers are handled by the School of Education. (Miami University-Ohio)

(8) Courses for teachers are handled by hurdle credit. (San Diego Evening College)

6. Do you use full-time instructors 17 part-time instructors 7 or both? 21

Institutions using both full and part-time teachers - University of South Carolina, North Carolina State University, Drury College, University of Oregon, Drake University, Pennsylvania State University, University of Georgia, Washburn University of Topeka, Orange County Community College, Union College, University of Utah, University of Maine, Xavier University, Rochester Institute of Technology, College of William & Mary, San Diego Evening College.

7. Do faculty members receive additional remuneration for teaching courses on TV?

 15
yes

Institutions - University of New Hampshire, Pennsylvania State University, St. Francis College (p. t.), University of Minnesota, Harvard University, University of Utah, University of Maine, University of Maryland, University of Washington, Rochester Institute of Technology, (or part of teaching load), Wayne State University, Washburn University of Topeka, University of Nebraska-Omaha, San Diego Evening College, University of Oklahoma (or reduced load).

 14
no

Institutions - University of South Carolina, New York University, Drake University, University of Georgia, Orange County Community College, Iowa State University, Union College, Pensacola Junior College, Texas Christian University, Modesto Junior College, Community College of Baltimore, Nassau Community College, Miami University, Georgia Southern College.

141

8. Is the teaching load reduced? $\dfrac{14}{\text{yes}}$

Number of Hours	School
(1) By the number of hours taught on TV.	University of South Carolina, Drake University
(2) Three 1/2 hrs. per week is counted as a full teaching load on TV and the teaching load on campus is reduced accordingly.	Union College, New York University
(3) Faculty members receive remuneration (extra) for teaching TV courses or receive a reduced teaching load.	Pennsylvania State University
(4) Faculty members receive additional remuneration for teaching TV courses and their regular load is reduced by one class.	University of Minnesota, Washburn University of Topeka
(5) ETV courses are counted as part of the regular teaching load.	Pensacola Junior College, Modesto Junior College
(6) Teaching load is reduced 20 per cent.	
(7) There is no set policy regarding the matter of reduction of teaching load and/or remuneration.	College of William & Mary, Georgia Southern College
(8) Teaching load is reduced by one course.	

9. Who handles the registration for your education television courses?

Evening Division Director/Dean $\dfrac{3}{3}$
Extension Division

College of Education $\dfrac{3}{4}$
University/Evening College

Admissions Office or Registrar   14

Oregon Educational Broadcasting   1

Office of Div. of Cont. Ed.   9

By correspondence instructor
or field offices (mail or group
registration)   1

Independent Study Division   1

Evening & Special Classes   1

Graduate School   1

No registration   2

What procedure is used for registration?

Standard registration procedure   25

Mail registration (& personal)   11

Same as for Extension classes   1

Instructor registers students at first
meeting of the class and forwards
materials back to the Div. of Continuing Education (University of New
Hampshire)   1

Tuition 19

10. How are your educational TV courses financed?

Other:

(1) Out of salary funds plus tuition. (Drake University)

(2) Through the total budget. (Va. Commonwealth University) (University of Nebraska-Omaha)

(3) Fees plus state appropriation. (North Carolina State University) (University of Georgia)
(University of Oklahoma)

(4) Registration fee plus funds from a small grant. (Utah State University)

(5) TV programs are a deficit operation - public relations value (New York University)

(6) TV programs are financed by grants, contracts, fees, and subsidies. (Penn. State Univ.)

(7) Student fees, grants, etc. (University of California)

(8) Most TV courses are budgeted - others are self-supporting (Orange County Comm. College)

143

(9) By tuition and allocation. (Iowa State University)
(10) Courses are financed by participating industry. (University of Toledo)
(11) Foundation grants. (Union College)
(12) By extension support and tuition. (University of Minnesota)
(13) ETV courses are undergraduate and are financed through our regular budget. (Pensacola Jr.)
(14) Educational TV programs are financed through state funds. (Univ. of Washington)
(15) Educational TV courses are financed by ETV budget, $25,000 revolving fund and tuition. (University of Maine)
(16) TV courses are financed partly by an administrative fund and/or partly by station funds. (St. Louis University - Metro) (San Diego Evening College) (Towson State College)
(17) Average daily attendance card-part of regular teaching load. (Modesto Jr. College)
(18) A budget, the TV Center Budget, is expected to be balanced by income. (Rochester Institute of Technology)
(19) The instructor's salary is paid on an overload basis; the commercial TV station absorbs other costs as a public service. (Wayne State University)

11. If your institution is located near the state line, do you charge out-of-state tuition? If so, is the out-of-state tuition the same as that for an on-campus student?

10 Out-of-state Tuition	15 No out-of-state Tuition
(1) University of New Hampshire	(1) University of Oregon
(2) The Pennsylvania State University	(2) Virginia Commonwealth University
(3) Orange County Community College	(3) University of Detroit
(4) Pensacola Junior College	(4) North Carolina State University
(5) Community College of Baltimore	(5) University of Minnesota
(6) Miami University - Ohio	(6) University of Utah

144

(7) Washburn University of Topeka (7) University of Maine
(8) San Diego Evening College (8) University of Maryland
(9) Dutchess Community College (9) Rochester Institute of Technology
(10) University of Oklahoma (10) Wayne State University
(11) Georgia Southern College
(12) Harvard University (Univ. Ext.)
(13) University of Nebraska - Omaha
(14) Drake University
(15) Utah State University

12. When do you schedule your educational TV courses?

Institution	Time of TV Course Offerings
(1) University of South Carolina	1:30 - 4:30 p. m. ; 6:30 - 9:30 p. m.
(2) Drury College	6 a. m. Saturday mornings - Station A 6:30 a. m. Saturday mornings - Station B
(3) New York University	6:30 - 7:00 a. m. (CBS)
(4) Drake University	6:30 - 7:30 a. m. (3 days per week - Sunrise Semester)
(5) Dutchess Community College	1:00 p. m. - 8:00 p. m. in cooperation with N. Y. U.
(6) University of Detroit	After elementary teachers are out of school
(7) Virginia Commonwealth University	T & Th - 3:30 - 4:00 p. m. ; M & W - 4:00 - 4:30 p. m.
(8) University of Denver	Programs conducted during day - times vary.
(9) North Carolina State University	Late afternoon 3 - 4 p. m. and 4 - 5 p. m.
(10) Utah State University	7 p. m. on closed circuit
(11) University of New Hampshire	4:00 to 6:30 p. m.
(12) Pennsylvania State University	3:00 - 3:30 p. m. ; 4:00 - 5:00 p. m. ; 6:30 - 8:00 p. m.
(13) University of Georgia	7:00 - 9:00 p. m.

(14) Orange County Community College — In the evenings
(15) St. Francis College — Late afternoons
(16) University of Toledo — 8:00 a. m., 12:30 p. m. and 3:30 p. m.
(17) Union College — Evening hours
(18) University of Minnesota — 9:00 – 10:00 p. m.
(19) Pensacola Jr. College — 8:30 – 10:00 p. m.; 9:00 – 10:30 p. m.
(20) University of Utah — 5:10 p. m. Monday through Thursday
(21) University of Maine — 3:30 – 4:00 p. m.; 6:00 – 7:00 p. m.
(22) St. Louis University — 6:30 – 7:00 a. m.
(23) Modesto Jr. College — 7:00 – 8:00 a. m.; 10:00 – 11:00 a. m.; 7:00 – 8:00 p. m.
(24) University of Maryland — M, T, and Th, 8:00 – 8:30 a. m.
T, 9:30 – 10:00 p. m.
M and Th, 2:30 – 4:00 p. m.
Th, 8:00 – 8:30 p. m.

(25) Community College of Baltimore — Day and evening on a repeat basis
(26) University of Washington — 7:00 p. m., Mon. 9:30 p. m., Thurs, 4:00 p. m.
M, W, & Fri. 12:30 p. m.; T & Th
(Series also run on commercial TV stations throughout the state at various times – usually in the early mornings.)

(27) Rochester Institute of Technology — Programs are scheduled at noon and in the evening.
(28) Wayne State University — 6:30 – 7:00 a. m., 7:00 – 7:30 a. m. Daily
(29) College of William and Mary — Programs are scheduled at times convenient to public school teachers (evenings and Saturdays)

(30) Nassau Community College — Normal classroom hours
(31) Georgia Southern College — After school hours
(32) Harvard University (Univ. Ext.) — 3:00 – 3:30 p. m.; 7:00 – 7:30 p. m.; 7:30 – 8:00 p. m.
(33) University of Nebraska-Omaha — Saturday – 8 a. m. (Coml. VHF Station) 13 weeks

(34) San Diego Evening College   Mondays - 8 p. m. (Univ. VHF Station) 13 weeks

(35) University of Oklahoma   6:00 - 7:00 a. m.

     Programs scheduled at various times.

Additional Comments on Educational TV Programs:

The program is increasing as funds and needs increase.   (University of South Carolina)

Graduate courses are offered by educational TV-financed by tuition--no out-of-state tuition. (University of Oregon)

TV programs offered by the State University of N. Y. are supervised by SUNY (Dutchess Community College)

Virginia Commonwealth University Health Services Division makes considerable use of TV in its normal instruction program. At the academic division, "we think educational television will play a larger role in adult education in the years ahead."   (Virginia Commonwealth University)

All ETV courses offered are produced by the Evening College.   (Pensacola Junior College)

The Education Department offers TV courses for teachers - the Evening College offers one course - How to Teach on TV for credit.   (Xavier University)

Normally, a course runs 13 weeks. The instructor normally functions as coordinator-moderator using a guest speaker/guest panel format.   (University of Nebraska-Omaha)

VIII. NON CREDIT PROGRAMS

1. Does your division or college offer non-credit courses ? $\underline{113}$ $\underline{34}$

         yes   no

2. If so, in what areas ?

   Business and Management Studies $\underline{100}$ Arts & Sciences $\underline{90}$

147

Other areas   48

	Engineering	Education
	52	53

3. Do you have a budget for your non-credit programs?

	Engineering	Education
	47 yes	35 no

   Is the program expected to pay for itself?

	Engineering	Education
	95 yes	6 no

4. What remuneration does your faculty receive for teaching a non-credit course?

Municipal or State Colleges and Universities

School	Amt. per Course	Amt. per hr.	No. of Sessions	Basis of Remuneration	
				Qual. of Instructor	Area of Instruction
1. Univ. of South Carolina	$200	-	16	x	x
2. Northern Illinois Univ.	-	$50	-	x	x
3. New York University	$450- $1000	-	14	x	x
4. Univ. of West Florida	-	$25	-	-	-
5. University of Oregon	-	-	-	x	x
6. Virginia Commonwealth Univ.	-	-	-		
7. University of Windsor	1/6 of base salary	$12- $20	6 - 14	x	x
8. Univ. of New Mexico	-	$12.50 per session	-	x	x
9. University of Kentucky	$400- $500	-	-	-	-
10. Idaho State University	$340	-	12	x	x

148

School	Amt. per Course	Amt. per hr.	No. of Sessions	Basis of Remuneration Qual. of Instructor	Area of Instruction
11. Utah State University	$120	$15	10	-	-
12. Univ. of Southern Miss.	$240	$20-$30	8	-	-
13. Univ. of New Hampshire	$500	-	10	x	x
14. Univ. of Tenn.-Nashville	$400	$12-$20	10	x	x
15. Univ. of Georgia	-	-	-	x	x
16. Joint Univ. Center(MSU/UT)	$450	-	10(3-hr)	-	-
17. Bklyn. Coll. of City Univ. of N.Y.	-	$17	-	-	-
18. Iowa State University	-	$25 1st hr., $15 2nd, to $100/day	-	-	-
19. Univ. of Toronto	-	$23.50 per/hr- 25 lect. $29 per/hr-Asst. Prof. $36 per/hr-Assoc. Prof. $51.50 per/hr-Prof.	25	x	x
20. Univ. of Toledo	$480-$960	$15 per/cr. hr. -	-	x	x
21. East Carolina Univ.	-	-	-	x	x
22. Univ. of Tenn.-Knoxville	-	$20 per/cr. hr. -	-	-	-
23. Ohio State Univ.	-	$25-$75 per/hr. -	-	-	x
24. Univ. of Cincinnati	-	$35 per/class hr. -	-	x	-
25. Univ. of Utah	-	$120-$238 per/cr.- hr. -	-	x	-
26. Univ. of Maine	-	$20-$24 per/hr. -	-	x	-

School	Amt. per Course	Amt. per hr.	No. of Sessions	Basis of Remuneration Qual. of Instructor	Area of Instruction
27. Memphis State Univ.	-	$20 per/contact hr.	-	x	-
28. Univ. of Maryland	-	$710 per/3 hr. crse. $785 per/3-hr. crse.-Asst. Prof. $875 per/3-hr. crse.-Assoc. Prof. $975 per/3-hr. crse.-Professor	-	x	-
29. Purdue Univ.-Calumet Campus	Based on: faculty, salary, contact hrs., numerical index value to the level of the course			x	
30. Univ. of Washington	-	$12-$18 per/ contact	-	-	x
31. Wayne State Univ.	(2-hr. crse. schedule) - $384 Asst &UCAE lect. $416-Instr.; $448-Asst. Prof. $512-Assoc. Prof. & UCLE lect. $576-Professor		16 weeks	x	x
32. College of Wm. & Mary	$675-$825 per/3-hr. course	-	-	x	-
33. East Tenn. Univ.	$150-$170 per/qtr.hr.	-	-	x	x
34. Univ. of Tenn.-Knoxville	$400	$20 per/hr.	20	-	-
35. Georgia Southern College	-	$10-$18 per/hr.	-	x	-
36. Washburn Univ. at Topeka	-	$10 per/hr.	-	-	-
37. Univ. of Oklahoma	-	$25-100 per/crse 1 hr. sessions	-	x	x

Private and Church-related Institutions

	School	Amt. per Course	Amt. per hr.	No. of Sessions	Basis of Remuneration Qual. of Instructor	Basis of Remuneration Area of Instruction
1.	Centenary Coll. of Louisiana	$250	–	15	–	–
2.	Drury College	$150	–	6	–	–
3.	Drake University	$600	–	15	–	x
4.	Roanoke College	–	$20 per/hr.	–	–	–
5.	George Washington Univ.	–	$35–$50	–	–	x
6.	Univ. of Denver	$100 min.	–	10	–	x
7.	Drexel University	–	–	–	–	x
8.	The American University	–	–	–	–	x
9.	PMC Colleges	Same as credit-level courses			x	–
10.	Sacred Heart Univ.	$600	–	–	–	–
11.	Philadelphia Coll. of Textiles	$550–$800	–	10	x	x
12.	Indiana Central College	$100–$400	–	6–15	–	–
13.	Baylor University	–	$25 1st hr., $15 2nd, to $100/day	–	x	–
14.	St. Joseph's College	$720–$1070	–	–	x	–
15.	St. Francis College	$250	$15	6	–	–
16.	Russell Sage College	$300–$350	–	–	x	–
17.	Union College	Varies	–	–	–	x
18.	Bryant College	$500–$1000	–	10–15	x	x
19.	Upsala College	$400–$500	–	–	x	–
20.	St. Louis Univ.-Metropolitan College	$250	–	10	–	–

School	Amt. per Course	Amt. per hr.	No. of Sessions	Basis of Remuneration — Qual. of Instructor	Area of Instruction
21. Texas Christian Univ.	$100 - 1 cl. session	-	-	x	x
22. Thomas More College	$178	-	-	x	x
23. Xavier University	$200	-	16	-	-
24. The New School	$500-$1500	-	15	x	-
25. Bradley University	-	$15-$20	-	x	x
26. Rochester Inst. of Techn.	-	$15	-	x	x
27. University of Tampa	$300-$500	-	8-10	x	-
28. Baldwin-Wallace College	-	$27.50	-	-	-
29. Tulane University	-	$30-$50 per/cl.	-	x	x
30. Hofstra University	$400	-	10	x	x
31. Northwestern University	$400	-	4	-	-
32. C. W. Post College	-	$25	-	-	-
33. Rider College	-	$25-$30	-	x	-
34. The Johns Hopkins Univ.	-	$225 up	10-15	x	x
35. Rockford College	-	$35 per/cl.	-	-	-

Private and State Community (Junior) Colleges

School	Amt. per Course	Amt. per hr.	No. of Sessions	Basis of Remuneration — Qual. of Instructor	Area of Instruction
1. County College of Morris	$180-$270	-	-	-	-
2. Bakersfield College	-	$8.83	-	-	-
3. Mohawk Valley Comm. Coll.	-	$9-$12	-	x	-
4. Orange County Comm. Coll.	$240	-	15	-	-
5. Queensborough Comm. Coll.	$210-$360	$14-$24	-	x	-

School	Amt. per Course	Amt. per hr.	No. of Sessions	Basis for Remuneration Qual. of Instructor	Area of Instruction
6. Northern Va. Comm. Coll.	$200–$500	–	10	–	x
7. Pensacola Junior College	–	$8.00	varies	–	–
8. Miami-Dade Junior College	–	$7.50	–	–	–
9. Modesto Junior College	–	$6–$13	–	–	–
10. Manhattan Junior College	–	$10	–	–	x
11. Comm. Coll. of Baltimore	$750	–	15	x	–
12. Southwestern Michigan Coll.	–	$7–$10	–	x	–
13. Jefferson State Jr. College	$225	–	10	–	–
14. Nassau Community College	–	$185–$230	–	–	–
15. Manatee Junior College	$700	–	15	x	–
16. San Diego Evening College	–	$9.86	–	x	–
17. South Texas Junior College	$480–$510	–	–	–	x

5. Does your division or college sponsor conferences and institutes?

$$\frac{82}{\text{yes}} \qquad \frac{32}{\text{no}}$$

If so, list the Conferences and Institutes Sponsored this Past Year by your Division or College.

1.	School	Title of Conference, Seminar or Institute
1.	University of South Carolina	1) Advanced Cosmetology Institute 2) Optometry Institute 3) Management Seminar 4) Legal Secretaries Conference 5) Business & Professional Women's Conference
2.	Drexel University	1) Liberty Bell Corrosion with the Philadelphia Chapter of the National Association of Corrosion Engineers
3.	The American University	1) Public Affairs Institute 2) Systems Practice for Managers 3) Environmental Systems Institutes 4) English Language Institutes 5) Administration of Justice Conferences
4.	Idaho State University	1) Association of Hospital Accountants 2) Idaho State Vocational Educators 3) Conferences for Nursing Home Administrators
5.	Dutchess Community College	1) Pre-School Parents Seminar 2) Environment Crisis Seminar

School	Title of Conference, Seminar or Institute
Dutchess Community College (Cont'd.)	3) Dental Hygienist Reference Workshop 4) Basketball Clinic 5) Parent Orientation to Special Preparation Summer Program
6. University of Rochester	1) Consortium Summer Program on Southeast Asia 2) Workshop in Programming Self-Instructional Materials 3) Workshop on Teaching Language in Secondary Schools 4) Individualized Reading Institute 5) Selected Topics in Reading Instruction 6) Teaching about Foreign Culture 7) Systems Application for School Principals
7. Drury College	1) Rhythmics Workshop 2) Testing Techniques Workshop 3) Instructional TV Workshop 4) Exceptional Child Workshop 5) Quality Control Seminar 6) Bob-White Quail Seminar 7) Stroke Patient Workshop
8. Drake University	1) Children's Emotional Health 2) Employee Mutual Insurance Institute 3) New Counselor Orientation Program 4) Jury Seminar 5) Head Start Supplementary Training

School		Title of Conference, Seminar or Institute
Drake University (Cont'd.)	6)	Students' United Nations Symposium
	7)	President's Commission on the 25th Anniversary of the United Nations
	8)	License Qualification Course for Iowa Insurance Agents
	9)	Communication Seminar
	10)	Ecology Seminar
	11)	Literature Seminar
	12)	Awareness Laboratory
	13)	Becoming Woman Workshop
	14)	Local Government Workshop
	15)	Social Welfare Practices
	16)	Banker's Life Speech Seminar
	17)	Teacher Education for Methodist School of Nursing
	18)	Supervisory Management Training for Women
9. The University of West Florida	1)	Florida Association of Science Teachers
	2)	Second Annual Manufacturers Conference
	3)	Case Studies in Industrial Management
	4)	Effective Communication for Managers
10. University of New Mexico	1)	Dental Seminar
	2)	Dental Hygienists Seminar
	3)	Hotel-Motel Management
	4)	Tax Assessors Conference
	5)	Air Frame and Power Plant Maintenance
	6)	Boiler Plant Operation
11. University of South Mississippi	1)	Vocational Rehabilitation Training Workshop

School		Title of Conference, Seminar or Institute
University of South Mississippi (Cont'd.) Total credit courses-11 Total non-credit courses-53 Total Activities, credit and non-credit-64 Total number of participants-9033	2) 3) 4) 5) 6) 7) 8) 9) 10) 11) 12) 13) 14) 15)	Drug Abuse Workshop Land Owners Conference 14th Annual Instrumental Conductors Conference Mississippi Conference on Social Welfare Mississippi School Counselors Workshop Workshop: Reading for the Disadvantaged Guidance Residence Seminar School Health Institute Aerospace Education Workshop Investigation of Sex Crimes Children's Book Festival Art Exhibit Internal Revenue Service Southern Fine Arts Festival (Partial Listing)
12. North Carolina State University Total of 95 conferences in 1971	1) 2) 3) 4) 5) 6) 7) 8) 9) 10) 11) 12) 13)	Nurseryman's Short Course Tree Improvement Agricultural Chemicals School Post Control Operators School Employment Security Commission How to Work Smarter Instead of Harder Noise and Hearing Conservation for Industry Public Works Conference Dairyman's Conference Experimental Stress Analysis Turfgrass Conference Sale Seminar Sport Fishing Short Course

School	Title of Conference, Seminar or Institute
North Carolina State University (Cont'd.)	14) Conference on Men's Knitting Suiting
	15) Maintenance of Commercial Vehicles
	16) Color Theory & Color Measurement
	17) Home Economics Workshop on Textiles
	18) Commercial Flower Growers
	19) Meter School
	20) Photographic Re-touching
13. New York University Many conferences and institutes	1) Annual Institute of Federal Taxation
	2) Annual Institute on Labor
	3) Biennial Institute on Charitable Foundations
14. University of Tennessee-Nashville	1) Warehousing Management
	2) Applied Work Measurement
	3) Conservation Education
	4) Decision Making
15. University of Arkansas 31 conferences and workshops offered	1) Lunch Room Management Workers
	2) Educational Secretaries Workshop
	3) Summer music camp
16. University of Hawaii	60 conferences conducted this past year
17. Orange County Community College	1) In-service Training of Instructors for Adults
	2) Institute of Marine Biology in-service workshop
	3) Health Education in the Public Schools
	4) Industrial Manpower Clinic
	5) Diabetic Workshop
	6) Fashion Show

School	Title of Conference, Seminar or Institute
Orange County Community College (Cont'd.)	7) High School Enrichment Program 8) Police and Youthful Offenders
18. Pennsylvania State University	Over 300 conferences and institutes offered
19. Indiana Central College	1) 12 Supervisory Institutes 2) 12 Management Development Programs 3) 6 Women's Programs
20. Memphis State University	50 conferences conducted during the year
21. St. Louis University (Metropolitan College)	24 conferences and Institutes were held this year
22. University of Georgia	1) Southeastern Law Enforcement Program - Annual Police Juvenile Officers Workshop 2) Community Development Program for Ministers - Religion, Government and Business in Contemporary Society 3) Annual Summer Conference of Georgia Association of Supervision & curriculum development 4) Short Course for Commercial Flower Growers 5) Georgia Pre-School Association Workshop 6) Seminar for Newly Appointed College Administrators 7) Realtors Institute 8) Workshop: Parole in the Criminal Justice System 9) 2nd Institute for Voter Registrars of Georgia

School	Title of Conference, Seminar or Institute
University of Georgia (Cont'd.)	10) Mathematics Education Workshop
	11) 1969 Annual Conference, Georgia Association of Colleges
	12) Grounds Maintenance Conference
	13) Junior College Administrative Team Conference Education Professional Development Act
	14) Institute for Teachers of Emotionally Disturbed Children
	15) Conference on Reproductive Problems in Animals
	16) 23rd Southern Industrial Editors Institute
	17) ASCA-Management Development Course V
23. University of Tennessee-Chattanooga	1) Pre-Retirement Planning
	2) Management Development
	3) Estate Planning
	4) Consumer Education
24. Bryant College	1) Law Enforcement Seminar
	2) Income Tax Seminars
	3) Marketing Seminars
	4) 15-week CPCD courses
25. Pensacola Junior College	1) Drug Abuse
	2) Mental Health
	3) National Security Seminar
	4) Travel Seminar
	5) Pilot's Confab
	6) Rock Hounds
26. University of Maine	1) Nursing Conference
	2) Purchasing
	3) Creativity
	4) Transportation Conference
	5) Engineering Conference

School	Title of Conference, Seminar or Institute
University of Maine (Cont'd.)	6) Veterinary Medicine Conference 7) Retailing 8) Literature 9) Graphic Arts
27. St. Louis University (Metropolitan College)	24 conferences and institutes were held this past year
28. University of Maryland	145 conferences and institutes offered this past year
29. Texas Christian University	1) Chamber of Commerce Institute 2) Civil Affairs Institute 3) Management Seminar 4) Numerous other meetings
30. University of Washington	103 conferences and institutes held this past year
31. Thomas More College	1) Institute on Religious Life "What's Happening in the Church?" 2) Introduction to Direct Supervision 3) Operation Access (admission to college) 4) Operation Second Chance (for continuation in college or readmission)
32. University of Tennessee-Knoxville	1) Applied Work Measurement and Methods Engineering 2) Quality Control Seminar 3) Production Planning and Control Seminar 4) Basic Management Analyst Training Program 5) Tennessee High School Journalism Institute I and II 6) Conference on Legal Services for the Appa-

School	Title of Conference, Seminar or Institute
University of Tennessee-Knoxville (Cont'd.)	lachian area 7) Small Business Management Seminar 8) Tax Forum 9) Flight Instruction-Instrument Seminar 10) Labor-Management Relations Clinic 11) Sex Education Workshop 12) High School Choral Camp
33. University of Richmond	Approximately 150 conferences were offered this past year
34. Ohio State University	1) Ohio School of Banking 2) Engineering & Technical Society 3) Pro Football Players 4) Publications 5) Consumer Economics 6) Upward Bound 7) NSF Mass Political Communications 8) NSF Summer Math Institute 9) Forensics 10) Squires 11) Chamber Music 12) Theater Arts 13) Wrestling Clinic 14) Japanese Teachers of English 15) Acid Mine Drainage 16) NSF Biology
35. Southwestern Michigan College	1) Art Education Workshop 2) Management Seminar 3) Para-professionals workshop 4) Drug Institute
36. Wichita State University	1) Community Improvement 2) Secretarial Seminar 3) Media and the Humanities

School	Title of Conference, Seminar or Institute
Wichita State University (Cont'd.)	4) Opportunities for Women 5) Extra Dimension
37. University of Tampa	1) American Institute of Real Estate Appraisers 2) Policy Community Relations Institute 3) Course in Real Estate 4) Fire and Casualty Insurance
38. Wayne State University Numerous additional conferences	1) Treatment of Rheumatic Arthritis 2) Michigan's Concern for Children and Youth 3) Behavior Modifications 4) Successful Programs 5) Industrial Toxology
39. Tulane University	1) ASHRAE-Symposium on Air Conditioning 2) IAHY-DITC Disability Insurance Research Seminar 3) American Institute of Real Estate Appraisers
40. Hofstra University	1) Incinerator Technology 2) Solid Wastes Technology 3) You and Your Heart 4) Man and Machine (Liberal Arts) 5) Short Conference with Professional Organizations
41. University of Louisville	1) Kentucky Association for Children with learning disabilities 2) Management Techniques 3) Television Seminar 4) Leadership Training Institute 5) Kentucky Youth Conference

School	Title of Conference, Seminar or Institute
42. Miami University-Ohio	1) Library Management 2) Middle Management 3) Extern Seminar for School 4) Economics for Clergy
43. Manatee Junior College	1) Teachers Aide Training Conference 2) An R. N. Nursing Workshop (in-service training) 3) Emergency Care Technology (ambulance, rescue workers, firemen, etc.)
44. University of South Florida	1) Techniques and Training for Competitive Swimming 2) Speed Reading Development 3) Creative Dramatics for Children 4) 7th Annual National Superintendent's Conference 5) Professional Development in Quality Control 6) Institute in Housekeeping Management and Supervision 7) Southeastern Conference for Cooperative Education Workshop 8) "What in the World" - lecture 9) Ultimate Strength Design Methods 10) Investment Seminars for Florida Trust Investment Officers
45. Washburn University of Topeka	1) Secretarial Seminars 2) Arts Council Seminars 3) Conferences on Aging 4) Urban Policy Conferences

School	Title of Conference, Seminar or Institute
46. University of New Hampshire (Partial Listing)	1) Third Annual Conclave for Applied Behavior Scientists 2) Poultry Health Conference 3) Accident Prevention Workshop 4) Early Childhood Conference 5) National Science Foundation 6) Public Library Techniques 7) Summer Youth Music School 8) New England Credit Union School 9) New Hampshire Association 10) New England Personnel and Guidance Conference 11) New England Parks and Recreation 12) New England Grange Lecturers
47. Idaho State University	1) Association of Hospital Accountants 2) Idaho State Vocational Education 3) Conference for Nursing Home Administrators
48. Seminole Junior College	1) Drug Seminar 2) Counseling Seminar 3) Quality Control Seminar
49. Rochester Institute of Technology	Numerous Conferences and Institutes
50. Queensborough Community College	1) Saturday Reading and Writing Institute 2) Community Leadership Conference 3) Secretarial Refresher Forum

School	Title of Conference, Seminar or Institute
51. Northern Virginia Community College	1) Flower Show Judges Forum 2) PTA Regional Conference for New Officers 3) V. A. Regional Conference for Supervisors and Curriculum Specialists
52. East Carolina University	1) State Personnel Management 2) Executive Development 3) School Administrators 4) Numerous other conferences
53. Baylor University	1) School of Alcohol & Narcotics Studies 2) Central Texas Regional Science Fair 3) Young Homemakers of Texas
54. University of Oklahoma	1) Over 500 conferences, institutes offered during last year

6. How much do you pay your clinicians for conferences and institutes?

Majority of responses: Varies according to background of clinicians and type of conference.

Other individual responses:

A. One day

$100	11	$50-$500	1
$175	1	$200	1
$100-$150	1	$25-$150	1
$150	2	$250	3
$25-$75	5	$50-$400	1

B. One week

$200	2	$500	2	$750	1

7. Are conferences sponsored by your division or college in cooperation with another college or does your division or college sponsor its own conferences using qualified faculty members in your own institution and/or visiting lecturers?

Cooperate with other colleges   <u>14</u>
Division or College sponsors its own   <u>32</u>
Both   <u>23</u>

8. Is your division responsible for the summer session at your institution?

<u>46</u>   <u>38</u>   <u>9</u>
yes   no   evening only

IX.   GENERAL

1. Is your institution participating in any of the following innovative practices?

A. Offering credit and/or non-credit courses in "store front" locations off-campus for economically deprived populations?   <u>29</u>   <u>50</u>
                                      yes   no

Institutions Offering Such Courses

(1) Bakersfield College - an Off-campus Course "Parent Education in the Ghetto"
(2) New York University
(3) Drake University
(4) University of New Mexico
(5) The American Univ.
(6) Idaho State Univ.
(7) North Carolina State Univ.
(8) Univ. of New Hampshire
(9) Northeastern Univ.
(10) Univ. of Tennessee-Nashville
(11) The Pennsylvania State University
(12) Univ. of Georgia
(13) Orange County Comm. College
(14) Memphis State Univ.
(15) Brooklyn College of City Univ. of N. Y.
(16) Modesto Junior College
(17) East Carolina Univ.
(18) Manhattan Comm. Coll.
(19) Bryant College
(20) Wichita State Univ.
(21) American International College
(22) Temple Univ. (Bus. Adm.)
(23) Univ. of Nebraska-Omaha
(24) San Diego Evening Coll.
(25) Univ. of Minnesota
(26) Pensacola Junior College

(27) Univ. of Cincinnati
(28) University of Utah
(29) University of Maine

B. To what extent do students at your institution participate in any discussions regarding the academic programs?

62	24	9
considerable	limited	no participation

How do they participate?

Students are members of the Academic Affairs Committee, Curriculum Committee, Senate, or other committees. 56
By means of questionnaires, surveys, personal conferences. 14
Evening student honor society. 1
Continuing Education or Evening Student Council. 5
Student-Faculty Relations Committee 5
Academic Dean(s) meet with student leaders 2-4 times per year. 3
Candidates for graduation make suggestions for future schedules, etc. 2

C. Do you have an Evening Division Advisory Committee? 24 81
       yes   no

Institutions Having an Advisory Committee

(1) Univ. of Oregon
(2) Marietta College-Ohio
(3) Sacred Heart Univ.
(4) Univ. of New Hampshire
(5) Mohawk Valley Comm. College
(6) Northeastern Univ.
(7) Univ. of Georgia
(8) Rollins College
(9) Wichita State Univ.
(10) Tulane University
(11) Baylor University
(12) Univ. of Arkansas
(13) Millard Fillmore Coll.
(14) St. Mary's Dominican College
(15) Univ. of Minnesota
(16) Univ. of Utah
(17) Modesto Jr. College
(18) Rockhurst College
(19) Rider College
(20) Temple University
(21) Univ. of Nebraska-Omaha
(22) Manatee Jr. College
(23) Dutchess Comm. Coll.
(24) LaSalle College

D. What other innovative practices are used at your institution?

(1) New York University - Faculty participation for part-time faculty, use of appointed or elected "ombudsmen" to whom a student can anonomously bring complaints or problems, publication of a newsletter, "Continuing Education", a "House Organ" entitled, "School Notes" and "Library Notes", a program of special events such as lectures, musical and dance programs, colloquia, art.

(2) Graduate courses for part-time students are offered both on and off-campus during the evening and can lead to degrees upon approval of the student program for adults.

(3) Marietta College-Ohio - Graduate programs for part-time evening students are cooperative programs with Ohio University (e. g. , MBA with graduate courses taught by Ohio University faculty) degree regulations by Ohio Univ. , registration and facilities provided by Marietta.

(4) Virginia Commonwealth University - Five classes taught by educational TV; 500-600 adult students attend classes on Saturday a. m.

(5) University of Windsor - Closed circuit TV is used for some instruction.

(6) George Washington University - The Master of Science in Administration program is a 36-hr. program in which the student may choose one of the thirteen areas of concentration with no thesis required for the benefit of part-time evening students.

(7) University of New Mexico - A study of the student profile during the last five years is in progress.

(8) University of Denver - Law students are participating as recorders and advisors for Model City Resident Committee. The University of Denver has a separate office of Conference Coordination which operates under the Vice-Chancellor for Public Affairs.

(9) The American University - Special programs on campus to assist the economically and educationally disadvantaged students fall under "PRIDE", and special programs to assist returning personnel to prepare for second careers fall under Strategy of Career Transition.

(10) Idaho State University - Student evaluation of faculty.

(11) Utah State University - Tele-lectures are used for off-campus courses, "quality" faculty are flown to two off-campus centers.

(12) Bakersfield College - An off-campus course "Parent Education in the Ghetto" is offered. For the past 14-15 years, 325 new courses have been tried in the evening. Many of these have moved into the regular program; some have expanded into a full curricula.

(13) Post Junior College - Students may walk in "off the streets" - there are no formal admission requirements.

(14) University of New Hampshire - Six M. Ed. programs are offered through the Div. of Continuing Education in cooperation with Education and Graduate School.

(15) Pennsylvania State University - The University does participate in "store front" credit and non-credit courses for the economically deprived populations. Currently, in operation is a computer-assisted instruction mobile van (computer plus 14 student stations in a 40' x 40' van).

(16) University of Georgia - Last year, the Center for Continuing Education, in cooperation with the Savannah State College (black) and the Armstrong State College launched an extensive non-credit program in a ten-block area of Savannah that, with the support of Title I program is carrying programs directly to the culturally "deprived" where they are - the program shows much promise; a proposal has been submitted to and approved by the top administration of the University for taking over and completely renovating a University facility (located adjacent to a deprived neighborhood) as a center for community-wide non-credit programs that would involve the economically and culturally deprived, as well as other income groups.

(17) University of California-Berkeley - Univ. Ext. - No degree oriented programs are offered to part-time students in the evening, but many are designed for graduates.

(18) Joint University Center - MSU/UT - Free noon-time lecture series are offered on Monday and Thursday each week.

(19) Orange County Community College - Credit and

170

non-credit courses are offered at off-campus locations for economically deprived populations in four major locations and on a collegiate bus.

(20) University of Missouri - Three remedial courses offered, free tutorial services, development of a viable student council and services are provided for evening students.

(21) Utica College - Syracuse University - About 60 graduate education courses and twenty graduate courses in other areas are offered in cooperation with Syracuse University - graduate courses are for residence credit.

(22) St. Joseph's College - An M. A. in General Education is offered part-time students in the Evening Division.

(23) University of Toledo - Honors students may participate in non-credit courses for enrichment.

(24) Russell Sage College - An M. S. degree in Nursing and an M. S. degree in Elementary Education are offered as graduate programs for part-time students.

(25) Millard Fillmore College - The institution does offer tutorial programs for the disadvantaged - some admission requirements are waived for this group of students.

(26) Suffolk University - Scholarship assistance is available to economically deprived individuals who are qualified to take college work. Interdisciplinary Senior Honors Program - students are placed in Social Work Agencies as part of their field experience course.

(27) Bryant College - Special off-campus and Saturday classes are offered by Law Enforcement Personnel.

(28) Pensacola Junior College - Audio-tutorial labs, closed and open circuit TV, directed study.

(29) University of Maine - An innovative practice used at this institution is a federal program in Model Cities area of the community. Four programs for part-time students are administered by the Evening Division; Masters of Business Administration, Sec. Education, Library Science and Engineering.

(30) Upsala College - The college has an Internship Program combining class study with field work.

(31) Modesto Junior College - Programs are offered for the disadvantaged and physically handicapped both high school level and lower college level.

171

(32) Manhattan Community College - The college administers three regional Opportunity Centers for the disadvantaged.

(33) Xavier University - Graduate programs for part-time students are administered through the graduate school with 3,000 registrants. An experiment of "Friday Night Adult Education Center" is now in progress.

(34) Metropolitan College-Boston University - There are special and new credit degrees in Urban Affairs (undergraduate and graduate) and Master of Liberal Studies.

(35) University of Washington - A recent innovation was to permit adults to register on a space available basis in all credit classes if they can obtain the permission of the instructor, by paying a regular fee through a highly simplified registration process.

(36) Rochester Institute of Technology is just beginning to use closed circuit TV both day and evening. "We have an IBM 1500 computer available to all, but specifically for students of the National Technical Institute for the Deaf."

(37) Southwestern Michigan College - The institution is instituting packaged independent study courses.

(38) Western New England College - Calculus and Physics are studied both half a night each, twice a week.

(39) University of Tampa - Students meet in weekly open meetings with the President, Vice-President, and department chairmen.

(40) Baldwin-Wallace College - An Experimental Learning Center is available to which students with special academic problems can be referred.

(41) Manatee Junior College - According to the Dean, the Evening College is "one department completely innovative." "We use a flexible schedule, trying out new needed community education needs."

(42) Springfield College - House workshops are held for library administrators.

(43) Harvard University - Univ. Ext. - Offering television courses for credit for the past 15 years. Television courses will be offered through two stations each term of this year for credit. These courses are prepared with the support of the U.S. Navy as part of the PACE program of college-level instruction.

(44) Rider College - Remedial programs are offered in Mathematics, English and Reading.

(45) University of Nebraska-Omaha - Extensive use of credit by examination, amnesty for poor past academic performance, flexibility of degree programming.

(46) University of Oklahoma - Special adult degree programs offered: Bachelor of Liberal Studies, Master of Living Sciences and Master of Arts in Government and Economics.

2. To whom are you as Director or Dean of the Evening Division, School or College, responsible?

Pres. or Chancellor	29	Dean, Faculty of A&S	4
Dean, Acad. Affairs	50	V. P. for Admin.	2
Acad. V. P., Provost		Dean, Div. of Cont.	
V. P. or V.-Chancellor	10	Ed.	2
Dean of College	13	Dir. Publ. Serv. -	
Dean of Instr., Dean of		Dean, School of	
Faculty	9	Bus. Adm.	1
		Mgt. Committee	1

3. What audio-visual and other technical instructional aids are used in your division or College of Continuing Education?

Most all schools have the usual audio-visual aids available to evening classes. A few schools have closed-circuit television. Six institutions have unusually well-equipped audio-visual departments:

1. New York University - about 200 special appearances on TV and radio as well as other instructional aids.

2. University of Windsor - Closed circuit TV and other equipment.

3. Utah State University - Tele-lecture, educational TV, two-way conference phones, and files. "We hope to add a tele-writer in the audio-visual and instructional aids area."

4.,5. Joint University Center - MSU/UT - Video tape TV, electro-writer, perceptoscope (to teach reading), 16mm film projector, slides and record players, etc.

6. University of Georgia - Both open and closed circuit television, slides, filmstrips, etc. are available for evening classes.

4. Do you have a chapter of Sigma Lambda at your institution?   13   75
yes   no

173

Institutions With Chapters

(1) University of Detroit
(2) George Washington Univ.
(3) St. Joseph's College
(4) Millard Fillmore Coll.
(5) Tulane University
(6) Fairleigh Dickinson Univ.
(7) C. W. Post College
(8) Univ. of Bridgeport
(9) Rider College
(10) American International College
(11) Univ. of Detroit (McNichols Evening Div.)
(12) Utica College
(13) PMC Colleges

5. In general, do you feel that the Evening Division or College is receiving adequate support?

67	51	6
yes	no	limited support

Does your administration recognize the need and importance of your adult education program?

78	42
yes	no

Comments:
(1) Support is dependent upon legislative apportionment. (University of West Florida)
(2) During the past two years, there has been a marked improvement in the stature of the College of Continuing Education and in the recognition accorded the Division at all echelons within the University. (The American University)
(3) Budget support, yes - scholarship support, no. (Metropolitan College - Boston University)
(4) In this college, the Evening College "supports" the day division. (Western New England College)

X. STUDENT RECRUITMENT

1. Publicity

	Much	Limited	Very Limited	None
Newspaper	141			
Radio	100	5		24
Television	67		8	35

174

2. Public Relations - special motivational appeals developed for:

| Industry | 95 | 16 | 3 |
| | yes | no | limited |

Organizations
| Chambers of Commerce | 73 | 14 | 11 |
| | yes | no | limited |

Clubs
| (Kiwanis, Rotary, etc.) | 77 | 13 | 8 |
| | yes | no | limited |

3. Typical publicity program or programs involving public relations:

(1) There is an office concerned with publicity and information which is concerned with press releases, newspaper articles, and television appearances, etc. Many brochures and fliers are sent to students as well as to industry and civic organizations. This is the office of Special Services to Business and Industry. (New York University)

(2) Marquee advertising is used along with spot radio announcements and newspaper publicity. (Rollins College)

(3) Student recruitment is done by quarter page ads placed in the newspaper before each session. (St. Joseph's College)

(4) The institution mails out 200, 000 pieces of promotional literature each year to business and industry and provides brochures and Sunday Supplements to the Chamber of Commerce. (University of Toledo)

(5) Plant papers are used for publicity. (University of Tennessee-Nashville)

(6) Participation in community and county career and education division programs for adults, group in formation sessions, College-for-a-Day program for adults. (Hofstra College)

(7) $7500 a year is budgeted for newspaper advertisement; $2, 200 a year for radio publicity. (Rider College)

American International College
Springfield, Mass.
Evening College

Total Enrollment 1,760 Day   Private Institution
                 1,075 Evening   Semester System
                 500 Off-campus

I. ADMISSION POLICIES

Deadline for application for admission to evening
classes is the day classes start. Students may register for
credit courses without transcripts. Non-matriculated students may take a maximum of eighteen semester hours. Admission requirements are high school graduation and in some
cases, specific course requirements. Mail registration is
used. There is an annual review of each student's record and an
interview with each student whose record is unsatisfactory.
Two special degree programs for adults are now in committee. Admission policies are set by the day school faculty.
Day and evening students may register for the same class
with permission. Orientation for evening students is held
a week before classes start. Evening students drop out if
they are doing unsatisfactory work making probation policies
unnecessary.

II. TERMINOLOGY

Title of Division: Evening College. Defined: College
which offers only on-campus evening credit courses.

III. FEES

Tuition fees are the same for day, evening, graduate
or undergraduate courses. Refunds are made on a graduated percentage basis.

IV. FACULTY AND FACULTY RECRUITMENT

Approximately 62% of the faculty teaching evening classes are full-time. Final authority to hire faculty lies with the
day school department chairmen, although some hiring is done
by the Dean of the Evening College. The Dean of the Evening
College can engage an instructor without the consent of the

department chairmen. No regular faculty meetings are held.
Faculty members are limited to one overload course per
semester; non-credit courses, conferences, etc. do not
count. Salary range for part-time faculty members is $600
to $775 for a three-hour course based upon rank. The
same salary scale applies to overloads.

V. SCHEDULING

The Dean of the Evening College is responsible for
the evening class schedule and has the authority to revise it.
Three-hour classes are scheduled once a week. Day and
evening classes are equal in terms of quality. There is a
Dean's List for evening students and there is an Honor Society: Alpha Sigma Lambda. No course required for a degree is ever cancelled but less than ten students gives option to cancel.

VI. ORGANIZATIONAL STRUCTURE

Ten staff members constitute the administrative staff
including staff not under the direction of the Evening College
Dean. The duties and responsibilities of the Dean are all
inclusive except for the service provided by the Registrar's
office, Business office and Director of Public Relations. The
Dean of Continuing Education is responsible for the non-credit
programs, conferences and institutes as well as extension.
The teaching staff consists of 116 part-time faculty members.
The following number of administrative staff are recommended for various sized student bodies: 2000 enrollment, two;
5000 enrollment, three, for credit programs; for non-credit
programs: 1000 enrollment, five, 2000 enrollment, eight.

VII. EDUCATIONAL TELEVISION PROGRAMS

The Evening College does not sponsor any educational
Television programs.

VIII. NON-CREDIT PROGRAMS

All non-credit courses are handled by the Dean of
Continuing Education.

IX. GENERAL

Special courses for economically deprived populations
are offered. Students participate in discussions regarding

the academic programs through the Evening Student Council and on Committee for Evening and Summer Curricula. The Evening College is receiving adequate support. The available audio-visual aids are used in the evening classes. The Dean of the Evening College is responsible to the President of the College.

X. STUDENT RECRUITMENT

Newspaper, radio and television publicity are used for student recruitment. Special motivational appeals are made to industry.

<u>The American University</u>
Washington, D.C.
College of Continuing Education

Total Enrollment 15, 326   Church-related Institution
Off-campus Enrollment 3, 134   Semester System
Non-degree Enrollment 5, 367

I. ADMISSION POLICIES

The deadline for application for admission for regular students is March 1 for freshmen, December 1 for freshmen transfers and graduate students, June 1 for transfer and graduate students--no undergraduate admission for summer. There is no deadline for admission for non-degree or "special" students. A student may register for credit courses before transcripts are submitted if he meets the non-degree admission criteria. Non-matriculating of "special" students may take eight courses (32 credit hours) for undergraduates and twelve credit hours for graduate students. Admission requirements for non-matriculating or "special" students is twenty-one years of age or older and in good standing at college previously attended. Regular student standards are set by the University's Committee on Admissions and are based primarily upon previous academic records, as well as test results, recommendations, and other pertinent information. Graduate students are required to maintain a "B" average; undergraduate students are required to maintain a "C" average. Mail registration for summer session only was conducted for the first time in 1970. Summer session schedule with application form was included in a Sunday supplement

to two major metropolitan newspapers. Registration forms
and confirmation of enrollment were handled by subsequent
correspondence. No ACT scores are required for admission;
only the CEEB if they are applying for freshman admission
and have completed secondary education within the past two
years. School college and ability tests are required as a
basis for admission. Adult degree programs include: Bachelor of Science in General Studies, Master of Science in
Teaching, BS in Administration of Justice, MS in the Administration of Justice. A Bachelor of Science in Technology
of Management as well as degrees in Environmental Systems
Analysis are being planned. The Faculty Committee on Undergraduate Admissions and Scholarships formulate the admission policies for regular degree students; College of Continuing Education for non-matriculating and/or "special" students. Students may enroll in day and evening classes whenever there is room. The advantage to a combined class is
that the educational needs of the adult student are better served
if he is given flexibility of enrolling in either or both day/
evening classes. A disadvantage is that the regular day students sometimes take evening classes and thereby displace
evening students. No separate orientation program is conducted for evening students. The college graduate who does
not meet academic standards for direct admission to a graduate degree program may apply for admission to a Graduate
Certificate Program administered by the College of Continuing Education. If he completes the Certificate Program with
a high enough grade average, he may be considered for admission to a graduate degree program.

II.   TERMINOLOGY

Title of Division: College of Continuing Education.
Defined: A college designed to act as a link between the
adult student and the University. CCE enables the adult student to make maximum use of University facilities. Continuing Education defined: The provision of a means for the
continued pursuit of learning--via non-degree, degree, and
non-credit programs.

III.   FEES

There is no fee differential between day and evening
classes but there is a fee differential between on and off-
campus courses since the overhead off-campus is lower.
Refunds are made on a graduated scale for the first six
weeks of classes during Fall and Spring semesters. Re-

funds are also made on a graduated scale for a shorter period during summer and special sessions.

IV. FACULTY AND FACULTY RECRUITMENT

There is no policy regarding the percentage of faculty
teaching evening classes. Two per cent of the budget is
spent on faculty recruiting. Part-time off-campus faculty
are hired by the Dean or Department Chairman approved by
the Dean of the College of Continuing Education. The Director cannot reject a faculty member who has been assigned to
teach evening classes; however, the recommendation is usually followed. No full-time faculty teach exclusively in the
evening. The Director cannot engage an instructor without
the consent of the department head if the department head is
outside the College of Continuing Education. Faculty meetings
are held as required. No distinction is made between day/eve-
ning faculty. Policies on overload teaching are determined
by individual teaching units of the University. Some departments permit overloads and others do not. Salary ranges:
full-time faculty teaching off-campus - $950; adjunct pro-
fessors - $950/3-cr. or course; lecturers - $715 per 3/cr.
or course.

V. SCHEDULING

The Director is responsible for the off-campus schedule only. There is no separate evening class schedule--day/
evening classes are included in the same schedule. Three-
hour classes are scheduled one night a week. Various projects are under way through our Labor Studies Center - Title
I projects - and a Research in Educational Technology is
planned. The day/evening classes compare equally in quality.
Most of the off-campus classes are taught by part-time faculty
and therefore vary in quality although we strive to maintain
high quality in all classes. Plans are underway to make
evening students eligible for the Dean's List. A Bachelor of
Science in Technology of Management degree is planned.
Classes are never conducted at a loss and very few at break-
even--if below break-even, the faculty is paid $100 per stu-
dent.

VI. ORGANIZATIONAL STRUCTURE

The administrative staff consists of twenty-eight staff
members. The teaching staff consists of nineteen full-time
and approximately 170 part-time faculty members. The Dean

is responsible for overall operation; four Assistant Deans -
Program Development, Off-Campus and Special Programs,
Administration Institutes and Management Programs; ten Di-
rectors - Center for Administration of Justice, Urban Communication Workshop, Neighborhood Campus Centers, Pride,
Urban Development Studies, Institute for Housing, Off-Campus, Business Council for International Understanding, Career
Development, English Language Institute; nine Assistant Directors - Center for Administration of Justice, Center for
Technology of Administration and English Language Institute;
Admissions - four advisement staff members (Admission and
registration functions for non-degree students are performed
primarily by academic advisors and representatives of Center
for Administration of Justice, English Language Institute,
Pride, Coordinator of Off-Campus Programs in cooperation
with the Admission and Registrar offices).

VII.   EDUCATIONAL TELEVISION PROGRAMS

No courses are offered in educational television.

VIII.   NON-CREDIT PROGRAMS

The Division offers non-credit courses in Education
and Technology of Management.   The Division sponsors conferences and institutes such as: Public Affairs Institute,
Systems Practice for Managers, Environmental Systems Institute, English Language Institute, Administration of Justice
Conferences.   Pay for clinicians varies from $25 up depending
upon many factors including qualifications of the clinician.
Some conferences are sponsored by the Division exclusively
and other times sponsored in cooperation with other colleges
and institutes using a combination of own faculty and visiting
lecturers.   Until the summer of 1971, the college was responsible for both on-campus and off-campus sessions.   For
1971 and the future, only the off-campus will be the responsibility of the Division.

IX.   GENERAL

Non-credit courses for the economically deprived populations are offered in the Neighborhood Campus Centers.
Students participate and are actively encouraged to participate
in discussions regarding the academic program.   This participation is conducted through faculty and advisement staff,
formal and informal student committees, questionnaires and
other student evaluating devices.   Special Programs on cam-

pus to assist the economically and educationally disadvantaged
student fall under Pride, and special programs to assist returning personnel to prepare for second careers fall under
Strategy of Career Transition. During the past two years
there has been marked improvement in the stature of the
College of Continuing Education and in the recognition accorded the Division at all echelons within the University community. The Director is responsible to the Vice-President
for Academic Affairs.

X. STUDENT RECRUITMENT

All special motivational appeals developed for public
relations is done by the University Office for Development
and University Relations. Newspaper, radio and sometimes
television are used as publicity for student recruitment.

<u>University of Arkansas</u>
Fayetteville, Arkansas
Division of Continuing Education

Total Enrollment 16, 000   Public-Land Grant
Evening Enrollment - No District   Institution
Evening College Program   Semester System

I. ADMISSION POLICIES

The deadline for application for admission to off-campus evening classes is August 22 (Fall) and January 6 (Spring).
A student may not register for credit courses without transcripts. Students may take an unlimited number of hours as
non-matriculating or special students. Admission requirements for non-matriculating students require a letter of good
standing if enrolled in another school--others full admission.
Regular students are required to submit complete official
transcripts through the various college deans. Students who
are rejected for regular classes are not advised to apply as
evening students. Registration by mail is optional; if used,
students complete the following information on cards pro-
vided--an application for admission or enrollment form, a
request to register for graduate credit form (if a graduate
registration), a sectional registration card. This is to be
returned to the Division of Continuing Education with payment
of the registration fee that is applicable. Probation and suspension policies are the same required by on-campus students.

The ACT or CEEB examination is required for the undergraduate program and GRE or MAT for the graduate program.
These are not used as a basis for placement but as a basis
for admission.   No separate degree program is offered for
evening students; graduate credit is limited to twelve semester hours when applied to University degree program.   No
degree granting program is in effect at the present time,
but plans are being made to offer a special degree program.
There is a faculty-student committee for the entire Continuing Education endeavor.

II.   TERMINOLOGY

Title of Division: Division of Continuing Education.
Many off-campus credit classes are administered by the Division as well as non-credit courses, conferences and institutes.

III.   FEES

The fees are the same for all students as the University of Arkansas does not operate a distinct Evening College
Program.

IV.   FACULTY AND FACULTY RECRUITMENT

There is no percentage of full-time faculty required
for the evening program.   The Dean or Department head of
the academic area involved has final authority for hiring full
and/or part-time faculty members.   No overload teaching is
allowed for off-campus teaching.   The salary range for part-
time faculty varies--all appointments are split appointments.

V.   SCHEDULING

The Director of the Division of Continuing Education
is responsible for the class schedule only for off-campus
offerings; the Deans of the Colleges are responsible for
course offerings on campus.   The procedure for compiling
class schedules are by demand and the Director has authority to revise the schedule.   Three-hour classes are scheduled one night per week.   Research projects at present consist of the Director's dissertation on An Analysis of the Role
and Scope of General Extension Services of the University of
Arkansas Division of Continuing Education.   Day and evening
classes compare favorably in terms of quality.   Part-time
evening students are not eligible for the Dean's List.   Usu-

ally 10 students are required to constitute a class but an instructor's compensation is not reduced when teaching less than ten, the class is dropped if too small.

VI.   ORGANIZATIONAL STRUCTURE

There are no full-time faculty members assigned to teach exclusively in the evening.   The Division does not have academic autonomy.   The Director of the Division is in charge of the Division.

VII.   EDUCATIONAL TELEVISION PROGRAMS

No courses are offered by the Division by educational television.

VIII.   NON-CREDIT PROGRAMS

Non-credit courses are offered in areas of Business and Management, Arts and Sciences, Engineering and Education.   This program is expected to pay for itself.   The remuneration for faculty is negotiated.   The Division sponsors conferences and institutes including thirty-one which were conducted between July 1, 1969 to June 30, 1970; including a Lunchroom Managers Workshop, Educational Secretaries Workshop and a Summer Music Camp.   Clinicians are paid through negotiation but pay does not exceed $100 per day. Conferences are sponsored by the Division in cooperation with other colleges.   This Division is not responsible for the summer session.

IX.   GENERAL

Credit and Non-credit courses are offered off-campus. Students participate in discussions regarding the academic program through committee membership.   Graduate programs are offered for part-time students (majority of evening students are graduate students).   The Director is responsible to the Academic Vice-President.

X.   STUDENT RECRUITMENT

Publicity used for recruitment is through newspapers and mailings.   Special efforts are made through industry, organizations, chambers of commerce, etc.

Aurora College
Aurora, Illinois
Evening Program

Total Enrollment 800   Church-related Institution
Evening Enrollment 350   Semester System

I. ADMISSION POLICIES

There is no deadline for admissions. A student may
register for credit courses before transcripts are submitted
and may take up to twenty hours of credit work as a non-
matriculate or "special" student. Regular students must
submit an application, high school transcripts, college transcripts if transfer student, take a standardized English test
and furnish references from employer. There are no special
requirements for non-matriculating or special students. Students who are rejected as regular students are advised to
apply as evening students and are automatically accepted for a
limited number of hours. (These students may register for
one course to prove their capabilities.) Mail registration
forms are printed in the evening brochures. The office staff
completes the registration forms and 50% of the tuition is required at the time of registration. Probation and suspension
policies for evening students are the same as for day stu-
dents--evening students carrying nine or more hours. The
ACT or CEEB are not required. English test is required at
time of matriculation and is used as a guide to placement
and advisement. All degree programs are identical to day
programs except one--a major in Industrial Management which
is not open to day students and represents a B. A. in Industrial Management. Distribution requirements for undergraduate degree: Humanities - 9, Social and Behavioral Sciences
- 9, Bible and Religion - 6, Physical Education - 4, Language or Alternative - 15, Natural Sciences and Math - 9.
The Director of the Evening Program and the Dean of the
College formulate the admission requirements. There are
no limitations to the number of day/evening combination students. No orientation program is held for evening students.

II. TERMINOLOGY

Title of Division: Evening Program. Defined: The
Evening Program is not a separate college, it is a part of
the total program and of immediate concern to the Dean; it
supplements and strengthens the day curriculum.

III. FEES

Evening students do not pay an application fee, college commons fee, health service fee, new student fee, or change of registration fee. Tuition charges are the same as for day students with these exceptions. A percentage of tuition is refunded based upon the number of sessions class has met before the student drops the course.

IV. FACULTY AND FACULTY RECRUITMENT

Approximately 31% of the faculty is full-time but there is no policy regarding percentage of full-time faculty teaching evening classes. The Dean of the College has the final authority for hiring faculty members. No full-time faculty is exclusively employed to teach evening classes. No regular faculty meetings are held for evening faculty. Salary range is $8 to $20 per class hour with no provision for overloads. (Overloads are discouraged as much as possible.)

V. SCHEDULING

The Dean of the College is responsible for the scheduling of evening classes. The Evening Director makes recommendations to the faculty who in turn recommends to the Dean of the College. The Director does not have the authority to revise the schedule. Three-hour classes scheduled two nights per week. Day and evening classes are comparable in quality. Part-time evening students are eligible for the Dean's List--anyone with a GPA of 3. 5 is eligible if he carries at least nine hours a semester. Seven to ten students constitute a class. An instructor's compensation is not reduced if he teaches a class below minimum size.

VI. ORGANIZATIONAL STRUCTURE

Three staff members - Director and two others - comprise the administrative staff. The teaching staff consists of sixteen full-time and thirty-five part-time faculty members. Since the Evening Program does not operate as a separate college, other offices absorb the additional work when the enrollment increases.

VII. EDUCATIONAL TELEVISION PROGRAMS

No educational television program is offered.

VIII. NON-CREDIT PROGRAMS

No non-credit programs are offered by the Evening Program.

IX. GENERAL

The Evening Program does receive adequate support. The Director is responsible to the Dean of the College. Audio-visual aids are available to the Evening College.

X. STUDENT RECRUITMENT

Display advertising in area papers, spot ads on area radio stations are used for student recruitment.

<u>Bakersfield College</u>
Bakersfield, Ohio
Continuing Education

Total Enrollment 6, 000   Community College-Public
Evening Enrollment 4, 770   Semester System

I. ADMISSION POLICIES

The deadline for admission for regular and non-credit students is two weeks after the opening day of the semester and after the first week of the summer session. Registration can be carried out before submission of transcripts; admission requirements for non-matriculating students: 18 years of age and have the ability to profit by instruction; for regular students: a physical examination, application and high school transcripts. There is no limit as to the amount of work for credit a non-matriculating student may take. Students are not advised to register for the evening division if they are rejected as regular students, but many enter this way and are automatically accepted. Mail registration has been tried but was not successful. Policies regarding probation and suspension for degree students are similar to regular students since an evening student may transfer to regular status; this is the same for non-degree students except for a tendency to be lenient since the course may be more practical. The SCAT and IGED are used for placement and advisement. An undergraduate degree, A. A. , is offered;

enrollment for full-time undergraduates is 5,100 and part-
time 4,700. The distribution requirements for the A.A. degree consist of a total of 62 semester units as follows: English, six units, Social Studies, 6 1/2-11 units, Health and
Physical Education, four-five units, Mathematics three units,
specific field of study, twenty units. There is no special degree program for adults. The Dean of Pupil Personnel formulates the admission policies for all categories of evening
students. Day students are admitted to the evening classes
if they have irreconcilable conflicts in the day program or if
their numbers are needed to keep the evening class operating.
The advantage of combined classes is that the younger students are exposed to a greater knowledge and experience of
the more mature students. An orientation program is in
effect each semester, and is recommended for new students.
There is no Evening Division Advisory Committee.

II.   TERMINOLOGY

Title of Division: Continuing Education. Defined:
Those courses or classes which are not a part of the regular
day program. The term "Continuing Education" is used to
describe any post-high school class. They may be taken for
credit and "we include some classes that do not offer credit
and some that may be taken where part of the students elect
credit and others do not. "

III.   FEES

No fees are charged in the Evening Division. There
are no refund policies for students who drop one or more
classes but remain in school.

IV.   FACULTY AND FACULTY RECRUITMENT

Any regular faculty member who is interested may be
employed. Approximately 65% of the faculty are full-time.
The Dean of Continuing Education has the final authority for
hiring full and/or part-time faculty for the evening classes.
In questionable cases, after conference with the President,
the department chairman is consulted. The Dean may reject a faculty member who has been assigned to teach evening classes. Full-time faculty members are not employed
to teach exclusively in the evening and the Dean may engage
an instructor if the department head refuses to do so. Regular faculty meetings are held at the beginning of the semester. With one or two exceptions, this Division holds to one

class or at the most four units with the exception noted a-
bove, in regard to faculty members' teaching classes as an
overload.   None of the budget is spent for recruitment.   Salary range for part-time faculty is $8. 83 per class hour.
Salary range for overloads is approximately 1/1000 of base
salary; however, none is paid less than $8. 83.

V.   SCHEDULING

The Dean is responsible for the evening class schedule.   This is accomplished by consulting with the faculty as
to what classes they wish to teach.   The department heads
are contacted for suggestions and possible new courses.   The
Dean may revise the schedule.   Three-hour classes are
scheduled two nights a week.   There is no research in progress.   A survey was made of faculty who taught day and evening classes--the result of their opinions as to difference in
quality was: nineteen instructors said evening classes were
superior, sixteen said classes in general were superior, and
twenty said the achievement was about the same.   Part-time
evening students are not eligible for the Dean's List.   At
least twenty-five have to enroll to constitute a class; though
if it is second or third semester course fewer may be required.   Compensation does not change for classes below the
minimum size.

VI.   ORGANIZATIONAL STRUCTURE

The administrative staff consists of two staff mem-
bers--one full-time and one part-time.   Teaching staff consists of 210 part-time faculty members.   The Dean has administrative and supervisory duties; the Associate Dean has
the similar duties assigned by the Dean.   For credit programs an administrative staff of one is required for an enrollment of 300; one [sic] for 1000 and two [sic] for 5000.

VII.   EDUCATIONAL TELEVISION PROGRAMS

None offered by Continuing Education.   This has been
done in the past and residence credit was given, which counted
toward a degree.   Such courses as history and economics
were tried in connection with national networks--discussion
sessions were held on campus.

VIII.   NON-CREDIT PROGRAMS

Non-credit courses are offered in the areas of Business

and Management and Parent Education. There is not a separate budget for the non-credit programs nor is it expected to pay for itself. Salary range is the same as reported above. Occasionally Continuing Education sponsors conferences such as Medical lecture series and Paleontological Biostratigraphy Seminars. Clinicians are paid $50 per night's lecture and this will be increased to $75 next year. Continuing Education is responsible for the Summer session.

IX. GENERAL

An off-campus course, Parent Education in the Black Ghetto, is offered. There is no formal structure for student participation regarding the academic program, but suggestions are welcomed. For the past 15 years about 325 new courses have been tried out in the evening. Many of these have moved into the regular program; some expanded into the full curricula.

X. STUDENT RECRUITMENT

Recruitment is done through newspaper, radio and TV publicity. Announcements to classes are made at the end of each semester. Brochures are mailed out and left in libraries. Special mailings are sent to industries.

Baldwin-Wallace College
Berea, Ohio
Division of Educational Services

Total Enrollment 3, 450   Church-related Institution
Evening Enrollment 1, 000   Quarter System
    (550 average per quarter)

I. ADMISSION POLICIES

The deadline for application for admission is usually two weeks preceding the quarter except for the summer. A student may register for credit courses prior to submitting transcripts with special permission only. Non-matriculating students may take an unlimited amount of credit courses. Admission requirements for "special" students include an undergraduate degree. High school graduation and good standing are required for admission to regular degree pro-

grams. Students who are rejected as regular students are
advised to apply as evening students. Mail registration is
used--all forms are mailed to students six to eight weeks
prior to the start of the quarter with a return deadline of
about four weeks before quarter begins and no pre-payment
required. A 2. 0 average is required on a 4. 0 system.
Those falling below 2. 0 are probationary and given special
conditions. No ACT or CEEB examinations are required.
The Adult College Aptitude test is required for all degree
students and is used for placement and advisement. A B. A.
and a B. S. are offered with an enrollment of ten full-time and
510 part-time students. The total number of hours required
to complete degree requirements is 186 quarter hours. The
College Admission Committee and the Director of the Evening
Session formulate the admission policies. The advantages of
a day/evening combination class are communications and
comparison of theoretical and practical knowledge while the
disadvantages are class grading curve sometimes is unfair to
evening students, and, some intimidation exists where classes
are out of balance. An orientation for evening students is
held one week before each quarter begins.

II.   TERMINOLOGY

Title of Division: Division of Educational Services.
Defined: Division includes Evening Session, Fall, Winter,
Spring and Summer sessions. Continuing Education defined:
At the higher education level is primarily a credit program
leading to or adding to a specific degree. Some short-term
objectives such as single courses, courses in series, non-
credit work, workshops, etc. should be included in a broad
definition.

III.   FEES

Evening classes are 80% of the day rate. A percentage
rebate is paid graduated according to time in class.

IV.   FACULTY AND FACULTY RECRUITMENT

A high percentage of full-time faculty is desired.
Sixty percent of the evening class faculty are full-time. Academic Dean has final authority in hiring full/part-time faculty
for the evening classes but in practice the hiring is handled
by the department head and Evening Session Director. A
part-time faculty member can be rejected by the Director but
full-time faculty rejection could not be made by the Director.

No full-time faculty teach exclusively in the evening. Faculty overloads consist of not more than one course per quarter. Ten percent of the budget is spent on faculty recruitment. Salary range for part-time faculty is $155 to $229 per contact hour; overload compensation is the same.

V. SCHEDULING

The Director is responsible for the evening class schedule with the assistance of the department heads. The Director does have the authority to revise the schedule within planned limitations (budget). Three-hour classes are scheduled one night per week. Day/evening classes are equal in terms of quality. Part-time evening students are eligible for the Dean's List with a 3.5 for each fifteen hours. Ten students are required to constitute a class. The instructor's compensation is not reduced if the class enrollment is less than ten.

VI. ORGANIZATIONAL STRUCTURE

The administrative staff consists of one staff member and sixty-five full-time, forty part-time faculty members. The Director of the Evening Session, Summer Session, Special Programs and Special Assignments is assisted by a part-time administrative assistant who carries out functional duties relative to various programs supervised by the Director. Two counselors spend only 8% of their time with the Division.

VII. EDUCATIONAL TELEVISION PROGRAMS

The Division of Educational Services does not offer educational TV courses.

VIII. NON-CREDIT PROGRAMS

Non-credit programs are offered in Business and Management and Arts and Sciences. This program is expected to pay for itself. Remuneration for full/part-time faculty teaching non-credit courses is approximately $27.50 per contact hour. The Division does sponsor conferences and institutes such as: The Institute for School Food Service, etc., using its own faculty or special lecturers. The Division does sponsor the summer session.

IX. GENERAL

The students participate in academic programs through
an evening student association.   An "Experimental Learning
Center" is available to which students with special academic
problems can be referred.   No graduate program is offered
for part-time students.   Stress on financial support is not
as adequate as it should be--but seems to compare favorably
to other institutions.   The Director is responsible to the
Academic Dean.   Technical aids are available for evening
classes.

X. STUDENT RECRUITMENT

Newspaper, radio advertising is used for student recruitment.

<u>Baylor University</u>
Waco, Texas
Evening Division

Total Enrollment 1100-1400   Church-related Institution
                                    Semester System

I. ADMISSION POLICIES

The deadline for admission is the same as for day
students - September 9 and January 27.   Summer session
deadline is June 8.   Students are rarely permitted to take
work for credit as non-matriculating or "special" students
and may not register for credit courses before transcripts
are submitted.   Admission requirements are not specifically
specified for non-matriculating or "special" students; regular
students must have a high school diploma and a satisfactory
ACT score and be in the upper half of the graduating class.
Students who are rejected for admission to regular classes
are not advised to apply for evening classes.   No mail registration is used.   A student is placed on probation when he
becomes twelve grade points deficient.   A student is suspended if the grade point deficiency is increased during probation.   The ACT and/or CEEB examinations are required
for students under thirty years of age and used as a basis
for admission.   No evening degree program is offered which
differs from the day degree program.   A B. A. and a B. S.
are offered for undergraduate and a M. S. and a M. A. are

offered for graduate degrees. There are 1233 students enrolled (Fall Quarter). A total of 124 hours is required to
complete the undergraduate degree and thirty to thirty-six
hours required for the graduate degrees. Areas of concentration are American Studies, Business, English, Math for
the undergraduate; American Studies, Business, Education,
Math and Physics for the graduate degree. Some consideration is underway for a special adult degree program. The
Dean of Admissions and the Dean of the Evening School are
responsible for formulating the admission policies. Evening
classes are best because of the presence of mature and experienced adult students. There is no orientation program
for evening students. An Evening Division Advisory Committee gives course of study advice.

II. TERMINOLOGY

Title of Division: Evening Division. Defined: to include the university college plus continuing education. Continuing Education defined: Non-credit courses, conferences,
and institutes plus credit programs leading to degrees for
adults.

III. FEES

There is no fee differential between day and evening
classes. Refund policies are handled the same as for day
students.

IV. FACULTY AND FACULTY RECRUITMENT

Approximately 95% of the faculty are full-time teaching evening classes. The President has the final authority
for hiring faculty members for evening classes. The Director can reject a faculty member who has been assigned
to teach evening classes. No full-time faculty are employed
to teach evening classes exclusively. The Director can engage an instructor with the recommendation of the Dean of
Instruction. No regular faculty meetings are held. Evening
classes are treated as part of a regular load and not as an
overload. Salary ranges for part-time faculty vary from department to department.

V. SCHEDULING

The Director is responsible for the evening class
schedule with requests and discussions through departments

and schools. Three-hour classes are scheduled two nights
per week with a few on one night--preferably two. The
day and evening classes are equal in terms of quality. Part-
time students are eligible for the Dean's List. Eight students constitute a class at the undergraduate level and five
on the graduate level.

VI. ORGANIZATIONAL STRUCTURE

The administrative staff includes four staff members:
the Dean who has the responsibility for administration and
procedures, the Assistant Dean as assigned by the Dean and
two other assistants. The teaching staff includes enough
faculty to teach 100 to 120 classes per semester with 95%
of the faculty being full-time.

VII. EDUCATIONAL TELEVISION PROGRAMS

There are no educational television programs offered.

VIII. NON-CREDIT PROGRAMS

Non-credit programs are offered in the areas of Business and Management, Arts and Sciences, and Education. No
budget is spent on non-credit courses--they are expected to
pay for themselves. Remuneration for faculty teaching non-
credit courses depends upon the class but is usually $20 for
each class session. Conferences and institutes offered during
the past year included a School on Alcohol and Narcotics
Studies, Central Texas Regional Science Fair, etc. The Division is responsible for the summer session.

IX. GENERAL

Students are encouraged to offer advice and suggestions regarding the academic program. Graduate programs
are offered to part-time students through the respective
schools. The Director is responsible to the Dean of Instruction and the President. Audio-visual aids are available.

X. STUDENT RECRUITMENT

Publicity is available through newspapers, radio, and
television as well as appeals which are made to industry and
organizations.

Boston College
Boston, Massachusetts
Evening College

Total Enrollment 10, 956   Private, Church-related
Evening Enrollment 1076   Institution
                                      Semester System

I. ADMISSION POLICIES

No deadline for application for admission, but entrance
examination is required. Students may register without transcripts as "special" students. There is no limit to amount
of hours taken as a non-matriculating or "special" student.
Admission requirements are high school graduation or equivalent. Tests required for degree students: SCAT Series II
and Kider-DD. E. There is no mail registration. Student is
required to maintain a "C-minus" average or be placed on
probation. At least a "C-minus" average required for graduation. No special degree program for adults and none is
considered. Admission policies are set by the Academic
Senate. There are mixed classes of day and evening students. There is an orientation program for evening students.

II. TERMINOLOGY

Title of Division: Evening College of Arts and Sciences and Business. Continuing Education has as its primary
objective to offer higher educational opportunities to working
men and women.

III. FEES

There is a tuition differential for day and evening students. Refunds are prorated by withdrawal date.

IV. FACULTY AND FACULTY RECRUITMENT

90% of the faculty teaching evening classes are full-
time faculty members. Authority to hire faculty lies with
Evening College Dean working through the Department Chairmen and College Deans. No full-time faculty members teach
exclusively in the evening. Most regular faculty teach in
evening as an overload. All faculty, whether teaching as an
overload or on a part-time basis, receive $52. 50 per eve-
ning of instruction. Programs are carefully planned. Pre-
registration takes place in May--"to give the Dean a feel";

if a course does not attract many at that time it is cancelled before the catalogue is published.

V.   SCHEDULING

The Dean of the Evening College is responsible for
the schedule.   Classes meeting one evening per week for two
and a half hours are preferable.   Day and evening classes
are of very high quality.   The public attending them are different so the participation and instruction differ.   Part-time
students are eligible for the Dean's List by completing three
courses with an 82% average or better in each semester in
which they complete the courses.

VI.   ORGANIZATIONAL STRUCTURE

Administrative Staff consists of Dean, Counselor and
four full-time secretaries with 80 part-time faculty members
each semester.   The Counselor's title is Coordinator of Student Services and works with student organizations, plans
career nights, orientation, etc.   The size of administrative
staff for administering evening credit programs is dependent
upon the ability of the staff.

VII.   EDUCATIONAL TELEVISION PROGRAMS

The Evening College does not offer any Educational
Television courses.

VIII.   NON-CREDIT PROGRAMS

Interested persons can audit a credit class but no non-
credit programs are offered per se.

IX.   GENERAL

The Evening College is receiving most encouraging
support.   The Dean is responsible to the Academic Vice-
President.

X.   STUDENT RECRUITMENT

Newspaper publicity is used.

Boston University
Boston, Massachusetts
Metropolitan College

Total Enrollment 28,000   Private Institution
Evening Enrollment 3,575   Semester System

I. ADMISSION POLICIES

There is a deadline for application for admission to
evening classes. Students may register for credit courses
without transcripts. Non-matriculated students may take two
courses (eight hours). Admission requirements for special
students include high school diploma; regular students, high
school grades, SAT, and performance. Mail registration is
used. Students must maintain a 2.0 for graduation. The
Bachelor of Liberal Studies, Bachelor of Urban Affairs and
Masters of Liberal Studies are offered as special degrees for
adults; 52 students are enrolled in the Masters program. A
"B" average or better in latter half of undergraduate program
is required to enter. Admission policies are set by the Faculty Board of the College. Day and evening students may enroll in the same classes. Evening students meet faculty and
staff at the general open house during registration. Distribution requirements for undergraduate degrees are: fourteen
courses; two English, four Humanities, four Social Sciences,
and four Sciences. Graduate degrees, MLS, three-year long
seminar in Humanities, Social Sciences and Sciences. Total
number of hours for completion of undergraduate work is 128
hours (32 courses) and graduate degree is 40 hours (10
courses). Admission requirements are the same for the
special degree programs as for the regular program. At
present, the percentage of day and evening students enrolled
is: 25% day and 75% evening. A student handbook has been
prepared for the purpose of orientation. ACT scores are required with some exceptions.

II. TERMINOLOGY

Title of Division: Metropolitan College. Defined:
Evening College which offers part-time evening education and
degree credit.

III. FEES

Day tuition is $58 per credit hour; evening tuition is
$40 per credit hour due to fewer services and facilities used

by evening students.   Refunds are made on a graduating scale.

IV.   FACULTY AND FACULTY RECRUITMENT

Approximately 55% of the faculty teaching evening classes are full-time.   Final authority to hire faculty lies with the Dean of the Metropolitan College.   The Dean can reject a faculty member assigned to teach evening classes and may engage an instructor without the consent of the department head but only if the department head refuses to staff evening classes.   Overloads of one course are permitted each faculty member per semester.   Salary range for part-time faculty is $160-$240 per credit hour.   Overloads paid as 10% of base pay for each course.

V.   SCHEDULING

The Registrar, Dean and Department Chairmen are responsible for the evening class schedule.   The Dean has the authority to revise the evening class schedule.   Three-hour classes are scheduled on both one and two nights per week.   Evening students are eligible for the Dean's List if they have a 3.3 in at least two courses per semester.   Approximately ten students constitute a class.

VI.   ORGANIZATIONAL STRUCTURE

The administrative staff consists of fourteen: the Dean with the overall administrative responsibility of the College, two Assistant Deans - Administrative and Student Affairs and Academic Affairs - and eleven additional staff members.   The teaching staff consists of 232 full-time and 189 part-time faculty members.

VII.   EDUCATIONAL TELEVISION PROGRAMS

Metropolitan College does not offer any educational television programs.

VIII.   NON-CREDIT PROGRAMS

Non-credit programs are offered in English for International Students.   Remuneration varies but does depend upon the qualifications of the instructor.   Metropolitan College is not responsible for the summer session.

IX. GENERAL

There are special and new credit degrees in Urban
Affairs (undergraduate and graduate) and Master of Liberal
Studies. The Evening Division is receiving adequate support.
The Dean is responsible to the Vice-President of Academic
Affairs. Audio-visual instructional aids are available for
evening classes.

X. STUDENT RECRUITMENT

Newspaper and radio publicity are used for student recruitment. Special motivational appeals have been developed
for civic organizations.

<u>Bradley University</u>
Peoria, Illinois
Evening College

Total Enrollment 5, 000   Private Institution
Evening Enrollment-Approx. 1, 000   Semester System

I. ADMISSION POLICIES

The deadline for application for admission is approximately one week before registration. Students may register
on a probationary basis before transcripts are submitted.
Non-matriculating or "special" students may take up to thirty
hours of work for credit. Admission requirements are high
school graduation and SAT scores. Students who are rejected as regular students are not advised to apply for evening classes. No mail registration is used. Probation and
suspension policies are the same as the day school. No ACT
or CEEB scores are required for admission. No special degree program for adults is offered in the evening. The Office of Admissions formulates the admission policies. Students may enroll in day and evening classes any time and all
times. No orientation program is held for evening students.

II. TERMINOLOGY

Title of Division: Evening College. Defined: this is
a misnomer. There are only part and full-time students--
no day/evening designations. Continuing Education defined:
parallel programs of credit and non-credit complimenting each

other and allowing adults to move from one to another program.

III. FEES

There is no fee differential for day and evening
classes. Refunds are made at the rate of 80% the first week,
60% the second week, 40% the third week and 20% the fourth
week.

IV. FACULTY AND FACULTY RECRUITMENT

There is no policy regarding percentage of full-time
faculty teaching evening classes--approximately 95% are full-
time. The Academic Vice-President has the final authority
for hiring faculty members. The Director cannot reject a
faculty member who has been assigned to teach evening
classes. No full-time faculty is employed to teach exclusively in the evenings. No regular faculty meetings are held for
evening faculty. Salaries are $200 per semester hour.
There are no overloads permitted. Part-time faculty are
paid $15 to $25 per clock hour for teaching non-credit
courses.

V. SCHEDULING

The Director is responsible for the evening class
schedule, in cooperation with the Deans of the various colleges. Three-hour classes are scheduled both one and two
nights per week with one night being preferred. Evening
classes are apparently superior to day classes. Part-time
students are eligible for the Dean's List. There is no set
rule as to numbers of students required to constitute a class.
The non-credit courses are based upon a "break-even" number.

VI. ORGANIZATIONAL STRUCTURE

Two staff members comprise the administrative staff
with a teaching staff of approximately 350 full-time teachers.
The Dean of the Evening College and an Assistant Dean, responsible for the evening college, summer school, conferences, continuing education and alumni education. The ideal
staff size is difficult to estimate as it all depends upon the
work done by regular university staff, etc.

VII.   EDUCATIONAL TELEVISION PROGRAMS

No educational television programs are offered but in the near future the University will have their own TV station.

VIII.   NON-CREDIT PROGRAMS

Non-credit programs are offered in Business and Management, Engineering, Arts and Sciences, Education and Interdisciplinary areas.   There is a budget for the non-credit programs but most pay for themselves.   Remuneration for faculty ranges from $15 to $25 per clock hour.   The College is just beginning to sponsor conferences, etc.   The College is responsible for the Summer session.

IX.   GENERAL

Students participate more and more each day in academic program discussions.   All part-time students, graduate and undergraduate, are administered to by the Evening College. The Dean of this Evening College reports to the Academic Vice-President.   The Evening College does not receive adequate support.   Audio-visual instructional aids are available for evening classes.

X.   STUDENT RECRUITMENT

Newspaper, radio and television publicity are used for student recruitment as well as direct mail to industry.

University of Bridgeport
Bridgeport, Connecticut
Evening Division

Total Enrollment 8, 500   Private Institution
Evening Enrollment 4, 300   Semester System

I.   ADMISSION POLICIES

Deadline for admission, two months prior to registration.   Students may register for credit without transcripts. Non-matriculating students may take up to 15-30 semester hours for credit.   Admission requirement is high school graduation.   Mail registration is used.   Students are warned when they drop below "C" or 2. 0 level.   Dismissal for all

students with 15 quality points deficiency.   No ACT or CEEB
tests required.   There is no special degree program.   Admission policies are set by the Academic Standard Committee
or regular faculty.   Mixed classes--day and evening students
are allowed to register for the same class if space is available because it allows more flexibility for evening students.

II. TERMINOLOGY

Title of Division: Evening Division.   Defined: a division of the University primarily concerned with a series of
credit and non-credit courses, conferences and institutes and
in addition, it actually encompasses all phases of part-time
study done by adults.

III.   FEES

Evening students pay tuition only.   They are only eligible for counseling services.   Refunds are based on full
tuition--after one week, 90%; two weeks, 80%; three weeks,
50%; longer, no refund.

IV.   FACULTY AND FACULTY RECRUITMENT

85% teaching evening classes are full-time.   Final
authority to hire evening faculty lies with Department Chairmen.   The evening faculty members are responsible to the
Department Chairmen.   Faculty meetings are held on Friday
and Saturday afternoons.   Salaries range from $170-$225 for
part-time and $150-$180 for overloads.

V.   SCHEDULING

The Director of the Evening Division is responsible
for the schedule.   Departments send suggestions concerning
problems with schedules directly to the registrar.   Three
credit-hour courses are held two nights a week.   There is
no difference in the quality of day and evening classes.   Part-
time students are eligible for the Dean's List.   We do have
a chapter of Alpha Sigma Lambda.   Classes are cancelled
when below the average minimum of 15 students.

VI.   ORGANIZATIONAL STRUCTURE

The Director "gets into everything"; the Assistant
Director counsels students, takes charge of mail registration, sits on Assistant Deans Council, assists in admission

procedures; Director of Non-Credit Programs and Evening
Student Affairs (new position) works in non-credit area and
formation of the evening student government.

VII. EDUCATIONAL TELEVISION PROGRAMS

No educational television programs are offered.

VIII. NON-CREDIT PROGRAMS

Non-credit courses are offered in Mathematics.   No
budget is set-up for non-credit courses--the program pays
for itself.   Remuneration for faculty depends upon qualification: has been tried on an overload basis but was not satisfactory.   No conferences or institutes are sponsored by the
Evening Division.   The Evening Division is not responsible
for the summer session even though most of the work is delegated to the Division.

IX. GENERAL

The Evening Division is receiving adequate support.
As Director of the Evening Division, he is responsible to the
new Vice-President for Academic Affairs.   Audio-visual aids,
e. g. , T. V. , projectors, etc.

X. STUDENT RECRUITMENT

Newspaper and radio publicity are used.   Public re-
lations--special motivational appeals have been developed for
industry and organizations (Chamber of Commerce, Kiwanis,
Rotarians.)

Brooklyn College of the City University of New York
Brooklyn, New York
School of General Studies

Total Enrollment 30, 000   Public Institution
Evening Enrollment 10, 000   Semester System

I. ADMISSION POLICIES

Application for admission to evening classes must be
made approximately one month before registration.   Students
may not register for credit courses without transcripts.

There is no limit to the amount of courses taken as a non-
matriculating student. Admission requirements for adults are
satisfactory high school or college records and evidence of
adequate preparation for specific courses. Qualifying examinations are required of adults in the evening division. Admission policies are set by the Director of Admissions and
a committee on Admission Requirements. Day and evening
students may enroll in the same classes with approval. Orientation programs are held each semester for evening students. Students must maintain a C average--or be subject to
dismissal. Suspension is governed by the Board of Higher
Education by-laws. Special evening degree programs for
adults are as follows: Small College Degree Program with
an enrollment of 4,290 full-time students and a Special Baccalaureate Program for Adults with 196 enrollees. Total
number of hours required to complete this degree is 128
hours. Areas of concentration are Afro-American, Anthropology, Art, Biology, Chemistry, Classics, Economics, Education, English, Geology, Health Education, History, Home
Economics, Information Science, Integrated Science, Judaic
Studies, Mathematics, Modern Languages, Music, Philosophy,
Physics, Political Science, Psychology, Puerto Rican Studies,
Social Sciences, Sociology, Speech and Theater. A special
degree program is being considered for the near future.
Broad guidelines of admission are established by the Board
of Higher Education for the City University of New York.
Adaptive modifications of those requirements are made through
the Faculty Council through its Committee on Curriculum and
Admission.

II. TERMINOLOGY

Title of Division: School of General Studies. Defined: "It's primary objective is to offer higher educational
opportunities to working men and women. "

III. FEES

Proportional refunds are made to students within the
first three weeks of the term.

IV. FACULTY AND FACULTY RECRUITMENT

There are approximately 60 full-time and 500 part-
time faculty members. Final authority for hiring faculty lies
with the teaching departments and the Dean of the School of
General Studies with approval by the Board of Higher Educa-

tion. The Dean can reject a faculty member who has been
assigned to teach evening classes. Sixty full-time faculty
members teach exclusively in the evening and are responsible
to their respective departments. Regular faculty meetings
are held once or twice yearly. Faculty members are allowed
to teach an overload of eight semester hours per year.

V. SCHEDULING

The Dean of the School of General Studies is responsible for the schedule of evening classes. Departments submit
tentative schedules to the Dean and revisions are made as
necessary. Three credit hour classes are scheduled twice
weekly. Part-time students are eligible for the Dean's List
with a 3.3 grade point average after completing thirty credit
hours.

VI. ORGANIZATIONAL STRUCTURE

A total of seventy-three staff members comprise the
administrative staff which includes 23 administrative, supervisory and counseling staff, 15 administrative clerical (10
full-time), 19 administrative, supervisory, counseling clerical, 19 registrar supervisory (17 full-time) and 12 part-time
staff members. The School of General Studies is headed by
a Director who is also Associate Dean of the Faculty in college-wide administration. The Director is directly responsible to the President of the College for the overall administration of the School including the baccalaureate programs of
instruction, for providing higher educational opportunities for
non-matriculated students and for disadvantaged groups, for
recommending part-time and full-time faculty members and
other administrative officers for appointment to the staff, for
supervision of the budget, etc. The Associate Director is
the deputy of the Director and acts for him during his absence. Responsibilities include the direction of the Small
College Program. There are two Assistant Deans of the
School of General Studies--one is responsible for Academic
Adjustments including probation and dismissal cases, consultation with students, etc. , and the other Assistant Dean is
responsible for Program Development and Community Relations. The SGS Registrar prepares the schedule of classes
each semester and makes all room assignments in addition
to all the normal registrar duties. The Director of Non-
Credit Programs supervises, staffs and works in the registration, setting and maintaining records of students in non-credit
adult education programs.

VII.   EDUCATIONAL TELEVISION PROGRAMS

No educational television programs are offered.

VIII.   NON-CREDIT PROGRAMS

Non-credit programs are offered in the area of Business and Management, Arts and Sciences, Education, Languages and Recreation.   The Program is expected to pay for itself.   Faculty receives remuneration at the rate of $17 per hour.   No conferences and institutes are sponsored by the Division.   Summer session is not the responsibility of the Division.

IX.   GENERAL

Some credit and non-credit courses are offered off-campus for economically deprived populations.   Students participate in discussion regarding academic programs by serving on faculty-student committees.   In general, evening divisions are not receiving adequate support.   The Dean is responsible to the President.   Complete audio-visual instructional aids are available to evening classes.

X.   STUDENT RECRUITMENT

Newspaper and radio publicity are used.   Special motivational appeals are developed for industry and organizations.

Bryant College
Providence, Rhode Island
Evening Division

Total Enrollment 1, 950   Private Institution
Evening Enrollment 1, 430   Semester System

I.   ADMISSION POLICIES

The deadline for application for admission to evening classes is about two weeks prior to registration.   Students may register for credit courses before transcripts are submitted and may take a maximum of twelve credit hours as non-matriculating students.   Admission requirements for students are high school graduation or equivalency; in law enforcement classes, students must be in some phase of law enforcement work; insurance classes, in insurance work, etc. Mail registration is used. A special degree program is not offered but there are special certificate programs for adults in various fields. Admission policies are formulated by the Vice-President of Academic Affairs and the Dean and Director of the Evening Division. Day and evening students may register in the same class with the Dean's permission. There is no orientation for evening students. Policies regarding probation and suspension require that a student complete four three-hour courses with grades of C or better; must have two years of high school algebra or take pre-college algebra course to remove probation. (This does not apply to non-degree students.) Degrees offered adults are undergraduate programs in A. S. B. A. and D. S. B. A., a major in Transportation and Traffic Management requiring no language courses and six hours of science in the B. S. B. A. and three hours of science in the A. S. B. A. The graduate degree offered is MBA. The total number of hours required to complete the B. S. B. A. is 120-123; for graduate degree 18 hours foundation and 30 hours advanced. Areas of concentration are: 120 credit hours in Accounting, 123 in Marketing, 120 in Transportation, 123 in Economics, and 120 in general studies. The admission requirements for the degree programs the same as above. The Director and Dean, with the Academic Vice-President, formulates the admission policies for evening students; the Dean and Academic Vice-President for the graduate program.

II. TERMINOLOGY

Title of Division: Evening Division of Bryant College. Defined: Division responsible for adult education, degrees and special courses, evenings and Saturdays, on and off campus. Continuing Education defined: Services to help a person who needs more knowledge during his lifetime than he can obtain in normal high school and college. With a rapid advance in technology, continuing education is of greater importance than at any other previous period in history.

III. FEES

Day students pay $45 per semester hour; evening students pay $16. 67 per semester hour. Refunds are made on a graduating percentage basis: 80% first week, 60% second week; 40% third week, no refund thereafter.

IV.   FACULTY AND FACULTY RECRUITMENT

Approximately 50% of the faculty teaching evening classes are full-time. Final authority to hire evening part-time faculty lies with the Director and Dean of the Evening Division. No full-time faculty members teach exclusively in the evening. The Dean can hire part-time instructors. Regular faculty meetings are held the week before each semester begins. Full-time faculty members are limited to teaching not more than two nights per week (six semester hours). Salary range for part-time faculty is $725 for three-hour courses. Fifteen students constitute a class. The instructor's compensation is not reduced when teaching a class below minimum size. Classes with less than twelve are usually cancelled. Approximately seven and one-half percent of the budget is spent on recruiting.

V.   SCHEDULING

The Dean of the Evening Division is responsible for the evening class schedule and has the authority to revise. Three-hour classes are scheduled both one and two nights a week. Day and evening classes are equal in terms of quality. There is no Dean's List.

VI.   ORGANIZATIONAL STRUCTURE

The administrative staff consists of five staff members. The teaching staff consists of thirty-five full-time and thirty-eight part-time faculty members. The Dean works with the department chairmen on faculty and with the curriculum committee on courses and degree content; the Director has charge of the administration of the evening division and the continuing education division, counsels evening students, works with the Dean and department chairmen on faculty, supervises registration and admissions. The Evening Division counsellor counsels evening students and reviews and evaluates transcripts of new students. Administrative staff required for the ideal evening credit program would be four for an enrollment of 800; 5 for enrollment of 1000, etc. For non-credit programs, an enrollment of 300 would require one staff member; enrollment of 1000 would require six staff members.

VII.   EDUCATIONAL TELEVISION PROGRAMS

The educational television courses are not offered by

the Division.

VIII. NON-CREDIT PROGRAMS

Non-credit programs are offered in the area of business and management. There is a budget for this program, but it is expected to be self-sustaining. Remuneration to faculty varies--$500-$1000 per course for 10-15 class sessions depending upon qualifications of instructors and area of instruction. The Evening Division sponsors conferences such as Law Enforcement Seminar, Income Tax Seminars, Marketing Seminars, and fifteen-week CPCU courses. Pay for clinicians varies--$0 to $100 a day. The Division is responsible for the summer session.

IX. GENERAL

Some special courses for economically deprived populations are planned. Day students participate in discussions regarding the academic program more than evening students. Special off-campus and Saturday classes are offered for Law Enforcement Personnel. The Dean of the Evening Division is responsible to the Vice-President for Academic Affairs.

X. STUDENT RECRUITMENT

This effort is carried out by extensive newspaper publicity, very limited radio and no TV coverage. Limited brochures are mailed to industry and personal contacts are made at various organizations.

<u>University of California</u>
Berkeley, California
University Extension

Total Enrollment 27, 000   State Institution
Evening Enrollment 40, 000 per year   Quarter System
   (equivalent of approx. 3, 000 full-time students)

I. ADMISSION POLICIES

The deadline for admission for non-degree or special students is the second meeting of any given course. Since all students are non-matriculating, transcripts are not ordinarily required. Each course carries its own pre-requisite

for admission.   Mail registration is used.   All admission
policies are formulated by the Academic Senate.   Day/eve-
ning combination classes are very limited but it is felt that
there is obvious advantages such as the stimulation of the
older by the younger, fostering relevance by exposure of the
day student to the non-cloistered evening student and a general narrowing of the generation gap.   The Academic Senate
Committee oversees the long-term policies and assures ex-
cellence for the University Extension.

II. TERMINOLOGY

Title of Division: University Extension.   Defined:
The Continuing Education and public service arm of the University.   Continuing Education defined: Non-degree oriented
adult education beyond but sometimes including the undergraduate level.   The University of California Extension is
not an evening college as such.   No degrees are granted and
students do not matriculate in the University.   Most of the
students already have degrees and are interested only in continuing education.   Extension credit is offered and is rarely
applied toward a degree either at the University or at other
institutions.

III. FEES

Fees are not comparable.

IV.   FACULTY AND FACULTY RECRUITMENT

No full-time faculty teaching at the University Extension.   The University Extension Dean has final authority for
hiring faculty members and delegates this responsibility to
the department heads.   Overloads are limited to a percentage
of annual salary.   There is no budget allocation for faculty
recruitment.   Part-time faculty salaries range from $15 to
$18 per classroom hour.

V.   SCHEDULING

The University Extension Dean is responsible for
scheduling evening classes but schedules are compiled by the
department heads and programmers in the various extension
academic departments.   Extension courses vary from course
to course in terms of quality... superior in some disciplines
... inferior in others.   Normally fifteen to eighteen students
must register to constitute a class.

VI. ORGANIZATIONAL STRUCTURE

The administrative staff consists of 280 staff members. All of the teaching staff are part-time. The Dean has overall administrative responsibility, the Assistant Deans have responsibilities of general administration with emphasis on academic matters and fiscal matters. The Evening Registrar is responsible for student enrollment, collection of fees, and recording of grades.

VII. EDUCATIONAL TELEVISION PROGRAMS

Educational television programs are offered from time to time for extension credit. Such credit may be accepted by our own institution or another institution but not automatically. Extension department head in the appropriate academic area is responsible for the program. Registration is handled by the Registrar. TV viewers are invited to write or phone for an enrollment application and follow usual procedures for registering.

VIII. NON-CREDIT PROGRAMS

Non-credit programs are offered in Business and Management, Engineering, Arts and Sciences, Education and other areas. The program is expected to pay for itself. The Extension is responsible for the sponsoring of conferences and institutes.

IX. GENERAL

No degree-oriented programs are offered to part-time students in the evening but many are designed for graduates. Dean of University Extension is responsible to the Chancellor of the University.

X. STUDENT RECRUITMENT

Newspaper advertisement is used for student recruiting. Direct mail is the most important recruiting medium.

Centenary College of Louisiana
Shreveport, Louisiana
Evening Division

Total Enrollment 956   Private, Church-related
Evening Enrollment 197   Institution
                                        Semester System

I. ADMISSION POLICIES

The deadline for application for admission to evening
classes is the date of registration; for 1970-71, September 11,
February 5, June 14. Students may enroll for credit without transcripts provided they sign an "eligibility statement"
and also authorize the college to send for their transcripts.
Non-matriculating or "special" students may take up to 24
hours before matriculating. However, this is discouraged
and all students are now matriculated. Admission requirements for regular degree students: must be graduate of a
recognized high school, submit a transcript or take and pass
the GED test, file an application, pay the fee, and have a
2. 0 grade point average in high school work. Admission requirements for non-matriculating or "special" students: must
meet the College's requirement of being a graduate of a recognized high school, present a high school transcript or GED
scores, must file an application and pay the enrollment fee.
Probation and suspension policies: if a student's cumulative
average falls below the standards set for the college: First
year (1-30 credits) 1. 6; second year (31-60 credits), 1. 8;
third year (61-90 credits), 1. 9; or if at the end of any year
his average is less than 2. 0 in his major, he is placed on
probation. Mail registration not generally used. However,
when exceptions are made, all requisites including transcripts,
etc. , must be met before registration is accepted. Forms
are returned with fee and registration is completed. No ACT
or CEEB examinations are required for admission to the evening division. No special degree program is offered for
adults. The Committee of Academic Policies formulated the
admission policies for evening students. Day and evening
students are encouraged to enroll in the same classes. The
advantage is a broader perspective and more incentive for
both to work harder. No orientation program is held for
evening students.

II. TERMINOLOGY

Title of Division: Evening Division. Defined: An ex-

tension of the college day into the evening. Definition of
Continuing Education: Adult education, non-credit, enrichment program.

III. FEES

There is no differential between day and evening
classes. Refund policies: if a student withdraws within a
week after the first class, 50% of the fee is refunded.

IV. FACULTY AND FACULTY RECRUITMENT

There is no policy regarding the percentage of full-
time faculty members teaching evening classes. Approximately 50% of the evening faculty are full-time. The Director of Evening Division has the final authority for hiring full
and/or part-time faculty members for evening classes. The
Director may reject a faculty member who has been assigned
to teach evening classes. The Director may engage an instructor without the consent of the department head if this
person refuses to staff these classes. Faculty meetings are
held with evening faculty at the beginning of each semester.
Faculty members are encouraged to participate in institutes
and conferences but not to teach a course as an overload.

V. SCHEDULING

The Director of the Evening Division is responsible
for the evening class schedule. Procedure for compiling the
evening schedule: a record is kept of all requests for courses
and collated with the recommended course offering by the department heads; the regular student body is polled for suggested courses. The Director has the authority to revise or
make additions to the evening class schedule. Three-hour
courses are scheduled either one or two nights a week.
Business courses generally meet two evenings per week.
Day and evening classes are equal in quality. Part-time evening students are not eligible for the Dean's List. A minimum of ten students is required to constitute a class.

VI. ORGANIZATIONAL STRUCTURE

The Director of the Evening Division is the only administrative officer in the Division, with a teaching staff of
approximately 15 full-time and 15 part-time faculty members.
The Director of the Evening Division has the following responsibilities: recruits students, plans the curriculum offer-

ings for each semester, hires and fires faculty, counsels students, plans degree programs, plans and directs the non-
credit offerings, acts as Registrar for the Division--main-
taining the records, transcripts, files, etc. on each Evening
Division student. He also collects all fees and makes a report to the Comptroller of the College. An administrative
staff of three members is recommended for an evening student body of 300.

VII. EDUCATIONAL TELEVISION PROGRAMS

The Evening Division does not sponsor any courses on
Educational Television.

VIII. NON-CREDIT PROGRAMS

The Evening Division offers non-credit programs in
Business and Management, Mathematics and Engineering.
The program must pay for itself as no budget is allowed for
these courses. Faculty members receive $250 per course
for fifteen class sessions. The Division sponsors conferences and institutes such as the following programs offered
this past year: Debate Forensic, Basketball Coach Institute
and Life Insurance. The Director of the Evening Division is
responsible for the summer session of the College.

IX. GENERAL

Students may participate in discussions regarding the
academic program to a limited degree. Students are polled
periodically. The Evening Division is not receiving adequate
support at the present time. The Director is responsible to
the Academic Dean of the College. Audio-visual aids and
other technical instructional aids are available for evening
classes.

X. STUDENT RECRUITMENT

Newspaper publicity (three paid ads per year) is used
together with radio and television "public service" publicity.
Special motivational appeals are developed for industry and
various civic organizations together with the Chamber of
Commerce. Rotary International sponsors a cultural exchange scholarship at the College.

Central Connecticut State College
New Britain, Connecticut
Evening Division, Extension, Summer Session

Total Enrollment 12, 200   Public Institution
Evening Enrollment 5, 500   Semester System

I. ADMISSION POLICIES

There are no admission deadlines. A student may
register for credit courses before transcripts are submitted
and may take up to thirty semester hours of credit work as
non-matriculating or special student. Admission requirements for non-matriculating and/or special students is only
high school graduation or the equivalency; for regular students, a 2. 0 CPA for consideration. Students who are rejected as regular students are advised to apply as evening
students and are automatically accepted, but must matriculate before completing thirty semester hours. Mail registration is used. Materials are mailed with announcement bulletins. Approximately one-half of the registration is received by mail. Matriculated students are subject to probation and suspension policies the same as for day students;
non-matriculated or special students are not subject to probation and suspension policies except that restriction is placed
on exceeding ten hours unless CCPA exceeds 1. 8. No ACT
or CEEB examinations are required. No undergraduate degree program is offered especially for adults; a graduate degree in Educational Guidance is offered. Students enrolled
fall quarter totalled 6700 full-time day students and 5804
part-time students. Distribution requirements for the undergraduate degree is eight hours Science, nine to twelve hours
Language, with a total of 132 semester hours for completion;
graduate degree requires thirty semester hours for completion. Areas of concentration are numerous--all type combinations are available. The Vice-President for Academic Affairs formulates the admission policies for evening students
and the Graduate Dean formulates policies for the graduate
students. Day/evening combination classes have the advantage
of setting good examples for day students. Counseling services serve as orientation for evening students.

II. TERMINOLOGY

Title of Division: Evening Division, Extension, Summer Session. Defined: Evening Division encompasses all
classes scheduled after 4 p. m. ; Extension covers all off-cam-

pus courses; Summer Session is the entire college summer program. Continuing Education defined: Any formal organization for any type of education beyond the secondary level.

III. FEES

Day students pay a flat rate of tuition; evening students pay by the semester hour. The day division is supported by state funds and the evening division is self-supporting. No refunds are made after the start of classes except in cases of illness or induction to the armed forces.

IV. FACULTY AND FACULTY RECRUITMENT

No attempt is made to have full-time faculty teach upper division classes. About 37% of the faculty is full-time. The Vice-President for Academic Affairs is responsible for hiring faculty members but the Director can reject a faculty member who has been assigned to teach evening classes. Graduate faculty is hired to teach exclusively in the evening. No regular faculty meetings are held with evening faculty. Departments are encouraged to integrate full and part-time faculty through meetings and conferences. Salary range for part-time faculty is $250 to $300 per semester hour. Regular faculty are not permitted an overload.

V. SCHEDULING

The Director, assisted by the Master Scheduler and the Dean, is responsible for the evening class schedule. Departments submit schedules to the Master Scheduler based upon the cycle pattern, Evening Division reviews and recommends or requests changes as needed. The Director has the authority to revise. Three-hour classes are scheduled one and two nights per week. Undergraduate students tend to register for two classes back-to-back when classes are scheduled two nights. Various research projects are in progress in addition to those already completed. Day and evening classes apparently are equal in quality. Part-time students are eligible for the Dean's List at the time of graduation only. (Standards are under revision). Twelve to fourteen students constitute a class but may be less in special areas.

VI. ORGANIZATIONAL STRUCTURE

Three staff members comprise the administrative staff. The Director, Assistant Director, and one full-time counselor. The ideal staff would be a Director or Dean, three assistants and one full-time counsel with a supporting staff of 4 to 6 people for an enrollment of 5000.

VII. EDUCATIONAL TELEVISION PROGRAMS

Closed circuit TV is used for instruction earning residence credit but not educational television per se.

VIII. NON-CREDIT PROGRAMS

Non-credit courses are offered in the areas of Social Sciences and Arts and Sciences. The program is expected to pay for itself but is often operated at a deficit which is charged off to community service. Remuneration for faculty teaching non-credit courses is $500 per course for fifteen class sessions depending upon qualifications of instructor and area of instruction. No conferences or institutes are sponsored by the Division. The summer session is the responsibility of the Division and is the "straw that really does it."

IX. GENERAL

One credit course under OEO is offered in a "store front" location for the economically deprived. Student participation is through committees. All the graduate offerings, except for a few full-time day offerings, are under the Division. The Director is responsible to the Vice-President for Academic Affairs. Excellent support is provided by the College A/V Services Department.

X. STUDENT RECRUITMENT

Newspaper is always used to recruit students. Radio is used upon occasion.

University of Cincinnati
Cincinnati, Ohio
Evening College

Total Enrollment 25,000   Public Institution
Evening Enrollment 7,661 credit   Quarter System
          2,000 non-credit

I. ADMISSION POLICIES

Deadline for application for admission is approximately
two days prior to registration. Students may register provisionally without transcripts. Students may take courses
approved by advisors without being classified as degree candidates. Admission requirements include graduation from an
accredited high school or the equivalent. Mail registration
is used; 45% of the student body take advantage of mail registration in the Fall Quarter. A special degree for adults
is offered: Bachelor of Science with an enrollment of 3000+.
Admission policies are set by the State of Ohio. Day and
evening students may enroll in the same class. When a student's average falls below 2.0 he is automatically dropped
from the degree candidate list. Hours required to complete
degrees are 86 to 120 for Associate and 186-224 for Bach-
elors. The Dean of the Evening College formulates admission
policies for the evening students.

II. TERMINOLOGY

Title of Division: Evening College. Defined: A college that offers its own associate and bachelor degrees, controls its own faculty and has identical status as other colleges.

III. FEES

All part-time fees are identical. Refunds: 100%
credit memo through fifth week, 80% cash first and second
week; graduated to fifth week and no refund after the fifth
week.

IV. FACULTY AND FACULTY RECRUITMENT

Two-thirds of the faculty are full-time and one-third
are part-time off-campus members. Final authority to hire
faculty lies with the Evening College Dean. Regular faculty
meetings are held as needed but kept to a minimum of once
a year. Faculty members are permitted to teach two hours
as an overload and in some cases up to four depending upon
individual situations. Salary ranges for part-time faculty are
$135-$200 per quarter hour; overloads $200 to $270.

V. SCHEDULING

The Dean of the Evening College is responsible for
the evening class schedule. Some three-hour classes are

scheduled one night a week and some on two nights. Part-
time students are eligible for the Dean's List after completing six quarter hours with a minimum of 3. 5 average.

VI. ORGANIZATIONAL STRUCTURE

The administrative staff consists of ten staff members
and the teaching staff consists of 423 part-time faculty members (209 full-time on overload and 215 part-time off-campus). Being municipally-owned and state supported there is
academic and administrative autonomy. The Dean is responsible for the overall policy of the Evening College and is liaison with top university administration and other colleges; the
Assistant Dean is responsible for non-credit programs of the
Evening College; one Associate Dean is responsible for the
operational aspects of the College and the other for the student counseling services. There are six assistants to the
Dean: three are responsible for operational aspects of the
College and two for counseling functions and the other for
public relations.

VII. EDUCATIONAL TELEVISION PROGRAMS

The Evening College does not offer any educational
television programs.

VIII. NON-CREDIT PROGRAMS

Non-credit courses are offered in Business and Management, Arts and Sciences and other community interest
courses in various areas. These programs are budgeted and
not necessarily expected to pay for themselves. Remuneration for full/part-time faculty is $35. 00 per class hour.

IX. GENERAL

Some non-credit courses are planned in off-campus locations for economically deprived populations. In general,
all evening divisions are not receiving adequate support. The
Dean of the Evening College is responsible to the Provost for
Academic Affairs. Audio-visual aids are available for all
evening classes.

X. STUDENT RECRUITMENT

Newspaper, radio and television publicity is used.
Special motivational appeals are developed for industry and

civic organizations.

<u>City College of New York</u>
New York, New York
School of General Studies

Total Enrollment 15, 000 approx.   Public Institution
Evening Enrollment 4, 200   Semester System

I.   ADMISSION POLICIES

There is a deadline for application for admission to
evening classes but exceptions are made.   Students may not
register for credit courses without transcripts.   Non-matriculated students may take an unlimited amount of work but
they must take courses required for a degree.   Admission
requirements are high school graduation and SCAT scores.
Mail registration is not used.   There is no special degree
for adults.   Admission policies are formulated by the college
as a whole for regular students and by the School of General
Studies in consultation with the General Admissions Office.
Day and evening students may enroll in the same class.
There is an orientation program for evening students.   Students must maintain a "C" average and a reasonable attendance record in order to prevent probation status.

II.   TERMINOLOGY

Title of Division: School of General Studies.   Defined:
Evening Session for same baccalaureate degrees as those offered during the day.   Continuing Education defined: All education, both formal and informal, continues some previous
education.

III.   FEES

Matriculated students pay no tuition; non-matriculated
students pay $18 per class hour.   City government has felt
that only those who met rigid entrance requirements were to
be given free tuition.   Refunds are made on a graduating percentage basis unless the student is entering the armed forces.

IV.   FACULTY AND FACULTY RECRUITMENT

Approximately 50% of the faculty teaching evening

classes is full-time; the same percentage of students who are
matriculated. Final authority to hire faculty lies with the departments. The Dean can reject a faculty member who has
been assigned to teach evening classes. Some full-time faculty members teach exclusively in the evening. They are responsible to their department chairmen. Regular faculty
meetings are not held. A maximum of eight hours is permitted as overload for one term. No budget is spent on recruiting. The salary range for part-time faculty is $16 to
$26 per contact hour. The same salary range is paid for
overloads. The number of students required to register for
a class varies with the subject; courses have been given six
students. The instructor's compensation is not reduced when
he teaches the class with few students.

V.　SCHEDULING

The Dean of the School of General Studies is responsible for the evening class schedule. The Dean has the authority to revise the evening class schedule in consultation with
the department chairmen. Three hour classes are scheduled
two nights a week. Part-time evening students are eligible
for the Dean's List with at least thirty-two hours with a 3. 2.
Motivation seems to be a very important factor in determin-
ing success. High school averages and "aptitude" tests do
not predict success.

VI.　ORGANIZATIONAL STRUCTURE

The administrative staff in the Evening Division consists of thirty staff members and forty-five full-time and two-
hundred and eighty-eight part-time teachers. The Evening
Division is not a branch of the State University. The administrative staff consists of the Dean who is chief executive
in charge of the Division, and Associate Dean who is responsible for the summer session, an Assistant Dean who is
mainly responsible for refunds and resignations (student) and
making admission decisions, one Associate Registrar (evening), Business Manager (evening) and secretarial assistance.
The Chief Business Officer of the College serves all Divisions. The ideal staff structure would be fourteen for an
enrollment of 2000, thirty for an enrollment of 5000.

VII.　EDUCATIONAL TELEVISION PROGRAMS

The School of General Studies does not offer courses
in educational television. The Division is responsible for the

summer session.

VIII. NON-CREDIT PROGRAMS

The School of General Studies does not offer non-credit programs.

IX. GENERAL

Students participate in discussions regarding the academic programs by meeting regularly with the Committee on Curriculum. In general, all evening divisions are not receiving adequate support. The Dean of the School of General Studies is responsible to the President of the College.

X. STUDENT RECRUITMENT

The School of General Studies does not have a student recruitment program.

<u>Community College of Baltimore</u>
Baltimore, Maryland
Division of Continuing Education

Total Enrollment 3800   Public Institution
Evening Enrollment 2600   Semester System

I. ADMISSION POLICIES

Students may register without prior application during the week before classes begin and with a penalty during the first week of classes. No transcripts are required for registration. There is no limit to the amount of work taken as a non-matriculating student. Regular admission requirements are high school graduation or equivalent and special interest in a certain field. Students are dismissed from school if they fail two courses; if they complete 30 credit hours with a quality point average of less than 1.5 or 45 credit hours with an average of less than 1.7 they are dismissed. Admission policies are set by the Administration Council of the College. There is no mail registration. Day students may enroll in evening classes if they are unable to schedule those classes during the day. Evening students may register for day classes after day students' registration. Orientation for evening students is held each semester. No special evening degree programs are offered.   The A. A. degree (undergraduate) requires 60 hours for completion.

II.   TERMINOLOGY

Title of Division: Division of Continuing Education of the Community College of Baltimore.   Defined: A Division of the College offering credit programs with the same standards as regular day courses on a part-time basis.

III.   FEES

Refunds are based on individual courses and a graduated percentage system is used.

IV.   FACULTY AND FACULTY RECRUITMENT

Five percent of the faculty teaching evening classes are full-time faculty members.   Final authority to hire evening faculty lies with the Dean of the Division of Continuing Education.   Regular faculty meetings are held at the beginning of each semester.   Regular faculty members are not permitted to teach overloads except on an emergency basis; laboratory assistants in the sciences and technologies are often used.   Part-time faculty salaries range from $200-$250 per credit hour depending upon the training and experience of the instructor; $150 per lab hour.

V.   SCHEDULING

The Dean of the Division of Continuing Education is responsible for the evening class schedule.   Three credit hour classes are scheduled one night per week.   Part-time evening students are not eligible for the Dean's List, but a special "HONOR ROLL" is compiled for the evening division students based on number of credits earned and grades. Minimum sized class is normally 15, but classes have met with as few as five students.

VI.   ORGANIZATIONAL STRUCTURE

The Dean of the Division of Continuing Education is responsible for administering the Division of Continuing Education; the Assistant Dean is responsible to the Dean; Director of Summer Sessions is responsible to the Dean and Assistant Dean; Director of Off-campus Conferences and Institutes fall into a separate division--Division of Community

Services--which is responsible to the President.

VII.   EDUCATIONAL TELEVISION PROGRAMS

Credit courses are offered by educational television earning residence credit. The credit earned does count toward a degree. Day faculty is responsible for supervising the courses. Full-time faculty receive a reduced on-campus teaching load of three credits, per TV course. The Division of Continuing Education handles the registration the same as for other courses. Only undergraduate courses are offered by TV and tuition finances the program. Out-of-state tuition charges are the same as on-campus tuition. Courses are offered day and evening on a repeat basis.

VIII.   NON-CREDIT COURSES

Non-credit courses are handled through another Division of the College. Remuneration for full or part-time faculty teaching non-credit courses is $750 per course for 15 class sessions--depending on the qualification of the instructor. The Division of Continuing Education is responsible for the Summer session.

IX.   GENERAL

The Division is receiving adequate support. The Dean of the Division of Continuing Education is responsible to the President of the College.

X.   STUDENT RECRUITMENT

Newspaper, radio and television publicity is used for student recruiting. Special motivational appeals have been developed for industry using brochures and supplements.

<u>County College of Morris</u>
Dover, New Jersey
Continuing Education Division

Total Enrollment 4, 295   Public Community College
Evening Enrollment 2, 211   Semester System

I. ADMISSION POLICIES

The deadline for admission application for Fall Semester is September 1 and for Spring Semester is January 1.
Students may register for credit courses before transcripts
are submitted. Non-matriculating or "special" students may
take twelve hours of work for credit. Admission requirements for non-matriculating or "special" students is proof of
high school graduation. Students who are rejected as regular
students are advised to apply for evening classes. Mail registration is used and always has been for part-time students.
Students are mailed sufficient scheduling and registration
forms with information for processing - on a first-come,
first-served basis. Academic probation and dismissal regulations: Probation: 0-18 hours, below 1. 4 GPA; 19-36 hours,
1. 6 GPA, 37-48 hours, 1. 8 GPA, 49 hours and above, 2. 0
GPA; Dismissal: a maximum of two successive semesters of
academic probation will be granted before dismissal from the
College. No ACT or CEEB examinations are required for
admission. The enrollment includes 1084 full-time and 2211
part-time students. Typical distribution requirements for
Associate Degrees for career students: Data Processing
Technology - Humanities, 6 hours, Social Science, 6 hours,
Business, 6 hours, Mathematics and Science, 6 hours; Data
Processing Courses, 33 hours, Electives, 8 hours; total
hours 65; Law Enforcement - Humanities, 12 hours, Social
Science, 21 hours, Mathematics and Science, 10 hours, Law
Enforcement, 18 hours, Electives, 6 hours - total hours, 67;
Biological/Medical Laboratory Technology - Humanities, 9
hours, Social Science, 6 hours, Mathematics and Science, 6
hours, Biology/Chemistry courses, 44 hours, Electives, 5
hours - total 70 hours; Electronics Technology - Humanities,
9 hours, Social Science, 3 hours, Mathematics, 22 hours,
Electronics, 30 hours, Electives, 5 hours - total 69 hours.
The Director of Continuing Education formulates the admission
policies for evening students. There is a minimal cross
registration between part-time and full-time students. No
orientation program is held for evening students. There is
no Evening Student Advisory Committee. Non-high school
graduates may be allowed to register for credit courses with
the prior approval of the Director of Continuing Education.

II. TERMINOLOGY

Title of Division: Continuing Education Division.
Defined: At this institution the term is synonymous with
part-time students interested in college credit work. Defi-

nition of Continuing Education: Continuing Education means
to this College that we extend ourselves to meet the educational needs of area residents who vary in age and educational purpose.

III. FEES

There is no differential in fees between day and evening classes. Refund policies: 50% of tuition is remitted
to all students who drop courses during the first week of
classes.

IV. FACULTY AND FACULTY RECRUITMENT

There is no policy regarding the percentage of evening
faculty members that are full-time faculty. Approximately
28% of the evening faculty are full-time faculty members.
The Dean of Instruction has the final authority for hiring
full and/or part-time faculty members for evening classes.
The Director of Continuing Education counsels and advises
the Dean of Instruction regarding the assignment of faculty
members for evening classes. Full-time faculty members
are used exclusively for evening classes in one special program and are responsible to the Dean of Continuing Education.
The Director may engage an instructor without the consent
of the department heads if this person refuses to staff certain classes. Regular faculty meetings are held for evening
faculty members prior to the Fall semester. Regular faculty
members receive extra compensation for teaching evening
classes on an overload basis based on academic rank. No
budget funds are used for recruitment purposes. The salary
range for part-time faculty members is $180 to $270 per
credit hour. Compensation for overloads range from $190
to $270 per credit hour.

V. SCHEDULING

The Director of the Continuing Education Division is
responsible for the evening class schedule. Procedure used:
"we analyze prior semester course offerings and requirements for the various degrees, figuring in attrition of student
body and schedule accordingly. " The Director has the authority to revise and make additions to the evening schedule.
Three-hour classes are scheduled one night per week which
is preferred by students and instructors. A comparison of
day and evening classes shows that in general the motivation
and maturity of the adult student produces a quality factor in

part-time students not ordinarily found in full-time students.
Part-time students (evening) are not eligible for the Dean's
List. No minimum number of students is required to constitute a class. An instructor's compensation is not reduced
for teaching small classes.

VI. ORGANIZATIONAL STRUCTURE

The administrative staff includes ten staff members
with a teaching staff of 31 full-time and 76 part-time faculty
members. The administrative staff includes: an Associate
Dean who has the major administrative responsibility for the
Continuing Education Division, a Director who has the major
responsibility of the day-to-day operation of the Division and
a Counselor/Evaluator who has routine administrative responsibility plus academic counseling of students. The suggested size of an administrative staff for various enrollments:
300-500, 1 administrator; 800-1000, 2 administrators; 2000,
4 administrators; 5000, 6 administrators for credit classes.
For non-credit courses, conferences and institutes: 200-1000,
1 administrator; 2000-5000, 2 administrators.

VII. EDUCATIONAL TELEVISION PROGRAMS

The Division of Continuing Education does not sponsor
educational television courses.

VIII. NON-CREDIT PROGRAMS

The Division of Continuing Education sponsors a few
non-credit programs in Business and Management, Engineering and developmental courses in Mathematics, Reading and
English. The program is expected to pay for itself. The
faculty remuneration is the same as for credit classes. No
conferences or institutes are sponsored by the Division. The
Division of Continuing Education is responsible for the summer
session.

IX. GENERAL

Students are voting members of academic committees.
The Division is receiving adequate stress and financial support. The Director of Continuing Education is responsible to
the Dean of Instruction. Audio-visual aids such as films,
slides, recorders, etc. are available for evening classes.
Closed circuit TV will soon be available.

X. STUDENT RECRUITMENT

The newspaper and radio are used for publicity purposes as well as special motivational appeals for industry
and civic organizations.

C. W. Post College
Long Island, New York
Adult Education and Special

Total Enrollment 11, 400   Private Institution
Evening Enrollment 4, 500   Semester System

I. ADMISSION POLICIES

There is no deadline for application for admission to
evening classes prior to registration. Non-matriculated students may register for credit courses subject to receipt of
transcripts and may take a maximum of thirty semester
hours.   Admission requirements are high school graduation
or equivalent.   Mail and in-person registration are used.
Students are dismissed after completing six semester hours
below 2. 0.   Students are allowed two semesters on probation
before suspension and/or dismissal.   Admission policies are
formulated by Admissions.   Full and part-time students may
enroll in the same classes.   There is no group orientation
for evening students.   Each applicant has personal inter-
views with an advisor at the time of application and at each
registration.   Non-degree or special students may be allowed
to complete in extremely severe cases.   No special degree
program is considered.

II. TERMINOLOGY

Title of Division: Adult Education and Special Programs.   Defined: Comprises all adult undergraduate students enrolled at C. W. Post College.

III. FEES

Tuition for day and evening classes are the same because the courses are exactly the same.

IV.   FACULTY AND FACULTY RECRUITMENT

Approximately 50% of the faculty teaching evening
classes are full-time. Final authority to hire evening faculty
lies with the Dean of the College but hiring is done by the
respective department chairmen. Some faculty members
teach exclusively in the evening. Regular faculty meetings
are not held. Faculty members are discouraged from teaching courses on an overload basis but may teach non-credit
courses with no objections. Salaries range from $175 to
$375 per credit by rank, overloads are paid at the rate of
$225-$375.

V.   SCHEDULING

The various department chairmen are responsible for
preparing the evening class schedule. Three-hour classes
are conducted on two nights a week. Part-time evening students are eligible for the Dean's List after completing twelve
hours with a 3. 5 average.

VI.   ORGANIZATIONAL STRUCTURE

The Division of Adult Education and Special Programs
is staffed with two administrators and two counselors. The
Division of Continuing Education (non-credit and summer
sessions) is staffed with two administrators. The Director
of Adult Education and Special Programs is also the Director
of the Center for Adult Studies with the responsibility of student services plus catalogs in program development. The
Assistant Director of the Division of Adult Education and
Special Programs serves staff support functions.

VII.   EDUCATIONAL TELEVISION PROGRAMS

There are no educational television courses offered.

VIII.   NON-CREDIT PROGRAMS

Non-credit courses are offered but are run through the
office of Continuing Education and Summer Sessions. The
areas offered are Business and Management, Arts and Sciences, Education, Engineering and other areas. Guidelines
are set up to make the program self-sufficient even though
there is budget available. Remuneration for faculty is $25
per contact hour which is a standard rate for all instruction.
The Office of Continuing Education does sponsor conferences

and institutes.   Recently the office sponsored the first Annual
Chiropractic Conference.   The Office of Continuing Education
and Summer Session is a separate campus operation from
the Adult Education and Special Programs Division.

IX.   GENERAL

Students participate in discussion regarding the aca-
demic programs through the school newspaper, the Adult
Student Government, and the honor society, Alpha Sigma
Lambda.   Audio-visual aids are available for evening classes.
The Director is responsible to the Vice-President for Ad-
ministration.

X.   STUDENT RECRUITMENT

Newspaper and radio publicity are used.   Special motivational appeals are developed for industry in the form of
personal letters and by membership in the Association of
Training and Development.   Personal visits to various civic
groups are made.

DeKalb College
Clarkston, Georgia
Evening Programs

Total Enrollment 5, 357   Public Institution
Evening Enrollment 1, 770   Quarter System

I.   ADMISSION POLICIES

The deadline for application for admission for all
categories of students is twenty days before registration each
quarter.   Students may not be admitted without transcripts.
Non-matriculating or "special" students may take fifteen hours
of work for credit.   Admission requirements are the same
for all students, with a fee of $10. 00 (admission) and a late
penalty fee of $25.   Students who are rejected as regular
students are not admitted automatically as evening students.
Mail registration is employed to some extent, but is limited.
All students must maintain a 1. 50 GPA to avoid probation.
Examinations such as the ACT and CEEB are required for
adults in the evening division, as well as other tests which
are all used as a basis for placement and advisement.   The
Evening Programs does not offer a degree program that dif-

fers from the day program.   The College Admission Committee formulates the admission policies for all students. Students may enroll in both day and evening classes as may be desired.   There is no orientation program for evening students and there is no Evening Division Advisory Committee.

II.   TERMINOLOGY

Title of Division: Evening Programs.   Defined: The regular college program is adopted to four evenings per week; 2-2:05 periods each evening.   Definition of Continuing Education: Inclusion of both credit and non-credit programs.

III.   FEES

There is no fee differential for day and evening classes.   Refund policies are 80% the first week and a sliding scale of 60-40-20 for the following weeks.

IV.   FACULTY AND FACULTY RECRUITMENT

Approximately 50% of the faculty for evening classes are full-time.   The County Personnel Director for the Board of Education has the final authority for hiring full/part-time faculty members for evening classes.   The Director may reject a faculty member who has been assigned to teach evening classes.   No full-time faculty members are employed to teach exclusively in the evening but two are used on a part-time basis.   They are responsible to the Director.   No regular faculty meetings are held.   Faculty members who teach an overload, in any area, receive extra pay; the unit basis is $450-$720.   None of the budget is spent for recruitment. The salary range for part-time faculty is $450 with a Master's, $750 with a Doctorate and three years' experience. The same pay scale is used for overloads.

V.   SCHEDULING

The Director is responsible for the evening class schedule.   The schedule is compiled by projections from previous quarters and the requests from students.   The Director has the authority to revise as necessary.   Five-quarter hour classes are taught two nights a week.   Part-time evening students are eligible for the Dean's List if they take ten hours with a GPA of 4.0 or fifteen hours with a GPA of 3.5. Eight or ten students must register to constitute a class.

VI. ORGANIZATIONAL STRUCTURE

The administrative staff consists of one staff member--the Associate Dean, who is in charge of the entire evening academic and non-credit courses. The Director of Adult Education Center plans and coordinates the programs at the county level. The Dean of the College has the general direction of all academic affairs. The College is one of seven centers. The ideal staff needed for evening credit programs with an enrollment of 5000, would be eight.

VII. EDUCATIONAL TELEVISION PROGRAMS

Educational television programs are not offered in the Evening Programs.

VIII. NON-CREDIT PROGRAMS

Non-credit programs are offered in the areas of Business and Management, Arts and Sciences, through the University Adult Education Department. This program is expected to pay for itself. Full/part-time faculty members are paid $4.00 per hour for two-hour courses and seven to nine class sessions. The remuneration depends upon the area of instruction. The Evening Program has sponsored conferences but the venture has not been successful. The summer session is not the responsibility of the Evening Programs.

IX. GENERAL

There are no courses offered in off-campus locations for the economically deprived populations. Student discussion regarding academic programs is limited. The Evening Programs does not receive adequate support in comparison with the day program. The Dean of the Evening Programs is responsible to the Dean of the College.

X. STUDENT RECRUITMENT

Student recruitment is handled through publicity in newspapers, radio and television as well as appeals through industry and organizations.

University of Denver
Denver, Colorado
Continuing Education

Total Enrollment 8, 926   Private, Church-related
Evening Enrollment 2, 922   Quarter System
(non-credit 735)

I. ADMISSION POLICIES

Deadline for application for admission to evening
classes is about one month prior to registration. Students
are registered provisionally before transcripts are submitted.
Non-matriculated students may take a maximum of fifteen
quarter hours. Applicants under twenty-one years of age or
those who have recently attended another college are not eligible for admission. Other students may take such credit
courses as their previous study or experience qualifies them
to take. All degree candidates must maintain a "C" average
to remain in good standing. There is no special degree for
adults. Admission policies are set by the Director of Admissions. Day and evening students may enroll in the same
classes. There is no orientation program for evening students. The policy of the University is to encourage unclass-
ified students enrolled in credit courses to matriculate.
"Special"/non-degree students are not encouraged to enroll.
Below "C" (2. 0) represents probation and after one quarter
suspension for one year.

II. TERMINOLOGY

Title of Division: Office of Continuing Education.
Defined: Continuing Education as used at the University of
Denver implies non-credit courses and programs. It is defined as educational opportunities offered for anyone whose
chief occupation or role in life is no longer that of a full-
time student. The definition applies to both credit and non-
credit programs.

III. FEES

There is no fee differential between day and evening
classes. Refunds are based upon a diminishing percentage
formula which extends through the third week of classes.
No limit is set on the extent of withdrawal (one, two or three
courses, etc.).

IV.   FACULTY AND FACULTY RECRUITMENT

Seventy-five percent of faculty teaching evening classes are full-time faculty members.   The deans of the respective colleges hire all faculty members who teach credit courses at night.   No regular faculty members participate in non-credit activity without special permission.   No regular faculty meetings are held.   Overloads involving the teaching of both credit and non-credit courses are discouraged by the administration.   Salaries range from $100 to $1000 depending upon load and course taught.

V.   SCHEDULING

The deans of the respective colleges are responsible for the scheduling of evening credit classes.   The Office of Continuing Education prepares the schedule of non-credit courses and programs.   Three credit hour courses are scheduled both one and two nights a week, depending on the subject.   The Office of Continuing Education of the University of Denver plans to cooperate with other schools in the Denver area on a project sponsored by the Adult Education Council of Metropolitan Denver which obtains information on enrollment trends.   Day and evening classes are equal in terms of quality since the same faculty teach both.   Part-time evening students are not eligible for the Dean's List.   Sixteen students must register for a $25 course; 14 for $30 course and 12 for $35 course.   Special courses range from 15 to 30 students.

VI.   ORGANIZATIONAL STRUCTURE

Coordinator of Continuing Education directs and administers the entire non-credit program.

VII.   EDUCATIONAL TELEVISION PROGRAMS

Credit courses are offered by educational television - residence credit - directed by Mass Communications and earning a B. A. degree.   Full-time faculty members receive no additional remuneration for teaching TV courses.   The University Registrar handles the registration and the courses are financed through regular tuition charges.   Program is always conducted during the daytime hours and varies in time from quarter to quarter.

VIII. NON-CREDIT PROGRAMS

Non-credit courses are offered in Business and Management, Education, Arts and Sciences, Engineering and Law.
A budget is available for these courses; however, they are
expected to pay for themselves. The faculty receive remuneration of $100 (minimum) per course for ten two-hour class
sessions. The Division does not sponsor conferences and
workshops. The University of Denver has a separate office
of Conference Coordination which operates under the Vice
Chancellor for Public Affairs. The Division is not responsible for the Summer Session.

IX. GENERAL

The deans of each college have a student advisory
council which meets regularly and participates in discussion
regarding the academic program. Law students are participating as recorders and advisors for Model City Resident
Committees. In general, all evening divisions are not receiving adequate support. The Coordinator of the Office of
Continuing Education is responsible to the Vice-Chancellor
for Academic Affairs. Audio-visual aids are available for
evening classes.

X. STUDENT RECRUITMENT

Newspaper, radio and television publicity is used,
along with special appeals to industry.

<u>University of Detroit</u>
Detroit, Michigan
Evening College of Business and Administration

Total Enrollment 9, 000   Private Institution
Evening Enrollment 1, 174   Semester System

I. ADMISSION POLICIES

There is no deadline for admission applications. Students may register for credit courses before transcripts are
submitted if supported by student's copy of transcripts on a
provisional basis. Non-matriculating or special students may
take up to twelve credit hours of work and the only requirement is high school graduation. Regular students rejected

for regular admission are not advised to apply as evening
students.   Mail registration is not used.   Probation occurs
when GPA falls below "C" and failure to raise the "C" results in dismissal.   No ACT or CEEB scores are required.
Special degree programs for adults are BBA for undergraduates with seventy full-time and 1104 part-time students.
Distribution requirements are according to AACSB standards -
40% non-business, 40% business and 20% float between liberal
arts and business with a total of 120 hours required for completion.   Areas of concentration are management, marketing,
finance and accounting.   The Admissions Committee formulates the admission policies.   There are no barriers for day/
evening combinations.   The experience has been that adults
plus full-time students make a good combination.   There is
no orientation for evening students.

II.   TERMINOLOGY

Title of Division: Evening College of Business and
Administration.   Defined: One of the co-equal colleges of
the University with an independent budget, curriculum, etc.
with the Dean reporting to the Academic Vice-President.
Continuing Education is extinct at the institution.

III.   FEES

The fee for day students is $55 per credit hour and
the evening students pay $42 per credit hour.   Part-time
students are mobile and the fee is priced accordingly.   Refunds are made on a scale published in the bulletin.

IV.   FACULTY AND FACULTY RECRUITMENT

Final authority for hiring full and part-time faculty
for evening classes is the Dean's with consent of the Vice-
President.   The Dean can reject a faculty member who has
been assigned to teach evening classes, and has exercised
this right frequently.   Two full-time faculty members teach
exclusively in the evening and are responsible to the Dean.
Regular faculty meetings are held for evening faculty at the
start of each semester.   No overloads are permitted.   Full-
time faculty teach evenings as part of their nine-hour load.
Virtually no budget is spent on faculty recruiting.   Salaries
are $250 per credit hour per semester.

V. SCHEDULING

The Dean is responsible for the evening class schedule. Revisions are made by the Dean without limitation other than budget. Three-hour classes are scheduled one night per week for scheduling convenience. Evening classes are superior to classes offered in the day in some instances but otherwise comparable. Part-time students are eligible for the Dean's List with six of 3. 0. There is no policy regarding class size--classes have been taught with as few as three students.

VI. ORGANIZATIONAL STRUCTURE

Administrative staff consists of Academic Dean, two assistant deans working basically with the student body, Director of Admissions and two general staff members. The teaching staff consists of seven full-time and 63 part-time faculty members.

VII. EDUCATIONAL TELEVISION PROGRAMS

The Evening College does offer credit courses on educational television. Students earn residence credit and courses do apply toward a degree. The Director of the Division of Education supervises the courses. The Dean supervises the registration in cooperation with the Education Division. The undergraduate courses are financed by tuition collected. Classes are scheduled after the elementary teachers are out of school. The Evening College does not offer any non-credit courses.

VIII. NON-CREDIT COURSES

None offered.

IX. GENERAL

A full consultation procedure is conducted with students. The level and quality of support to the Evening College is satisfactory. The usual film strips, projectors, etc. are available for evening classes. The Evening College does have an active chapter of Alpha Sigma Lambda.

X. STUDENT RECRUITMENT

Newspapers are the major source of publicity for student recruitment. Approximately 5% of the budget is spent

on student recruiting.   Very poor results have been derived
from 40 "spot" announcements on radios "back" station.   No
TV publicity is used.   Special motivational appeals are made
to industry.

University of Detroit
Detroit, Michigan
McNichols Evening Division

Total Enrollment 9, 000   Church-related Institution
Evening Enrollment 900   Trimester System

I.   ADMISSION POLICIES

There is no deadline for application for admission to
evening classes.   Students may not register for credit classes
before transcripts are submitted.   Non-matriculating or
special students may take up to twelve hours of work for
credit.   Admission requirements: regular degree students -
high school graduation with a "C" average; non-matriculating
students - high school graduation.   Students who are rejected
for admission as regular students are not advised to apply
for evening classes.   Mail registration is not used.   Probation and dismissal policies: below 2. 0 average results in
probation; dismissal is at the discretion of the Director.
For non-degree or special students a 1. 75 average is required
after completing twelve hours.   No ACT or CEEB scores are
required for admission to evening classes.   No evening degree program for adults is offered.   The Council of Deans
formulates the admission policies for evening students.   Day
and evening students may enroll in the same class.   Advantages of day/evening combination classes are that students
learn more in discussion situations and exchange different
points of view.   An orientation program is held for evening
students during registration.   There is no evening advisory
committee.   Each student is interviewed by admissions personnel and also by evening division personnel.

II.   TERMINOLOGY

Title of Division: McNichols Evening Division (of the
Arts and Sciences College).   The Division is part of the College.   Definition of Continuing Education: Includes both credit
and non-credit courses for persons over twenty-one years of
age.

III. FEES

There is a fee differential between day and evening classes: $42 per credit for evening and $55 for full-time day students. This differential is justified because evening students have less access and use of various campus facilities.

IV. FACULTY AND FACULTY RECRUITMENT

There is no policy regarding the percentage of faculty members teaching evening classes that are full-time faculty members. The evening sections are part of the regular schedule. Approximately 99% of the evening faculty are full-time faculty members for evening classes. The Director may reject a faculty member assigned to teach evening classes. No full-time faculty members are employed to teach exclusively in the evening. Regular faculty members are paid overload rate for teaching credit or non-credit courses or participating in institutes, seminars and conferences. The salary range for part-time faculty is $250 per credit; $300 for overloads.

V. SCHEDULING

The Director is partially responsible for the evening class schedule together with the department chairmen. The department issues the tentative schedule and the Director adjusts with the cooperation of the department chairmen. The Director has the authority to revise as necessary. Three-hour classes meet one and two nights per week depending upon the class. In the opinion of the Director, one night is preferred. Day and evening classes are comparable. Part-time evening students are eligible for the Dean's List by taking nine hours with a 3.0 average. A minimum of ten students is required to constitute a class. The instructor's compensation is not reduced when teaching a class below minimum size.

VI. ORGANIZATIONAL STRUCTURE

The administrative staff consists of three staff members with a teaching staff of 100 full-time and four part-time faculty members. The Division is headed by the Director who has the administrative responsibility for the Division. He is assisted by an Assistant Director and one other administrator. The ideal size of an administrative staff for

various-sized student bodies is: 300-800 enrollment, 3 staff
members; 1000 enrollment, 5 staff members for both credit
and non-credit programs.

VII.   EDUCATIONAL TELEVISION PROGRAMS

The McNichols Evening Division offers credit programs using educational television.   Students may earn residence credit by taking these courses and the credits will
apply toward a degree.   The Director of the Division of Education supervises the educational television.   The Director
of the Evening Division and the Division of Education handle
the registration.   Regular registration procedure is used but
it is held off-campus.   Only undergraduate courses are offered using educational television.   No out-of-state tuition
is charged.   Educational television courses are held for
elementary teachers immediately after their classes are
finished.

VIII.   NON-CREDIT PROGRAMS

No non-credit courses are offered by the Evening Division.   The Division is responsible for the summer session
at the University.

IX.   GENERAL

No graduate programs are offered for part-time stu-
dents which are administered by the Evening Division.   The
Director is responsible to the Dean of the Arts and Sciences
College.   Audio-visual aids are available for evening classes.
There is an active chapter of Alpha Sigma Lambda.

X.   STUDENT RECRUITMENT

The Evening Division uses the local newspaper for
publicity purposes.

Drake University
Des Moines, Iowa
University College

Total Enrollment 5, 000   Private Institution
Evening Enrollment 2, 500   Semester System

I. ADMISSION POLICIES

A student may register for credit courses without
transcripts. A student may take a maximum of thirty semester hours in the non-matriculated status. Admission requirements for non-matriculating students are high school
graduation or equivalent and a probable chance of success;
regular students must meet the regular admission requirements for the University. Students must maintain a 2. 0 or
"C" average or better; one or two semesters of probation
are permitted. Admission policies are set by the University
Admissions Committee. Day and evening students may enroll in the same classes with approval of their advisors.
Youthful students are encouraged to apply for admission before starting their program, while more mature students usually matriculate after accumulating some credits. Probation and suspension policies for evening students are the same
as for day students; repeated low grade point averages (less
than 2. 0) for two successive semesters results in probation;
suspension follows if conditions of probation are not met. A
committee is currently studying the possibility of an evening
degree program for adults. The Council of Deans formulates
the Admission Policies for evening students: The Dean of
the College for regular degree students; the Dean of University College for special or non-degree students.

II. TERMINOLOGY

Title of Division: University College-Center for Continuing Education. Defined: University College is one of
nine colleges which offers evening, Saturday, and extension
classes. The Center for Continuing Education develops programs with business, industry, community services, and
other groups of a non-credit nature. Continuing Education is
a series of learning situations aimed at solving problems
recognized by the learner as needing solutions. This includes both formal and informal experiences moving a person
from where he is in the direction of some desired goal.

III. FEES

Evening classes are $16 per semester hour less than day classes. Refunds are based on a diminishing scale of 90% for the first week to 0% after five weeks.

IV. FACULTY AND FACULTY RECRUITMENT

Faculty recruiting falls under the Development Budget. Sixty percent of the faculty teaching evening classes are full-time. Final authority to hire evening faculty lies with other Deans and Dean of University College. The Dean of University College has the authority to reject a faculty member assigned to teach evening classes. Full-time faculty members teaching only in the evening are responsible to their college deans respectively. Overloads are permitted for all faculty members if it does not interfere with the full and effective performance of the individual's responsibility to the University. Salaries range from $600 to $750 per three semester course. Policies preclude overload for "courses". Only for continuing education programs are extra compensations permitted.

V. SCHEDULING

The Dean of University College is responsible for the evening class schedule, and has the authority to revise it. Three credit hour courses are scheduled one and two nights a week. Day and evening classes are equal in terms of quality. Part-time evening students are not eligible for the Dean's List.

VI. ORGANIZATIONAL STRUCTURE

The administrative staff consists of seventeen including seven secretaries: the Dean has overall responsibility; two Assistant Deans who have general supervisory responsibility for a segment of the total operation plus input into democratic decision making process; two Directors with responsibility of coordinating and programming; two coordinators handling Urban Affairs and Employment Security Training with appropriate contacts with clientele and program planning and execution; three Directors for admissions, counseling and placement of evening students. The teaching staff consists of 80 full-time and 75 part-time faculty members. The full-time faculty is furnished by other colleges.

VII. EDUCATIONAL TELEVISION PROGRAMS

The Sunrise Semester is the educational television program which is one fourteen-week course offered for extension credit 6:30 to 7:30 a. m. three days per week. Supervision of the educational television course lies with the commercial and/or ETV station personnel; non-credit courses offered by television is supervised and moderated by a faculty member. Faculty members teaching courses on TV are given token remuneration and carry a reduced teaching load for regular on-campus classes. All credit teaching by full-time faculty is a part of a load depending upon credit hours of course. Registration for the educational television program is handled by the University College the same as other courses. Tuition income out of budgeted salary funds finance the TV courses. Actually this is a continental classroom sunrise semester offering. The non-credit offering was developed by the University College and was entitled "Search for Creativity. "

VIII. NON-CREDIT PROGRAMS

Non-credit programs are offered in the areas of Business and Management, Arts and Sciences, Education, and Journalism as well as Fine Arts. There is a budget for non-credit courses, only, the programs are expected to pay for themselves. Faculty does not receive remuneration for a non-credit course as they are a part of the regular load for full-time faculty. Part-time faculty receive $600 per course for fifteen class sessions and this salary is dependent upon the area of instruction. This division sponsors conferences such as: Children's Emotional Health, Employee Mutual Insurance Institute, New Counselor Orientation Program, Jury Seminar, etc. The clinicians receive $100 per day normally, but salaries vary with program, discipline and the group being served. These conferences are sponsored by this division using qualified faculty members of the institution. Summer sessions are not a responsibility of this division.

IX. GENERAL

Some courses for economically deprived populations are planned. Students are included on all university committees and the Senate. The evening division is receiving adequate support. The Dean of University College is responsible to the Provost. Audio-visual instructional aids are available for evening classes.

X. STUDENT RECRUITMENT

Newspaper, radio and television publicity are used.
Special motivational appeals have been developed for industry
in the form of posters, schedules and brochures.

Drexel University
Philadelphia, Pennsylvania
Evening College

Total Enrollment 11, 025   Private Institution
Evening Enrollment 2, 879 undergraduate   Quarter System
              1, 500 graduate

I. ADMISSION POLICIES

Deadline for application for admission is approximately
two weeks prior to registration.   Students may not register
for credit courses without transcripts.   Admission requirement for non-matriculating students is bachelor's degree;
regular students must be high school graduates and show
satisfactory performance on qualification test.   A 2. 0 quality
point average is required for graduation; non-degree students
must complete each course satisfactorily.   Admission policies
are set by the Admissions Committee of the Evening College.
Day and evening students may register in the same classes
with permission by their respective deans.   Orientation for
evening students is on registration day.   The Evening College
program offers courses leading to the BS degree but no
special evening degree program for adults is offered per
se--each of the six undergraduate colleges offer its own
degree program.   Probation and suspension policies are:
27-50 hours with a minimum of 1. 6 average, 90-110 hours
with a 1. 88 average, over 150 hours with a 2. 0 average;
failure to achieve the minimum cumulative average upon entering an interval defined by the number of credit hours completed will result in probation.   If the minimum average
specified has not been attained by the end of the interval, the
student will be dismissed for poor scholarship.

II. TERMINOLOGY

Title of Division: Evening College.   Defined: Com-

pletely autonomous under program of studies offered after
6 p. m.

III. FEES

Evening students pay $25 per quarter hour plus an-
nual institute fee of $35; part-time day students pay $45 per
quarter hour plus institute fee of $30, $50, or $70, depend-
ing upon credit carried or quarter of study. No cash refunds are made; tuition credit of 75% is given if withdrawal
is in first two weeks of class, 50% in third and fourth weeks,
25% in fifth and sixth week, none after the sixth week.

IV. FACULTY AND FACULTY RECRUITMENT

Twenty-five percent of faculty teaching evening classes
in Business Administration are full-time and fifteen percent
over all.   Final authority for hiring evening faculty lies with
the Dean of the Evening College.   General faculty meetings
are held yearly and department meetings as often as necessary.   Faculty members are permitted to teach on an overload basis a maximum of two evenings per week at three
periods per evening.   Part-time salary ranges from $30 to
$66 per three-hour evening instruction.   No overloads are
permitted.

V. SCHEDULING

The Dean of the Evening College is responsible for
the evening schedule.   Three-credit hour classes are scheduled one night a week.   Part-time evening students are eligible for the Dean's List after completing 6 1/2 quarter
hours with a 3. 5 quality point average.   Required courses
are offered on a predetermined schedule regardless of the
number of students enrolled.   Elective courses need a minimum of twelve students to constitute a class; however,
electives are often offered with fewer than twelve at the
Dean's discretion.

VI. ORGANIZATIONAL STRUCTURE

Twenty staff members are included on the administrative staff.   Teaching staff includes 285 part-time faculty and
two full-time plus twelve from the College of Business Administration.   The Dean is responsible for the overall administration of the Evening College and is assisted by nineteen others "too numerous to mention. "

VII. EDUCATIONAL TELEVISION PROGRAMS

No courses are offered on Educational Television.

VIII. NON-CREDIT PROGRAMS

Non-credit courses are offered in Engineering and other areas. This program is self-supporting. Remuneration for faculty varies with the course. The Division does offer conferences and institutes such as the Liberty Bell Corrosion Course in cooperation with the Philadelphia Chapter of National Association of Corrosion Engineers.

IX. GENERAL

Day students participate more in discussions regarding the academic program than evening students. Much emphasis is placed on leadership development through co-curricular and extra-curricular activities. The evening division is receiving adequate support. The Dean of the Evening College is responsible to the Vice-President for Academic Affairs and directly to the President in major decisions. Most audio-visual instructional aids are available to evening classes.

X. STUDENT RECRUITMENT

Newspaper publicity is used. Special motivational appeals are made to industry and professional organizations.

Drury College
Springfield, Missouri
Continuing Education Division

Total Enrollment 1, 005   Private Institution
Evening Enrollment 1, 205   Semester System

I. ADMISSION POLICIES

All students must be registered by the first night of class. Students may register for credit courses without transcripts. Non-matriculated students may take eight hours a semester to a total of 94 hours before matriculation is required. Admission requirements are completion of registration cards and admissibility to previous college attended.

Mail registration is used. Students must maintain at least a
2. 0 after a total of twelve semester hours or they are placed
on scholastic probation. A special degree for adults is offered: The Bachelor of Science Degree, with an enrollment
of 160 per semester. Admission requirements for the special
degree are previous transcripts on file; 2. 0 average overall
required; admission test scores should be good. Admission
policies are set by the Continuing Education Council. Day
and evening students do not usually register for the same
classes. Orientation is held at the beginning of each semester. Degree students are placed on probation below 2. 0
for twelve hours but no suspension policy is used. Of the
1205 enrollment in the special Bachelor of Science program,
42 are full-time and 1163 are part-time students. Distribution requirements for the special degree program are: a
minimum of 12 hours in each of the three divisions, Arts-
Humanities, Social Sciences, Science-Math. A total of 124
hours (semester) are required to complete the special degree with a minimum of 18, maximum of 30 hours, in the
major. A 2. 0 grade point average, acceptable scores on
admission tests and good grades while at Drury are the requirements for the special degree program.

II. TERMINOLOGY

Title of Division: Evening College of Continuing Education Division. Defined: A program for adults 18 years of
age or older not in full-time school. For individuals who
cannot pursue an educational program in the regular session
of the college. The program will provide stimulus and leadership in the cultural and intellectual life of the surrounding
community.

III. FEES

Evening fees are set by the credit hour; day fees are
by semester to cover 12 to 16 semester hours. Refunds are
made on a graduating percentage basis: full refund after 1st
meeting, no refund after the sixth meeting.

IV. FACULTY AND FACULTY RECRUITMENT

Fifteen percent of the faculty teaching evening classes
are full-time faculty members. Final authority to hire faculty
lies with the Continuing Education Council. The Director of
the Adult Education Division may reject a faculty member assigned to teach evening classes. Some full-time faculty mem-

bers teach exclusively in the evening and are responsible to
the Director of the Continuing Education Division. Regular
faculty members meet once each semester. Faculty members are welcome to participate in seminars and conferences
and only limited by a sense of moderation.

V. SCHEDULING

The Director of the Adult Education Division is responsible for the evening class schedule. The Schedule of
Evening Classes is planned by the Dean's staff. Three credit
hour courses are scheduled one night a week. Day and evening classes are equal in terms of quality but different instructional methods are used. Part-time evening students
are eligible for the Dean's List with at least eight hours a
semester with a grade point average of 3. 3 or higher. Normally ten students must register to constitute a class. Part-
time faculty receive salaries from $112 to $250 per semester
hour; regular day faculty receive $144-$250 per semester
hour for teaching overloads.

VI. ORGANIZATIONAL STRUCTURE

Ten staff members comprise the administrative staff
of the Division, with 20 full-time and 70 part-time teaching
staff. The Dean is responsible for overall supervision and
public relations, the Associate Dean is responsible for the
day-to-day routine of the Evening College, the Director of
Non-credit Programs, Director of Conferences and Institutes
have responsibility of coordinating the summer institutes,
evening college student affairs, government contracts and
comptrollership, Director of Extension coordinates the off-
campus residence center, orders all books, and handles all
veteran affairs. Registrar and assistant are caretakers of
student records.

VII. EDUCATIONAL TELEVISION PROGRAMS

Credit courses are offered via educational television.
Students do earn residence credit. In addition to sixteen
half-hour telecasts, each course contains several meetings
on campus. The Dean and Assistant Dean of Continuing Education are responsible for supervision of the TV courses.
Both full and part-time faculty are used to teach the TV
courses. The regular Evening College staff handles the registration and courses are financed through the tuition.

Course 1 - 6:00 a. m. Saturday mornings on Station A;
Course 2 - 6:30 a. m. Saturday mornings on Station B.

VIII.   NON-CREDIT PROGRAMS

Non-credit courses are offered in Business and Management, Arts and Sciences and other areas.   There is a budget for non-credit courses but they are expected to pay for themselves initially.   Remuneration for faculty teaching non-credit courses is $25. 00 per session or $150 per course for six class sessions.   The Division does sponsor the conferences and institutes such as: Rhythmic Workshop, Testing Techniques Workshop, Instructional Television Workshop, Exceptional Child Workshop, Bob-White Quail Seminar, Stroke Patient Workshop.   Clinicians are paid from $50 to $100 per day.   The Division uses qualified faculty members as well as visiting lecturers.

IX.   GENERAL

A student council is being organized in order for students to participate in discussions regarding the academic program and the Student Senate offer suggestions.   The Residential Center is ninety miles from the campus.   In general, all evening divisions are not receiving adequate support.   The Director of Continuing Education Division is responsible to the President of the College.   Audio-visual instructional aids are available for evening classes.

X.   STUDENT RECRUITMENT

Newspaper, radio and television publicity are used. Special motivational appeals have been developed for industry and civic organizations.

Dutchess Community College
Poughkeepsie, New York
Office of Continuing Education

Total Enrollment 4, 405   Public Institution
Evening Enrollment 2, 363   Semester System

I.   ADMISSION POLICIES

Deadline for application for admission to evening

classes is about two weeks prior to registration. Students
may register for credit courses without transcripts. There
is no limit to the amount of work taken as non-matriculated
students. Admission requirements for regular students are
acceptable college transcripts or high school graduation or
equivalency. Mail registration is used. There is no special
degree for adults. Admission policies are set by the Board
of Trustees of the state. Day and evening students may
register in the same classes. There is no orientation for
evening students. Matriculated students are automatically on
probation when GPA is less than 1. 80. No special adult degree program is being considered. The Board of Trustees
formulates the admission policies, along with the President
and Deans.

II. TERMINOLOGY

Title of Division: Office of Continuing Education.
Defined: Educational opportunities for area residents whose
daily responsibilities prevent them from attending the College's day division as full-time students and who seek to
complete initial higher educational objectives, update skills
and techniques and seek cultural enrichment.

III. FEES

Part-time students pay a $3. 00 college fee; full-time
students pay a $25 college fee. Refunds are made on a
graduating percentage basis.

IV. FACULTY AND FACULTY RECRUITMENT

Over half (55%) of the faculty teaching evening classes
are full-time. Final authority for hiring faculty lies with
the Dean of Continuing Education. Regularly scheduled faculty
meetings are held evenings. When faculty members teach on
an overload basis, they are compensated for expenses in-
curred. No budget is established for faculty recruiting.
Salary ranges from $220 to $270 per credit hour for part-
time faculty and is the same for overloads.

V. SCHEDULING

The Dean of Continuing Education is responsible for
the evening class schedule, and has the authority to revise
it. Three credit hour classes are scheduled one night a
week. Day and evening classes are equal in terms of quality.

Part-time evening students are eligible for the Dean's List with twelve credit hours and a 3. 2 GPA or better. A minimum of ten students are required to constitute a class.

VI. ORGANIZATIONAL STRUCTURE

The administrative staff consists of a Dean who is responsible for developing and operating The Office of Continuing Education and the Summer School and for providing adequate programs to meet the needs of part-time adult students; two Assistant Deans assist the Dean--one is responsible for the summer school and the other for short-term courses; the Director of Admissions and Registrar are shared with the day division.

VII. EDUCATIONAL TELEVISION PROGRAMS

Educational television programs are offered by the State University of New York and supervised by SUNY. Registration is handled through the DCC Office of Continuing Education. Programs are scheduled afternoons and evenings from 1:00 p. m. to 8:30 p. m. Out-of-state tuition charge is the same as that for on-campus students.

VIII. NON-CREDIT PROGRAMS

Non-credit courses are offered in Business and Management, Education, Engineering, Arts and Sciences and other areas. The program is expected to pay for itself. Approximately $660 per course for one class session, depending upon experience, is paid full or part-time faculty teaching non-credit courses. Conferences and institutes are sponsored by the Office of Continuing Education such as: Preschool Parent Seminar, Environmental Crisis Conference, Dental Hygienist Refresher Workshop, Basketball Clinic, Parent Orientation to Special Preparatory Summer Programs. Clinicians are paid from $25 to $75 per day for these conferences and workshops. Summer session is the responsibility of the Office of Continuing Education.

IX. GENERAL

Students participate in discussion regarding the academic program through the Evening Student Association. The evening division is receiving adequate support. The Dean of Continuing Education is responsible to the President. Complete audio-visual instructional aids are available for evening classes, including closed circuit television.

X.   STUDENT RECRUITMENT

Newspaper, radio and television publicity is used.
Special motivational appeals have been developed for industry
and civic organizations.

East Carolina University
Greenville, North Carolina
University College

Total Enrollment 10, 085   Public Institution
Evening Enrollment 820   Quarter System

I.   ADMISSION POLICIES

There is no deadline for application for admission for
evening classes.   Students may register for credit courses
before transcripts are submitted on Conditional Admission.
Non-matriculating or "special" students may take up to thirty-
five quarter hours for credit.   The admission requirements
for non-matriculating or "special" students are: high school
graduation and eligibility to return to the last school in which
student was matriculated--same requirements for regular
students.   Students who are rejected as regular students are
advised to apply as evening students though they are not automatically accepted.   Mail registration is not used.   The policies regarding probation and suspension require all evening
students to meet the same academic requirements as day students.   The ACT or CEEB are not required for adults in the
evening division.   The evening degree program is the same
as the day degree program.   The Campus Admissions Committee formulates the admission policies for all evening students.   The day and evening students are enrolled in the
same classes without restriction.   In the opinion of the University College, there are two advantages to combined classes,
namely: "insures potential small evening classes materializing and department chairmen take a greater interest in the
program. "   There is no orientation program for evening students.

II.   TERMINOLOGY

Title of Division: Division of Continuing Education,

under the Division of the Continuing Education is the University College.   Defined: University program to provide specialized services for adult students.   Continuing Education defined: Education is life long for adult students.   It may be credit, non-credit, short courses or conferences and institutes.

III.   FEES

There is no fee differential between day and evening classes.   The refund policies for evening students who drop one or more classes but remain in school are based upon class meetings held prior to the withdrawal.

IV.   FACULTY AND FACULTY RECRUITMENT

Approximately 50% of the faculty for evening classes are full-time faculty members.   The Board of Trustees has the final authority for hiring full and/or part-time faculty for evening classes, although the Director of the Evening Division may reject a faculty member who has been assigned to teach in the evening.   The Director does employ full-time faculty to teach exclusively in the evening--with the consent of the department head.   No regular faculty meetings are held.   Very little of the budget is spent on recruitment. The salary range for part-time faculty is $10 to $20 per contact hour and is the same for overloads.   If the faculty is paid by the course, the compensation is $480 to $960. Ten students constitute a class but an instructor's fee is not reduced for teaching a class with less.

V.   SCHEDULING

The Director is responsible for the evening class schedule which is compiled by student surveys.   The Director has the authority to revise the schedule.   It is preferred that three-hour classes meet one night per week.   The day and evening classes are the same in terms of quality.   Part-time students are not eligible for the Dean's List.

VI.   ORGANIZATIONAL STRUCTURE

The administrative staff is comprised of five - the Dean with overall responsibility, Associate Dean who is responsible for undergraduation instruction, and three program Directors.   The teaching staff consists of eleven full-time and twenty-six part-time faculty members.   It is estimated that the ideal administrative staff size for an evening credit program with an enrollment of 800 would be six staff members.

VII. EDUCATIONAL TELEVISION PROGRAMS

University College does not offer any courses in educational television.

VIII. NON-CREDIT PROGRAMS

The University College offers non-credit courses in Business and Management, Arts and Sciences, Education and other areas. There is a budget for these programs although this program is expected to pay for itself. The remuneration to faculty is the same as for teaching a credit course. The University College sponsors conferences and institutes as: State Personnel Management, Executive Development, School Administrators, plus many others. Qualified faculty members are used as well as visiting lecturers. The University College is not responsible for the summer session.

IX. GENERAL

The University College offers courses in "store front" locations for economically deprived populations. The students on all committees participate in discussions regarding the academic program. There is no graduate program for part-time students. The Evening Division is not receiving adequate support as in comparison to the day program. The Administration does recognize the need however. The Director is responsible to the Dean of Continuing Education. Audio-visual aids are available for evening classes.

X. STUDENT RECRUITMENT

Publicity in newspapers, radio and television is used for student recruitment.

East Tennessee State University
Johnson City, Tennessee
School of Continuing Education

Total Enrollment 10,000   Public Institution
Evening Enrollment 2,500   Quarter System

I. ADMISSION POLICIES

Deadline for application for admission to evening classes is two weeks prior to registration. However, this deadline is not enforced. Registration process will not be considered complete if a student registers before transcripts are submitted. Non-matriculated students may register for credit work but they are cautioned that credit is not applied toward a degree unless approved by the appropriate college dean when they do matriculate. Freshmen must maintain a grade point average of 1. 5; sophomores 1. 8; juniors 2. 0. There is no special degree program for adults; none is being planned in the immediate future. Admission policies are set by the Dean of Admissions. Day and evening students may enroll in the same classes with approval. There is no orientation for evening students. Everything within reason is done to maintain evening degree programs that are an integral part of the total University.

II. TERMINOLOGY

Title of Division: School of Continuing Education. Defined: A division through which educational services of the University are extended to individuals and groups other than day students. Includes both credit and non-credit programs.

III. FEES

There is no fee differential between day and evening classes. Refunds are made only if classes are cancelled. Students withdrawing from all classes receive refunds according to a published schedule.

IV. FACULTY AND FACULTY RECRUITMENT

50-90% teaching evening classes are full-time faculty members. Final authority to hire faculty lies with the President upon recommendation by the Dean of the School of Continuing Education. Some full-time faculty members teach exclusively in the evening and are responsible to the Dean of the School of Continuing Education. Faculty meetings are held with certain groups. No teaching overloads are permitted. Expenditures for recruitment are limited to occasional display advertising and bulletins published quarterly. The salary range for part-time faculty is $150-$170 per quarter hour. Regular faculty members may teach one off-campus

class per year for added remuneration ranging from $100-
$210 per quarter hour.

V.   SCHEDULING

The Dean of the School of Continuing Education is responsible for the evening class schedule and has the authority
to revise it.   Three credit hour courses are scheduled both
one and two nights a week.   A study is planned to compare
day and evening classes, procedures and results.   Part-time
evening students are eligible for the Dean's List with a 3. 5
GPA after carrying 14 quarter hours.

VI.   ORGANIZATIONAL STRUCTURE

The School of Continuing Education has an administrative staff of four members, with a teaching staff of 14 full-
time and 33 part-time faculty members.   In addition, the
schools employ 10 clerks to assist in the program.   The institution does not have academic or administrative autonomy.
It is an integral part of the total university program.   The
School is headed by a Dean with a Director and Assistant
Director of the Kingsport University Center and a Director
of Non-Credit Program who is the coordinator of Non-Degree
Programs.

VII.   EDUCATIONAL TELEVISION PROGRAMS

The School of Continuing Education does not sponsor
Educational Television courses.

VIII.   NON-CREDIT PROGRAMS

The school offers non-degree courses in Business and
Management and in Personal Development.   There is no budget provided for these courses; the program is expected to
pay for itself.   Faculty are paid the same hourly rate as
for summer school teaching, and the remuneration depends
upon the qualifications of the instructor.   The school sponsors conferences and institutes as a part of the non-degree
program.   Clinicians are paid from $25-$150 per evening
session for conferences depending upon their qualifications
and the demand.   The School of Continuing Education is not
responsible for the Summer school.

IX. GENERAL

Students are invited to suggest additions or modifications of academic programs. There is a Center at Kingsport which is involved with the University of Tennessee. The evening division is receiving adequate support. The Dean of the School of Continuing Education is responsible to the Dean of University Faculty and the President of the University. Complete audio-visual instructional aids are available at each Center of the University. The minimum class size is 12 for the lower division, eight for the upper division and five for the graduate classes.

X. STUDENT RECRUITMENT

Newspaper, radio and television publicity are used. Special motivational appeals have been developed for industry and various civic organizations.

Fairleigh Dickinson University
Rutherford, New Jersey
University Evening Division

Total Enrollment 19,000   Private Institution
Evening Enrollment 9,000   Semester System

I. ADMISSION POLICIES

There is no deadline for application for admission to evening classes. Students may register for credit courses on a provisional basis before transcripts are submitted. Non-matriculating or "special" students may take unlimited hours of course work for credit. Admission requirements: high school diploma or equivalent. Students who are rejected for admission as regular day students are advised to apply as evening students, but admission is not automatic. Mail registration is used. An inquiry post card (with return) is mailed to the student, followed by a "kit" if requested. Probation and dismissal policies require a student to maintain a 2.0 cumulative average. A student is dismissed only after a long process of probation. No ACT or CEEB examination is required for admission. No special degree program is offered for adults. The total enrollment includes 9000 undergraduates and 3000 graduate students in the evening. There are 128 semester hours required to complete the degree pro-

gram.   The University Educational Policies Committee formulates the admission policies for evening students.   Day and
evening students may enroll in the same classes on a 50/50
basis.   No orientation program is held for evening students.

II.   TERMINOLOGY

Title of Division: University Evening Division.

III.   FEES

There is no fee differential for day and evening classes.

IV.   FACULTY AND FACULTY RECRUITMENT

There is no policy regarding the percentage of evening, full-time faculty members.   Approximately 25% of the
evening faculty are full-time faculty members.   The department chairmen have the final authority for hiring full/part-
time faculty members for evening classes.   The Dean of the
University Evening Division has authority to reject a faculty
member who has been assigned to teach evening classes.   No
regular faculty meetings are held for evening faculty.   No
part of Evening Division budget is spent on recruitment.   Salary
range for part-time faculty is $8 to $12 per hour and the
same for overloads.

V.   SCHEDULING

Department Chairmen are responsible for the evening
class schedule.   The Dean of the University Evening Division
has the authority to revise the schedule as necessary.   Three-
hour classes are scheduled one night per week.   Day and evening classes are equal in quality.   Part-time students are
eligible for the Dean's List.   A minimum of ten students
required to constitute a class.   The instructor's salary is
not reduced if he teaches the class below minimum size.

VI.   ORGANIZATIONAL STRUCTURE

The University Evening Division has an administrative
staff of five staff members with a teaching staff of 900 part-
time faculty members.   The Division is headed by a Dean
who has the responsibility for all-university direction and
supervision.   The Assistant to the Dean gives personal assistance and acts as a "deputy" for the Division.   The Director is in charge of the evening division on one campus (there

are four campuses).

VII.   EDUCATIONAL TELEVISION PROGRAMS

The University Evening Division does not sponsor educational television programs.

VIII.   NON-CREDIT PROGRAMS

The University Evening Division does not offer any non-credit programs.

IX.   GENERAL

Students at the University do have a considerable amount of opportunity to participate in discussion regarding the academic program.   No graduate programs for part-time students are offered in the Evening Division.   The Evening Division is receiving adequate financial support.   The Dean of the Evening Division is responsible to the President and the Provost.   There is an active chapter of Alpha Sigma Lambda.

X.   STUDENT RECRUITMENT

Newspaper, radio and television are used for publicity. Special motivational appeals are developed for industry, the Chamber of Commerce and various civic organizations.

George Washington University
Washington, D. C.
College of General Studies

Total Enrollment 14, 000   Private Institution
Evening Enrollment 24, 000   Semester System

I.   ADMISSION POLICIES

There is no deadline for admission applications.   Students may register for credit courses before transcripts are submitted.   Non-matriculating or "special" students may take an unlimited amount of work for credit.   There are no admission requirements for undergraduates other than high school diploma or equivalency; graduate students requirement is 90 semester hours with a "B" average.   Rejected students

(regular) are not advised to apply as evening students.   Pre-
printed forms are mailed and returned to a central registration location as a form of mail registration.   Probation and
suspension policies are: SGBA undergraduate - 12 hours between 1. 5 and 2. 0, SGBA graduate - 6 hours or more between 2. 5 or 3. 0; Columbian College - 2 grades of "F" in
one semester; suspension results if a SGBA graduate student
fails to meet probation requirements of 6 hours or more below 2. 50 and SGBA undergraduate student fails to meet probation requirements of 12 hours or more below 1. 5.   ACT
and CEEB examinations for adults are not required.   Graduate degree candidates are required to take ATGSB which is
used as a basis for admission.   Evening degree programs
for adults offered are BGS, BSGS, BSG&CS, BSO, BSEH for
the undergraduate and an MSA for graduate students.   Undergraduate degree students totalled 2, 000 in the Fall and graduate students totalled 4, 500.   (75 full-time and 6, 425 part-
time).   Distribution requirements for undergraduates are:
Communications - 12, Humanities - 12, Natural Sciences -
6 to 8, Mathematics - 6, Social Sciences - 12, Electives -
10-12, Concentration - 24, Related Area - 18, Electives -
18; for graduates: Communications - 6, Humanities - 6,
Natural Sciences - 6 to 8, Mathematics - 9, Social Sciences
- 12, Business and Economics - 15 to 18, Electives - 4 to
9, Concentration - 33, Related Electives - 27.   Total number of hours to complete a degree (undergraduate) is 120 and
36 for graduate.   Areas of concentration are BGS - History,
Math, Political Science, Psychology - 24 hours; BSGS - Accounting, Business Administration - 24 hours; BSGCS - 60
hours Cartography, Geodesy; BSO - Oceanography, 60 hours;
BSEH - Environmental Health, 25 hours.   The Deans of the
concerned college or school in conjunction with the University
Admission Office formulate the admission policies.   Combined day/evening classes create a learning experience of
more breadth for the student.   There is no orientation for
evening students.

II.   TERMINOLOGY

Title of the Division: College of General Studies.
Defined: College is concerned with all off-campus part-time
education programs.   Continuing Education defined: To provide educational programs and associated student services to
satisfy the needs of this adult population.

III. FEES

There is a fee differential for day/evening classes. The off-campus tuition is $50.00 per hour and on-campus tuition is $68.00 per hour plus $3.50 per hour for center fee. The off-campus programs do not use the campus facilities. Refunds are based upon a refund schedule starting at 90% after last class.

IV. FACULTY AND FACULTY RECRUITMENT

The Dean of the College has the final and full authority to hire faculty members for evening classes. No full-time faculty members teach exclusively in the evening. Regular faculty meetings are held at the beginning of each semester. Regular faculty members are permitted to teach one class (credit or non-credit) as an overload. No budget is set up for recruitment. Salary ranges from $700 to $1000/3 semester hours for part-time faculty and the same for full-time depending upon academic rank.

V. SCHEDULING

The Dean is fully responsible for the evening class schedule. Compiling the evening class schedule involves a procedure of coordinating with the field education officer and the university with the CGS staff. Three-hour class periods are scheduled one night a week. Day and evening classes compare favorably in terms of quality. Part-time evening students are eligible for the Dean's List and are required to have twelve hours of 3.5 (Columbian College students must have honors in at least 60% of 15 hours of course work). Twelve students must register on the undergraduate level to constitute a class. Instructor compensation is not reduced if he teaches a class below minimum size.

VI. ORGANIZATIONAL STRUCTURE

The administrative staff consists of thirty staff members with 410 (active) part-time faculty members. The Dean is responsible for the overall operation of the College of General Studies; the Assistant Dean operates as Director of Credit Programs and assumes the role of Dean in his absence; Directors are responsible for a significant segment of the operation as presently organized by the Assistant Directors.

VII. EDUCATIONAL TELEVISION PROGRAMS

The College of General Studies does not offer any educational television programs.

VIII. NON-CREDIT PROGRAMS

Non-credit programs are offered in Business and Management, and in Arts and Sciences. Programs are budgeted to pay for themselves. Faculty remuneration ranges from $35 to $50 per course. Conferences and institutes are sponsored by the College. Educational conference with area school superintendents and staff development officers was the highlight of the past year.

IX. GENERAL

The Master of Science in Administration program is a 36-hour program in which a student may choose one of thirteen areas of concentration with no thesis required for the benefit of part-time evening students. The need for adult education programs is recognized and adequate support is given to the evening program. The Dean is responsible to the Vice-President for Academic Affairs. No audio-visual instructional aids are used. A chapter of Alpha Sigma Lambda is active on campus.

X. STUDENT RECRUITMENT

Newspaper advertising, spot announcements on three major radio stations are used as publicity for student recruitment.

<u>Georgia Southern College</u>
Statesboro, Georgia
Department of Evening Studies

Total Enrollment 5, 900   Public Institution
Evening Enrollment 255   Quarter System

I. ADMISSION POLICIES

There is no deadline for application for admission to evening classes. A student may register for credit courses before transcripts are submitted. Non-matriculating or "special" students may take up to fifteen quarter hours. The admission requirements for regular degree students are the Dean's approval; for "special" students, twenty-three years of age or special recommendation. Students are not advised to apply for evening classes when they are rejected as regular students. Mail registration is not used. Probation and suspension regulations for evening students are the same as for the day students except more time is allowed. The CEEB examination is required and is used for placement and advisement only--not for admission purposes. No special degree program is offered for adults. The Dean of Continuing Education formulates the admission policies for evening students with the assistance of a committee. Day and evening students may enroll in the same classes. An orientation program is held for evening students.

II. TERMINOLOGY

Title of Division: Department of Evening Studies. Defined: All aspects of a complex program. Continuing Education defined: All aspects of programs - credit and non-credit - and special services.

III. FEES

There is no fee differential for day and evening classes. Refund policies for evening students are the same as for day students.

IV. FACULTY AND FACULTY RECRUITMENT

There is no policy regarding the percentage of full-time faculty members who teach evening classes. No full-time faculty members teach evening classes. The Department Head has the final authority for hiring full/part-time faculty members for evening classes. About 10% of the budget is spent for recruitment. Part-time faculty members receive $600 per course and the same salary is paid for overloads.

V. SCHEDULING

The Director of Continuing Education is responsible for the evening class schedule. The procedure for compiling the evening class schedule is based upon the requests and needs of the students. The Director has the authority to revise the schedule as needed. Three-hour classes are sched-

uled two nights per week.   Day and evening classes are the
same in quality.   Part-time evening students are eligible for
the Dean's List; a full-load equivalent is required.   A minimum of ten students are required to constitute a class.   The
instructor's compensation is not reduced when teaching a
class below minimum size.

VI.   ORGANIZATIONAL STRUCTURE

The Department of Evening Studies is headed by a
Dean.   There are two staff members and a teaching staff of
fifteen part-time faculty members.   The institution does not
have academic or administrative autonomy.   Ideally, with an
evening enrollment of 300 to 500, there should be two administrative staff members for the credit program; 6 to 8
staff members for the non-credit programs, conferences and
institutes.

VII.   EDUCATIONAL TELEVISION PROGRAMS

The Department of Evening Studies offers credit and
non-credit courses using educational television.   Students
may earn residence credit which may apply toward a degree.
The department concerned supervises its own courses.
Only full-time faculty members participate in the program.
Faculty members do not receive remuneration (additional)
for teaching TV courses.   Their regular teaching load is reduced by one course.   The Registrar handles the registration
for the educational television courses.   Courses are scheduled "after school hours. "   No out-of-state tuition is charged.

VIII.   NON-CREDIT PROGRAMS

Non-credit programs are offered in Business and
Management, Arts and Sciences, and in Education.   The program is expected to pay for itself.   Faculty members receive from $10 to $18 per hour for each class.   The remuneration depends upon the qualifications of the instructor.
The Department also sponsors conferences and institutes.
Clinicians receive $100 per day for conferences.   Confer-
ences are generally sponsored in cooperation with other divisions or colleges.   The Department is not responsible for
the summer session.

IX.   GENERAL

The institution does participate in offering credit and

non-credit courses in "store front" locations off-campus for
the economically deprived populations.   Students are requested
to support discussions regarding the academic program.   Education offers about twenty courses per year on the graduate
level for part-time students in the evening.   The Evening
Division is receiving support adequately.   The Dean is responsible to the Vice-President for Instruction.   Audio-visual
aids are available to evening classes.

X.   STUDENT RECRUITMENT

Newspaper, radio and television publicity is used.
Direct contact is made with business and industry and with
the Chamber of Commerce to publicize academic and non-
academic programs.

University of Georgia
Athens, Georgia
Center for Continuing Education

Total Enrollment 21, 873   Public Institution
Evening Enrollment 480   Quarter System
(1, 035 off-campus)

I.   ADMISSION POLICIES

Deadlines for admission are September 3, December
10, March 2, May 26; however, deadlines are waived when
the case justifies.   Students may register "tentatively" before transcripts are received; however, transcripts must be
submitted within 14 days or registration is cancelled.   Non-
matriculating and/or special students may take up to 45
hours (qtr. hrs.) of work for credit.   The admission requirements for non-matriculating/special students are high school
graduation, 21 years of age and exhibition of marked degree
of maturity, CEEB, SAT score of 750 or above.   (Sixteen
acceptable high school units, except for mature adults.)   Admission for regular students is above average high school
record, CEEB total of 950 or predicted grade point average
of 2. 0 (sixteen acceptable high school units.)   Students who
are rejected for regular admission are advised to enroll as
evening students, but are not automatically accepted.   A student failing to make an average of 1. 7 in any quarter except
summer is placed on probation unless his cumulative average
is 2. 5 on all work.   Student remains on probation until he

makes a 2. 0 average. If a student fails to get off probation
during a second consecutive probation quarter, he is dismissed; he is also dismissed if his average drops to a 0. 7
in any quarter. ACT or CEEB examination for adults in the
evening division is required, and used as a basis for admission as well as placement and advisement. No evening
degree program for adults is offered. The Evening School
Admission Committee in consultation with the University's
Director of Admissions formulate the admission policies.
Any day student may enroll in evening classes with written
permission of his Dean. Evening students must gain formal
admission to the University before they can take classes offered by the day division. The combined class gives more
flexibility to meet student needs, the "cross-fertilization"
factor is advantageous. No orientation program is conducted
for evening students but an individual pre- and post-admissions counseling is provided along with orientation information through a newsletter. An informal advisory committee
reviews procedures and policy, course offerings and dis-
cusses problems.

II.   TERMINOLOGY

Title of Division: Center for Continuing Education.
Defined: A program for credit and non-credit courses, institutes, conferences, seminars, and other educational services designed to meet the unique needs of adults who wish to
continue their education. For the most part the clientele of
continuing education are adults whose primary occupation is
other than that of going to school. Our "other educational
services" include adult educational counseling, educational
television, Independent Study, individual reading programs
for adults, travel advisory services, etc.

III.   FEES

There is no fee differential for those students taking
less than 12 quarter hours of work. However, regular students who take more than 12 hours, do get a reduction in
the standard charge of $11. 00 per quarter hour. Instructional
costs for University Evening Classes are covered entirely by
student fees; while day students instructional costs are financed largely by allocations from state funds. Present
policy on refunds permits "no refund for reduction of class
load. " However, consideration is being given to a change
of this policy to allow exception when reduction in load is
necessitated by change of work assignment, etc.

IV.   FACULTY AND FACULTY RECRUITMENT

There is no policy regarding the percentage of full-time faculty teaching in the evening except that "we strive to have as many full-time faculty members teaching in the evening as possible." Approximately 43% of the faculty were full-time during the Fall quarter of 1970. Final authority for hiring full and/or part-time faculty members for evening classes lies with the Vice-President for Instruction and Vice-President for Services with recommendations from the Director/Associate Director of the Center of Continuing Education. The Director can reject a faculty member who has been assigned to teach evening classes. Three full-time faculty members are employed to teach exclusively in the evening--at the Waycross Center--and they are responsible to the Director of the Center for Continuing Education. No regular faculty meetings are held for evening faculty. Regular faculty members are encouraged to teach in all credit, non-credit, institutes, seminars and conferences; for credit courses permission must be given by the Dean and Department Head with a limit of one course per quarter. Budget does not carry a specific item for recruitment of faculty. It is estimated that about 8-10% of a Director or Extension Coordinator's time is spent on recruitment. Salary range for part-time faculty is $550 flat fee for non-lab five-quarter hour course, $340 for a three-quarter hour course, $100 additional for five-quarter hour lab course.

V.   SCHEDULING

The Director of University Evening Classes on campus, off-campus center Directors, and Extension Coordinators are responsible for class schedules at off-campus locations. Students are polled for determined needs, review of degree requirements is made in various subject matter areas, staff availability is determined, review of current students course profiles and prior quarters' offerings prior to compilation of evening class schedule which takes into account projected needs of students on the basis of these things. The Director does have the authority to revise a class schedule but very rarely has occasion to do so. Three-hour classes are scheduled two nights per week. This method of scheduling is preferred by students and faculty as a convenience in traveling where two or more persons ride together. The three-hour classes are completed at the end of six weeks. It is felt that evening classes are superior due to a higher motivation but high quality is strived for both in day and evening classes.

Part-time students are not eligible for the Dean's List but
an Honors List is provided for those with a 3. 4 on ten quarter hours.   Fifteen students constitute a class but in exceptional cases a class is taught with a minimum of 10-12
students.   Instructor's compensation is reduced for teaching
lesser classes.   Income from a specific class must cover
all direct instructional costs including instructor's salary and
travel.   If a class of ten students is permitted, and travel
and other direct costs amount to $75, the instructor will
have to agree to teach the class for a salary of $475 (i. e.
$550 less $75.)

VI.   ORGANIZATIONAL STRUCTURE

An administrative staff of sixty-two (some of which
are joint-staffed with other units of the University) includes:
Vice-President for Services with overall responsibility for
approval of Center's budget, staff appointments and promo-
tions, and major policy changes; Director of Center for Continuing Education with overall responsibility for the administration of the Center staff and programming; three Associate
Directors of the Center--Instruction, Managerial Services
and Communication Services; two Directors of Adult Educa-
tion--one administers off-campus center at Waycross and one
administers off-campus center at Thomasville; Coordinator of
Off-Campus Programs with direct responsibility for all off-
campus non-credit program planning, scheduling, budget
making, etc. ; Assistant Director for Conferences and Institutes with direct responsibility for residential conferences,
workshops, institutes and seminars; Assistant Director for
Extension with direct responsibility for off-campus centers
and extension classes; Director of University Evening Classes
who is in charge of admissions, registration, scheduling,
faculty recruitment and records for University Evening
Classes; Assistant Director for Inter-institutional Programs
who is in charge of Title I and Title VIII State Agency Operation and personnel who are joint-staffed with other institutions of higher education; Assistant Director for Program
Development and Evaluation who is responsible for new program development and program evaluation; Coordinator of
Governmental Training who is responsible for all kinds of
governmental training; Supervisor of Independent Study who
handles correspondence study and Adult Advisory Service,
etc.   A staff of ten is required to administer an evening
credit program with an evening enrollment of 5, 000.

VII.   EDUCATIONAL TELEVISION PROGRAMS

Non-credit courses are offered by educational television. (The School of Journalism is responsible for all
credit subject-matter courses relating to television programming via on-campus closed-circuit television.) The Associate
Director for Communications Service and the relevant faculty
members involved are responsible for supervising the television courses. Both full and part-time faculty are used for
the television courses. Faculty members do not usually receive additional remuneration for teaching courses on TV.
Registration is handled either by the University Extension
Office or the Independent Study Department. In some cases
the Extension Coordinator met with local discussion groups
who were receiving lectures, etc. by television; in other
cases registration materials and course outlines were ex-
changed via mail. Financing is in part from state funds and
in part by student fees. Courses are scheduled from 7 to 9
p. m.

VIII.   NON-CREDIT PROGRAMS

The Division offers non-credit programs in the areas
of Business and Management, Arts and Sciences, Education,
Veterinary Medicine, Gerontology, Governmental Training,
Civil Defense, Community Development, etc. The non-credit
program is budgeted as part of University Extension but is
expected to pay for itself. Remuneration for faculty teaching
non-credit courses is from $12 to $35 per contact hour depending upon the qualifications of the instructor and the area
of instruction. Two hundred ninety-eight conferences were
sponsored or co-sponsored by the Center for Continuing Education last year. Almost all of these conferences were conducted in the Center Building. The vast majority of conferences are conducted under a joint sponsorship arrangement.
The Center is not responsible for the summer session.

IX.   GENERAL

Last year the Center for Continuing Education, in cooperation with the Savannah State College (black) and the Armstrong State College launched an extensive non-credit program
in a 10-block poor area of Savannah that, with support from
Title I, is carrying programs directly to the culturally deprived "where they are." Program shows much promise!
The Director of University Evening Classes, with Directors
of the two off-campus centers, encourage both students and

faculty-student groups to enter into dialogue with them from time to time concerning how the evening program can better meet the needs of its students. A proposal has been submitted to and approved by the top administration of the University for taking over and completely renovating a University facility (located adjacent to a deprived neighborhood) as the center for a community-wide non-credit program that would involve the economically and culturally deprived, as well as other income groups. Following a nine-months study in 1963-64 by a committee appointed by the Dean of the Graduate School, the Center for Continuing Education was given the overall facilitative management responsibility for all off-campus and irregular graduate study by teachers, government officials, and other part-time graduate students. Since that time this program has grown from 600 to 7000+ students. It is felt that adequate stress and financial support are not comparable to the day program but the University administration is quite generous. The Dean of the Center for Continuing Education is responsible to the Vice-President for Services. Both open and closed-circuit television, slides, film strips, etc. are available for evening classes.

X. STUDENT RECRUITMENT

Newspaper publicity is rather widely used for student recruitment by the University Public Relations Department. Spot announcements are frequently used along with television to a limited degree. Announcement brochures developed for each program are mailed to potential students. Personal contacts with industrial officials, talks, etc. are used as special motivational appeals.

Harvard University
Cambridge, Massachusetts
University Extension

Total Enrollment 6,000   Private Institution
                                              Semester System

I. ADMISSION POLICIES

There is no deadline for application for admission to classes taken through the University Extension. Students may register for credit courses before transcripts are submitted. A few Extension students are admitted as "special" students to the Faculty of Arts and Sciences and take some of their work in regular day classes.   There is no limit to the amount of work taken as non-matriculating students.   Students may apply for admission to candidacy for the degree of Associate in Arts in Extension Studies or Bachelor of Arts in Extension Studies on one of the following bases: a) those who have had no previous college work must satisfactorily complete the equivalent of one year of college work - four full courses or eight half-courses - under the Commission or in the Harvard Summer School.   When a student is admitted to the degree, these courses count retroactively; b) those who have had previous college work and wish to have it evaluated for possible transfer credit must satisfactorily complete two full courses or four half-courses under the Commission or in the Harvard Summer School before presenting official transcripts of this work.   College catalogs for the years attended must be supplied also.   There is a very informal structure as far as admission to degree candidacy and rate of progress toward the degree is concerned. The Administrative Board for University Extension formulates the admission policies.   The A. A. in Extension Studies, representing the equivalent of two years of college work, was instituted in 1971.

II.   TERMINOLOGY

Title of Division: University Extension, within the Faculty of Arts and Sciences.

III.   FEES

There is a fee differential between day and evening students.   No course fee (tuition, lab, conference or credit) will be refunded after October 15, 1971 for fall and through-year courses, or after February 18, 1972 for spring term courses.   The basic tuition is $5 per term, plus registration, conference, and lab fees.

IV.   FACULTY AND FACULTY RECRUITMENT

All instructors in University Extension are "part-time" but are normally full-time in their day faculties.   The Director invites faculty to teach and the approval of the program each year, including the instructor, is given by the Faculty of Arts and Sciences at Harvard.   A reception is held for the Extension faculty annually.

V.   SCHEDULING

The Director of University Extension is responsible for the scheduling of classes.   Classes are normally held one night per week.

VI.   ORGANIZATIONAL STRUCTURE

The administrative staff consists of a Director, an Assistant to the Director, and an Administrative Assistant who have overall administrative responsibility.   Teaching staff consists of all part-time faculty members.

VII.   EDUCATIONAL TELEVISION PROGRAMS

Educational television programs are offered for Extension credit.   Credit does count toward a degree.   The Administrative Board supervises the program.   Part-time faculty members are used for the educational television programs and they receive additional remuneration for teaching the courses.   The Extension office handles all registration. Financing is supported by the U. S. Navy for the PACE program.   Programs are scheduled from 3 to 3:30 and 7 to 7:30 p. m.

VIII.   NON-CREDIT PROGRAMS

University Extension does not offer any non-credit programs per se--no differential from credit courses.   No conferences or institutes are offered by the Extension.   The summer session is not the responsibility of Extension.

IX.   GENERAL

Students discuss the academic program with their instructors.   Harvard has been offering television courses for credit for the past fifteen years.   The administration does recognize the need and importance of the program in adult education.   The Director of University Extension is responsible to the Dean of the Faculty of Arts and Sciences.

X.   STUDENT RECRUITMENT

Some publicity is given to the courses offered through University Extension in newspapers and through radio and television.

University of Hawaii
Honolulu, Hawaii
Division of Continuing Education and Community Services

Total Enrollment 24, 000   Public Institution
Evening Enrollment 3, 500   Quarter System
(plus 15, 000 attending various activities
in one quarter)

I. ADMISSION POLICIES

There is no rigid deadline for application for admission. Students may not register for credit courses before transcripts are submitted except non-matriculated graduate students who can present diploma with high SAT scores may be accepted without transcripts. Students may take a certain amount of work as non-matriculating or "special" students. Regular student admission requirements include fair high school record, 800 SAT, transfers of 2. 0 GPA; graduate students must have proof of degree. Mail registration has been used for a special group of late afternoon courses for in-service teachers but normally an in-person registration is preferred. Degree students must earn 2. 0 after 24 credits; if below 1. 7 student is suspended. The CEEB exam is required and is used as a basis for admission. The TOEFL is used for advisement. A special degree program for adults is being considered at the undergraduate level. There are no restrictions for day/evening students enrolling in the same class except on maximum total student load - permission of the Dean is required if day and evening load is over 18 credits. Evening classes are accelerated in four - ten week sessions. No orientation program is conducted for evening students but a counseling service is provided. Since about forty percent of the evening students are servicemen there is a need for simple, rapid admission procedures--keeping consonant with the effort to maintain the same standards as the day school.

II. TERMINOLOGY

Title of Division: College of Continuing Education and Community Service. Defined: Theoretically, any educational activity undertaken by a person who is now or has been for some time not primarily a student. Practically, any activity differing in time, place, or format from the normal degree programs.

III. FEES

Day students pay $9 per credit for part-time, under-
graduates $116 full-time, graduates $103 and evening $20
per credit (out-of-state, both, $30 per credit).   The fee dif-
ferential is due to the lack of sufficient legislative appropriations.   Refund policies for evening students: 75% refund
for the first week, 37 1/2% refund for the second week (of
10 week sessions).

IV.   FACULTY AND FACULTY RECRUITMENT

Approximately 65% of the faculty are full-time.   Final
authority for hiring full and/or part-time faculty members
for evening classes lies with the College after departmental
approval.   No full-time faculty members are employed to
teach exclusively in the evening.   The Director cannot engage an instructor without the consent of the department head.
No regular faculty meetings are held with evening faculty.
Full-time faculty are allowed to teach nine credits per year
as an overload.   Evening and summer session, non-credit
courses usually count as one credit, other activities do not
count.   Salary range for part-time faculty is $490 for Pro-
fessors, $260 for Instructors.   Overloads are paid same.

V.   SCHEDULING

The Director is responsible for the evening class
schedule.   Program Director makes tentative schedule, negotiation takes place with departments for staff, courses are
added or deleted by request and/or need.   Three-hour
classes are scheduled on two nights per week.   Every effort
is made to keep quality at least at par with the day school
and it is believed that, since there is more freedom of
choice with instructors, the evening classes are often better.
Part-time students are not eligible for the Dean's List.   Ten
students normally constitute a class...on rare occasion a
teacher is paid all tuition receipts less 10%.

VI.   ORGANIZATIONAL STRUCTURE

Administrative staff consists of thirty-two staff mem-
bers and the teaching staff includes 160 part-time teachers.
The Dean has general responsibility and is the liaison with
University administration; the Associate Dean is the Fiscal
Officer and Personnel Manager; the Assistant Dean is re-
sponsible for services, advising and administration; five Di-

rectors - Courses and Curricula, Special and Professional
Programs, Community Services, Center for Governmental
Development, Center for Labor-Management Training; three
Directors - Non-Credit Programs, Evening Credit Programs,
Teachers Credit Programs; three Counsellors and eighteen
coordinators, twenty-one secretarial and other civil service
staff.

VII. EDUCATIONAL TELEVISION PROGRAMS

No educational television programs are offered.

VIII. NON-CREDIT PROGRAMS

Non-credit programs are offered in the area of Business and Management, Engineering, Arts and Sciences, Education and other areas.   Programs are expected to pay for
themselves.   Remuneration is first ten paid course fees plus
35% of all paid course fees over the fifteenth.   The Division
does sponsor conferences and institutes - sixty were conducted during the past year.

IX. GENERAL

Day school students serve on university committees,
student senate, etc.   The Director is responsible to the
Vice-President for Academic Development.   Audio-visual aids
are available.

X. STUDENT RECRUITMENT

Newspaper publicity is used.

Hofstra University
Hempstead, L. I. , New York
University College

Total Enrollment 8, 000 undergraduates   Private Institution
Evening Enrollment 2, 000 undergraduates Semester System

I. ADMISSION POLICIES

Deadline for application for admission is about one
week prior to the start of the semester.   Students may register for credit courses without transcripts but they must be

received by the end of the semester. Admission requirements are high school graduation or GED and advisement
test or satisfactory record from previously attended colleges.
There is no "special" student category at this institution.
Students may register by mail only if a formal plan of studies
has been worked out for them.   The student receives a copy
of it for reference when filling out the mail registration forms.
Students must maintain a 2. 0 in order to remain in school.
(Transcripts are reviewed annually at the end of the Spring
semester).   A special degree for adults is not offered or
considered.   Admission policies are set by the Dean of University College with Faculty Admission Committee and the
Director of Admissions.   Day and evening students may enroll in the same classes.   Orientation for evening students
is held at the beginning of each semester.

II.   TERMINOLOGY

Title of Division: University College (credit program);
The Institute for Community Education (non-credit).   Defined:
College of the University offering programs and courses for
adults.   Continuing Education is any involvement of adults in
education--undergraduate, graduate, credit and non-credit
work; workshops, conferences, seminars, etc.

III.   FEES

Refunds are made based on the date of withdrawal.

IV.   FACULTY AND FACULTY RECRUITMENT

60% teaching evening classes are full-time.   The final
authority to hire part-time evening faculty lies with Department Chairmen with final approval of the Dean of University
College.   Faculty members are responsible to the Department Chairmen and the Dean.   No faculty meetings are held
for evening faculty members.   Faculty members are permitted to teach three credits on an overload basis, non-credit
courses are subject to Department Chairman's approval.   Recruitment is at the department level.   The salary range for
part-time faculty--$200 per credit hour ($600 for a three-
hour course) to $275 per credit hour; the same salary for
overloads.

V.   SCHEDULING

The Dean of University College is responsible for the

evening class schedule. Three credit hour classes are scheduled two nights a week. Part-time students are not eligible
for the Dean's List; there is a special Honor's List for part-
time students which is annual and based on a minimum of
twelve credits with a 3. 3 average.

VI. ORGANIZATIONAL STRUCTURE

The University College has an administrative staff of
five full-time and eight part-time staff members with a teaching staff of 238 full-time and 225 part-time faculty members.
The administrative staff includes: Dean - a) general supervision of University College (adult branch of the University),
the Graduate Program, and Summer Session, b) liaison with
community projects; cooperative college center, OEO, Health
and Welfare Council, etc. ; Associate Dean - a) responsible
for evening undergraduate students; e. g. , advisement system,
b) represents the Dean at key faculty committees, primary
responsibility is the non-credit area; Assistant to the Dean -
a) counsels adults attending day classes, responsible for University College and Summer Session bulletins, b) coordinator,
Liberal Arts in extension, plans and coordinates the non-
credit Liberal Arts program, under the general supervision
of the Associate Dean, Director of non-credit programs (major part of the responsibilities of one Associate Dean), c)
Coordinator (part-time), conferences and institutes (non-credit), one part-time coordinator, extension--coordinates credit
extension program; four part-time advisors--general advisement of evening and graduate students; Admissions (evening
students) responsible to Dean of Admission and Registrar
(evening), responsible to the Registrar.

VII. EDUCATIONAL TELEVISION PROGRAMS

University College does not offer any courses in Educational Television.

VIII. NON-CREDIT PROGRAMS

The University College offers non-credit courses in
Business and Management, Education, Arts and Sciences,
Engineering and Systems and Programming.   This program
is expected to pay for itself.   The remuneration the faculty
(full or part-time) receive for teaching a non-credit course
is $400 per course for 10 class sessions.   The remuneration
depends upon the qualifications of the instructor.   University
College does sponsor conferences and institutes, namely (in

the past year): "Incinerator Technology, Solid Wastes Technology," "You and Your Heart," "Man and Machine (liberal
arts)," and "Short Conferences with Professional Organizations." Clinicians for a conference are paid approximately
$100 per day, regardless of duration, using qualified faculty
members or visiting lecturers. University College is responsible for the Summer session.

IX. GENERAL

Students are being selected for participation on all
faculty committees in order to take part in discussions regarding the academic program. The evening division is receiving adequate support except in the area of scholarships.
The Dean of University College is responsible to the Provost.

X. STUDENT RECRUITMENT

Newspaper advertisements and feature stories are
used. Special motivational appeals have been developed by
a number of methods: participation in community and county
career and education clinics, talks to various groups, group
information sessions and college-for-a-day program for a-
dults.

Idaho State University
Pocatello, Idaho
Division of Continuing Education

Total Enrollment 8,500   Public Institution
Evening Enrollment 1,000   Semester System

I. ADMISSION POLICIES

There is no deadline for admission. A student may
register for credit courses before transcripts are submitted.
A student may take work for credit as a non-matriculating
or "special" student until ready to apply for graduation. A
student must be a high school graduate to qualify for admission. Students rejected for admission as regular students
are advised to apply as evening students and are automatically
accepted. Mail registration is used for off-campus courses
only. Probation and suspension policies are established by
the University. ACT or CEEB examinations are not required
for adults in the evening division. No special degree program

for adults is offered or considered for the future. The administration formulates all admission policies. Students are free to enroll in either day or evening classes or both. There is no orientation program for evening students.

II. TERMINOLOGY

Title of Division: Continuing Education. Defined: Evening and Extension Classes: on-going process furthering the educational aspirations and needs of the community.

III. FEES

There is no tuition differential for day and evening classes. No refunds are given after the third week; prior to the third week refunds are made on a sliding scale.

IV. FACULTY AND FACULTY RECRUITMENT

Final authority for hiring full and/or part-time faculty members lies with the departments. The Director of the Division can reject a faculty member assigned to teach evening classes. No full-time faculty teach evening classes exclusively. The Director cannot engage an instructor without the consent of the department head. No regular faculty meetings are held for evening faculty. Overloads for regular faculty members are allowed with the permission of the department chairmen. Salary for part-time faculty members ranges from $170 to $185 a semester hour.

V. SCHEDULING

The Director is responsible for the evening class schedule which is compiled from surveys, demand, and course sequence. Two nights per week are preferred for three-hour classes but the Division has been successful with the three-hour one-night classes also. Part-time students are eligible for the Dean's List based upon twelve hours/semester with a GPA of 3.33. Twelve students constitute a class. The instructor's compensation is reduced when he teaches a minimum size class--receiving all student fees paid if less than the normal salary.

VI. ORGANIZATIONAL STRUCTURE

The administrative staff consists of the Director who is responsible for 1000 students per semester plus an additional 1000 off-campus.

VII.   EDUCATIONAL TELEVISION PROGRAMS

The Division of Continuing Education does not offer
any educational television programs.

VIII.   NON-CREDIT PROGRAMS

Non-credit programs are offered in the areas of Business and Management, Engineering, Arts and Sciences, Education and other areas.   This program is expected to be
self-supporting.   The remuneration is $340 per course for
twelve class sessions depending upon the qualifications of the
instructor and the area of instruction.   The last three conferences held were: Association of Hospital Accountants with
seventy-five enrollees, Idaho State Vocational Educators with
500 people, and Conference for Nursing Home Administrators
with 75 enrollees.   Clinicians for a conference receive $100
a day or $500 per week.   The Division is not responsible
for the summer program.

IX.   GENERAL

Non-credit and/or credit programs are offered off-
campus for economically deprived populations.   Student participation in the academic program discussions is minimal.
Other innovative practices used at the institution include student evaluation of faculty.   No graduate programs for part-
time students are administered by the Evening Division.   Adequate support is given to the Evening Division.   The Director
is responsible to the Academic Vice-President.   All audio-
visual and other technical facilities are available to the Evening Division.

X.   STUDENT RECRUITMENT

Listings in sports or society newspaper sections and
radio announcements are used for student recruitment.   TV
has been tried with little indicated success.

Indiana Central College
Indianapolis, Indiana
Evening and Graduate Division

Total Enrollment 2, 393   Church-related Liberal Arts
Evening Enrollment, 1257   Semester System

I. ADMISSION POLICIES

There is a deadline for admission to evening classes; students may not register for credit courses without transcripts. Non-matriculating students may take a maximum of thirty hours. Admission requirements are high school graduation and successful completion of the SAT tests. Mail registration is used. Admission policies are set by the College Administration and Faculty. Some classes are mixed with day and evening students. There is no orientation for evening students. Probation and suspension are determined according to the academic index. Suspended students are ineligible to return. Non-degree and/or special students are suspended if after two semesters they have not earned an index of "C". Evening degree programs for adults are: Associate in Science and Associate in Finance at the undergraduate level and a Master of Arts at the graduate level. Fall semester enrollment was 397 part-time students. Distribution of requirements for the undergraduate degrees are thirteen hours of liberal arts and fifty-five hours of subject area; graduate degree is twenty hours liberal arts and eight hours subject area and four hours research with a total of seventy-two hours to complete the undergraduate degree and thirty-two hours to complete the graduate degree. Admission requirements for the special degree program at the undergraduate level is high school graduate; for the graduate level, college graduation, GRE score and recommendations. A special degree program for adults in Police Administration is under consideration.

II. TERMINOLOGY

Evening Division: An administrative term used to distinguish between the day and evening programs. Continuing Education defined: Credit and non-credit college work offered for those actively engaged in work and/or other full-time pursuits.

III. FEES

The Evening Division fees are less than day school.
No refunds made on tuition two weeks after classes begin.

IV. FACULTY AND FACULTY RECRUITMENT

Thirty-three percent of the faculty teaching evening
classes is full-time.   Final authority to hire full-time faculty
lies with the academic dean; part-time faculty, evening division dean.   Regular faculty meetings are held annually.   The
faculty is permitted to teach one overload course.   Salary
ranges from \$120 to \$185 per credit hour for part-time faculty.   Overloads are paid at \$190 per credit hour.

V.   SCHEDULING

The Dean of the Evening Division is responsible for
the schedule.   Class schedules compiled on the basis of regular rotation and special need.   Three-hour credit classes
are held one night a week, four and five hour classes meet
twice a week.   Part-time evening students are eligible for
the Dean's List after completing fifteen hours with a 10. 500.
Normally, ten students constitute a class.   If a class is
taught with less than 10, the instructor is paid 85% of the
tuition received for the class.

VI.   ORGANIZATIONAL STRUCTURE

The administrative staff consists of seven staff members and a teaching staff of seventy-one part-time faculty
members.   The Dean is responsible for faculty, staff, schedule and budget; the Director of Student Services is responsible
for admissions, counseling, matriculation and registering;
the Director of Non-Credit Programs is responsible for industrial relations, continuing education, etc.

VII.   EDUCATIONAL TELEVISION PROGRAMS

No educational television programs are offered.

VIII.   NON-CREDIT PROGRAMS

Non-credit programs are offered in the areas of Business and Management, Arts and Sciences and other areas.
These programs are expected to pay for themselves.   Faculty
receives remuneration at the rate of \$100 to \$400 per course

for six to fifteen class sessions.   The Division is responsible
for conferences and institutes such as the twelve supervisory
institutes,   twelve management development programs and six
women's programs offered during the past year.   Conferences are sponsored in affiliation with the University of
Chicago's Industrial Relations Center.

IX. GENERAL

The Master's degree program in the area of Liberal
Arts is offered in the evening.   The Evening Division is
receiving adequate support.   The Dean of the Evening Division is directly responsible to the President of the College.
Audio-visual aids such as films and film strips are used in
instruction.

X. STUDENT RECRUITMENT

Newspaper, radio and television publicity is used.
Public Relations special motivational appeals have been developed for industry, Chamber of Commerce, Kiwanis and
other such organizations.

Iona College
New Rochelle, New York
Division of Business Administration

Total Enrollment 3, 223   Private Institution
Evening Enrollment 856   Semester System

I. ADMISSION POLICIES

Deadline for application for admission to evening
classes is about one month prior to registration.   Students
may not register for credit courses without transcripts.
Students may not take courses for credit without being matriculated unless they have a letter of permission from their
college.   Admission requirements for regular students are
high school graduation and college board scores.   Mail registration is not used.   Admission policies are set by the
Committee on Administration.   Day and evening students may
enroll in the same classes.   There is no orientation for evening students.   A student is placed on probation as soon as
his index falls below 2. 0 (C); if he does not improve after
guidance and several warnings he faces suspension.   A B. A.

and a B. B. A. are offered for undergraduates, an MBA for graduates. Fall quarter enrollment was 300 undergraduates and 572 graduates. Distribution requirements for undergraduate degrees are: Liberal Arts 50%, Business 50%, Major in Business 18-24 credits in major field with a total of 128 hours to complete (48 hours to complete graduate work). Areas of concentration are Accounting - 24 credits, Finance - 18, Marketing - 18. A special degree program for adults is being considered in the School of General Studies. The Committee of the Faculty formulates the admission policies for regular degree students and the Admissions Committee formulates the requirements for non-matriculating, non-degree and/or special students.

II. TERMINOLOGY

Title of Division: Division of Business Administration. Defined: "It refers to the fact that a B. B. A. degree is offered in the evening."

III. FEES

Day students pay a "flat" tuition rate, evening students are charged by the semester hour. Refunds are made at a graduating percentage rate.

IV. FACULTY AND FACULTY RECRUITMENT

Approximately 90% of the evening classes are taught by full-time faculty members. Final authority to hire evening faculty lies with the Director of the Division of Business Administration. The Director can reject a faculty member who has been assigned to teach evening classes. No regular faculty meetings are held. No regular faculty are permitted overloads. Salaries range from $210 to $300 per credit hour.

V. SCHEDULING

The Director of the Division is responsible for the evening class schedule. Three-hour classes are scheduled two nights per week. Day and evening classes are equal in terms of quality. Part-time evening students are eligible for the Dean's List with a 3. 4. Eight students constitute a class. Instructor compensation is not reduced when teaching a class below minimum size.

VI.   ORGANIZATIONAL STRUCTURE

One staff member is the Director who coordinates the program after consultation with the Deans and department chairmen.   Teaching staff includes five full-time and seven part-time faculty members.

VII.   EDUCATIONAL TELEVISION PROGRAMS

No educational television programs are offered by the Division.

VIII.   NON-CREDIT PROGRAMS

Non-credit programs are not offered by the Division.

IX.   GENERAL

Students participate in discussions regarding academic programs through membership on certain College Committees. The Evening Division is receiving adequate support.   The Director of the Division is responsible to the Dean of the Day School.   The Division is responsible for the summer session.

X.   STUDENT RECRUITMENT

Newspaper and radio publicity is used.   Special motivational appeals are developed for industry and civic organizations.

Iowa State University
Ames, Iowa
University Extension

Total Enrollment 19, 620   Public, land-grant Institution
                                      Quarter System

I.   ADMISSION POLICIES

Applicants for admission must submit the required applications for admission and the necessary official transcripts to the Admissions Office at least ten days prior to the beginning of the orientation.   A student may register for credit courses without transcripts only as a "restricted non-

degree" student. Special students may take an unlimited
amount of hours for credit - the special student is considered
a student who is not working toward a degree and who takes
classes on a "sporadic" basis and is highly selective. Admission requirements for regular students include a certificate of high school credits, including a complete statement
of the applicant's high school record, rank in class, certification of graduation and standardized test scores. Applicant
normally must be in the upper half of his graduating class.
Mail registration is used. Retention policy requires a student to maintain a 2. 0 average. Admission policies are the
same for evening students as for regular students. Day and
evening students may enroll in the same classes. The Dean
of Admissions formulates the admission policies for regular
and special, non-degree students. The Dean of Graduate
College formulates the admission policies for the evening
graduate students. No orientation program is held for evening students. There is no special degree program for adults
at present but it is being considered for the near future.

II.   TERMINOLOGY

Title of Division: Extension Courses and Conferences
as a Department of University Extension. Defined: Administration and Supervision of all off-campus credit courses
and some off-campus non-credit classes and on-campus cred-
it/non-credit conferences and institutes. Adult education implies "Quantitative educational experiences as a vital part of
continuing education, i. e. , learning new skills, up-dating old
ones, new techniques, etc. Qualitative educational experiences
are the second part of any continuing education, personal development, growth and maturity. This can involve both positive and negative influences on us as individual members of
society.

III.   FEES

Day and evening students pay the same fees. Refund
policies permit ten percent of the total fee to be deducted
for each class meeting attended through the fifth class meeting. No refund will be made if a student withdraws after the
fifth class session.

IV.   FACULTY AND FACULTY RECRUITMENT

There is no policy regarding the percentage of evening
faculty members that must be full-time. No full-time faculty

members teach exclusively in the evening. No strict policy exists for faculty members teaching an overload - some faculty receive payment on an overload basis.

V. SCHEDULING

Departments are responsible for the evening class schedule. The schedule is compiled through the Admissions Office. Day and evening classes are equal in quality. Part-time students are not eligible for the Dean's List.

VI. ORGANIZATIONAL STRUCTURE

No information available.

VII. EDUCATIONAL TELEVISION PROGRAMS

University Extension offers courses in educational television. There is no distinguishing between "residence" and "extension." All credit courses are of the same quality on and/or off campus. I. S. U. records a number of credit and non-credit courses on video tape for replay at locations throughout the State. These courses do count toward a degree if approved by the Students Committee. Full-time faculty members are used for these courses. The faculty members do not receive additional remuneration for teaching TV courses. The Extension courses, conferences, on TV are registered the same as any on-campus registration. Both graduate and undergraduate courses are offered. The educational television courses are financed by the tuition and allocations. Closed circuit type is used.

VIII. NON-CREDIT PROGRAMS

Non-credit courses are offered in Engineering and Agriculture and are expected to pay for themselves. The faculty receives $25 for the first hour, $15 for the second hour to a maximum of $100 per day. The remuneration depends upon the qualifications of the instructor. The University Extension also sponsors conferences and institutes for which most of the clinicians do not receive compensation but speakers outside the University are paid (including travel). Most of the conferences originate in the various colleges or extension departments; University Extension does not often sponsor its own conferences. The University Extension is not responsible for the summer session at the institution. Approximately 180 on-campus non-credit short courses and

conferences were held in 1969-1970; over 100 off-campus
non-credit courses were held during the same period.

IX. GENERAL

Most departments have student representatives on
various departmental committees.   The Leader of Extension
courses and conferences reports to the Dean of University
Extension.

X. STUDENT RECRUITMENT

Newspaper, radio and television are used.   Contacts
are made with business and industry.

Jefferson State Junior College
Birmingham, Alabama
Division of Continuing Education

Total Enrollment 4, 500	Public Institution
Evening Enrollment 1, 800	Quarter System

I. ADMISSION POLICIES

The registration deadline is not rigidly enforced... a
student can register on registration night... however, the
official deadline is ten days in advance of registration for all
quarters.   The transcripts must be on file before the end of
the quarter.   Admission requirements for regular students
are high school diploma or GED equivalency.   "Special" students are those who are planning to transfer to a four-year
college but do not follow the Freshman Studies Program.
Students who are rejected for regular admission are not advised to apply for admission to evening classes.   Mail registration is not employed; however, the subject is under study.
Probation and suspension policies require a 2. 0 average -
under 1. 5 for a given quarter - constitutes dismissal after
two quarters of probation.   These policies apply to all students.   The ACT or CEEB examinations are not required for
adults in the evening division; Math and English placement
tests are required and used as a basis for placement and
advisement only.   The evening degree program for adults is
no different from the day degree program.   Number of students enrolled in the Fall Quarter 1970 totalled 180 full-time,

1621 part-time--all undergraduates. The distribution requirements for undergraduate degrees are: English, 20 quarter
hours, Fine Arts, 5 quarter hours, Speech, 5 quarter hours,
Social Sciences, 20 quarter hours, Natural Sciences/Math,
20 quarter hours, HPR, 6 quarter hours. These requirements are for University Parallel Programs. There are no
plans for offering special degree programs for adults in the
near future. The State Board of Education formulates the
admission policies for all students. All classes are open to
all students. The disadvantage of combined classes is that
with a high percent of young students, adults do not respond
freely in class; the advantage is that with the small number
of young students they are more serious and try to keep up
with the adults. An orientation program for evening students
is conducted one week before registration. There is no Evening Division Advisory Committee.

II. TERMINOLOGY

Title of Division: Division of Continuing Education.
Defined: College credit programs after 4:00 p. m. as well
as all non-credit courses regardless of the time. Continuing
Education defined: Any learning experience that takes place
after the normal years for high school and college.

III. FEES

The fee for full-time students is $67. 50 per quarter
(12 or more hours) and part-time students pay $33 for five
hours, $63 for ten hours. Most evening students attend
part-time. The fee is set by the State Board of Education.
Full-time students who drop classes but stay in school are
refunded on a sliding scale--part-time students receive no
refund.

IV. FACULTY AND FACULTY RECRUITMENT

No policy is in existence for the percentage of faculty
for evening classes. Approximately 60% of the evening faculty members are full-time. The Academic Divisional Chairmen have the final authority for hiring faculty members and
the Continuing Education chairman has the final authority to
hire part-time faculty. The Director of the Evening Division
may reject a faculty member who has been assigned to teach
evening classes. Full-time faculty members are employed
to teach exclusively in the evening and are responsible (administratively) to the Director, and, (academically) to the

Divisional chairmen. The Director may engage an instructor
without the consent of the department head. Regular faculty
meetings are held twice quarterly. The State Board of Education disallows payment for overloads--instructors teaching
non-credit courses are given reduced loads. Recruitment is
not a budget item. Salary range for part-time faculty is:
B. A., $400; M. A., $450; M. A. + 30, $500; Ph. D., $550.
Faculty receive no payment for overloads.

V.   SCHEDULING

The Director is responsible for the evening class
schedule and has the authority to make revisions as necessary.
The five-hour classes meet two nights per week. Day and
evening classes compare equally in terms of quality. Part-
time evening students are not eligible for the Dean's List.
(requires 12 qtr. hrs. and a 3.0 average on a 4.0 scale.)
Generally, twenty students must register to constitute a class
except in specialized areas where twelve are required.

VI.   ORGANIZATIONAL STRUCTURE

The Continuing Education program has an administrative staff headed by a Director together with a Director of
Adult Education and four staff members. The teaching staff
consists of twenty-four full-time faculty members and forty-
eight part-time faculty members. Other staff members are:
Director of Extension, Registrar (evening) and Director of
Student Services. It is recommended that the following staff
members are required to accommodate certain enrollments:
300-500 students - 1; 800 students - 2; 5000 students - 6.
These recommended numbers are assuming that there is only
one campus location.

VII.   EDUCATIONAL TELEVISION PROGRAMS

The Division of Continuing Education does not have
educational television courses.

VIII.   NON-CREDIT PROGRAMS

A budget is provided for non-credit courses and programs are offered in the areas of Business and Management
and Arts and Sciences. Faculty members receive $225 for
ten two-hour class sessions. The Evening Division is not
responsible for the summer session.

IX. GENERAL

Credit and non-credit courses are being offered in two locations off-campus for the economically deprived populations. Students are surveyed at least once each year to obtain student opinions regarding class hours, days, breaks and schedules together with a faculty evaluation form. The Evening Division is not receiving adequate support in comparison with the day program. Not all top administrators recognize the need for adult education programs. The Director is responsible to the Dean of Instruction and the Dean of Students. Films and TV are used as audio-visual aids.

X. STUDENT RECRUITMENT

Student recruitment is handled through publicity in local newspapers, radio and television. Public relations efforts are directed toward industry and civic organizations.

The Johns Hopkins University
Baltimore, Maryland
Evening College

Total Enrollment 11, 800   Private Institution
Evening Enrollment 7, 500   Semester System

I. ADMISSION POLICIES

There is no deadline for application for admission-- applications are not accepted unless they can be processed before registration however. Undergraduate students may register for credit courses without transcripts. There is no limit to the amount of work taken as non-matriculating students; only sixteen credits taken under that status may be applied toward a certificate or degree. Admission requirements are high school graduation, in good standing at previous college attended and specific course prerequisites. Mail registration is used. Students must maintain satisfactory academic and conduct records. All records are reviewed each term by the Academic Standing Committee. Students at the graduate and undergraduate level are dropped or placed on probation if the academic performance falls below an acceptable level for the particular program. Day and evening students do not enroll in the same classes because the programs are basically different and are constructed for the

particular public they serve.   There is no orientation program for evening students.   Nineteen undergraduate and fourteen graduate programs are offered to adults in the Evening
College.   These are only offered in the evening.   Enrollment
for fall was: part-time 5, 480, undergraduate 3, 753 and
graduates 1, 727.   A special degree for graduate students is
offered with the total number of hours variable with each
program.   Admission requirements are the same.   New programs will be added as the ability and demand grow.   The
Evening College administrative staff, with the Advisory
Board's approval, formulates the admission policies for the
evening students.

II.   TERMINOLOGY

Title of Division: Evening College.   Defined: A program for part-time higher education for adults.   Emphasis
is placed on work toward certificates and degrees.

III.   FEES

Tuition is $30 per semester credit in the evening and
$80 per contact hour during the day (part-time).   No refunds
are made after classes begin.

IV.   FACULTY AND FACULTY RECRUITMENT

Approximately 40% of the faculty teaching evening
classes are full-time.   Final authority to hire evening faculty lies with the Dean of the Evening College.   No full-time
faculty members teach exclusively in the evening.   Regular
faculty meetings are held usually in the fall.   Faculty members who teach courses on an overload basis are paid accordingly but are not required to teach more than one course
per term during the academic year.   Approximately 2. 5% of
the budget is spent on faculty recruiting.

V.   SCHEDULING

The Dean of the Evening College is responsible for
the evening class schedule.   The Dean has the authority to
revise the schedule when necessary.   Three-hour classes are
scheduled one and two nights per week.   "The day and evening programs are different and they are offered for very
different publics.   The basic philosophy is quite different for
the two programs. "   Both programs are of very high quality.
There is no Dean's List.

VI. ORGANIZATIONAL STRUCTURE

The administrative staff consists of eight staff members. The Dean has overall responsibility for the operation of the Evening College, academic and administrative leadership, planning programs, outside and faculty relations, budget, executive operations within the University; the Associate Dean is responsible for the day-to-day operations of the program, particular direction of the graduate programs, program planning, advising students, faculty and staff members, recruitment of faculty and general operation of the program and admission of graduate students. There is a Director for each of the major divisions within the Evening College. They plan the program and staff within the particular division, new programs within the division and student advising. There is a particular section of the University Registrar's office devoted to the Evening College work where registration and records are handled. The Administrative Assistants have general administrative duties within the Evening College. Administrative staff required for various enrollments depend entirely upon the administrative organization and the philosophy under which it operates. The teaching staff consists of 321 instructors.

VII. EDUCATIONAL TELEVISION PROGRAMS

No educational television programs are offered.

VIII. NON-CREDIT PROGRAMS

Non-credit programs are offered in the areas of arts and sciences and speed reading. There is a budget but the program is expected to pay for itself. Remuneration for instructors is on a scale per course for ten to fifteen class sessions, depending upon qualifications of the instructor as well as the area of instruction. No conferences are sponsored by the Evening College. The salary scale depends upon education and full-time position--from $225 up per semester hour of contact. Approximately ten students must register to constitute a class. The Evening College is responsible for the summer session.

IX. GENERAL

Some surveys are done from time to time which enable students to participate in discussion regarding the academic programs. The Evening College is essentially one of-

fering credit courses to be applied toward degrees and certificates; graduate programs are being stressed more and
more.   The Dean of the Evening College is responsible to
the President of the University.

X. STUDENT RECRUITMENT

Newspaper publicity (especially during the summer
and before major registration periods) is widely used. Special motivational appeals have been developed for industry,
especially with training directors and professional organizations.

Joint University Center (MSU/UT)
Memphis, Tennessee

Total Enrollment 26, 000   Public Institution
Evening Enrollment 5, 000   Quarter System

I. ADMISSION POLICIES

The deadline for application for admission to evening
classes for all students is before the first class meets for
all quarters.   A student may register for credit courses before transcripts are submitted (tentative pending receipt of
transcripts) and may take ninety quarter hours for credit as
a "special" student.   The requirements for non-matriculating
students are: first-time students, over 21 years of age,
good standing at previously attended colleges or universities.
The requirements for regular students are: first-time students, in-state high school grade point average of 2. 25 on a
4 point scale or 17 ACT composite; transfer, thirty-six
quarter hours with a GPA of 1. 5, eighty-four quarter hours
with a GPA of 2. 0.   Students who are rejected for admission
as regular students are not advised to apply as evening students and are not automatically accepted as such.   Mail
registration is used as follows: two weeks before "in person" registration, student must write, telephone, or visit
office to get forms; one week before "in person" registration
forms must be in the office.   Probation consists of failing
majority of courses any one quarter and dismissal occurs
when thirty-six hours are attempted with a GPA of less than
1. 5, eighty-four hours with less than 2. 0 GPA--but there
are exceptions for special cases.   Non-degree student requirements are the same as for degree students.   The ACT is not

required for special students but is required for all degree
students. The Center does not offer any degree--a student
may earn ninety quarter hours of transfer credit. The number of full-time students enrolled during the Fall Quarter
was 39 full-time and 1,150 part-time (undergraduate 1,159,
graduate 30). Consideration is being given to a special degree program for undergraduate adults. The Admissions
Office at the University of Tennessee-Knoxville formulates
the admission policies for the evening students. No day
classes are offered except on Saturday mornings.

II. TERMINOLOGY

Title of Division: Joint University Center (MSU/UT).
Defined: The Joint Center grew out of a former extension
center - offering only evening classes and no degree. The
Center is supported one-half by Memphis State University
and one-half by the University of Tennessee. Continuing Education defined: Any educational activity undertaken by an
adult who has finished his full-time, formal, traditional
schooling; includes conferences, self-study, seminars, lectures, educational television and is a process, not a teaching method.

III. FEES

The Center provides for a partial refund, the amount
of which is determined by the number of classes in which
the student remains enrolled.

IV. FACULTY AND FACULTY RECRUITMENT

The percentage of full-time faculty teaching in the
evening is approximately 8% by head and 28% based on total
classes offered. The resident department heads have final
authority for hiring full and/or part-time faculty. Faculty
are not assigned to classes by any one person; the process
is initiated by the Director. Full-time faculty members are
employed who teach exclusively in the evening. These faculty members are responsible to the Director. Regular faculty meetings with evening faculty members are usually held
prior to the Fall Quarter. Credit or non-credit courses are
counted as part of the regular load; participating in institutes,
seminars, conferences is encouraged but cannot exceed eight
hours a week (averaged over nine months). Percentage of
budget for recruitment: direct costs - none, indirect costs
(administrative time, etc.) - 10%. There is no salary

range - $450 for thirty hours class instruction with no incre-
ment added for degrees or professional rank. The same
applies to overloads.

V. SCHEDULING

The Director is responsible for the evening class
schedule which is compiled by full-time faculty and administrative staff. The Director has the authority to revise,
make additions or deletions to the schedule. Three-hour
classes are scheduled one night per week. Research is being conducted by one staff member working on his doctoral
dissertation concerning selection of courses by administrators.
No comparison has been made between day and evening
classes. Part-time evening students are not eligible for the
Dean's List. Total enrollment which must average sixteen
students ranges from four to forty students. The instructor's
compensation is not reduced if he teaches a class below minimum size.

VI. ORGANIZATIONAL STRUCTURE

The administrative staff consists of four staff members and the teaching staff consists of six full-time and 65
part-time faculty members. The institution does not have
academic or administrative autonomy. Duties and responsibilities of the staff include overall responsibilities by the
Director including teacher recruiting, budget preparation,
course selection in adult education; the Assistant Director
recruits teachers and supervises admissions, publicity (mailing lists) and librarian; the Associate Director directs non-
credit programs and conferences, organizes and creates programs, recruits and supervises teachers and prepares publicity; Assistant Business Manager supervises cashier and
bookstore management, acts as liaison with building manager
and purchasing. The ideal size of an administrative staff
depends greatly on assistance received from parent institution, e. g. , who handles registration, develops publicity,
oversees admission and records, etc. ; however, for an enrollment of 800-1000 four staff members should be sufficient;
5000 enrollment five staff members.

VII. EDUCATIONAL TELEVISION PROGRAMS

The Joint University Center (MSU/UT) does not offer
any educational television courses.

VIII. NON-CREDIT PROGRAMS

Non-credit courses are offered in the areas of Business and Management, Arts and Sciences, Engineering and other areas. There is a budget for non-credit programs. Faculty receive $450 per course for ten three-hour sessions. Remuneration does not depend upon the qualifications of the instructor or upon the area of instruction. No conferences and institutes are sponsored by the Center.

IX. GENERAL

No off-campus courses offered for economically deprived population are in progress. Students participate only informally in the academic program. Free noon-time lecture series are offered Monday and Thursday each week. No graduate program is offered for part-time students. The administration recognizes the need for adult education programs. The Director is responsible to the Management Committee comprised of three members from Memphis State and three from the University of Tennessee. The following audiovisual aids are used: video tape TV, electro-writer, perceptoscope (brand name) to teach reading, 16 m. m. film projector, slide projector, record player, etc.

X. STUDENT RECRUITMENT

Newspaper and radio are used for publicity. Special direct mail to industry and organizations (mostly trade/professional organizations) is used as publicity.

<u>University of Kentucky</u>
Lexington, Kentucky
Evening Class Program

Total Enrollment 17, 000   Public Institution
Evening Enrollment 1, 350   Semester System

I. ADMISSION POLICIES

There is no deadline for admission to evening classes. Students may register for credit courses before transcripts are submitted. "Special" or non-matriculating students may take work for credit with no limitations. Non-degree students must be eligible for credit at time of enrollment in

order to meet admission requirements. Evening students
must maintain a 2. 0 grade point average. There is no mail
registration. No ACT or CEEB examinations are required
for admission. There is no special degree program for
adults and none are being considered. Admission policies
are set by the Dean of Admissions. Day and evening students may enroll in the same classes if space is available.
No orientation program is held for evening students. No
evening advisory committee has been formed.

II. TERMINOLOGY

Title of Division: Evening Class Program, University
Extension. Defined: Non-degree students meeting classes
after 5:00 p. m. Continuing Education defined: An educational program that includes both credit and non-credit
classes.

III. FEES

There is no fee differential between day and evening
classes. Refunds are made on the basis of one-half of tuition from one day of class to mid-semester.

IV. FACULTY AND FACULTY RECRUITMENT

The Chairmen and the Dean of the respective colleges
have final authority for hiring full and/or part-time faculty
members for evening classes. The Director may not reject
a faculty member who has been assigned to teach an evening
class. No full-time faculty members teach exclusively in
the evening. The Director may not hire an instructor without the consent of the department or Dean. No regular faculty meetings are held for evening faculty. All faculty members teaching in the Evening Class Program are on an overload basis. No budget is spent for recruiting. The overload pay is based upon course level--100-400 level $220/cr. ,
400-500 level $240/cr. , 600-800 level $260/cr.

V. SCHEDULING

The Director is responsible for evening class schedules. All schedules are approved by the chairman and Dean
of the respective departments prior to final compilation. The
Director does have the authority to revise the schedule. All
three-hour classes are scheduled two nights per week. Part-
time students are not eligible for the Dean's List. Twelve

or fifteen students must register to constitute a class. Instructor's compensation is not reduced if he teaches a class
below the minimum size.

VI.   ORGANIZATIONAL STRUCTURE

The administrative staff consists of two staff members and the teaching staff consists of 75-90 part-time faculty
members.   The Director is responsible for preparation of
course offerings, counseling, registration of students and
has complete financial responsibility.   The Director is assisted by a secretary.

VII.   EDUCATIONAL TELEVISION PROGRAMS

There are no educational television programs offered.

VIII.   NON-CREDIT PROGRAMS

Non-credit programs are offered in the areas of Business and Management, Engineering and other areas.   These
programs are expected to support themselves.   Remuneration
for faculty (full or part-time) is $450-$500 per course depending upon the area of instruction.   The Division does not
sponsor conferences and institutes.

IX.   GENERAL

No graduate program for part-time students is administered by the Division.   In general, the Division does
not receive adequate support in comparison with the day program.   The Director is responsible to the Dean of University
Extension.   Audio-visual aids are available to evening classes.

X.   STUDENT RECRUITMENT

Newspaper and radio publicity are used for student
recruiting.

LaSalle College
Philadelphia, Pennsylvania
Evening Division

Total Enrollment 6, 500 (Day /Eve)   Church-related Institution
Evening Enrollment 3, 148   Semester System

I.   ADMISSION POLICIES

Deadline for application for admission is eight days before classes begin. Students may not register for credit courses without transcripts. Non-degree students may take a maximum of eight hours of credit work and must already have a bachelor's degree. Students must maintain 1.00 after 30 semester hours; 1.50 after 60 hours; 1.75 after 90 hours. There is no special degree program for adults. Admission policies are set by the Evening Division Committee. Day and evening students may enroll in the same classes when courses correspond. Orientation for evening students is held before registration.

II.   TERMINOLOGY

Title of Division: LaSalle College Evening Division. Defined: Regular collegiate degree-oriented programs offered in the evening.

III.   FEES

Day school students pay an annual fee of $1,600; evening students pay $38 per credit hour. Refunds of 90% are made in the first week of classes; 80% in the second week; 70% in the third week; 60% in the fourth week; 50% in the fifth week; 40% in the sixth week; 30% in the seventh week; none thereafter.

IV.   FACULTY AND FACULTY RECRUITMENT

Thirty-three percent of the faculty teaching evening classes are full-time. The final authority to hire evening faculty lies with the Dean of the Evening Division. Some full-time faculty members teach exclusively in the evening and are responsible to the Dean of the Evening Division. The salary range for part-time faculty is $650 through $1,344 for 3 credit hour courses; the range is $864 through $1,792 for 4 credit hour courses. No overloads are permitted. Generally ten or more students are required to constitute a class. The instructor's compensation is not reduced when he teaches a class below minimum size. Regular faculty meetings are held.

V.   SCHEDULING

The Dean of the Evening Division is responsible for

the evening class schedule.   Three credit hour classes are
scheduled two nights per week.   Part-time evening students
are eligible for the Dean's List after completing 30 hours
with a minimum of 3. 40.

VI.   ORGANIZATIONAL STRUCTURE

The administrative staff consists of three members:
the Dean is responsible for all academic matters, and, for
the quality and performance of the faculty, students and curriculum; the Director of Admissions is responsible for
scheduling and processing all admissions; the Registrar
is responsible for all student records.   The teaching staff
consists of 83 full-time and 129 part-time faculty members.

VII.   EDUCATIONAL TELEVISION PROGRAMS

The Evening Division does not offer an educational
television program.

VIII.   NON-CREDIT PROGRAMS

The Evening Division does not offer any non-credit
programs.

IX.   GENERAL

Students participate in discussions concerning academic
programs through the Academic Affairs Committee and Student Congress.   The Evening Division is receiving adequate
support.   The Dean of the Evening Division is responsible to
the Academic Vice-President.   Audio-visual instructional aids
are available for evening classes.

X.   STUDENT RECRUITMENT

Newspaper and radio publicity are used.   Special motivational appeals have been developed for industry.

Louisiana State University
Baton Rouge, Louisiana
University College

Total Enrollment 18, 887   Public Institution
Evening Enrollment 1, 381   Semester System

I. ADMISSION POLICIES

There is no deadline date for application for admission
to evening classes.   Non-degree students may register for
credit courses without transcripts.   A total of nine semester
hours may be taken as a non-degree student in summer only.
Admission requirements for non-matriculating students is a
statement of good standing from the last college attended.
No mail registration is used.   A "C" average must be maintained by all students.   If a student drops ten quality points
below 2. 0 he is placed on probation.   If he does not make a
"C" average after being placed on probation, he is dropped
from the University.   The Bachelor of Science in General
Studies and Bachelor of Science in Law Enforcement are offered as special degree programs for adults.   Enrollment
for the Bachelor of Science in General Studies program is
1, 381.   Students must have forty semester hours in one area
of Humanities, Social Sciences or Natural Sciences, and must
have eighteen hours in each of the other two areas.   The remaining hours are electives to complete a total of 128 hours
for the degree.   Admission policies are set by the Director
of the University College.   Day and evening students may enroll in the same class.   No orientation program is held for
evening students.

II.   TERMINOLOGY

Title of Division: University College.   Defined: Full-
time college for students seeking a General Studies Degree or
a Degree in Law Enforcement.   The term Continuing Education may be applied to any type of education for students or
individuals not enrolled on a full-time basis.

III.   FEES

There is no fee differential between day and evening
classes.   Refunds of 90% are made before classes begin;
75% during the first two weeks; 50% during the third and
fourth week; none thereafter.

IV.   FACULTY AND FACULTY RECRUITMENT

Final authority for hiring evening faculty lies with the
Office of Academic Affairs.   The Director of University College may not reject a faculty member who has been assigned
to teach evening classes.   No full-time faculty members
teach exclusively in the evenings.   Faculty members may

teach an equivalent of three credit hours on an overload basis. No budget funds are used for recruitment purposes.

V. SCHEDULING

Department Chairmen are responsible for the evening class schedule. Three-hour classes are scheduled one and two nights per week. Part-time evening students are eligible for the Dean's List with a grade point average of 3. 5.

VI. ORGANIZATIONAL STRUCTURE

The University College has an administrative staff of three and one-half members. As a part of the state university system the institution has administrative autonomy. The University College is headed by a Director who is responsible for the organization and administration of the College.

VII. EDUCATIONAL TELEVISION PROGRAMS

University College does not sponsor any educational television programs.

VIII. NON-CREDIT PROGRAMS

University College does not sponsor any non-credit programs and is not responsible for the summer session.

IX. GENERAL

The Evening Division is receiving adequate support. The evening students have no opportunity to express opinions regarding academic programs. The Director of University College is responsible to the Dean of Academic Affairs.

X. STUDENT RECRUITMENT

Special motivational appeals are made to industry.

Louisiana State University in New Orleans
New Orleans, Louisiana
Evening Division

Total Enrollment 9, 000   Public Institution
Evening Enrollment 1, 200   Semester System

I.   ADMISSION POLICIES

There is no deadline for application for admission to
evening classes.   Students may register for credit courses
before transcripts are submitted.   A total of twelve hours
may be taken as a "special" student.   Admission requirements for regular and non-matriculating students (resident of
state) include a statement of good standing from the last institution attended.   The admission requirements vary for out-
of-state students.   The ACT is required for admission but
is not used as a basis for admission but for advisement.   No
mail registration is used.   The Board of Supervisors of the
University formulate the admission policies.   Day and evening students may enroll in the same classes.   The policies
regarding probation and suspension for degree students are
the same as for day students and depend upon the student's
status in the Junior Division or a Senior College.   An orientation program for evening students is held just prior to
registration.

II.   TERMINOLOGY

Title of Division: Evening Division.   Defined: The
administrative unit which keeps the academic records of students taking classes at night.   Continuing Education defined:
Continuing Education is a life-long project--either for credit
or non-credit, either formally or informally.

III.   FEES

There is no fee differential for day and evening
classes.   A refund for reduction of hours carried is made
if the drop occurs before the date specified to add courses
for credit.

IV.   FACULTY AND FACULTY RECRUITMENT

All evening classes are taught by the regular faculty.
The Dean of each college hires his own faculty.   No full-
time faculty members teach exclusively in the evening.   No
regular faculty meetings are held for the evening faculty.
The Dean of each senior college is responsible for any overloads taught by his own faculty.   The salary range for part-
time faculty varies with rank and course load as determined
by the department chairman.   No salary is paid for overloads.   Eleven students must register for an undergraduate
course to constitute a class.   The instructor's compensation

is not reduced when he teaches a class below the minimum
size.   Small classes are cancelled.

V.   SCHEDULING

The department chairmen submit a schedule for evening classes to the Dean of Academic Affairs; approval follows.   Three-hour classes are scheduled two nights per week.
There is no difference in quality between day and evening
classes.   Part-time students (evening) are not eligible for
the Dean's List.

VI.   ORGANIZATIONAL STRUCTURE

The size of the administrative staff of the Evening
Division is two, namely; Director who administers the duties
of the Evening Division and a Counselor.   Faculty members: 97.

VII.   EDUCATIONAL TELEVISION PROGRAMS

There are no educational television programs offered.

VIII.   NON-CREDIT PROGRAMS

The Evening Division does not offer any non-credit
courses.

IX.   GENERAL

Students do not participate in any discussions regarding academic programs.   In general, the evening division
could use more support in terms of additional programs and
financing.   The Director of the Evening Division is responsible to the Dean of Academic Affairs.   The Evening Division
is not responsible for the summer session at the institution.

X.   STUDENT RECRUITMENT

Newspaper articles are used for publicity but no advertising is permitted.   Public service announcements are
prepared for radio and television.

<u>University of Louisville</u>
Louisville, Kentucky
University College

Total Enrollment 10, 000   Private Institution
Evening Enrollment 2, 300   Semester System

I. ADMISSION POLICIES

There is no deadline for application for admission to
evening classes.   Non-degree students may register for
credit courses without transcripts and may take a maximum
of twelve hours.   Regular students must have been in the
upper half of their high school graduating class.   There is
no special degree program for adults.   Admission policies
are set by the faculty.   Day and evening students may register in the same class.   Orientation for evening students is
held during the Fall and the Spring.   Mail registration is
used only for academically qualified students.   Effective
August 1970 the University converted to a 4. 0 system.   Ten
points deficit is probationary status; excess of twenty points
deficit is dismissal.

II. TERMINOLOGY

Title of Division: University College.   Defined: Encompasses all Continuing Education Programs.

III. FEES

Evening students do not pay the student activity fees
that day students pay.   Refunds are made on a graduating
percentage basis.

IV. FACULTY AND FACULTY RECRUITMENT

Approximately 40% of the faculty teaching evening
classes are full-time.   Final authority to hire evening faculty lies with the Dean of University College, and he may
reject a faculty member assigned to teach evening classes
or engage an instructor without the consent of the department chairmen.   Regular faculty meetings are held every
Fall.   Each full-time faculty member may teach one course
per semester on an overload basis and may participate in
non-credit courses as needed.   There is no budget for faculty recruiting.   Salaries range from $215 to $305 per credit
hour.   Only full-time faculty teach overloads.

V. SCHEDULING

The Dean of University College is responsible for the evening class schedule and has the authority to revise as needed. Three-hour classes are scheduled both one and two nights a week. Part-time evening students are eligible for the Dean's List with a "B" average after completing seven hours. Five or six students are needed to constitute a class. The instructor's compensation is reduced if he teaches a class below minimum size; 74% of resident rate tuition for each student and usually it is handled on an individual basis.

VI. ORGANIZATIONAL STRUCTURE

The administrative staff consists of fifteen staff members and the teaching staff consists of 157 full-time and 123 part-time faculty members. The institution does have academic and administrative autonomy. The Kentucky State Council on Higher Education is the general policy control for the university's organization. The Dean supervises all aspects of the University College program; the Assistant Dean plays an advisory role in policy and supervision of faculty relations, students and administrative institutions within the University; the Director of Audio-Visual Program and the Director of Upward Bound Program, the Director of Non-Credit Programs have the responsibility of administering selection and operation of non-credit programs. The ideal size of administrative staff to administer to 2000 students would be six.

VII. EDUCATIONAL TELEVISION PROGRAMS

A credit course is offered in commercial television but no additional television programs are offered.

VIII. NON-CREDIT PROGRAMS

Non-credit programs are offered in the areas of Business and Management, Arts and Sciences, Education and Engineering. A budget is provided for the non-credit programs. Remuneration to faculty for teaching a non-credit course varies and does depend upon the qualifications of the instructor as well as the area of instruction. The University College does sponsor workshops, conferences and institutes such as: Kentucky Association for Children with Learning Disabilities, Management Techniques for Hospital Supervisors,

Television Seminar, Kentucky Youth Conference, Leadership
Training Institute, etc.   Clinician fees vary from conference
to conference.   University College is responsible for the
summer session.

IX.   GENERAL

The evening division is receiving adequate support.
The students have little opportunity to participate in discussions regarding the academic programs.   The Dean of University College is responsible to the President of the University.   Audio-visual aids are available for evening classes.

X.   STUDENT RECRUITMENT

Newspaper and radio publicity is used for student recruitment.

Loyola University
Chicago, Illinois
University College

Total Enrollment 14, 669   Church-related Institution
Evening Enrollment 2, 534   Semester System

I.   ADMISSION POLICIES

Deadline for application for admission for evening students is registration day.   Students may register for credit
courses without transcripts.   Admission requirements are
high school graduation or equivalent or in good standing at
college previously attended.   There is no limit to the amount
of work as a non-matriculating student, only that he remains
in good academic standing.   Mail registration is used.   Students must maintain a 2. 0 average to remain in good standing.   Students on probation at another institution must wait
one year before making application to University College.
The same applies to students dropped for poor scholarship.
Loyola students who have been put on probation or dropped
for poor scholarship must wait six months prior to making
application to the division.   There is no special degree program for adults in the evening.   Admission policies are set
by the Committee on Admissions.   Day and evening students
may enroll in the same class with permission.

II. TERMINOLOGY

Title of Division: University College. Defined: The part-time, degree-granting division which offers classes in the late afternoon, evenings, and on Saturdays.

III. FEES

Day students are charged $50 per semester hour; evening students, $40. Refunds are based upon a graduated percentage basis.

IV. FACULTY AND FACULTY RECRUITMENT

Approximately 50% of the evening faculty are full-time. Final authority to hire evening faculty lies with the Committee on Faculty appointments. The Dean of the University College can reject a faculty member assigned to teach evening classes. The salary range for full-time faculty is $500-$600 per three-hour course--the same applies to part-time faculty. Overloads for faculty members are not permitted. Ten students constitute a class but an instructor's compensation is not reduced when teaching a class below the minimum size.

V. SCHEDULING

The Dean of the University College is responsible for the evening class schedule. Three-hour classes are scheduled both one and two nights per week. Part-time evening students are eligible for the Dean's List and a 3.2 or better after twenty semester hours is required.

VI. ORGANIZATIONAL STRUCTURE

The Evening Division has four staff members which include a Dean, an Assistant Dean and two support staff. The Evening Division has a teaching staff of ninety-three full-time and seventy part-time faculty members. The recommended size of an administrative staff of an evening credit program would be one staff member for an enrollment of 300; six staff members for an enrollment of 5000. The Division is responsible for the summer session.

VII. EDUCATIONAL TELEVISION PROGRAMS

No educational television programs are offered at the

University College.

VIII.   NON-CREDIT PROGRAMS

Non-credit courses are not offered at University College.

IX.   GENERAL

The Evening Division is receiving adequate support. The Dean of the University College is responsible to the Academic Vice-President.

X.   STUDENT RECRUITMENT

Newspaper and radio publicity are used.

Loyola University
New Orleans, Louisiana
Evening Division

Total Enrollment 4, 500   Church-related Institution
Evening Enrollment 1, 300   Semester System

I.   ADMISSION POLICIES

There is no deadline for application for admission and students may register without transcripts. Admission requirements are high school diploma, examination or advanced standing. Admission policies are set by the University Committee on Admission Policies and Standards. Students falling below 2. 0 are placed or admitted on "probation." Those failing to remove the deficiency within the stated period, or who fail to make reasonable progress in that direction are excluded. Bachelor degrees are offered to evening students only in Social Studies, Liberal Studies, Commercial Science and Police Science. The distribution requirements for these undergraduate degrees include: English, 12 hours; Math, 6 hrs., Speech, 3 hrs., History, 6 hrs., Language, 6 hrs., Science, 8 hrs.; field of concentration twenty-one hours with some variation. The areas of concentration include Social Studies, Humanities and Business - a total of 128 semester hours is required for the degree. Admission requirements for the special degree program includes fifteen acceptable high school units, advanced college standing, or by examination. Day and evening students may enroll in the same class only with the permission of the Director of the Evening Division. Orientation for evening students is held the day before the opening of each semester.

II. TERMINOLOGY

Title of Division: Evening Division which like other schools and colleges is answerable to the Academic Vice-President. Continuing Education is credit or non-credit (creditable courses not now being applied to a degree) courses scheduled by adults.

III. FEES

Part-time day students pay $50 per semester hour; evening students pay $22 per semester hour. Refunds of 80% are made during the first week; 60% during the second and third week; 40% during the third to fifth week and none thereafter.

IV.   FACULTY AND FACULTY RECRUITMENT

Ten faculty members teaching evening classes are from the day faculty. Five full-time faculty members teach exclusively in the evening. Regular faculty meetings are held each semester. Faculty members are paid $500 for three-semester hour courses taught on an overload basis. The budget for recruitment is not included in the Evening Division budget - it is handled by the Academic Vice-President through his budget.

V. SCHEDULING

The Dean of the Evening Division is responsible for the evening class schedule and has the authority to revise or make additions as needed. Three-hour classes are scheduled both one and two nights per week. Part-time evening students are eligible for the Dean's List after completing nine semester hours with a 3. 0 average.

VI. ORGANIZATIONAL STRUCTURE

The Evening Division has an administrative staff of three members; with a teaching staff of ten full-time and sixty-five part-time faculty members. The Division is headed by a Dean with two assistant Deans who counsel students in regard to degree requirement fulfillment.

VII.   EDUCATIONAL TELEVISION PROGRAMS

The Evening Division does not sponsor educational
television courses.

VIII.   NON-CREDIT PROGRAMS

All regular courses may be taken for non-credit.   No
special non-credit programs are offered.   The Evening Division is responsible for the summer session.

IX.   GENERAL

Candidates for graduation make suggestions for future
schedules.   The Evening Division is receiving adequate support.   The Dean of the Evening Division is responsible to
the Academic Vice-President.   Audio-visual aids are available for evening classes.

X.   STUDENT RECRUITMENT

Newspaper, radio and television publicity are used.

University of Maine
Portland, Maine
Continuing Education

Total Enrollment 31, 000   State Institution
Evening Enrollment 21, 000   Semester System

I.   ADMISSION POLICIES

There is no deadline for application for admission to
evening classes.   A student may register for credit courses
before transcripts are submitted.   A student generally takes
30 hours of work for credit as non-matriculating or "special"
student.   The requirements for admission for non-matriculating or "special" students are high school diploma and fulfill
any prerequisite the course may require.   Regular students
meet the university admission requirements or complete the
deferred degree program of thirty hours selected by the academic unit.   Students who are rejected for admission as regular students may be advised to apply as evening students;

and are automatically accepted.   Mail registration is used
for matriculated students who have been approved by an academic advisor.   Policies regarding probation and suspension
are the same as those for the day program for degree students; non-degree students are reviewed by the Continuing
Education Division Counsellor and staff.   The ACT or CEEB
are not required for adults in the evening division.   No other
tests are required.   Evening programs for adults are the
same as in the day.   There are plans for offering a special
degree program for adults in the evening session.   The admission policies for evening students are formulated by the
faculty with advice from the CED staff.   Many day students
are enrolled in the evening programs.   This helps to bridge
the generation gap; learning from each other.   There is no
orientation program for evening students.

II.   TERMINOLOGY

Title of Division: Continuing Education Division.
Defined: Programs offered in the late afternoon and evening
primarily for the adult--on and off-campus.   In addition, responsible for developing and administering seminars, short
courses and workshops in response to the community's needs.
Continuing Education defined: Credit and non-credit courses,
seminars, workshops offered for adults, primarily in the
late afternoon and evening.

III.   FEES

For the part-time student there is no difference in
fees.   The maximum tuition is the same.   A registration
fee is retained before classes begin.   One-half is retained
when dropping out the first month, one-third returned during
the second week, one-sixth returned after the third week,
no refund after the third week.

IV.   FACULTY AND FACULTY RECRUITMENT

The department head and the Dean of the academic
unit have the final authority for hiring full and part-time
faculty members.   Approximately 60% of the faculty are full-
time.   The Director may not reject a faculty member who
has been assigned to teach evening classes.   No full-time
faculty members are employed who teach exclusively in the
evenings.   Regular faculty meetings are not held.   Faculty
members may teach one overload course per semester.
None of the budget is spent for recruitment.   Salary range

for part-time faculty members (non-university visiting faculty) is $630 to $900. Salary for overloads is one-twelfth of their salary with a maximum of $1250 for three-credit course.

V.   SCHEDULING

The Dean is responsible for the evening class schedule. The Dean has the authority to revise or make additions to the schedule. Three-hour classes are scheduled one night per week. From a learning point of view, two nights are better if the student takes one course per night. There is no research going on at the present time. Day and evening classes compare equally in quality. Part-time students who carry twelve hours and have a 3.0 grade point average are eligible for the Dean's List. The number of students required to constitute a class is determined by the individual student need. An instructor's compensation is not reduced when teaching a class of reduced size.

VI.   ORGANIZATIONAL STRUCTURE

The administrative staff consists of thirteen staff members. This institution has administrative autonomy. The Director's title will be changed to Vice-President. The Assistant Director does programming and advising. The Director of Adult Education Center directs programs on five campuses. The duties of the Director of Conferences and Institutes is self-explanatory. The Director of Counselling counsels students and formulates policies and procedures in the area. For administering and directing non-credit courses, conferences, etc., for an enrollment of 500, one staff member is required.

VII.   EDUCATIONAL TELEVISION PROGRAMS

Credit and non-credit courses are offered in educational television. Residence credit may be earned counting toward a degree. The Evening Continuing Education produces and administers these programs with the approval of the academic units. Both full-time and part-time faculty are used and they receive additional remuneration for teaching courses on TV. Continuing Education Division handles the registration for these courses in the same manner as other courses. Undergraduate courses are offered in educational television which are financed by FTV budget--$25,000 revolving fund and tuition. An out-of-state tuition fee is not charged. Educational television courses are scheduled from 3:30 to 4:00 p. m. and from 6 to 7 p. m.

VIII. NON-CREDIT PROGRAMS

Non-credit courses are offered in the areas of Business and Management, Arts and Sciences, and Education. The program is expected to pay for itself. Faculty receive $20 to $24 per hour and this depends upon the qualifications of the instructor. The following conferences were sponsored by the evening division: Nursing, Purchasing, Creativity, Transportation, Engineering, Veterinary Medicine, Retailing, Literature and Graphic Arts. Clinicians are paid from $50 to $400 per day. Continuing Education sponsors conferences and co-sponsors with units in and out of the University. The Division is responsible for the summer session.

IX. GENERAL

The University offers credit and/or non-credit courses in "storefront" locations off-campus for economically deprived populations. Students have little opportunity to participate in discussions regarding the academic program. One innovative program sponsored by the institution is a federal program in the Model Cities area of the community. The graduate programs for part-time students are administered by the Continuing Education Division including: Master of Business Administration, Secondary Education, Library Services and Engineering.

X. STUDENT RECRUITMENT

Recruitment is done through newspapers, radio and television publicity.

Manatee Junior College
Bradenton, Florida
Evening College

Total Enrollment 2, 500
Evening Enrollment 1, 000
    (plus 600 senior citizens in
    non-credit courses)

Public Junior College
Semester System

I. ADMISSION POLICIES

The deadline for application for admission to evening
classes for regular degree students is thirty days prior to
the beginning of classes; for non-degree or "special" students
there is no deadline. However, there are less than fifty
special students enrolled each semester. A student may
register as a non-matriculating student before transcripts are
submitted and may take up to fifteen semester hours before
he must matriculate. Auditors may take courses without
submitting transcripts as space permits. Admission requirements for regular students include a minimum of 150 on the
Florida State-Wide Twelfth Grade Placement Test - for entrance to a degree program (500 is the top score). To enter
as a non-matriculating student one must be a high school
graduate or GED equivalent. Students who are rejected as
regular students are not advised to enroll in evening classes.
However, they may enter the Basic Studies (Pre-College)
Prep Program. Students may register by mail for non-
credit courses for adults. A student failing to maintain a
2. 0 any one semester is placed on automatic probation; if
his grades average below 2. 0 a second semester, a student
is dropped for one semester and must petition for readmission. The ACT or CEEB examination is not required for
adults who apply for admission to evening classes. The
SCAT is required for matriculated students and used for
placement in English and Mathematics. No special degree
program is offered for adults, but they may complete either
an Associate in Arts (2 yr. LAS transfer) or an Associate
in Science degree (2 yr. occupational terminal). During the
Fall Semester of 1970, the enrollment in degree programs
included 1845 full-time and 640 part-time students. Sixty-
four semester hours are required for graduation including
thirty-six hours of General Education for all A. A. degree
candidates. The Registrar and the Dean of Special Education
formulate the admission policies for evening students. Day
and evening students may enroll in the same classes. Day
students gripe, "adults are too eager beaver" while adults
gripe "young day students are 'hep' and test-wise--too much
competition. " No orientation program is conducted for evening students. An Evening Advisory Committee is a part of
the committee structure - on call for new curricula.

II. TERMINOLOGY

Title of Division: Evening College of Manatee Junior
College. Defined: Evening College of the Division of Contin-

uing Education. Continuing Education defined: "could be all
the way from credit courses leading to a degree to the other
extreme of a series of non-credit adult continuing life-long
education. "

III. FEES

There is no fee differential for day and evening
classes.   There is a full-time fee for all students, or a
part-time fee for students taking less than twelve semester
hours at "X" dollars per semester hour (presently $10).
Refund policies: 100% within the first week of class, down
to 0%.

IV.   FACULTY AND FACULTY RECRUITMENT

Approximately 75% of the evening faculty are full-time
faculty members.   The final authority for hiring full/part-
time faculty lies with the Dean of Special Education which
includes the evening college and summer school.   The Dean
may reject any faculty member who has been assigned to
teach evening classes.   No full-time faculty teach exclusively
in the evening.   The Dean may hire an instructor without
departmental consent if this person refuses to staff certain
classes.   No regular faculty meetings are held for evening
faculty.   After the orientation interview, faculty members
are kept aware of policies by an up-dated Evening Faculty
Policy Handbook.   Faculty members are paid for teaching
credit and non-credit courses if it is beyond a full-time regular load - at the rate of $700 for a three-hour class for
Ph. D's or $600 for Master's degrees.   The same salary
scale applies to overloads and part-time faculty members.
No budget is needed for recruitment since faculty members
are attracted to the State of Florida.

V.   SCHEDULING

The Dean of Special Education is responsible for the
evening class schedule.   The Dean initiates the request to
Department Chairmen, sets a deadline date, and suggests
needed course offerings to be offered at certain hours.   According to the Dean, some negotiation is necessary.   Three-
hour classes are scheduled either one or two nights per
week, depending upon the class.   Two nights are preferable
for learning but one night for student convenience.   Day and
evening classes are the same in quality.   Part-time students
are eligible for the Dean's List after taking twelve hours with

a 3. 0 average. The minimum class size is fifteen for regular classes, ten for technology classes (with a state fund
supplement). An instructor's compensation is not reduced
if he teaches a class below minimum size, however, his
salary is pro-rated if the course is less than a semester in
length, e. g. , ten weeks of the fifteen week semester with
2/3 of the regular class payment.

VI. ORGANIZATIONAL STRUCTURE

The Evening College is administered by a Dean and
an Assistant Dean. The teaching staff consists of one full-
time and twenty-seven part-time faculty members. The College has academic and administrative autonomy within the
State Guidelines limits. In addition, there is a Coordinator
of the College's Senior Citizen Programs which attracts about
1000 students over sixty-five years of age.

VII. EDUCATIONAL TELEVISION PROGRAMS

The Evening College does not sponsor any educational
television programs.

VIII. NON-CREDIT PROGRAMS

Non-credit programs are offered in Business and
Management, Arts and Sciences, Education and special
courses for the Community upon request. A budget is provided for the non-credit programs but these courses are expected to pay for themselves. Faculty members receive the
same remuneration for teaching a non-credit course as for
a regular course - $700 per course for fifteen three semester
hour sessions. The remuneration depends upon the qualifications of the instructor. The College does sponsor some conferences and institutes such as: the Teacher Aide Training
Conference, and RN Nursing Workshop (in-service training)
and Emergency Care Technology (Ambulance, rescue work-
ers, firemen, etc.) The College endeavors to obtain professionals locally to participate in special conferences for
"prestige" and "service. " Conferences are sometimes held
in cooperation with another institution. The Dean is responsible for organizing the summer session.

IX. GENERAL

Students do have an opportunity to participate in discussions regarding the academic program since they "sit" on

every major committee of the whole College.   As far as innovative practices are concerned, flexible scheduling, trying
out new, needed community education.   There are two staff
members and one and one-half secretaries working on this.
The Evening Division is receiving fine support - including
presidential support.   The College has a Media Center where
the latest audio-visual equipment is available to faculty and
students.   There is a chapter of Phi Theta Kappa, the Junior
College Scholarship Honorary Fraternity at Manatee Junior
College.

X. STUDENT RECRUITMENT

Newspaper and radio publicity is used together with
special contacts with industry and civic groups.

Manhattan Community College
New York, New York
Division of Evening and Continuing Education

Total Enrollment 9, 300   Public Institution
Evening Enrollment 5, 600   Semester System

I. ADMISSION POLICIES

Because of limited facilities, there is no deadline for
application for admission to evening classes for regular students but there is a deadline (based on a first-come, first-
served basis) for non-degree or "special" students (with
credit).   Students may register for credit courses before
transcripts are submitted.   A student may take 10 hours for
credit as a non-matriculating or "special" student.   A high
school diploma or General Equivalency Diploma is required
for admission.   Students who are rejected for admission as
regular students are advised to apply as evening students and
are automatically accepted.   There is no mail registration
for credit courses.   The policy regarding probation and dismissal for degree students is 1. 5 index, and none for non-
degree or "special" students.   No ACT is required for adults
in the evening division.   There is no evening degree program
for adults which is different from the day degree program.
No special degree program is planned for adults in the near
future.   The Faculty Council formulates the admission policies for the evening students.   Day and evening students may
enroll in the same class only in special cases.   Combining

day and evening students in classes has many advantages for
both groups. During the 2nd week of the semester there is
an Orientation Program for evening students. There is no
Evening Division Advisory Committee.

II. TERMINOLOGY

Title of Division: Evening and Continuing Education.
Defined: includes credit and non-credit courses offered on
and off-campus during the afternoon and evening. Continuing
Education: all courses and programs other than the regular
day credit offerings.

III. FEES

Non-matriculating students pay tuition; matriculating
students do not. Students who drop within three weeks receive a partial refund.

IV. FACULTY AND FACULTY RECRUITMENT

There is no policy regarding the percentage of faculty
for evening classes that are full-time faculty members; 40%
are full-time. Department Chairmen have the final authority
for hiring full and/or part-time faculty members for evening
classes. The Director of the Evening Division can reject a
faculty member who has been assigned to teach evening
classes. There are no full-time faculty members who teach
exclusively in the evening. The evening director cannot engage an instructor without the consent of the department head
if the person refuses to staff classes. No faculty meetings
are held for evening faculty. Regular faculty may teach one
course per semester as an overload. No budget is provided
for recruitment. Salary range for part-time faculty: $14-
$25 per hour. The same amount is paid for faculty over-
loads.

V. SCHEDULING

The Director is responsible for the evening class
schedule. Departmental chairmen submit request for courses
to be offered. The Director has the authority to revise or
make additions to the evening class schedule. Three-hour
classes are scheduled two nights per week. This is preferable to one night per week. There are no research projects
completed, or in progress at the institution. Evening students are academically superior to day students. Part-time

students are eligible for the Dean's List.   Twelve hours are
required with a 3. 3 index.   Fifteen students constitute a
class.   The instructor's compensation is not reduced when
he teaches the class below the minimum size.

VI.   ORGANIZATIONAL STRUCTURE

There are five staff members on the administrative
staff in the Continuing Education or Evening Division.   The
teaching staff has 173 part-time faculty members.   The institution has academic autonomy and administrative autonomy.
The Dean is the supervisor and administers the Evening and
Continuing Education Division.   He develops community service programs.   It is recommended that an institution have
one administrative officer for a student body up to 800, two
administrative officers for a student body of 1000, three administrative officers for a student body of 2000 and four administrative officers for a student body of 5000.   For non-
credit programs: 300-1000 students, one staff member;
2000 students, two staff members and 5000 students, three
staff members.

VII.   EDUCATIONAL TELEVISION PROGRAMS

There are no courses in Educational Television.

VIII.   NON-CREDIT PROGRAMS

The Division does offer non-credit courses in special
areas.   The program is expected to pay for itself.   The
faculty receives $16 per hour for teaching a non-credit
course.   Remuneration depends upon the area of instruction.
The Division does not sponsor conferences and institutes.
The Division is not responsible for the Summer session.

IX.   GENERAL

The College administers three Regional Opportunity
Centers.   Students participate on the Faculty Council and
Standing Committees.   There are no graduate programs for
part-time students administered by the Evening Division.   In
general, the evening division is not receiving adequate support (in terms of adequate stress and financial support) in
comparison with the day program.   The administration recognizes the need and the importance of the adult education programs.   The Director or Dean of the Evening Division is
responsible to the President.   The same equipment which is

used by day sessions is used in the Division of Continuing
Education--8 mm. projectors, phonographs, video-tape re-
corders, etc.   There is no active chapter of Alpha Sigma
Lambda.

X. STUDENT RECRUITMENT

Newspaper publicity is used.

Marietta College
Marietta, Ohio
Evening School

Total Enrollment 1, 900   Private Institution
Evening Enrollment 500   Semester System

I. ADMISSION POLICIES

There is no deadline for application for admission.
A student may register for credit courses before transcripts
are submitted and may take eighteen hours of credit work as
a non-matriculating student.   Non-matriculating students are
required to have a high school diploma as a requirement for
admission and regular students must have satisfactory completion of six (or less) evening school courses.   Students who
have been rejected are not advised to apply as evening students.   Occasionally a registration form has been printed into the regular bulletin of course offerings.   No policies are
necessary regarding probation and dismissal--there is a
natural attrition.   No examinations or tests are required for
adults in the evening division.   The evening program differs
from the day program in that there is a general "area of
concentration" rather than majors at the bachelor's level.
Also offered is an A. A. (Liberal Arts of Business Administration).   There are 519 part-time undergraduate students
enrolled. For undergraduate degrees the distribution requirements are: 48 semester hours in a first elected division and 12 semester hours in each of the two remaining
divisions.   A total number of 120 semester hours are required to complete the degree.   The area of concentration
with the credit requirements are 18 semester hours in any
department feasible within the evening school offerings.   No
special degree program is offered.   Admission to a degree
program is by "proving one's self in the Evening School. "
Admission policies are formulated by the admissions com-

mittee.   Enrollment of day and evening students in the same
class is limited only by facilities and expediency.   Combined
classes with day and evening students is mutually beneficial--
experience vs. talent.   No orientation program is held.   The
Evening Division Advisory Committee reviews the operation
and poses suggestions.   Any person with a high school diploma may register for evening school courses but formal
matriculation for a degree is dependent on proven ability.

II.   TERMINOLOGY

Title of Division: Evening School.   Defined: A program of credit courses offered in the evening primarily to
serve the adult community.   Continuing Education defined:
on-going enlightment--credit, non-credit or both.

III.   FEES

The fee differential for day and evening classes is
$45 per semester hour for day and $35 per semester hour
for evening.   This is justified in that the adult clientele is
less affluent.   There is no refund on the 1/3 down payment;
refund on a decreasing percentage basis is made up to six
weeks and no refunds thereafter.

IV.   FACULTY AND FACULTY RECRUITMENT

The Director has the final authority for hiring full
and/or part-time faculty members for evening classes and
may reject a member who has been assigned to teach an
evening class.   No full-time faculty teach exclusively in the
evening.   The Director may engage an instructor without the
consent of the department head.   No regular faculty meetings
are held.   Faculty members are limited to the teaching of
one course.   None of the budget is spent on recruiting.   A
salary range of $700 to $950 per course applies to part-time
faculty and is the same for overloads.

V.   SCHEDULING

The Director is responsible for the evening class
schedule--faculty preference is given consideration when ex-
pressed.   Revisions may be made by the Director.   Three-
hour classes are scheduled one night per week--a pro and
con arrangement.   A research project has been completed
consisting of a summary of course offerings and enrollment
over the past 10 years.   Day and evening classes are bal-

anced in terms of quality. No Dean's List is published. At least seven students must register to constitute a class. An instructor's compensation is not reduced if he teaches a class with fewer than seven.

VI. ORGANIZATIONAL STRUCTURE

The administrative staff consists of the Director who is responsible for the overall administration of the Evening School and a secretary who assists the Director. The teaching staff totals forty part-time faculty members. The ideal administrative staff size would be eight staff members for every 5000 students.

VII. EDUCATIONAL TELEVISION PROGRAMS

The Evening School does not offer any courses on educational television.

VIII. NON-CREDIT PROGRAMS

Non-credit courses are practically non-existent. The Evening School does not sponsor conferences or institutes, and is not responsible for the day summer session but there is an evening summer session which is independent of the day session.

IX. GENERAL

Students participate in discussions regarding academic programs. Graduate programs for part-time evening students are cooperative programs with Ohio University (e. g. , MBA, with graduate courses taught by Ohio University faculty with Marietta responsible for registration, facilities, etc.) The Evening School receives adequate support. The Director is responsible to the Dean of the College. Audiovisual aids are available.

X. STUDENT RECRUITMENT

Student recruiting is accomplished through the newspaper, radio and industry.

University of Maryland
College Park, Maryland
University College

Total Enrollment 32, 000   State Institution
Evening Enrollment 12, 000   Semester System

I. ADMISSION POLICIES

Deadline for application for admission is prior to registration for non-adults; adults may register for credit courses without transcripts but must have submitted academic documents by the end of the first semester and may take an unlimited amount of hours as special students. Admission requirements include high school graduation and good standing at college previously attended; non-adults must be graduates of an approved high school and have a "C" average in the last two years and upper half of the graduating class and/or good standing in previous college attended. GED equivalency may be substituted for high school diploma. No mail registration is used but a mail registration procedure is under development. A student is dismissed after completing 12 to 20 hours with a GPA of below .35; 21 to 35 hours of 1.35; 36-50 hours below 1.65; 51-65 hours below 1.80; 81+ hours below 1.95. A special degree program for adults is offered: Bachelor of Arts (General Studies curriculum-enrollment 12, 000). A special degree program is being considered at graduate level: M.S. in Social Science, M.A. in Liberal Studies; at undergraduate level a B.A. (Political Science concentration). Admission policies are set by the Dean, Chancellor and general administration. Day students may enroll in evening classes with permission of their Dean.

II. TERMINOLOGY

Title of Division: University College (three credit divisions operating in Maryland and three credit divisions overseas plus a conference and institute division and a residential center for adult education). Defined: A service-oriented administrative unit facilitating the continuing education responsibilities of the University which also grants degrees. University College serves as the State Agency for Community Service and Continuing Education (Title of Higher Education Act of 1965).

III.   FEES

Graduate students pay higher tuition than part-time day or evening students.   Refunds of 80% are made before 10% of the classes are over.

IV.   FACULTY AND FACULTY RECRUITMENT

Approximately 40% of the evening classes are taught by full-time faculty.   Final authority to hire faculty lies with the department chairmen.   Some full-time faculty members teach exclusively in the evening.   They are responsible to the Chancellor of the University College, administratively, and to the department chairmen, academically.   Faculty members are limited to an overload of the equivalent of six semester hours in an academic year.   Part-time faculty salaries range from $710 for instructor to $975 for full professor.

V.   SCHEDULING

The Chancellor of University College is responsible for the schedule.   Directors coordinate courses, then a consolidated list is sent to departments with requests to staff; three-hour courses are scheduled either one or two nights per week.   Part-time students are eligible for the Dean's List after completing fifteen semester hours with a 3.5 average.

VI.   ORGANIZATIONAL STRUCTURE

Twenty-two staff members including the Chancellor and Dean's office comprise the administrative staff.   Full-time faculty members total 28 and 550 part-time faculty - some of whom teach more than one course.   There is administrative autonomy.   The Dean is responsible for stateside and overseas programs.   There are two assistant Deans-- one responsible for academic affairs and the other responsible for overseas programs.   In addition there is a Chancellor, three Directors, three assistant Directors, a Director of Adult Education Center, a Director of Conferences and Institutes, three Assistant Directors of Conferences and Institutes, a Registrar who is responsible for all university college stateside registrations and a business manager who handles finance and budget matters.

VII. EDUCATIONAL TELEVISION PROGRAMS

Educational television programs in Mathematics are offered for residence credit which may be applied to a degree.   The program is supervised by the Math Department. Full or part-time instructors are approved by the Mathematics Department.   Classes meet with the instructor five times during the course.   The instructors receive special remuneration for teaching TV courses.   Registration is in person and is handled by the University College.   Financing is covered by tuition.   Classes are scheduled on Mondays, Tuesdays, and Thursdays from 8 to 8:30 p. m. on Mondays, 9:30 to 10 p. m. on Tuesdays, 3:30 to 4 p. m. on Wednesdays and Thursdays.

VIII. NON-CREDIT PROGRAMS

Non-credit programs are offered in Business and Management, Arts and Sciences, Education and other areas. The program is expected to pay for itself.   Faculty remuneration is the same as for the credit courses - pro-rated and equivalent of three-hour courses.   There have been 145 conferences and institutes offered by the University College.

IX. GENERAL

Special eight week terms are offered at military centers.   In general, evening divisions do not receive adequate support from all academic departments.   The Chancellor is responsible to the President and the Vice-President. Audio-visual aids are used.

X. STUDENT RECRUITMENT

Newspaper publicity is used (three ads per year) as well as radio and television occasionally.

Memphis State University
Memphis, Tennessee
Division of Continuing Studies

Total Enrollment 18, 000   Public Institution
Evening Enrollment 6, 000+   Semester System

I. ADMISSION POLICIES

There is no deadline for application for admission to
evening classes.   Students may register for credit courses
before transcripts are received and take a maximum of 18
semester hours as non-matriculating students.   Admission
requirements for special students is high school graduation
or at least 21 years of age; for regular students, acceptable
CEEB scores, high school transcript, health card, etc.   Students must maintain a 2. 0 average to remain in good standing.   A special degree program for adults is being considered.
Admission policies are set by the Admissions Standing Committee.   Day and evening students may enroll in the same
classes; approximately one-half of the evening students take
some day courses.   Orientation for evening students is held
prior to registration.

II. TERMINOLOGY

Title of Division: Division of Continuing Studies.
Defined: Division offering functions to service needs of students who do not choose to make college work a full-time
objective.

III. FEES

Refunds are made on a graduating percentage basis of
80% to 0% declining weekly from the first day of class.

IV. FACULTY AND FACULTY RECRUITMENT

Approximately 75% teaching evening classes are full-
time.   The final authority to hire evening faculty lies with
Department Chairmen and College Deans.   Regular faculty
meetings are held with department chairmen and deans.
Faculty members may teach one course per academic year
on an overload basis.   The salary range for part-time faculty
is $590 per three semester hour course.   The salary paid
to faculty for overloads is $285 high to $150 per semester
hour according to rank and degree.   No overloads are permitted except for extension courses, and the salary is the
same as that for Summer school.   Faculty is paid $590 per
three semester-hour course.   To constitute a class, there
must be an enrollment of 12 lower division students, eight
upper division students or six graduate students.   The instructor's compensation is not reduced when he teaches a
class below the minimum size.

V. SCHEDULING

The Director of the Division of Continuing Studies is partially responsible for the evening schedule. Schedules are submitted to the Registrar by the department chairmen. Three credit-hour classes are scheduled both one and two nights a week. Day and evening classes are equal in all respects in terms of quality. Part-time evening students are eligible for the Dean's List with a 3.4 after completing 15 semester hours.

VI. ORGANIZATIONAL STRUCTURE

The size of the administrative staff in Division of Continuing Studies is as follows: five administrative staff members and six clerical staff members. The teaching staff consists of 700 full-time instructors and the number of part-time instructors varies. The duties of the five administrative staff members are: namely, Director, Chief Administrator of Personnel, program administration and budget; Assistant Director, serves as extension director, also administers several budgets within the division, manages the office; Director of Non-Credit Programs, programs, prepares literature, hires teachers and administers registrations; Director of Conferences and Institutes and Director of Extension, organizes classes, hires teachers, registers students, etc.

VII. EDUCATIONAL TELEVISION PROGRAMS

Courses are offered in Educational Television which are credit courses and students earn residence credit. Attendance for on-campus sessions is sufficient to be acceptable to accrediting agencies.

VIII. NON-CREDIT PROGRAMS

The Division of Continuing Studies offers non-credit courses in Business and Management, Arts and Sciences, Education, Engineering and others. There is a budget for non-credit programs although this program is expected to pay for itself. For teaching a non-credit course the full or part-time faculty receive $20 per contact hour (class sessions vary). The remuneration depends upon the qualifications of the instructor. The Division of Continuing Studies sponsors more than 50 conferences per year. A clinician for a conference receives on the average $150 per day. The Division uses the qualified faculty members of the Institution or visiting lecturers.   The Division is also responsible for the Summer session at the institution.

IX.   GENERAL

Some off-campus special courses are being offered for economically deprived populations.   Students participate very little in discussions regarding the academic program. The evening division is receiving adequate financial support but, in general, all evening divisions do not receive adequate professional support.   The current annual budget is $7500. The Director of the Division of Continuing Studies is responsible to the University Provost.   Audio-visual instructional aids are available for evening classes.

X.   STUDENT RECRUITMENT

Newspaper publicity is used.

<u>Miami University</u>
Oxford, Ohio
Residence Credit Center

Total Enrollment 16, 258   Public Institution
Evening Enrollment 3, 400   Quarter System

I.   ADMISSION POLICIES

There is no deadline for application for admission to evening classes.   A student may register for credit courses before transcripts are submitted.   Non-matriculating or "special" students may take up to ten quarter hours for credit.   "Special" students must be twenty-four years of age or older for admission.   Regular degree students must have earned a high school diploma or the equivalent.   Students who are rejected for admission as regular day students are not advised to apply for evening classes.   Mail registration is used for the first quarter only.   Probation and dismissal policies require a 1. 7 average for freshmen and a 2. 0 for upper-division students.   No ACT or CEEB examination is required for admission to evening classes.   No special degree program for adults is offered.   The Dean of Educational Services together with the University Council formulates the admission policies.   The Graduate Council and Dean of Edu-

cational Services formulate policies for graduate admission.
Day and evening students may enroll in the same classes.
No orientation program is held for evening students.   An
Evening Advisory Committee has the responsibility of recom-
mending schedules and curriculum needs.

II.   TERMINOLOGY

Title of Division: Academic Centers changing to Residence Center by the Board of Regents.   Defined: Any part-
time program in the late afternoon or evening.   Definition of
Continuing Education: Education provided for those persons
not following a full-time program for credit or non-credit.

III.   FEES

The fee for part-time students is one-tenth the fee
for full-time students per hour.   The refund policies apply
the same to evening students as to day students.

IV.   FACULTY AND FACULTY RECRUITMENT

No firm policy has been established regarding the
percentage of faculty for evening classes that are full-time.
Approximately 25% of the evening faculty members are full-
time.   The Departmental Chairmen and Deans have the final
authority for hiring full/part-time faculty members for evening classes.   The Dean of the Residence Center has the
authority to reject a faculty member who has been assigned
to teach evening classes.   Some full-time faculty members
teach exclusively in the evening and are responsible to the
departments.   The Dean cannot engage an instructor for evening classes without the consent of the department chairmen.
No regular faculty meetings are held for evening faculty.
Faculty members may teach one class per week as overload
in some departments.   Other departments do not permit this
practice.   No budget is spent on recruiting.   The salary
range for part-time faculty is from $170 to $310 per credit
hour and the same schedule applies to overloads.

V.   SCHEDULING

The Associate Dean of Educational Services is responsible for the evening class schedule.   He confers with the
Director of branch campus, the department chairmen and
deans of divisions using program sequences and student survey results as a guide.   The Dean has the authority to revise

the schedule.   Most of the three-hour classes meet one night
per week--some departments insist on two meetings per week.
Some research projects in adult education have been completed or are in progress.   Part-time evening students are
eligible for the Dean's List.   Students must take a minimum
of nine hours and earn a 3. 0 grade point average.   The minimum number of students required to constitute a class is
ten; however, exceptions are made for various reasons.   An
instructor's compensation is not reduced for teaching a class
below the minimum size.

VI.   ORGANIZATIONAL STRUCTURE

The Residence Credit Center has an administrative
staff of seven headed by a Dean together with an Associate
Dean, Director, Assistant Director, Director of Admissions,
Registrar and Business Manager.   It is recommended that
an administrative staff of fifteen be employed for a student
enrollment of 2000 and a staff of four to handle non-credit
courses, conferences, institutes with a student body of 2000.

VII.   EDUCATIONAL TELEVISION PROGRAMS

The Residence Credit Center does sponsor Educational
Television courses for credit.   Students may earn residence
credit which will count toward a degree.   The Director of
Radio-TV Department (speech) supervises the educational
television program.   Courses for teachers are handled by
the School of Education-learning laboratory and formal courses
are offered.   Full-time faculty members are used.   Faculty
members do not receive additional remuneration for teaching
courses on TV.   The Registrar handles registration for the
TV courses which are all under-graduate courses.   Out-of-
state tuition is charged for credit courses.

VIII.   NON-CREDIT PROGRAMS

The Residence Credit Center offers non-credit courses
in Business and Management, Humanities and Education.   The
program is expected to be self-supporting.   The remuneration
for faculty members varies with the course and is dependent
upon qualifications of instructor.   The Center cooperates with
the various departments in offering non-credit courses.   The
Residence Credit Center is responsible for the summer program and for conferences and institutes.   Clinicians receive
4% of their base salary for participation.

IX.   GENERAL

Students do have the opportunity to express themselves regarding evening courses.   They are surveyed each quarter for desired or needed courses.   Some graduate programs are offered for part-time students in Education and in a few departments of Arts and Sciences (English and History). Such programs are being planned in Business Administration. The Evening Division is receiving adequate support.   The Administration is beginning to recognize the need and importance of the adult education program.   The Dean of the Residence Center is responsible to the Executive Vice-President for Academic Affairs.   Evening instructors have full access to teaching aids including equipment, planning and consultation as well as reproduction.

X.   STUDENT RECRUITMENT

Newspapers, radio and television publicity are used. Special motivational appeals are developed for industry, civic organizations and the Chamber of Commerce.

<u>Miami-Dade Junior College</u>
Miami, Florida
Special Programs Division

Total Enrollment 8,100   Public Institution
Evening Enrollment - not stated   Semester System

I.   ADMISSION POLICIES

There is no deadline for application for admission; a student may register for credit courses without transcripts. A limit of twelve hours may be taken as a non-matriculating student.   Admission requirements for special students include: 18 years of age or older; for regular students: high school graduation or GED.   All students must maintain a 1.5 upon completion of seventy-two hours; no probation policy for non-degree or special students.   A special degree program is not offered.   Admission policies are formulated by the President's Council.   There are no restrictions on day and evening students enrolling in the same class.

II. TERMINOLOGY

Title of Division: Division of Special Programs.
Defined: Any education program scheduled evenings, weekends and off-campus for persons beyond what was formerly
regarded as "normal" school age.

III. FEES

Refund policies: 100% first five days of class; 50%
after fifth but before end of the tenth day; none thereafter.

IV.   FACULTY AND FACULTY RECRUITMENT

Faculty teaching evening classes total approximately
90% full-time.   Final authority to hire evening faculty lies
with department chairmen.   Faculty may not teach overload
except with consent of the academic dean.   Salary for part-
time faculty ranges from $550 to $750 for three-hour course;
$7. 50 per hour for non-credit courses.   Overloads, when
permitted, are paid at the rate of 3/4 of one months salary
for a three-hour course.

V.   SCHEDULING

The Dean of the Special Programs must approve the
schedule but the department chairmen are responsible for it.
The Director frequently amends the schedule.   Three-hour
classes are scheduled either one or two nights per week.
Fifteen students constitute a class.

VI.   ORGANIZATIONAL STRUCTURE

The Evening Division has an administrative staff of
three with a teaching staff of 200-300 part-time faculty members.

VII.   EDUCATIONAL TELEVISION PROGRAMS

The Evening Division does not sponsor educational
television programs.

VIII.   NON-CREDIT PROGRAMS

Non-credit courses are offered in Business and Management, Arts and Sciences, Education.   Faculty members
are paid at the rate of $7. 50 per hour.   There is a budget

for non-credit programs, however, the program very nearly
pays for itself. Remuneration does not depend upon qualifications of the instructor or upon the area of instruction.
The Division does not sponsor conferences or institutes and
is not responsible for the summer session at the institution.

IX. GENERAL

Special Programs Division is receiving adequate support. The Director of Special Programs Division is responsible to the Academic Dean. Complete audio-visual services
are available to all instructors.

X. STUDENT RECRUITMENT

Newspaper, radio and television (Junior College Forum) publicity are used.

Millard Fillmore College
State University of New York
Buffalo, New York
Division of Continuing Education

Total Enrollment 23,900   Public Institution
Evening Enrollment 5,100   Semester System

I. ADMISSION POLICIES

Deadline for application for admission is August 1 for
fall semester, December 1 for spring semester. Up to
twelve hours may be taken as a "special" student. The admission requirements for non-matriculating or "special" students include a degree or a demonstrated need for the course
desired; for regular students: H. S. diploma or GED; transfer students: overall average of "C" or better. No ACT or
CEEB scores are required. Students who are rejected as
regular students are sometimes advised to enroll in evening
classes but are not automatically accepted. Only students on
a continuing basis are given advance registration materials
to be filed by mail if they wish. New students must register
in person. The institution is on a 100% machine basis.
There are no policies regarding probation and suspension for
non-degree or "special" students. If degree students fall
below a 2. 0 they are placed on probation and continued failure results in dismissal. The evening degree program for

adults does not differ from the day degree program.   Distribution requirements for undergraduate degrees include 32
semester hours outside the area of concentration.   No graduate program is offered.   The college is considering offering
a special degree program for adults to be offered in the near
future.   The Dean and his staff formulate the admission policies for evening students with the permission of the Faculty
Senate.   Evening students receive priority for enrollment in
evening classes - day students may enroll as space permits.
The advantage of a combined class is the exchange of ideas
between young students and the working students; disadvantage
is the generation gap in some cases.   An orientation program
is held for evening students in the fall and spring semesters.
There is an Evening Division Advisory Committee whose
function is to advise the Dean of future plans of the evening
division, review policies, etc.   Admissions are limited to
students living in a fifty mile radius of campus.

II.   TERMINOLOGY

Title of Division: Division of Continuing Education.
Defined: Educational opportunities offered by the University
beyond those offered in articulated day school programs.
Continuing Education defined: All educational opportunities
beyond articulated daytime programs.

III.   FEES

The same fees are paid by part-time and full-time
students--day or evening.   Student activity fees do differ,
i. e. , compulsory athletic fee is paid by day students only.
A graduated refund policy is used.

IV.   FACULTY AND FACULTY RECRUITMENT

Approximately 50% of the evening faculty are full-
time.   The Division tries to keep an even 50/50 distribution
of day/evening faculty.   The final authority for hiring full
and/or part-time faculty members for evening classes is by
joint appointment with the day division deans and departmental chairmen.   The Director of the Evening Division can
reject a faculty member who has been assigned to teach evening classes.   The Evening Division does not employ any
full-time faculty members who teach exclusively in the evening.   The evening class Director can (reluctantly) engage
an instructor without the consent of the department head if
this person refuses to staff the evening classes.   Regular

faculty meetings are held with evening faculty--once in the fall and once in the spring. N. Y. State insists that all overload work be discouraged and eliminated as quickly as possible--"which hasn't been accomplished as yet. " No budget is allotted for recruitment. Salaries range from: Instructors-$280 an hour (semester), lecturers-assistant professors-$350 an hour (semester), associate professors-$450 an hour (semester), professors-$600 an hour (semester). Faculty are paid on 1-2-3-4-contact-hour basis. Most courses are of four semester hour credits. Overloads for full-time faculty strongly discouraged as a matter of state policy.

V. SCHEDULING

The Dean of the Continuing Education Division is responsible for the evening class schedule in the institution. The procedure for compiling the schedule is a joint effort with the day division. Opinions are divided regarding three-hour class scheduling--one or two nights a week. The day and evening classes are considered equal in terms of quality. Part-time students with eight hours of 3. 0 or better are eligible for the Dean's List. Usually ten students constitute a class.

VI. ORGANIZATIONAL STRUCTURE

The administrative staff consists of ten staff members. The teaching staff consists of 150 full-time and 150 part-time faculty members. "We all do some of everything and coordinate our efforts to keep all operations functioning normally and smoothly. " The institution is under the supervision of the state university (to some extent) and the budget is an all university budget. The ideal administrative structure would be twelve professional and twelve clerical staff for an enrollment of 5000.

VII. EDUCATIONAL TELEVISION PROGRAMS

The Division of Continuing Education does not offer any courses in educational television. However, other school offerings are accepted.

VIII. NON-CREDIT PROGRAMS

The Division of Continuing Education offers non-credit programs in Business and Management, Arts and Sciences, Engineering and Education. The program is expected to pay for itself.   The Division does sponsor conferences and institutes.

IX.   GENERAL

Students participate extensively in discussions regarding the academic program.   The institution offers tutorial programs for the disadvantaged and some admission requirements are waived for this group of students.   In general, the administration does recognize the need and importance of adult education programs but adequate stress and financial support has not yet been realized.   The Dean of Continuing Education is directly responsible to the President.   There is an active chapter of Alpha Sigma Lambda, the Evening Honor Society.

X.   STUDENT RECRUITMENT

All forms of publicity are used for student recruitment - newspaper articles, advertisements, radio and television, as well as mailings to industry and publicity materials prepared for organizations in the city.

University of Minnesota
Minneapolis, Minnesota
Department of Evening Classes and Special Classes

Total Enrollment 48, 000+   Public Institution
Evening Division Enrollment 35, 000+   Quarter System

I.   ADMISSION POLICIES

There is no deadline for application for admission and students may register for credit courses without transcripts. Non-matriculated students may take an unlimited amount of work for credit.   There are no admission requirements for evening classes.   Mail registration is used.   Students request registration material, fill out forms and submit with tuition fees.   Students who are rejected as regular students are advised to apply as evening students and are automatically accepted.   A special degree program for adults is being considered for the near future.   Day and evening students may enroll in the same classes during the evening except for matriculated students.   There is an Evening Division Advisory Committee, namely, The Student Advisory Board, whose membership includes students, evening class instructors, and representatives of the office of the Dean of Extension. A Board was formed to serve students, faculty of evening classes.

II. TERMINOLOGY

Title of Division: Department of Evening and Special Classes.

III. FEES

Evening class tuition is $13 per credit hour; day class tuition reaches its maximum at twelve credits. There is a refund for classes dropped by evening students who drop one or more classes but remain in school.

IV. FACULTY AND FACULTY RECRUITMENT

Approximately 80% of the evening faculty are full-time. Final authority to hire evening faculty lies with the Director of Evening Classes. The Director may reject a faculty member assigned to teach evening classes. Some full-time faculty members teach exclusively in the evening. No regular faculty meetings are held. The salary range for part-time faculty and for overloads is $207-$319 per credit hour. The number of students who must register for a class before the class is taught is generally ten to twelve depending upon the course. The instructor's compensation is not reduced when he teaches a class below the minimum size.

V. SCHEDULING

The Director of Evening Classes is responsible for the evening class schedule with contact being established with each academic department. The Director has the authority to revise the evening schedule. Three hour classes are scheduled one night a week. Day and evening classes are comparable in terms of quality. Part-time evening students are not eligible for the Dean's List.

VI. ORGANIZATIONAL STRUCTURE

The administrative staff in the Department of Evening Classes consists of eitht staff members and 1000 part-time teachers. In the director's estimation, only one staff member is required for a credit program enrollment of 300-500.

VII.   EDUCATIONAL TELEVISION PROGRAMS

The Department of Evening Classes offer credit courses in educational television.   Full-time faculty is used. Faculty members receive additional remuneration for teaching courses on TV and their regular on-campus class load is reduced by one class.   The Evening and Special Classes handle the registration for the educational television courses; it is generally handled by mail, but also is done in person. Both graduate and undergraduate courses are offered in educational TV.   These courses are financed by extension support and student tuition.   The TV courses are scheduled 9 to 10 p. m.   Residence credit is awarded toward degrees.

VIII.   NON-CREDIT PROGRAMS

The Department of Evening Classes offers non-credit courses in Business and Management, Arts and Sciences, Engineering and others.   There is a budget for this non-credit program.   The Division of Evening Classes also sponsors conferences and institutes.

IX.   GENERAL

Some special courses are offered in "store front" locations for economically deprived populations.   Students participate very little in discussions regarding academic programs.   The Student Advisory Board deals with such matters. There is a graduate program offered for part-time students, Phase I of the MBA program, which is administered by the Evening Division.   In general, all evening divisions are not receiving adequate support.   The Director of the Department of Evening Classes is responsible to the Associate Dean of the Division.   Audio-visual instructional aids are available for use in the evening.

X.   STUDENT RECRUITMENT

Newspaper, radio and television publicity are used. Special motivational appeals have been developed for industry and civic organizations.

Mississippi State College for Women
Columbus, Mississippi
Continuing Education

Total Enrollment 2, 657   State-supported Institution
Evening Enrollment 322   Semester System

I. ADMISSION POLICIES

There is no deadline for application for admission for evening classes. The only admission requirements are that the person be 21 years of age if non-matriculating or special students and a high school graduate, if a regular degree student. Students who are rejected for regular admission are not advised to apply for evening classes. No mail registration is used. There are no policies regarding probation and suspension. The ACT or CEEB are not required for admission. No orientation program is conducted for evening students.

II. TERMINOLOGY

Title of Division: Continuing Education. Defined: Very important position in the educational program.

III. FEES

There is no fee differential between day and evening classes. Refund policies are the same as for day students.

IV. FACULTY AND FACULTY RECRUITMENT

There is no policy regarding the percentage of full-time faculty teaching evening classes. The Dean of Faculty has the final authority for hiring faculty members. No full-time faculty are employed to teach exclusively in the evening. The Director cannot engage an instructor without the consent of the Dean and the Department chairmen. No regular faculty meetings are held. Regular faculty members are paid for overloads.

V. SCHEDULING

The Director is responsible for compiling the evening schedules which are submitted by the Dean of Instruction and the department heads. The Director does have the authority to revise as necessary. Three-hour classes are scheduled

one night per week. Part-time students are not eligible for
the Dean's List. Eight students constitute a class; however,
an instructor's compensation is not reduced when teaching
less than eight students.

VI. ORGANIZATIONAL STRUCTURE

Two staff members comprise the administrative staff:
the Dean makes final decisions on policy and approves faculty
and the Director also supervises instruction and employs
faculty. The teaching staff consists of eight part-time faculty members. The Registrar keeps records and the Business
Manager collects fees. The ideal staff is two for an enrollment of 300.

VII. EDUCATIONAL TELEVISION PROGRAMS

There are no educational television programs offered
at the institution.

VIII. NON-CREDIT PROGRAMS

Non-credit programs are offered in the areas of Arts
and Sciences and Education. There is no budget set up for
the program--classes are to be self-supporting.

IX. GENERAL

No off-campus classes are conducted. Graduate programs are offered for part-time students subject to the approval of the Dean of the Graduate School. The evening division is not receiving adequate support but the need is recognized by the administration. The Director is responsible
to the Academic Dean. All audio-visual aids are available
for evening classes.

X. STUDENT RECRUITMENT

Newspaper advertisement, radio spot announcements
and TV spot announcements are used for student recruitment.

University of Missouri
St. Louis, Missouri
Evening College

Total Enrollment 9, 681   Public Institution
Evening Enrollment 2, 383   Semester System

I. ADMISSION POLICIES

There is no deadline for admission; a dateline is used depending upon the last day of regular registration. A student may not register for credit courses before transcripts are submitted. Students may take a certain amount of work as a non-matriculating or "special" student. Admission requirements for a non-matriculating or "special" student are: a person over twenty-one years of age who does not qualify for admission as a regular student, but who by reason of special preparation or attainment may be judged qualified to pursue certain courses. This student will be admitted as a "special" student though not as a candidate for degree. An applicant who is not in good standing at the school previously attended is not eligible for admission. Regular degree students must have a high school diploma and must have been in the upper 2/3 of his class; transfer students must have a 2. 0 average. Students who are rejected for admission as regular students are not advised to apply as evening students. Students do not register for credit courses by mail. However, they are expected to meet with advisors. No ACT or CEEB examination is required. The Missouri College Placement Test is used in Mathematics and English. No evening degree program is offered. Enrollment for Fall (Evening College) was 463 full-time and 1920 part-time. The graduate program is administered by the Graduate School. Requirements for degree: three courses in Humanities, three in Math Proficiency, one course which meets State requirements, forty-two hours in Arts and Science for the B. S. degree and an additional thirteen hours in a language for the A. B. degree. Generally, a beginning student (with less than twelve hours completed) is placed on probation if his grade point average is less than 1. 75. Several graduate degrees are offered by the Graduate School in the evening. There are no graduate degrees especially designed for evening students. Some consideration is being given to offering a special degree program for adults. The University Faculty establishes the minimum admission requirements for all divisions. Students may enroll in day and/or evening classes as space permits. Combined classes provide flexibility for scheduling

classes. "One disadvantage is that we sometimes have pressure to take more students in the evening classes than can
be accommodated. " There is no orientation program for evening students--it has been tried on a voluntary basis but student participation was not high. The Evening College Faculty
has three standing committees - Committee on Policies and
By-Laws, Curriculum Committee and Committee on Academic
Advisement - which meet regularly. A new admission policy recently approved by the faculty is awaiting approval by
the Board of Curators and includes: Applicants over twenty-one
years of age, veterans, etc. , who may not qualify for admission as a regular student may be admitted by virtue of
special preparation or attainment as "special students". This
new feature is an outgrowth of a study made by the Evening
College relating to the academic performance of adults.

II.   TERMINOLOGY

Title of Division: Evening College. Defined: Em-
braces all undergraduate programs offered in the evening
after 5 p. m. Education is thought of as education regardless of time, age or format. In the strictest sense, continuing education suggests extending some level of competence
or achievement already attained.

III.   FEES

Part-time students (day and evening) pay $29 per
credit hour, full-time students (eight hours or more) pay
$230 per semester. Refunds are made on a percentage ba-
sis; 75% through fourth week, 50% through eighth week, 25%
through twelfth week, assuming that the student is carrying
less than eight semester hours.

IV.   FACULTY AND FACULTY RECRUITMENT

As a policy, "we are shooting for 75% full-time and
25% part-time faculty. " Approximately 52% of the courses
are presently taught by full-time regular faculty. Departments hire full-time faculty with approval of the respective
Dean. The Evening Dean approves recommendations for part-
time faculty. The Dean can reject a faculty member who
has been assigned to teach evening classes. A few faculty
may teach only in the evening but are hired by the department. Regular faculty meetings are conducted at least three
times a year. Instructors may teach one class each year as
an overload. Faculty in rank teach evening classes as part

of the regular load and rarely on an overload basis.   Funds
for recruitment are allocated by the departments.   Salary
range for part-time faculty is: Professor - $1210 for a
three-hour course, Associate Professor - $1105, Instructor -
from $720 to $770.

V. SCHEDULING

Schedules are worked out by the Dean in cooperation
with the department chairmen.   Much time is spent in gen-
erating and analyzing the data.   Revisions, additions and
deletions are brought to the attention of the department chairmen.   Three-hour classes are scheduled two nights per week.
Two nights are preferred from an educational standpoint.   Research projects are underway as follows: Predictors of Academic Success among Evening College Students, Financial
Needs Analysis of Evening Students, Personal Data Relating
to Evening Students, Survey of Students who left the Evening
College, Employment Status of Evening Students.   Day and
evening classes are comparable in terms of quality.   Part-
time students are eligible for the Dean's List with nine hours
of 3. 2 or better on a 4. 0 scale.   Ten students constitute a
class; however, there is considerable latitude here, depending upon the various circumstances.   Salary for instructors
is determined by rank and hourly load--no adjustment is
made when class is less than ten.

VI. ORGANIZATIONAL STRUCTURE

Three full-time administrators and one full-time
counselor assisted by two part-time and three full-time secretaries and nine part-time clerks comprise the administrative staff.   Teaching staff includes eighty-one full-time and
seventy-nine part-time faculty.   In most areas the institution
has academic and administrative autonomy.   All campuses
are subject to the policies of the Board of Curators and di-
rectives of the President.   The Dean plans instructional program, budget, is liaison with departments, recruitment, directs research; the Associate Dean assists with the instructional program, publications and mailings, research, and assists with advisement; the Assistant Dean is responsible for
student advisement, transcripts, evaluations, student records,
class schedules, and student organizations.   The ideal staff
size is four or five staff members for an enrollment of
2000-3000 with much depending upon the supporting services
provided by the institution.

VII.   EDUCATIONAL TELEVISION PROGRAMS

No educational television programs are offered by the
Evening College.   All off-campus course work is administered by the Extension Division.

VIII.   NON-CREDIT PROGRAMS

Non-credit courses are offered through the Extension
Division.

IX.   GENERAL

Innovative practices are: three remedial courses,
free tutorial services, development of a viable student council and services provided for evening students.   Graduate
programs are available for part-time students in several
areas; however, they are administered by the Graduate
School.   Support is probably better than most but still not
as strong as desired.   The Dean of the Evening College is
responsible to the Dean of Faculties and through him to the
Chancellor.   A wide variety of instructional aids are available and delivered to the classroom upon request.

X.   STUDENT RECRUITMENT

Course schedules are mailed each semester to students, former students, business establishments and institutions.   The newspaper is used for publicity.

Modesto Junior College
Modesto, California   95350
Evening Program

Total Enrollment 5, 200   Community College
Evening Enrollment 9, 000   Semester System

I.   ADMISSION POLICIES

There is no deadline for admission and a student may
register before transcripts are received.   An open door policy is used for non-matriculating or "special" students.   A
student must be 18 years of age or older and must be able
to benefit by instruction.   Regular students who are rejected
are not advised to apply as evening students.   They are,

however, accepted by special arrangement. Mail registration is used. Probation for degree students at 2. 0; below
1. 5 disqualifies and student must petition for re-admission. No
ACT or CEEB scores are required; other tests required for
placement and advisement. The regular degree program available to adults: an A. A. and an A. S. degree, which require six
units of Social Science, six units of English and/or Speech,
two units of Health Education; twenty units of major and electives to complete 62 hours for degree. No special degree
program for adults is considered. The Evening College Administration and Dean of Admissions assist in formulating
admission policies for evening students. A preference is
given evening students (evening only) in the evening college.
No orientation program is conducted for evening students.
An Advisory Committee guides, advises, recommends programs, staff and facilities for the Evening College.

II. TERMINOLOGY

Title of Division: Modesto Junior College-Evening
Program. Defined: a comprehensive educational endeavor
to serve the needs of the community. Continuing Education
defined: A comprehensive offering of classes that fulfill the
need of working people--vocational, academic or developmental in nature.

III. FEES

Registration fee for evening students is $1. 00 plus a
material fee for laboratory classes due to reduced state support for evening classes. No refund is provided unless the
class is cancelled.

IV. FACULTY AND FACULTY RECRUITMENT

The Dean of Evening College has the authority for
hiring or rejecting full/part-time faculty members for evening classes. 30% of the faculty are full-time. There are
no full-time faculty members teaching exclusively in the evening. The Dean may reject a faculty member who has been
assigned to teach evening classes or engage an instructor if
necessary if Department Head does not furnish an instructor.
Regular faculty meetings are held weekly. Part-time faculty
salary ranges from $6. 50 to $13. 00 per hour. Overloads
are not permitted.

V.   SCHEDULING

The Dean is responsible for scheduling evening classes
in cooperation with the evening college administration and department chairmen.   The Dean does have authority to revise,
add or delete, the evening class schedule.   The three-hour
classes are scheduled one night and two nights per week depending upon the class.   Part-time evening students are eligible for the Dean's List if they have 30 units at 3.2 GPA.
Twenty students must register to constitute a class.   The
hourly rate of instructor compensation is independent of class
size.

VI.   ORGANIZATIONAL STRUCTURE

The administrative staff consists of four staff members: Dean, Assistant Dean and two coordinators with a
part-time faculty of 300.   The recommended administrative
staff would be three for each 5000 students.

VII.   EDUCATIONAL TELEVISION PROGRAMS

Non-credit courses are offered in educational television as community service programs.   These courses are
the responsibility of the program supervisor.   A regular
teaching load is reduced 20% for those teaching courses on
TV.   The Evening Division handles registration.   Programs
are scheduled at 7:00 to 8:00 a. m. , 10:00 to 11:00 a. m. ,
and 7:00 to 8:00 p. m.

VIII.   NON-CREDIT PROGRAMS

Non-credit programs are offered in business and management, engineering, arts and sciences, and other areas.
All such programs are state funded.   Faculty receive $6 to
$13 per course hour.   Special conferences and institutes
sponsored by the Evening College this past year included
reading, mathematics, electronics, and real estate appraisers.
Summer session is not the responsibility of the Evening College.

IX.   GENERAL

Courses are offered for the economically deprived
populations.   Students are represented on curriculum committees.   Programs are offered for the disadvantaged and
physically handicapped both high school level and lower col-

lege level. The administration does recognize the need and
the importance of adult education. The Dean is responsible
to the College President. The usual audio-visual aids are
available.

X.   STUDENT RECRUITMENT

All news media is used for student recruitment.
Brochures are mailed to industry and organizations.

<u>Mohawk Valley Community College</u>
Utica, New York
Continuing Education

Total Enrollment 2, 200   Public Community
Evening Enrollment 2, 800-3, 400   Quarter System

I.   ADMISSION POLICIES

Deadline for application for admissions is the second
week of class.   A student may register for credit courses
before transcripts are submitted.   Non-matriculating or
"special" students may take up to 15 hours of work for credit.
The only admission requirement for non-matriculating or
"special" students is some indication of ability for success.
Regular students rejected for admission are advised to apply
as evening students but are not automatically accepted but
take programs advised by counselors.   No mail registration
is used.   Students on probation are dismissed after two
quarters if grades are not improved.   No ACT or CEEB examinations are required.   New York State Regents Scholarship Exam is required and used as a basis for admission.
No special evening degree program is offered adults.   During
fall quarter the enrollment was 75 full-time and 3400 part-
time students.   Distribution requirements vary with degree.
The Admissions Committee formulates the admission policies
for evening students.   The Division of Continuing Education
formulates the admission requirements for non-matriculating
or "special" students.   Students may enroll in day and/or
evening classes with no limitations.   Day students are able
to get courses not offered days and students benefit from a
more heterogeneous group.   An orientation program is conducted in August.   An Evening Division Advisory Committee
advises on policies, practices and evaluations.

II.   TERMINOLOGY

Title of Division: Continuing Education.   Defined: To
serve the educational needs of the community not presently
being met by any other educational institution.   Continuing
Education defined: A program constantly introducing new
programs which may or may not become part of regular degree programs.

III.   FEES

There is no fee differential between day and evening
classes.   Refunds are made 80% the first week and 50% the
second week.

IV.   FACULTY AND FACULTY RECRUITMENT

Full-time faculty teach only one course per quarter
in the evening.   Approximately 5-10% of the faculty are full-
time.   The Director of Continuing Education has the final
authority for hiring full-time or part-time faculty members
for evening classes.   The Director can reject a faculty member assigned to teach evening classes.

V.   SCHEDULING

Past experience plus requests from department heads
determine the evening class schedule.   Three-hour classes
are offered both one and two nights and there is no preference.   A study of part-time adult students in a Community
College is being made.   Day and evening classes are the
same quality.   Part-time students are eligible for the Dean's
List with 12 hours and a 3. 0 average.   A class of six or
less will be taught--instructor's compensation remains con-
stant.

VI.   ORGANIZATIONAL STRUCTURE

The administrative staff consists of four with a teaching staff of 200 part-time faculty members.   There is academic and administrative autonomy.   The Dean is assisted
by the Assistant Dean and two Assistant Directors, with two
counselors assisting students.

VII.   EDUCATIONAL TELEVISION PROGRAMS

There are no educational television programs offered

by the Division of Continuing Education.

VIII. NON-CREDIT PROGRAMS

Non-credit courses are offered in the areas of Business and Management, Engineering, Arts and Sciences, and other areas. The program generally pays for itself. Remuneration to faculty is $9-12 per contact hour, depending upon the qualifications of the instructor. Continuing Education does sponsor conferences and institutes, such as: Insurance Agency Personnel, Conference on Research in Continuing Education, etc. Clinicians are paid up to $100 per day. The Division is responsible for the Summer session.

IX. GENERAL

Off-campus vocational courses are planned through vocational education funds for the economically deprived populations. No graduate programs are offered. Adequate support and stress are given to continuing education. The Dean is responsible to the President. Audio-visual and other technical instructional aids are available.

X. STUDENT RECRUITMENT

Newspaper, radio, television as well as special motivational appeals to local organizations, Chamber of Commerce, etc. are used for student recruiting.

Nassau Community College
Garden City, New York
Evening and Extension Division

Total Enrollment 12, 000   Public Institution
Evening Enrollment 7, 256   Semester System

I. ADMISSION POLICIES

Deadline for application for admission for classes is June 1, September-October for non-matriculating students. Students may take up to eighteen hours as "special" students. Admission requirements include a high school diploma or equivalency for "special" students and an 82 average and 450/450 board scores for regular students. No CEEB is required for adults but placement tests in Reading and English

are required. No mail registration is used. Retention policies: Open - with advisement and counseling used to determine continuation of enrollment. The Dean of the Evening
and Extension Division formulate the admission policies.
Day and evening students may enroll in the same class by
special permission. An orientation program for evening students is scheduled for four evenings a week. The evening
program for adults does not differ from the day program.
The same areas of concentration are offered in the evening
as in the day. There are no plans for offering a special degree
program for adults. A college-wide committee formulates the
admission policies for all students.

II. TERMINOLOGY

Title of Division: Evening and Extension Division.
Defined: The Evening and Extension Division is the administrative unit of the college which initiates, guides, facilitates
and provides leadership in a many-faceted program for those
persons not regularly enrolled as day students on the campus.

III. FEES

There is no differential in fees between day and evening classes. Applications for refunds are referred to a
committee. If withdrawals are beyond the control of the students, the fee is refunded.

IV. FACULTY AND FACULTY RECRUITMENT

There is no policy regarding percentage of faculty for
evening classes that are full-time faculty members. At the
present time 30% are full-time. The Dean of the Division
has the authority to hire full and part-time faculty members.
There are no full-time faculty members who teach exclusively
in the evening. Regular faculty meetings are held for evening faculty in September, February, and June. Faculty
members may teach an overload limited to eighteen hours
over an academic year. None of the budget is spent on recruiting.

V. SCHEDULING

The Dean is responsible for the evening class schedule.
Three-hour classes are scheduled on two nights per week.
A research project has been completed on the Cooperation
Opportunity in Public Education (COPE). Day and evening

classes are comparable in terms of quality.   Evening students are eligible for the Dean's List.   Twelve hours are required with a 3.25 GPA.

VI.   ORGANIZATIONAL STRUCTURE

The administrative staff numbers eight and the teaching staff consists of 600 part-time faculty members.   There is academic and administrative autonomy.   Responsibilities of staff: The Dean of Instruction and an Assistant Dean are responsible for part-time faculty, the Directors of Special Programs as Police Science and other special areas, and four others - one administrative office, (independent study,) and three administrative assistants.

VII.   EDUCATIONAL TELEVISION PROGRAMS

One credit course in educational television, which earns residence credit, is beginning German.   Students must be regularly attending NCC students.   Students attend a regular class session, go to the language lab and watch TV tapes. These credits do count toward a degree.   Faculty (full-time) supervise the educational television programs as a part of their regular load.   Registration is held during the regular registration period.   Only undergraduate courses are offered in this area and are financed by tuition.   Out-of-state tuition is not charged because out-of-state students may not register - only those presently attending NCC.   The program is scheduled during normal classroom hours.

VIII.   NON-CREDIT PROGRAMS

Non-credit courses are offered in the area of Arts and Sciences.   Faculty members are paid part-time rates per instructional (contact) hour; $185-$230 per contact hour depending upon instructor's step.   No budget is provided for non-credit courses; they are expected to pay for themselves. Conferences and institutes are not sponsored.   The Division is responsible for the summer session.

IX.   GENERAL

Limited opportunity is given students to participate in discussions regarding the academic program, but they do serve on the Curriculum Committee.   Adequate support is given to the evening program.   The Dean is responsible directly to the President of the College.

X.   STUDENT RECRUITMENT

Newspaper articles and advertisements are used for publicity purposes as well as radio.

University of Nebraska
Lincoln, Nebraska
University Extension Division

Total Enrollment 20, 800   Public Institution
Evening Enrollment 6, 000   Semester System

I.   ADMISSION POLICIES

There is no deadline for application for admission. A student may register before transcripts are submitted and may take an unlimited number of courses for credit as a non-matriculating or "special" student.   The only admission requirement is that the student meet the prerequisite requirement.   Students who are rejected as regular students are not advised to enroll in the evening division.   Mail registration is used on a very limited basis.   In special cases forms are sent to persons to be completed and returned.   No ACT or CEEB examination is required.   A special degree program for adults is being considered but still very tentative. The Extension Division and the various colleges formulate the admission policies.   There is no limit to the extent of day/evening combinations.   It is felt that the combination classes are disadvantaged by a difference in interests, backgrounds, and maturities.   There is no orientation program for evening students.

II.   TERMINOLOGY

Title of Division: Department of Class Programs - University Extension Division.   Defined: This is an administrative unit within the Extension Division.   Continuing Education defined: Any organized program of education provided for persons not regularly enrolled in a formal program of education.

III.   FEES

Day classes are charged at a rate of $14 tuition plus $5. 25 fees per credit hour; evening classes at a rate of $17 per credit hour. Evening classes do not provide the services for which fees are charged.   Tuition is higher because of larger degree of self-support.   Refunds are paid per class at a rate of 80% for the first week, 60% second week, 40% third week and 20% fourth week.

IV.   FACULTY AND FACULTY RECRUITMENT

Approximately 75% of the faculty teaching evening classes is full-time.   Department heads have the final authority in hiring faculty members to teach credit classes; University Extension Division has the final authority in hiring faculty members to teach non-credit courses.   The Director can reject a faculty member who has been hired to teach evening classes.   No faculty member is hired to teach exclusively in the evening.   No regular faculty meeting is held for evening faculty.   Approximately 1% of the budget is spent on recruitment.   There is no part-time faculty employed.   Salary for faculty overloads is $850 per three semester hour course.

V.   SCHEDULING

The head of Class Programs, who reports to the Director, is responsible for the evening class schedule.   Tentative schedules are proposed by the Extension Division;   additions and/or deletions are made by conference with the department chairmen.   The Director has the authority to revise the schedule as necessary.   Three-hour classes are scheduled one and two nights per week but one night is preferred.   There are no research projects underway at this time.   Part-time students are not eligible for the Dean's List.   Twelve students constitute a class.   Instructors teaching less than twelve students are paid on a salary prorated with class size.

VI.   ORGANIZATIONAL STRUCTURE

Two staff members comprise the administrative staff. The Director has general administrative responsibilities and the Assistant Director has responsibility of supervising evening classes along with three other areas of responsibilities. The teaching staff consists of 110 faculty members.   The institution does not have academic autonomy but is administratively autonomic.

VII. EDUCATIONAL TELEVISION PROGRAMS

No educational television programs are offered by the Extension Division.

VIII. NON-CREDIT PROGRAMS

Non-credit programs are offered in the area of Business and Management. The non-credit program budget is part of the evening budget but classes are expected to pay for themselves. Remuneration to faculty varies with the area of instruction. The Division is not responsible for conferences, institutes, or summer sessions.

IX. GENERAL

Part-time graduate programs are offered off-campus. Adequate support and stress are not received. The Director is responsible to the Director of University Extension. Audio-visual aids are available to evening classes.

X. STUDENT RECRUITMENT

Newspapers are the source of publicity for student recruitment. Special motivational appeals are developed for industry and organizations.

University of Nebraska at Omaha
Omaha, Nebraska
College of Continuing Studies

Total Enrollment 13, 000+   Public Institution
Evening Enrollment 1, 095 full-time   Semester System
                   2, 382 part-time

I. ADMISSION POLICIES

The deadline for application for admission is three weeks prior to registration. A student may register for credit courses before transcripts are submitted, provided the student completes a standard-type card form certifying that the transcript(s) will be received within an eight day or four week period, as well as good standing at former institution. Non-matriculating or "special" students may enroll as full-time students taking up to seventeen hours for credit. The

admission requirements for non-matriculating or "special"
students require high school graduation (or GED equivalent);
for regular students: high school graduation plus completion
of ACT unless the student has 58 semester hours of acceptable transfer credit.   Students who are rejected for admission as regular students are advised to apply in the evening
but are not automatically accepted.   Mail registration is
used.   Retention policies require a student to achieve a graduated grade point average depending upon the number of hours
accepted, i. e. , 12-16 hours with a 1. 2 GPA; 58 hours and
over with a 2. 0 GPA.   In addition, students applying for admission to the Bachelor of General Studies program may receive Academic Amnesty.   No ACT or CEEB are required
for adults in the evening.   The adult degree (Bachelor of
General Studies) is available to day and evening students.
This degree differs in a number of ways from other degree
programs.   The BGS degree requires the successful completion of 125 semester hours of credit.   At least thirty of
the 125 credits must be earned in courses at the junior-
senior level.   Core requirements: English Composition, 6
hours, Social Sciences, 12 hours, Natural Sciences/Math,
9 hours, Humanities, 12 hours.   Areas of concentration are
thirty hours for first minor, twelve hours for second minor,
thirty-two hours of electives for a total of 125 hours.   The
College is not involved with graduate students, courses or
degrees.   College of Continuing Studies students who wish to
earn the Bachelor of General Studies degree must apply for
and be formally admitted to candidacy as a specific pre-requisite for the degree.   The admission policies for the evening
students are formulated by a committee structure through the
University faculty, administration and regents.   Day and evening students may enroll in the same class with the exception
of young freshmen who are not supposed to take night classes.
In our opinion, the advantages and/or disadvantages of the
combined classes are intellectual exchange, cross-fertilization, inter-group understanding stimulating faculty.   There is
an Evening Division Advisory Committee whose functions are:
General policy review determination, etc.

II.   TERMINOLOGY

Title of Division: College of Continuing Studies: Defined: Makes higher education available to any functioning
adult who does not find his needs met by the regular traditional structures and programs of the University.   Continuing
Education defined: Within the University - providing oppor-

tunities for on-going education for functioning adults whose
education needs are not met by the regular, traditional academic programs of the institution.   These programs are taken
for credit or credit-free.

III.   FEES

There is no fee differential for day and evening
classes.   A full refund will be made for withdrawal before
classes start, 75% for withdrawal during first and second
week, 50% refund for withdrawal during third and fourth week
and 25% withdrawal during fourth through eighth week; no refund after the eighth week.

IV.   FACULTY AND FACULTY RECRUITMENT

Approximately 75% of the faculty for evening classes
are full-time faculty.   The Dean of the College has final
authority for hiring full/part-time faculty members for evening classes although the Director may reject a faculty member who has been assigned to teach evening classes.   Regular faculty meetings with the evening faculty are held annually for this College; Academic Departments are urged to include them.   The faculty members teaching credit courses
are controlled by the Dean of the various colleges.   Non-
credit courses are controlled by the College of Continuing
Studies.   There is a minimal percentage of the budget spent
for recruitment.   The salary range for part-time faculty is
$600 to $800 per three-hours.   The salary paid the faculty
for overloads is 3% of regular contract salary for each one
hour of teaching load.   Twelve students must register to
constitute a class.   The class taught below minimum size requires reduced compensation to the instructor.

V.   SCHEDULING

The Dean or Director is not responsible for the evening class schedule.   Each college within the University is
responsible for the evening class schedule.   It is the tradi-
tion of the institution that virtually all courses shall be available.   The procedure for compiling the evening class schedule involves varying consultation with CCS, academic departments submit schedules to the Dean, Deans submit schedules
to Registrar, Registrar prepares for printer.   Three-hour
classes are scheduled two nights per week.   The research
projects completed or in progress are a comparison of the
Academic Performance of Students Who Have Earned Degree

Credit Through CLEP General Examination Battery vs. Those Students Who Have Not, in cooperation with Educational Testing Service. Day and evening classes are equal in terms of quality. Part-time evening students are eligible for the Dean's List. Number of hours required are twelve with a grade point average of 3. 0 on a 4. 0 scale. The following procedure is used for adjustment of remuneration for small classes: Part-time contracts are "contingent" upon enrollment. If the class is small, the CCS Dean and the Dean of the College offering the course will consult. Decision may be made to cancel, operate at full salary, or it will be the instructor's option to accept an amount equal to tuition generated by the class.

VI. ORGANIZATIONAL STRUCTURE

The administrative staff consists of six staff members. The teaching staff consists of 300 full-time and 100 part-time faculty members. The College does have academic and administrative autonomy. The Dean has overall supervisory responsibility; one Assistant Dean supervises the academic programs and one supervises the Community Service Programs; a Director and one Assistant of Military Programs; a Director of Adult Academic Programs (civilian); a Director of Conferences and Institutes; a Director of Continuing Engineering Programs; a Counselor for Military Programs; and a Program Coordinator for the Community Services Division.

VII. EDUCATIONAL TELEVISION PROGRAMS

Educational Television Programs are offered for credit and non-credit. No distinction is made between credits earned day/evening or on/off campus. The University has a standard contractual policy with all TV instruction. Full-time faculty members teach the program. Faculty members receive additional remuneration for teaching courses on TV. The Registrar handles registration of credit educational TV courses; no registration is involved for the non-credit courses. Only undergraduate courses are offered occasionally on educational TV. The program is financed by the regular budget and courses are scheduled on Saturdays from 8 a. m. and Mondays from 8 p. m. for thirteen weeks. The instructor normally functions as the coordinator-moderator using a guest speaker/guest panel format.

VIII. NON-CREDIT PROGRAMS

Non-credit courses are offered in the following areas:
Business and Management, Arts and Sciences, Engineering,
Education and others.   This program is expected to pay for
itself.   Remuneration for faculty (full/part-time) is negotiated
and varies from program to program.   The Division sponsors conferences and institutes.   The clinicians receive various amounts.   The Division is not responsible for the summer session.

IX.   GENERAL

The institution offers credit and non-credit courses
in "store front" locations off-campus for economically deprived populations.   Students participate in discussions regarding the academic program in limited way but participate
heavily in the non-credit program.   Other innovative practices
used at the institution include extensive use of credit by examination, CLEP, amnesty for past poor academic performance and flexibility of degree programming.   In general, it
is felt that the evening division is receiving adequate support.
The Director is responsible to the Dean of Academic Affairs
and the President.   The usual audio-visual aids are used in
the College of Continuing Studies.

X.   STUDENT RECRUITMENT

The newspaper, radio and television are used as publicity for student recruitment.

The New School
New York, New York
A Division for Social Research

Total Enrollment 12, 369   Private Institution
Evening Enrollment 10, 000   Semester System

I.   ADMISSION POLICIES

Deadline for application for admission is two weeks
after classes begin (credit students) and three weeks after
classes begin for students enrolling for non-credit.   Students
may register before transcripts are submitted.   Admission
requirements include high school graduation--no ACT or CEEB

is required.   No special adult degree program is offered,
but one is being considered.   The faculty formulates the admission policies for the evening students; the Dean's office
for non-matriculating, or "special" students.   No Orientation
Program is scheduled for evening students.

II.   TERMINOLOGY

Title of Division: A division of the New School for
Social Research.   Defined: "Covers all non-degree courses--
includes certificate programs (day and evening). "

III.   FEES

The evening tuition is per course and by credit.   The
institution gives a proportional refund depending on date of
withdrawal up to the 3rd week of classes.

IV.   FACULTY AND FACULTY RECRUITMENT

There are no full-time faculty teaching evening classes.
The authority to hire faculty lies with the Dean.   No regular
faculty meetings are held for evening faculty.   No overloads
are permitted.   Part-time faculty are paid $500-$1500 per
course.   Ten students constitute a class, but the instructor's
compensation is not reduced if he teaches a class below the
minimum size.

V.   SCHEDULING

The Dean is responsible for scheduling.   Evening
classes are submitted by the faculty but the schedule is medi-
ated by necessity of space allocation.   Three-hour classes
are scheduled one night per week.

VI.   ORGANIZATIONAL STRUCTURE

There are 20 members on the administrative staff of
the evening division (includes department heads).   The teaching staff consists of 500 part-time faculty members.   The
division is headed by a Dean: academic and fiscal.   The assistant dean works under supervision of the Dean who is responsible for all matters.   Additional administrative officers
include the Director of Admissions (Evening) Evening Registrar
and Chairman of the various academic divisions along with administrative officers.

VII.   EDUCATIONAL TELEVISION PROGRAMS

No courses are offered by Educational Television.

VIII.   NON-CREDIT PROGRAMS

The Division offers non-credit courses in Business
and Management and Arts and Sciences.   This program is
expected to pay for itself.   The remuneration the faculty
members receive for teaching a non-credit course is $500-
$1500 per course for 15 class sessions, depending upon the
qualifications of the instructor.   The Division does not sponsor conferences or institutes.

IX.   GENERAL

In general, adequate support is given to the evening
program.   The Dean is directly responsible to the President
of the School.   The division is responsible for the Summer
session.

X.   STUDENT RECRUITMENT

Newspaper articles and advertisements are used for
publicity purposes.   Special motivational appeals are developed
for industry as well as for various civic organizations.

<u>University of New Hampshire</u>
<u>Durham, New Hampshire</u>
Division of Continuing Education

Day Enrollment 9, 000   Public Institution
Evening Enrollment 2, 000   Semester System
Total Enrollment 11, 000   (credits)

I.   ADMISSION POLICIES

The week before classes is the deadline for admission
applications.   A student may register for credit courses before transcripts are received.   Non-matriculating and/or
"special" students may take 26 hours of work for credit.
Admission requirements for "special" students are 18 years
of age or high school graduate (for regular students admission requirements are varied.)   Students rejected for admission as regular students are advised to apply as evening stu-

dents and are automatically accepted.   Mail registration is
used.   Registration materials are sent to students; materials
are returned along with a check for tuition and fees by a
designated date.   Probation and suspension policies are the
same as for the day division.   The ACT and/or CEEB examinations are optional.   An evening degree program for adults
is offered--Associate Degree in Applied Business with an enrollment of 87 part-time undergraduate students.   Distribution requirements are: 50% technical, 25% general education
and 25% elective (general education or technical.)   Sixty-four
hours are required to complete the degree with concentration
of ten courses (40 credits) in ABM and 2 courses (8 credits)
in Communications.   Admission requirements for the special
degree program are high school graduation or the equivalency.
The Executive Committee, Division of Continuing Education,
recommend admission policies.   Restrictions on the day/eve-
ning student combination is that no more than one-third of
the class can be made up of day students.   The advantage to
a day/evening combination is that evening students, older,
more practical and experienced, can tie theory and practice
together--older ideas take on a new meaning.   An orientation
program is conducted for evening students via the Annual
Bulletin.   A Division of Continuing Education Executive Committee functions for the purpose of program development, review and update of policies and procedures.

II.   TERMINOLOGY

Title of Division: Division of Continuing Education.
Defined: providing meaningful and effective educational opportunity and dissemination of information beyond normal programs of instruction . . .   provides a spectrum of services
and programs to New Hampshire citizens not regularly enrolled in on-campus programs.

III.   FEES

Evening students pay $100 a course; day students pay
$120 a course.   Evening charges are by course while day
charges are by credit hour if students load is eight credits
or less.   Refund policies dictate that 1/2 of tuition can be
refunded during first two weeks of class and nothing thereafter.

IV.   FACULTY AND FACULTY RECRUITMENT

There is no policy regarding percentage of faculty for

evening classes.   Approximately 90% of the evening faculty
are full-time faculty members.   The Director of the Division
of Continuing Education has the final authority to hire faculty
members to teach evening classes.   The Director can reject
a faculty member who has been hired to teach in the evening.
No full-time faculty members teach exclusively in the evening.   Regular faculty meetings are held each semester.
Faculty is allowed to teach one course a semester as an
overload.   No budget is spent for recruitment.   Salary range
for part-time faculty is: $1000 to $2000; overloads are
paid: $1100 Instructor; $1400 Assistant Professor; $1700
Associate Professor; $2000 Professor.

V.   SCHEDULING

The Director is responsible for the evening class
schedule in cooperation with the department heads and Deans.
Three-hour classes are scheduled one night per week.   Day
and evening classes are comparable in terms of quality.   No
part-time student (non-matriculated) is eligible for the Dean's
List.   Almost all courses are guaranteed.

VI.   ORGANIZATIONAL STRUCTURE

Six staff members make up the administrative staff:
the Director and four Assistant Directors--responsible for
credit courses, summer session, short courses and certificate
program, and conferences.   The teaching staff includes 100 part-
time faculty members, 90% of which are day division faculty.
The Division has administrative autonomy for associate degree programs, non-credit courses, and conferences.

VII.   EDUCATIONAL TELEVISION PROGRAMS

Credit courses are offered by educational television
earning residence credit toward a degree.   The Director of
Instructional Services, N. H. Network, supervises the program using part-time faculty.   Additional remuneration is
paid the faculty for teaching courses on TV.   The Division
of Continuing Education handles the registration--the Instructor registers students at the first class and forwards all
materials back to the Division of Continuing Education.   The
program is self-supporting.   Courses are scheduled 4 to
6:30 p. m.

VIII. NON-CREDIT PROGRAMS

Non-credit programs are offered in the areas of Business and Management, Engineering, Arts and Sciences, Education and Health Sciences. There is a budget set aside for the program, but overall the program is expected to pay for itself. Remuneration for faculty ranges from $20 to $30 per class hour or $500 per course for 10 class sessions of 2 1/2 hours each. Remuneration does depend upon the qualifications of the instructor. In addition to 61 short courses offered, 27 conferences and institutes were offered during the past year. The Division is responsible for the summer session.

IX. GENERAL

The institution is participating in "store front" locations off-campus for the economically deprived populations. Six M. Ed. degree programs are offered through the Division of Continuing Education in cooperation with the Department of Education and Graduate School. There is not sufficient stress or financial support given to the Division even though the need is recognized. The Director is responsible to the Academic Vice-President. All audio-visual facilities are available through the UNH Media-Services Center.

X. STUDENT RECRUITMENT

Newspaper, radio and television are used to recruit students. Special program brochures are developed for business and industry and Cooperative County Agents.

The University of New Mexico
Albuquerque, New Mexico
Division of Continuing Education

Total Enrollment 17,000   Public Institution
                                                       Semester System

I. ADMISSION POLICIES

The deadline for application for admission to evening classes is July 15 for the fall semester and January 1 for the spring semester. A student may register for credit courses before transcripts are submitted if he is a non-de-

gree student. Non-matriculating or "non-degree" students
may take up to thirty hours of work for credit. Admission
requirements: regular students must be high school graduates and age 19 or 21. Students who are rejected as regular students are advised to apply as evening students. (They
are not automatically accepted however.) No mail registration is used. Probation and dismissal requirements: students must maintain a "C" average. No ACT or CEEB examinations are required for admission to evening classes but
are used for placement and advisement purposes. No special
degree program is offered for adults. An AA degree is being
considered for the future. Admission policies are the same
for both day and evening students.

II. TERMINOLOGY

Title of Division: Continuing Education. Defined:
non-degree students, off-campus centers and programs, extension courses, correspondence courses, non-credit courses,
conferences and seminars.

III. FEES

There is no fee differential between day and evening
classes. The refund policies are the same as for day students.

IV. FACULTY AND FACULTY RECRUITMENT

The Director of Continuing Education has the final
authority to hire full and/or part-time faculty to teach non-
credit courses. No full-time faculty is employed to teach
exclusively in the evening. Such teaching is in addition to
the normal duties and pay is in addition to normal salary.
There is no budget for recruiting. Salary is $12.50 per
contact hour. The Director is responsible for the non-credit
program.

V. SCHEDULING

The Director is responsible for the non-credit class
schedule. Three-hour classes are scheduled one night per
week. Normally 16-18 students constitute a class.

VI. ORGANIZATIONAL STRUCTURE

The administrative staff of the Division of Continuing

Education consists of five staff members. The Director has the overall responsibility for the Division. He is assisted by an Assistant Director, a Director of Non-Credit Programs, a Director of Conferences and Institutes, a Director of Extension, and an Independent Study Registrar who handles all correspondence courses and student records.

VII. EDUCATIONAL TELEVISION PROGRAMS

The Division of Continuing Education offers no educational television programs.

VIII. NON-CREDIT PROGRAMS

The Division offers non-credit programs in Business and Management, Arts and Sciences, Education, Engineering and Crafts. A budget is provided for these programs but the courses are expected to pay for themselves. Faculty members receive $12.50 per class session. The Division sponsors conferences and institutes including such topics as: dental seminars, Dental and Hygienists seminar, Hotel-Motel Management, Tax Assessors Institute, Power Plan Maintenance, Boiler Plant Operation, etc. Varied amounts are paid to clinicians for conferences depending upon the type of conference and travel involved. The Division is not responsible for the summer session.

IX. GENERAL

The Division participates in offering credit and/or non-credit courses in "store front" locations for economically deprived populations. Students are members of all committees. All audio-visual aids are available for evening classes except closed circuit TV. A student profile during the last five years is in progress.

X. STUDENT RECRUITMENT

Newspaper, radio and television are used for publicity purposes. Special motivational appeals are developed for industry, civic organizations, Chamber of Commerce, etc.

New York University
New York, New York
School of Continuing Education
and
Extension Services

Private Institution
Semester System

NOTE: The material submitted from New York University pertains solely to the School of Continuing Education and Extension Services which
is largely devoted to non-credit courses, lecture series, workshops, conferences, and institutes; these last year accounted for 33,795
registrations of a total of 37,000 registrations.   The remaining 3,000 registrations
were in four special degree programs.

I.   ADMISSION POLICIES

Applications are ordinarily received before June 1 for
the fall semester; no student is admitted without application,
transcripts and relevant test scores.   There are no non-degree or special with credit.   Admission requirements for the
different degree programs vary according to the special case.
Degree programs are: Associate in Arts (evening degree
program for adults), Associate in Applied Science (Business)
for adults, Associate in Applied Science in Early Childhood
Education and Social Work (daytime program with sections
for adults and sections for recent high school graduates),
New York University Opportunities Program (for those with
grades ordinarily less than 10% of ordinary admission requirements).   There is no mail registration for credit courses.
Special Degree enrollment: 181-Associate in Arts (evening);
132-Associate in Applied Science (Business - evening); 60-
Associate in Applied Science.   The fourth special degree program involves 53 students with the majority attending on
Martin Luther King, Jr., scholarships.   Admission policies
are set by the faculty of the school - AA, AAS (Business)
high school graduation or equivalent, plus, adult admission
test.   Part-time students may enroll only for evening courses;
day students can schedule some evening courses if it is more
convenient.   There is an orientation program for day and
evening students, respectively, enrolled in each degree program.   Students below 2.0 (C) are probationary; below 2.0
a second semester are suspended.   Disciplinary action is in

the form of committee hearing. Undergraduate degrees in
each program require a minimum of 52 of 64 to a maximum
of 64 of 64 hours of required courses. Total number of
hours to complete a degree is 64-68 credits. Special degree
program requirements for admission are: (AAS - public
service) persons without a high school education are admitted
and given one year to acquire high school equivalency. Areas
of concentration include liberal arts, business, pre-physical
therapy, teacher aids, social work assistants, pre-respiratory therapy. A special degree program for adults is being
considered.

II. TERMINOLOGY

School of Continuing Education and Extension Services:
a general way of indicating that a considerable range of activities will be found here that are found in other institutions
by many other names. Continuing Education tends to mean
non-credit courses, conferences, institutes, etc. , especially
for people who already have one or more college degrees--
particularly professional ones.

III. FEES

There is no fee differential between day and evening
credit courses. Students are charged a "flat" tuition rate
because they schedule a "regular program. "

IV. FACULTY AND FACULTY RECRUITMENT

It is against University rules for any member of any
faculty to be used on an "overload" basis except in the School
of Continuing Education and Extension Services or in Education Field Services or through a temporary ruling of the
Chancellor. Faculty members are hired on recommendation
of the Dean to the Chancellor and the Board of Trustees.
Faculty meetings are held four times a year as established
by the Agenda Committee and additional faculty meetings are
sometimes called. No budget is established for recruiting.

V. SCHEDULING

The Dean of the School of Continuing Education and
Extension Services is responsible for the schedule. The program administrator or department head turns in "room cards"
requesting space for his class. After approval of the Curriculum Committee for any new courses or changes in fees,

etc. , the recommendations are submitted to the Chancellor
and the Board of Trustees for formal approval.   Most of the
classes are two hours (meeting once a week) or four hours
(meeting twice a week).   The few three hour classes are
scheduled once a week in the evening or twice a week in the
daytime.   Research has been completed as follows: A History
of the Division of General Education, New York University,
1934-59, Ed. D Thesis submitted by Anne Freidus; Patterns
of Educational Use of a Televised Public Affairs Program,
A Study of METROPOLIS: Creator or Destroyer, sponsored
by the University Council on Education for Public Responsibility; Study Director: Harry L. Miller, New York University's Harlem Seminars, a narrative account of a Title I,
Higher Education Act of 1965, project under the direction of
Dr. Harry L. Miller; Survey of University Adult Education
in the Metropolitan Area of New York, a study made possible
by a grant from the Fund for the Advancement of Education -
Ford Foundation under the direction of Mrs. Caroline Ellwood; An Evaluation of the MIND Adult Education Center on
West 114th Street in Harlem, an evaluation of a novel attempt at pre-vocational basic education for residents of 114th
St. between 7th and 8th Avenue by MIND, Inc. , a subsidiary
of Corn Products Corporation.   Evening classes are better
than day because they are taken by more interested students
with a greater diversity of background.   There is no dean's
list.   Ten to fifteen students must register to constitute a
class.   Salary ranges from $450 to $1000 per course depending upon many factors.

VI.   ORGANIZATIONAL STRUCTURE

      The administrative staff consists of fifty-five persons
with a teaching staff of 138 full-time and 826 part-time.   As
a private institution, we do have academic and administrative
autonomy.   The Dean of Continuing Education has overall
policy and administrative responsibilities and is Chairman of
the faculty; the Vice-Dean is the Dean's alter ego and is responsible for the day-to-day administration and budget control; three Associate Deans - Director of the Division of
Business and Industry (non-credit), Director of the Division
of Continuing Education (non-credit) and the Director of Associate in Arts Degree Program for Adults; the Assistant
Dean and Director of American Language Institute (non-credit);
the Assistant Dean and Director of Community Services (non-
credit); and Assistant Dean and Director of Special Events
and Public Information; Director of College Preparatory and
Foreign Language Program (non-credit); Director of Safety

(non-credit, undergraduate and graduate credit); Director of Reading Institute (non-credit); Director of Opportunities Program; Director of Institute on Federal Taxation; Directors of Associate in Applied Science (business), Associate in Applied Science (public service) and Associate in Science; Director of Town Hall; Assistant Director of the Division of Continuing Education, Division of Business and Management; Associate Director of the Institute of Federal Taxation; Assistant Directors of Associate in Arts Degree Program, Center for Safety, American Language Institute, Town Hall; the Director of Admissions; Registrar and Recorder.

VII. EDUCATIONAL TELEVISION PROGRAMS

Two non-credit courses a semester are offered on television. Credit courses offered can also be taken for residence credit in Washington Square College. The Dean of Continuing Education along with the Dean of Washington Square College is responsible for the supervision of the television programs. Three half-hours a week are counted as a full teaching load when handling the television program and the teaching load on-campus is reduced accordingly. Registrar's office handles all TV registration. The TV programs are a deficit operation (PR value). Programs are scheduled from 6:30 to 7:00 a. m. Courses can be carried on any CBS station. "We invite any college to use the courses as their own without fee to us and one free syllabus is supplied with final permission to copy. "

VIII. NON-CREDIT PROGRAMS

Non-credit programs are offered in education, business and management, arts and sciences, reading, graphics, publishing, languages, real estate, mortgage borrowing, etc. Income from these courses is budgeted directly and indirectly plus overhead expenses. Faculty (full or part-time) receive $450 to $1000 per course for fourteen class sessions. Remuneration depends upon the qualifications of the instructor. The School of Continuing Education does sponsor conferences and workshops with the principal ones of last year being Annual Institute of Federal Taxation, Annual Institute on Labor, Biennial Institute on Charitable Foundations. Salary range for instructors of these conferences and institutes range from $0 to $250 per day.

IX.   GENERAL

The Division is experimenting with non-credit courses
for economically deprived students in off-campus locations.
Innovative practices include: faculty participation for part-
time faculty; various programs have appointed or elected
faculty "ombudsmen" to whom the student can, anonymously
and without prejudice, bring complaints or problems; a newsletter "Continuing Education" is published eight times a year
for circulation to faculty and students; a "house organ" called
"School Notes" is circulated at irregular intervals to the office staff and administrators of the school - mailing list of
172: "Library Notes" reviews significant books or reading
material and is circulated at irregular intervals to administrators and full-time faculty; a program of special events -
lectures, musicals, colloquia, etc. , - is announced through
the newsletter.   During the current year approximately 50
events will be open to faculty and students of the school without charge.   The Dean of the Division is responsible to the
President and Chancellor of the University.   There are about
200 special appearances on television and radio yearly as
well as other instructional aids.

X.   STUDENT RECRUITMENT

There is an office concerned with publicity and information which is concerned with press release, newspaper
articles, radio and television appearances, etc.   In addition
to the general bulletin there are many brochures and fliers
sent to students as well as industry and organizations.   There
is an Office of Special Services to Business and Industry.

<u>University of North Carolina</u>
<u>Chapel Hill, North Carolina</u>
Evening College

Total Enrollment 15, 500   Public Institution
Evening Enrollment 650   Semester System

I.   ADMISSION POLICIES

The deadline for application for admission to evening
classes coincides with the date of registration.   Students may
register for credit courses before transcripts are submitted
but all transcripts, confidential rating sheets, etc. , must be

in within three weeks.   No work may be taken for credit as
a "special" student.   Regular students are admitted who score
800 or higher on the CEEB, and graduate in the 50th percentile of their high school graduating class unless it has
been over five years since they graduated from high school.
Students are required to take placement tests in language,
mathematics, etc. , as part of the admission process for
placement and advisement.   Regularly enrolled students whose
programs have been approved by an advisor may register by
mail.   Retention policies: after six semester hours, 1. 0;
after twelve semester hours, 1. 25; after twenty-four semester hours, 1. 50; after forty-eight semester hours, 1. 9.   A
special degree program for adults is being considered for
the near future.   The faculty committee on admissions formulate the admission policies for the evening students as well
as for regular students.   Evening College students may enroll in day classes with the approval of the Director of the
Evening College and the Chairman of the Department.   No
orientation program is held for evening students.

II.   TERMINOLOGY

Title of Division: Evening College.   (A part of the
College of Arts and Sciences administered by an official of
the Extension Division).   Defined: A general (two-year)
program for adult students.   Continuing Education defined:
as indicated above, as synonymous with adult education and
as adult education in one's professional or vocational field.

III.   FEES

There is no fee differential between day and evening
classes.   Refund policies: "We charge one-tenth of the tuition for the course for each week attended and refund the
remainder. "

IV.   FACULTY AND FACULTY RECRUITMENT

Approximately 5% of the evening faculty members are
full-time.   The Chancellor of the University has the final
authority for hiring full/part-time faculty for evening classes.
No full-time faculty members teach exclusively in the evening.   Faculty meetings are held for evening faculty once
each semester.   Regular faculty members may teach in the
Evening College as part of their regular load but not on an
overload basis.   Salaries range from $900 to $1600 per
course.

V. SCHEDULING

The Director of the Evening College has the responsibility for the evening class schedule, but as a matter of
convenience, he follows the regular University schedule.
Staff members prepare the schedule for the Director's approval.   Three-hour classes are scheduled two nights a week
with one or two exceptions.   Day and evening classes compare favorably in quality.   Part-time evening students are
not eligible for the Dean's List.   A minimum of ten students
are required to constitute a class; however, exceptions are
made.

VI. ORGANIZATIONAL STRUCTURE

Six staff members comprise the administrative staff.
There is a teaching staff of 34 part-time faculty members.
The University is not a branch of the State University and
therefore is not autonomous.   The Director has overall administrative responsibility for Evening College; the Assistant
to the Director is responsible for admission of students, development of procedures and processes of admission, assists
and works with other advisory staff of the Evening College;
one advisor who advises students, the Registrar who is responsible for registration of students and maintenance of student records, one Administrative Secretary responsible for
managing the Evening College and secretary to the Director.

VII. EDUCATIONAL TELEVISION PROGRAMS

No educational television program is offered through
the Evening College.

VIII. NON-CREDIT PROGRAMS

Non-credit programs are not offered except in developmental areas.

IX. GENERAL

Students participate in discussions regarding academic
program only on an informal basis.   The Evening College is
receiving adequate stress and support from the administration.   The Director is responsible to the Dean of Arts and
Sciences and to the Director, Extension Division as Associate Director of the Division.

X. STUDENT RECRUITMENT

The newspaper is used for promotion releases for special programs. Spot announcements are made on radio and television regarding programs to be offered in the Evening College. Brochures are prepared for distribution to industry and various civic organizations and the Chamber of Commerce.

North Carolina State University
Raleigh, North Carolina
Division of Continuing Education

Total Enrollment 13, 340   Public Institution
Evening Enrollment 1, 000   Semester System

I. ADMISSION POLICIES

There is a deadline for admission for regular students before registration; however, there is no deadline for non-degree (special) students. Students may register for credit courses before transcripts are submitted. Non-matriculating or "special" students may take two courses per semester - there is no limit to the number of hours they take as "special" students. Admission requirements for regular degree students: high school diploma and a predicted grade point average of 1. 6 based upon the CEEB examination. For non-matriculating students: high school diploma, 21 years of age, and student must not have been suspended within the last three years. Students who are rejected for admission as regular students are not advised to apply to take evening courses. Mail registration is used. The application is included in the catalog; when it is received, the applicant is cleared for admission by the Admission and Records Office. The class schedule and registration materials are mailed back to the student who doesn't need to come to the campus until the first day of classes. Probation and suspension regulations: probation below 2. 0 (C) average and dismissal when the student is more than 25 quality points below the required average. No ACT or CEEB examination is required for adults in the evening division. No special degree program is offered for adults. The Admissions Office formulates the admission policies with the Provost's assistance. The graduate school formulates the admission policies for graduate students. Day and evening student enrollment is permitted. No orientation program is held for evening students.

II. TERMINOLOGY

Title of Division: Division of Continuing Education.
Defined: "Generally our charge is to make available to the
citizens of this state, wherever and whenever needed, the resources of the University - short courses and conferences
are only one of a variety of means used to achieve the above
objective. "

III. FEES

Non-academic fees are reduced or waived for those
taking less than seven hours.   Justification is that occupied
adults cannot take advantage of the activities for which non-
academic fees are charged.   Refunds are not made after the
first two weeks of class except by special appeal to the Refund Committee.

IV. FACULTY AND FACULTY RECRUITMENT

There is no policy regarding the percentage of full-
time faculty members who teach evening classes.   However,
approximately 90% of the evening faculty members are full-
time.   The departments have the final authority for hiring
full and/or part-time faculty members.   The Director of
Continuing Education cannot automatically reject a faculty
member for evening classes, but can influence the retention
of a faculty member who has been found deficient.   No full-
time faculty members teach exclusively in the evening.   The
Director of Continuing Education cannot engage a faculty member without the approval of the department chairman.   No
regular faculty meetings are held for evening faculty members.   Faculty members are allowed to teach credit or non-
credit classes as an overload but the amount of extra compensation allowed during the year is restricted to a maximum
of 20% of the nine month salary.   There is no separate evening class budget.   Salaries for part-time faculty members
are determined and paid by the departments.   Full-time faculty members teach in the evening as part of their regular
load.

V. SCHEDULING

The Director of Continuing Education is not responsible
for the evening class schedule.   This responsibility lies with

the department and the registration office.   Procedure for
scheduling evening classes begins with the departments send-
ing their class schedules to the Registrar who compiles and
mails catalogs.   The Director of Continuing Education does
have the authority to revise or make additions to the evening
class schedule.   Three-hour classes are scheduled one or
two nights per week depending upon the class.   Two nights
are preferable.   Day and evening classes are the same in
quality.   Part-time evening students are not eligible for the
Dean's List.   A minimum of ten students is required to constitute a class.   The instructor's salary is not reduced if he
teaches a class below minimum size.

VI.   ORGANIZATIONAL STRUCTURE

The Division of Continuing Education has an administrative staff of four with a teaching staff of ninety full-time
and ten part-time faculty members.   The institution does not
have academic and administrative autonomy.   The Division
is headed by an Administrative Dean for University Extension
who has the overall responsibility for all extension work including Continuing Education.   In addition to the Administrative Dean, there is a Director of Continuing Education who
has the general responsibility for credit, non-credit and TV
activities of Continuing Education, two Assistant Directors -
one for credit work and one for non-credit work, conferences,
etc. , and a Director of Conferences and Institutes who has
the overall responsibility for administration.   The ideal staff
for 1000 students would be five staff members.

VII.   EDUCATIONAL TELEVISION PROGRAMS

Non-credit courses are offered through the Division
of Continuing Education.   The Director of ETV supervises
the educational television courses with the assistance of a
Television Advisory Committee.   Both full-time and part-
time faculty members participate in the program.   Faculty
members receive extra compensation for teaching non-credit
courses on TV.   The Division of Continuing Education handles
registration for these courses.   Educational TV courses are
financed by registration fees paid by the students and by a
state appropriation.   No out-of-state tuition is charged for
these courses.   Educational television courses are scheduled
in the late afternoon from 3 to 4 and 4 to 5 p. m.

VIII.   NON-CREDIT PROGRAMS

Non-credit programs are offered in the areas of Business and Management, Engineering and Arts and Sciences. Faculty members receive $30 per contact hour.   Clinicians for conferences are paid on an hourly basis.   Typical activities for 1971 include: Nurserymen's Short Course, Tree Improvement, Pork Producers, Construction Management, Motor Fleet Maintenance Management, Sale Seminar, Public Works Conference, Industrial Communications, Forecasting Techniques, Industrial Noise Control Techniques, AAMA Textile Fundamentals, Work Simplification and Measurement, Turfgrass Conference, Flower Show School-Course V, Engineering Economy and Electric Systems Supervision Conference.   The Division of Continuing Education is responsible for the Summer School.

IX.   GENERAL

The Division of Continuing Education occasionally offers credit work and/or non-credit work - courses in "store front" locations off-campus for economically deprived populations.   Many school committees have student members; some recommended by the student senate.   Innovative practices include a liaison committee who meets with the administration including student and faculty senate members.   In general, the Evening Division is not receiving adequate support and stress.   The Director of Continuing Education is responsible to the Administrative Dean for Extension and the Provost.   Audio-visual aids are available for evening classes.

X.   STUDENT RECRUITMENT

Newspaper, radio and television publicity is used. Special motivational appeals are developed for industry and civic organizations in the city.

Northern Illinois University
DeKalb, Illinois
College of Continuing Education

Total Enrollment 20,719   Public Institution
Evening Enrollment 3,700   Semester System

I. ADMISSION POLICIES

There is no deadline for applications for admission to evening classes except in Graduate School. Students may register for credit courses before transcripts are submitted. Non-matriculating or "special" students may take up to 12 semester hours for credit before they are required to matriculate. High school graduation is required for admission as a "special" student. For regular students, they must be in the upper 50% of their graduating class. For Graduate School, students must have earned a 2.5 average for their last two years as an undergraduate student. There is no mail registration. Scores on ACT or CEEB are not required for admission. The Admissions Committee formulates the admission policies for evening students. Day and evening students may enroll in the same classes. No orientation program is planned for evening students. Policies regarding probation and suspension: degree students - undergraduate 2.0 (4.0 scale); graduate - 3.0 GPA (4.0 scale). Twelve semester hours below "B", 6 semester hours below "C" constitute academic dismissal. There are no non-degree students and the evening degree program for adults does not differ from the day program. No plans are in view for a special degree program for adults. Admission policies for all students are formulated by an administrative committee.

II. TERMINOLOGY

Title of Division: College of Continuing Education - with Evening Division. Evening Division defined: A division serving the part-time evening students on campus. Definition of Continuing Education: All types of formal and informal education taken after the completion of the uninterrupted formal schooling.

III. FEES

There is no fee differential between day and evening classes. Students have ten days to drop all courses with a full refund.

IV. FACULTY AND FACULTY RECRUITMENT

Ninety-nine percent of the faculty teaching evening classes are full-time, but no full-time faculty members teach exclusively in the evening. The department heads and the Dean of the College of Continuing Education have the re-

sponsibility for hiring full and/or part-time faculty.   No
regular faculty meetings are held for faculty teaching evening
classes.   Faculty members receive extra pay for an overload.   They are limited to the equivalent of one overload
class per year.   Twelve percent of the budget is spent for
recruiting.

V.   SCHEDULING

The Dean of Continuing Education is responsible for
the evening class schedule.   The departments initiate the
schedule of evening classes and the Dean approves.   Most
three-hour classes are held one night per week with a few
classes meeting two nights per week.   Evening classes are
equal or better in quality than day classes.   Part-time evening students are not eligible for the Dean's List.

VL   ORGANIZATIONAL STRUCTURE

The administrative staff is composed of ten staff
members and courses are offered through the academic departments.   There is academic autonomy in the area of non-
credit courses and administrative autonomy in that the Dean
reports to the Provost.   The Dean is the administrative head
of the College of Continuing Education, the Director of Adult
Education is responsible for the non-credit programs, the
Director of Conferences and Institutes is responsible for
conferences, workshops, seminars and institutes, Director
of Extension is responsible for off-campus credit courses.
Other staff members include the Director of Industrial and
Business Services and Director of Law Enforcement Institute.
An administrative staff needed for administering the evening
credit program with an enrollment of 2,000 is four.

VII   EDUCATIONAL TELEVISION PROGRAMS

The College of Continuing Education does not offer
any educational television programs.

VIIL   NON-CREDIT PROGRAMS

Non-credit courses are offered in the areas of Business and Management, Arts and Sciences and Education.   A
budget is provided only for administration.   Remuneration
for faculty varies--approximately $50 per contact hour and
this depends upon qualifications of the instructor and the area
of instruction.   Conferences and institutes are sponsored by

an academic department--not the evening division. Conferences sponsored by the evening division are planned in cooperation with another college.

IX. GENERAL

Students do not participate in any discussions regarding the academic program. In general, the administration recognizes the need and importance of the evening program. The Dean of Continuing Education is responsible for the Provost.

X. STUDENT RECRUITMENT

Newspaper ads and announcements are used for publicity with announcements on radio and TV. Special programs are planned for industry with publicity coverage.

Northern Virginia Community College
Annandale, Virginia
Continuing Adult Education and Community Services

Total Enrollment 9, 779   Public Institution
Evening Enrollment 5, 510   Quarter System
    (includes day students taking
    one or more courses at night)

I. ADMISSION POLICIES

There is no deadline for applications for admission to evening classes. Students may register for credit courses before transcripts are submitted. Non-matriculating or "special" students may take up to forty-five quarter hours for credit before matriculating. Admission requirements for non-matriculating or "special" students require a $5. 00 application fee and registration for classes; for regular students: "Open-door" - high school diploma or equivalency. No mail registration is used. Scores on ACT or CEEB are not required for admission. The Admissions Committee formulates the admission policies for all students. Day and evening students may enroll in the same class. No orientation program is held for evening students. Any student who fails to maintain a cumulative grade point average of 1. 5 will be placed on probation. Failing to maintain a 1. 5 the next quarter results in suspension for normally two quarters unless appealed and accepted. This is true for non-degree students also. The evening program is an extension of the day program with additional special interest courses for credit and non-credit.

II.   TERMINOLOGY

Title of Division: Continuing Adult Education and Community Services.

III.   FEES

There is no fee differential between day and evening classes.   No refund is given after the first week of classes.

IV.   FACULTY AND FACULTY RECRUITMENT

Approximately 20% of the faculty teaching evening classes is full-time.   No full-time faculty members teach exclusively in the evening.   Faculty meetings for evening faculty are held once quarterly.   Full-time faculty members may teach an overload.   Part-time faculty are paid $100-$200 per quarter hour.   Additional pay is given for coming to campus more than one time per week.   The same pay is given for overloads.   Lecturer's salaries are based on rank and experience.   (They are not paid by the course.)

V.   SCHEDULING

The Coordinator of Continuing Education and Community Services is responsible for scheduling evening classes, in coordination with the Scheduling Committee and Department Chairmen or Coordinators.   The schedule is submitted from the various departments and divisions, using "experience figures" from the previous quarter and adding additional courses.   Three-hour classes are scheduled one night a week. Evening classes compare very favorably with day classes in quality with a "top-notch" part-time staff.

VI.   ORGANIZATIONAL STRUCTURE

The Director is responsible for evening and Saturday credit offerings and all Community Services and non-credit offerings.   The Assistant Director has the support of the Director.   NVCC has two campuses, two Directors, two Assistant Directors.   For credit programs with an enrollment of 300, one staff member is required.

VII. EDUCATIONAL TELEVISION PROGRAMS

Educational television programs are an extension of the day programs. Students earn residence credit and credit will count toward a degree. Both full-time and part-time faculty are used.

VIII. NON-CREDIT PROGRAMS

Non-credit programs are offered in the areas of Business and Management, Arts and Sciences, Education and Engineering as well as other areas. This is expected to be a self-sustaining effort. Remuneration to faculty is $200 to $500 per course for ten class sessions. The Division does sponsor conferences, such as: Flower Show Judges Symposium, P. T. A. Regional Conference for New Officers, V. A. Regional Conference for Supervisors and Curriculum Specialists. Honorariums for clinicians varies. The evening division is not responsible for the summer session.

IX. GENERAL

More stress and financial support is needed, but the administration does recognize the need and importance of adult education programs since the "objectives of the Community are clearly drawn to reflect emphasis on adult education." The Coordinator of Continuing Education and Community Services is responsible to the Dean of Instruction.

X. STUDENT RECRUITMENT

All the media for publicity are used - newspaper stories and advertisements, radio and television announcements. Special motivational appeals are developed for business and industry and for various civic organizations and the Chamber of Commerce.

Northeastern University
Boston, Massachusetts
University College

Total Enrollment 40, 000
Evening Enrollment 12, 500

Private Institution
Quarter System

I. ADMISSION POLICIES

The last day of registration is the deadline for ad-
mission--admission is accomplished at the same time as
registration.   A student may register for credit courses before transcripts are submitted.   Non-matriculating/special
students may take 40 quarter hours of credit work.   There
are no admission requirements for non-matriculating/special
students.   Regular students must satisfactorily complete 40
quarter hours with an average of 2.0 or better and have evidence of high school graduation.   Students who are rejected
as regular students are automatically accepted as evening
students for at least the first 40 hours.   Mail registration
is used--packets are mailed to former students and are received by the students early in August.   Packets must be
returned no later than a specific date in late August.   This
system is most effective.   A Degree student whose average
drops below 2.0 and shows no improvement is placed on probation and is faced with possible dismissal.   There are no
probation or suspension policies for non-degree or special
students.   No ACT or CEEB examination is required for
adults in the evening division.   Proficiency tests in Mathematics and English are used for placement and advisement
only.   An Associate in Science and Bachelor of Science degree program are offered for adults in the evening: one
hundred seventy-four quarter hours are required for completion.   Admission policies are formulated by the part-time
division with advice from the day colleges.   Currently an experiment is being made with one campus--allowing day students into certain sections of our part-time program.   An
orientation program is conducted for evening students prior
to the start of classes in the Fall.   An Evening Division
Advisory Committee promotes cooperation and understanding
between different portions of the part-time operations and
registrar.

II. TERMINOLOGY

Title of Division: University College.   Defined: Uni-
versity College covers part-time undergraduate offerings in
Business, Liberal Arts, Law Enforcement and Allied Health
Sciences.

III. FEES

Students in the regular day program of the University
pay approximately twice the fee of students in the part-time

program.   The part-time program is not entitled to most of
the extra curricular benefits and activities and the cost of
instruction is less.   Refunds are made: 100% during the
first week of the quarter, 75% during second week, etc.   Tuition refunds will be granted only on the basis of the date ap-
pearing on the official withdrawal application.

IV.   FACULTY AND FACULTY RECRUITMENT

There is no policy regarding the percentage of faculty
for evening classes that must be full-time faculty members.
At the present time, 25% of the liberal arts faculty is full-
time; less than 1% of the faculty in business and management is full-time.   The Dean of University College has the
authority for hiring full and/or part-time faculty members
for evening classes.   Full-time faculty members are employed to teach exclusively in the evening.   Faculty meetings
for evening faculty are held in the early fall and late spring.
The University College uses full-time faculty members on a
limited basis and pays them for the overload.   (No more
than one course per quarter).   Salary ranges from $15 to
$22.50 per hour for part-time faculty.

V.   SCHEDULING

The Dean of University College is responsible for the
evening class schedule.   Schedules are compiled by the program director in cooperation with the department consultant.
As a result of University College's development in the past
three years, the quality of evening classes is reaching a
comparable level for both day and evening.   Ten students
constitute a class.   Part-time students are eligible for the
Dean's List with a 3.0 GPA after 18 hours.   Three-hour
classes meet once a week for 100 minutes.   A doctoral student is presently conducting a research project on student
attitudes.

VI.   ORGANIZATIONAL STRUCTURE

The administrative staff consists of 13 staff members,
with a teaching staff of 150 full-time and 450 part-time faculty members.   The Dean has overall responsibility; four
Assistant Deans are all program directors.

VII.   EDUCATIONAL TELEVISION PROGRAMS

No educational television programs are offered.

VIII. NON-CREDIT PROGRAMS

No non-credit programs are offered.

IX. GENERAL

Student members are included on all curriculum committees.   Credit and/or non-credit courses are offered in
"store front" locations off-campus for the economically deprived populations.   No graduate programs are offered for
part-time students.   The Director of the University College
is responsible to the Academic Vice-President.   Audio-visual
aids are available for evening classes.

X. STUDENT RECRUITMENT

Newspaper publicity is used for student recruitment.
Special motivational appeals are developed for industry and
organizations.

Northwestern University
Chicago, Illinois
Evening Division

Total Enrollment 19, 000 annually   Private Institution
Evening Enrollment 3, 208 part-time   Semester System

I. ADMISSION POLICIES

The deadline for application for admission is approximately two weeks before registration.   Students may register
for credit courses without transcripts and may take an unlimited amount of credit work as non-matriculated students.
Admission requirements are high school graduation or twenty-
one years of age and acceptable other college transcripts.
Mail registration is used for former students.   Students are
placed on probation with below a "C" average and are dismissed if it is not maintained.   Students admitted on probation are limited to one course.   Admission policies are set
by the Dean and his advisory council.   Day and evening students are allowed to enroll in the same classes.   There is
no orientation program for evening students.   A Ph. B. and
a B. S. in General Education are offered with an enrollment
of 3,180 undergraduates and 28 graduate students.   The Ph. B.
requires twelve hours of language.   There are no language

requirements or lab science requirements for the undergraduate. Graduate students are not under the control of the Evening Division; the 28 graduate students are registered through the Graduate School office.

II. TERMINOLOGY

Title of Division: Northwestern University Evening Division. Defined: Each of the five day divisions is academically responsible for its own evening program which is identical to the day program leading to a degree.

III. FEES

Evening students pay less than half the tuition day students pay; lab fees, etc. are exactly the same. Evening students do not get to use the full facilities of the college as day students do.

IV. FACULTY AND FACULTY RECRUITMENT

Approximately 25% of the evening faculty members teaching evening classes are full-time. Final authority to hire evening faculty lies with the Dean of the Evening Division. The Director of the Evening Division can reject a faculty member assigned to teach evening classes and can engage an instructor without the consent of the department chairmen. Regular faculty meetings are not held. Faculty members who teach may not teach more than one four-hour course or two two-hour courses on an overload basis during an academic year: this does not include non-credit courses. Salary range for part-time faculty is $550 to $800 per two semester hour courses - once a week; overloads range from $650 to $800 depending upon the rank of the instructor . . . $650 for assistant professors up to $800 for full professors.

V. SCHEDULING

The Dean of the Evening Division is responsible for the evening class schedule and may revise as necessary. Three-hour classes are scheduled one night a week. Day and evening classes are of similar quality; the best students, academically, are in the evening division as well as the worst. There is no Dean's List. Classes are rarely cancelled; often carry classes with as few as five students. The instructor fee is not reduced when he teaches a class below minimum size.

VI. ORGANIZATIONAL STRUCTURE

The Evening Division staff consists of three (3) members: a Dean who is responsible for the entire evening program - budgets, recruitment, program planning, etc.; an Assistant Dean who handles admissions, counseling, publications, etc.; a Registrar who is responsible for keeping academic records of part-time students. The teaching staff consists of 150 part-time instructors. "In our estimation, the desired staff for 5,000 students - credit or non-credit - would be four."

VII. EDUCATIONAL TELEVISION PROGRAMS

The Evening Division does not offer any educational television program.

VIII. NON-CREDIT PROGRAMS

Business and Management and Arts and Sciences offer non-credit courses. These courses are expected to pay for themselves. Full or part-time faculty receive remuneration of $400 per course for four class sessions. The Evening Division is not responsible for the conferences and institutes and are not responsible for the summer session of the institution.

IX. GENERAL

Twice a year, the Deans meet with all evening students to discuss the academic program. In general, all evening divisions are not receiving adequate support. The Dean of the Evening Divisions is responsible to the Vice-President and Dean of Faculty. Audio-visual instructional aids are used in evening classes.

X. STUDENT RECRUITMENT

Newspaper, radio and television publicity is used. Special motivational appeals are made to industry.

Ohio State University
Columbus, Ohio
Division of Continuing Education

Total Enrollment 21, 000+   Public Institution
Evening Enrollment 533 (credit)   Quarter System

I. ADMISSION POLICIES

The deadline for application for admission to evening classes is the first night of classes. A student may register for credit courses before transcripts are submitted. Students may take an unlimited number of hours for credit as a non-matriculated student. For admission, a non-matriculated or special student must be a high school graduate (in some exceptional cases, a student may still be attending high school). The same admission requirements apply to degree students. Students who are rejected as regular degree students are not advised to apply for evening classes. No mail registration is used. The ACT or CEEB examination is not required for adults. There is no special program for adults offered in the evening. The number of students enrolled in the fall were 835 undergraduates and 363 graduates. No orientation program is held for evening students. There is no evening division advisory committee.

II. TERMINOLOGY

Title of Division: Continuing Education. Defined: The Division allows (mainly) adult students to continue their education during the evening while working at their professions during the day. Continuing Education defined: Both credit and non-credit courses offered to students. These courses have been designed to meet the special needs of individuals in the area of business, industrial, and professional groups.

III. FEES

There is a fee differential between day and evening students - for the undergraduate resident students. The main campus fee is somewhat higher per hour. There is no fee differential for undergraduate, non-resident and graduate students. There is no deadline for refunds. By a certain date, a full refund is given; by another day, an 80% refund is given. After that time there is no refund.

VI. FACULTY AND FACULTY RECRUITMENT

There is no policy regarding the number or percentage of full-time faculty members who teach evening classes.   The Director of Extension has the final authority for hiring full/part-time faculty members for evening classes.   The Director may reject a faculty member who has been assigned to teach evening classes; but may not engage an instructor without the consent of the department head.   No full-time faculty members teach exclusively in the evening.   No regular faculty meetings are held for evening faculty.   Overloads are permitted but no faculty member may earn more than 20% beyond the contract amount specified for his full-time services to the University.   The salary paid for overloads depends upon faculty rank and the number of hours per course.   The salary range for teaching off-campus as an overload per contact hour is as follows: $235 - instructor, $250 - assistant professor, $270 - associate professor and $280 for full professor.   Salary for teaching on-campus is: $220 - instructor, $230 - assistant professor, $245 - associate professor, $260 - full professor.   Part-time faculty receive the following for teaching on any campus: $190 - Master's degree or equivalent, $216 - A. B. D. (all but dissertation), $230 - Doctoral degree or equivalent.   No budget is spent for recruitment.

V.   SCHEDULING

The Assistant Director for Continuing Education is responsible for the evening class schedule.   The Director has the authority to revise the schedule.   Three-hour classes are held one night a week.   Research projects in adult education have been completed or are in progress.   Day and evening classes compare favorably in quality.   Part-time students are not eligible for the Dean's List.   There is no set number of students required to constitute a class; depends upon the number of resident and non-resident students. Classes must pay for themselves.   If an instructor teaches a class below minimum size, his compensation is sometimes reduced.

VI.   ORGANIZATIONAL STRUCTURE

The administrative staff consists of four staff members with a teaching staff of thirty-forty part-time faculty members.   The staff consists of an Assistant Director for Continuing Education with the overall administrative responsibility for the Division, two coordinators of Conferences and

Institutes, a Director of Independent Study through Correspondence.

VII. EDUCATIONAL TELEVISION PROGRAMS

The Division of Continuing Education does not offer any TV courses.

VIII. NON-CREDIT PROGRAMS

Non-credit programs are offered in the following areas: Business and Management, Engineering, and other areas. A budget is provided for these programs, but the program is expected to pay for itself. The remuneration for teaching non-credit courses depends upon the qualifications of the instructor. The Division of Continuing Education sponsors conferences and institutes, such as: R & D Management Program, Polymer Seminars, Chemical Engineering Seminars, Newsphoto Editors Conference. Thirty-one institutes, clinics and special conferences were offered during the past summer. Clinicians are generally paid $200 per day or $1000 per five days. Conferences are sponsored by the Division and also co-sponsored with another college within the University. The Division is not responsible for the summer session.

IX. GENERAL

The Division is not offering any credit or non-credit courses in "store front" locations off-campus for the economically deprived populations. Students have no opportunity to discuss the academic program with anyone except their advisors. The Division is not receiving adequate financial support and the administration does not, at this present time, recognize the need and importance of the adult education program. The Assistant Director is responsible to the Dean of Off-campus Academic Programs.

X. STUDENT RECRUITMENT

The newspaper, radio and television are used for student recruitment purposes. Special motivational appeals are developed for industry and civic organizations.

University of Oklahoma
Norman, Oklahoma
Division of Public Services

Total Enrollment 18, 000   Public Institution
                                                  Semester System

I. ADMISSION POLICIES

The deadline for application for admission to evening
classes is the first day of class or at the time of enrollment
for all semesters.   A student may register for credit courses
before transcripts are submitted.   Non-matriculating or "special" students may take a certain amount of work for credit.
The admission requirements for non-matriculating or "special" students are: high school graduates and in upper-half
of the class or upper one-half of ACT.   The admission requirements for transfer students are: good standing and "C"
(2. 00) GPA.   For regular students there are the same requirements as non-matriculating or "special" students.   No
mail registration is used at the institution.   The policies regarding probation and dismissal for degree students, non-degree or "special" students are: 30-36 hours, 1. 40 GPA; 37-
72 hours, 1. 60 GPA; 73-108 hours, 1. 80 GPA; above 108
hours, 2. 00 GPA based on a four-point grade system.   The
ACT or CEEB examination is only required for beginning
students and is used as a basis for admission.   There is an
evening degree program for adults which is different from
the day degree program, both for undergraduate or graduate
students.   The degree is The Bachelor of Liberal Studies for
undergraduate students.   The Master of Liberal Studies and
Master of Arts in Government and Economics are graduate
degrees offered for evening students.   The number of students enrolled in the Fall quarter: full-time, 1014; part-
time, 1622; undergraduate, 1532; and graduate, 1104.   The
distribution requirements for the undergraduate degrees and
graduate degrees vary.   The special degree program for
graduate students is administered by the graduate school.
The total number of hours required to complete the degree
for undergraduate and graduate students is not in terms of
credit hours.   The admission requirements for the special
degree program for graduate students is 3. 00 GPA and graduate of a regionally accredited institution.   Additional special
degree programs for adults (undergraduate and graduate) may
be offered in the near future.   The Board of Higher Regents
formulates the admission policies for all evening students.
Day and evening students may enroll in the same class by

permission, the advantages being broader offerings and time convenience. There is an evening division advisory committee.

II. TERMINOLOGY

Title of Division: Division of Public Services. Defined: Continuing Education and Extension. Continuing Education defined: any formal education above high school, either credit or non-credit.

III. FEES

There is some fee differential between day and evening classes: same fees for some classes, others vary from standard of $14 to $75 a credit hour, and some require extra fees. Adults must pay full cost but there is a difference of opinion about this. The refund policies for evening students who drop one or more classes but remain in school are: first week, 80% to the fourth week, 50% by the sixth week, 25%, after the sixth week, none.

IV. FACULTY AND FACULTY RECRUITMENT

There is no policy regarding the percentage of faculty for evening classes that are full-time faculty members as all members of the faculty for evening classes are full-time. The final authority for hiring full and/or part-time faculty members for evening classes is a joint decision of the department and program director. The director of the evening division can reject a faculty member who has been assigned to teach evening classes. Full-time faculty members who teach exclusively in the evening are employed, and they are responsible to both the department and director. The policies regarding regular faculty members teaching credit or non-credit courses or participating in institutes, seminars and conferences as an overload is limited to 1/4 of their annual salary. No percentage of the budget is spent for recruitment. The salary paid the faculty for overloads ranges from $125 per credit hour to the equivalence of regular salary.

V. SCHEDULING

The Director is responsible for the evening class schedule in the institution. The procedure for compiling the evening class schedule primarily demands analysis. The Director has the authority to revise or make additions to the

evening class schedule.   Three-hour classes may be scheduled one or two nights per week, depending on many factors.
In comparison of day and evening classes in terms of quality,
the evening classes are considered better.   Part-time evening students are not eligible for the Dean's List.   The number of students who must register to constitute a class depends on the basic need in the overall program.   The instructor's compensation is not reduced when he teaches a
class below the minimum size.

VI.   ORGANIZATIONAL STRUCTURE

There are approximately 150 staff members in evening division plus a teaching staff of four full-time and 100
part-time members.   The institution has limited administrative autonomy as a branch of the state university.   The administrative staff consists of: Vice-President, Director, Assistant Director/Directors, Director of Adult Education Center, Director, Admissions (Evening students), Registrar (Evening), and Business Manager (Evening).   It is estimated the
size of administrative staff required for administering an
evening credit program would be: (Credit program only) 300
enrollment--one staff member plus one staff member for administering, organizing and being responsible for non-credit
courses, conferences and institutes; 500--one plus one; 800--
two plus one; 1000--two plus two; 2000--five plus three;
5000--eight plus six.

VII.   EDUCATIONAL TELEVISION PROGRAMS

Credit and non-credit courses are offered in Educational Television and students earn residence credit which
counts toward a degree.   The department offering the courses
supervises the educational television courses.   Full-time faculty members are used.   The campus handles registration
for educational television courses.   The same procedure is
used as for other registration except mail registration may
be used.   Both graduate and undergraduate courses are offered and are financed by a State Grant and fees.   The institution is located near the state line, and out-of-state tuition is charged the same as for on-campus students.   The
schedule for educational TV courses varies.   The educational
television program is a State-wide cooperative program of
three major institutions.

VIII. NON-CREDIT PROGRAMS

The evening division offers non-credit courses in Business and Management, Arts and Sciences, Engineering, Education and in other areas. This program is expected to pay for itself. The remuneration the faculty receives for teaching a non-credit course is $25-$100 per course for one-hour class session. The remuneration depends upon both the qualifications of the instructor and the area of instruction. The division sponsored over 500 conferences and institutes this past year. The faculty used for these conferences or institutes are qualified faculty members of the institution or visiting lecturers. The division is not responsible for the Summer session at the institution.

IX. GENERAL

Students participate some in discussions regarding the academic program. The innovative practices used at the institution are many--degree programs, class arrangements and methods. The graduate programs offered for part-time students which are administered by the evening division are: Master of Liberal Studies and Master of Arts in Public Administration and Economics. In general, it is felt that the evening division is not receiving adequate support (in terms of adequate stress and financial support) in comparison with the day programs. The administration does recognize the need and the importance of the adult education programs. The director of the evening division is responsible to the Vice-President. Audio-visual and other technical instructional aids are used in the division.

X. STUDENT RECRUITMENT

Publicity by newspaper, radio and TV is used for student recruitment. Special motivational appeals are developed for industry and civic organizations.

Old Dominion College
Norfolk, Virginia
Division of Continuing Education

Total Enrollment 10, 500   Public Institution
Evening Enrollment 2, 400-3000   Semester System

I.   ADMISSION POLICIES

The deadline for admission to evening classes for
regular and non-credit or special students is as follows:
Fall, August 1, Spring, January 8, Summer, June 11.   Last
day of registration is deadline date for all special cases only.
A student, classified as a special student, may register for
credit courses before transcripts are submitted but must be
on file within six weeks at which time he is reclassified as
credit status.   Special students may take eleven semester
hours for credit.   Admission requirements for non-matriculating students are the same as regular with exception that
they may be admitted with a GED average not less than 60+8
units of high school credit.   Admission requirements for
regular students are high school graduate with sixteen units;
twelve of which are academic and satisfactory SAT scores,
"C" or above high school grades.   Engineering students need
four units of advanced high school math.   Mail registration
is not used.   Retention policies for evening students are the
same as for regular students.   The ACT or CEEB examination for adults is not required; however, tests in math or
other specific courses as stated in the catalog are given if
deemed necessary.   These are used as a partial basis for
admission and placement/advisement purposes.   No special
degree program for adults is offered at the present time but
is a possibility for the future.   The admission policies for
all categories of students are formulated by the Academic
Council and Council of Deans.   More than one-half of an evening student's load must be evening classes.   There is no
restriction on day students taking evening classes.   Advantage
of the combined class with day and evening students is the
competition with mature evening students.   There is no orientation program.   Evening students in Extension classes
are immediately classified as special students with no credit.
If in six weeks acceptable credentials are on file the student's
status is changed to credit.   If not acceptable, student receives no credit.

II.   TERMINOLOGY

Title of Division: Division of Continuing Education.
Defined: Evening classes, non-credit seminars, institutes
and workshops.   Vocational campus offerings, also extension
and public service offerings covering previous categories.
Continuing Education is best defined as being programs of
educational endeavor, involving credit, non-credit seminars,
institutes, workshops, etc. designed to meet the needs of the

public or organizations.

III. FEES

There is no fee differential between day and evening classes. Students are classified as resident or non-resident in graduate courses on campus. Non-resident charged $40/ credit hour. All full and part-time day students are classified as resident and non-resident. No part-time evening classified for tuition purposes as state resident. Refund policies are: before first class meeting full refund less $5. 00. During the first week 2/3 is refunded; during the second week one-third is refunded. There is no refund after the second week.

IV. FACULTY AND FACULTY RECRUITMENT

There is no policy regarding the percentage of faculty for evening classes that are full-time. The percentage of full-time is one-third to one-half. The Dean and Department Chairmen have the final authority for hiring full and/or part-time faculty for evening classes. The Director may reject a faculty member if valid reason is given. No full-time faculty members teach exclusively in the evening. The Director cannot engage an instructor without the consent of the department head. No regular faculty meetings are held. Faculty, full-time, are limited to three semester hours, overload only in Extension, not on campus. All overloads must have the approval of the Chairman, Dean and final approval of the Provost. The salary range for part-time faculty is fixed. For overloads faculty members are paid $600 for three hours of undergraduate courses and $675 for three hours of graduate courses. Twelve students must register in order to constitute a class.

V. SCHEDULING

The director, in cooperation with the chairman and the Dean is responsible for the evening class schedule and the school or department originates the schedule. The Director has the authority to revise the schedule, if need be, through schools and the Provost. Three-hour classes are scheduled one and two nights per week; the preference being two nights on campus except some graduate courses. Day and evening classes are equal in terms of quality. Part-time evening students are eligible for the Dean's List by completing 18 hours with a GPA of 3. 50.

VI. , VII. & VIII.

No information received.

IX. GENERAL

Students participate in discussion regarding the academic program only through the regularly scheduled meetings of the Honors Society. There are no course offerings,
credit or non-credit, off campus for economically deprived
populations. This division is receiving adequate support in
comparison with the day program and the administration recognizes the need and importance of adult educational programs. The Director is responsible to the Academic Dean
or Provost.

X. STUDENT RECRUITMENT

Student recruitment is carried on by newspaper articles and by contact with business and industry and civic organizations.

Orange County Community College
Middletown, New York

Total Enrollment 5, 846   Public Institution
Evening Enrollment 3, 812   Semester System

I. ADMISSION POLICIES

The deadline for application for admission to evening
classes is first week of classes. Students may register for
credit courses before transcripts are submitted. Non-matriculating or "special" students may take an unlimited number of courses, provided they maintain acceptable grades.
The Admission requirements for non-matriculating students
is high school diploma or equivalency. For regular students,
the SUNY Admissions Examination is required plus a high
school diploma and the guidance counselor's recommendations.
Retention policies vary depending upon grade point after
twelve credit hours; dismissal or suspension if less than 1. 75

after two semesters.   The ACT or CEEB is not required.
A special degree program for adults is being considered.
The admission requirements are formulated by the registrar's
office and admissions office jointly for evening students.
Day and evening students may enroll in the same class.   Evening students may attend the orientation program for full-
time students held during the day.   Degree students with a
GPA of at least 2. 0 may be dismissed, suspended or placed
on probation.   Distribution requirements: A. A. degree - 12
English, 12 Social Science, 9 Math and/or Science, 6 Humanities, 21 Electives; A. A. S. degree - 6 English, 6 Social
Sciences, 6 Math and/or Science, 20 credit of major concentration, 20 credits electives (minimum of 60 hours).   Admission requirements for the special degree programs: high
school graduation or equivalency.   Students wishing to take
more than eleven credit hours in a semester must be admitted through the Office of Admissions-Registrar.

II.   TERMINOLOGY

Title of Division: Division of Continuing Education.
Defined: Credit and non-credit courses offered after 4:30
p. m. (on and off-campus) and special interest courses.

III.   FEES

There is a fee differential between full-time and part-
time students.   Full-time students (in-state) pay $200 and a
$20 activity fee; part-time students (in-state) pay $17 per
credit hour.   Refund policies: Prior to first class, 80%,
after two weeks, no refund.

IV.   FACULTY AND FACULTY RECRUITMENT

Approximately 50% of the faculty for evening classes
are full-time faculty members.   The Director of Continuing
Education has the final authority to hire full and/or part-
time faculty for evening classes.   No full-time faculty teach
exclusively in the evening.   Faculty meetings are held once
a year.   Faculty members receive a separate salary for
overloads depending upon rank.   Faculty is responsible to
the Division Chairmen and Dean.   Salaries range from $240
to $345 per credit hour for part-time faculty.

V.   SCHEDULING

The Dean of Continuing Education is responsible for

the evening class schedule together with the recommendations
of the various divisions and areas of interest. Each division recommends credit and non-credit courses; the Associate Dean of Continuing Education recommends off-campus and
non-credit courses. Most three-hour classes are scheduled
one night a week. A research project has been completed
on a "Five-Year Prediction of Continuing Education Programs at Orange County Community College" by Howard C.
Smith, Jr. Day and evening classes are equal in terms of
quality. Part-time evening students are not eligible for the
Dean's List. Ten students constitute a class.

VI. ORGANIZATIONAL STRUCTURE

The administrative staff consists of four staff members: the Dean who establishes policies, aims and objectives;
the Associate Dean who executes policies and objectives as
related to non-credit, community services and off-campus
courses; Coordinator of Special Projects who establishes conferences, seminars, etc. and supervises Independent Study;
Coordinator of Women's Programs who establishes courses
(credit and non-credit) for women and supervises funded programs for disadvantaged. Non-credit programs are unique,
changing and often non-recurring. For this reason, they are
more difficult to establish and supervise (requiring more time
and a larger staff than credit courses which are more standardized and often recurring). Teaching staff includes 259
part-time faculty members. County Community College has
academic and administrative autonomy but is governed by the
Board of Trustees and employees of the County of Orange.

VII. EDUCATIONAL TELEVISION PROGRAMS

Educational television programs - non-credit - are
offered via video tape internally and on CATV. The Director
of Instructional Media Center is responsible for supervising
the program. Both full and part-time faculty are used.
Registration is handled through the Admissions Office via
mail or on-campus registrations. Programs are scheduled
in the evenings.

VIII. NON-CREDIT PROGRAMS

Non-credit programs are offered in the areas of Business and Management, Arts and Sciences, Education, Engineering and wherever there is a need or an interest. There
is a budget to cover expenses of the program even though

some are self-supporting.   All faculty are part-time faculty and remuneration is $240 per course for fifteen one-hour class sessions.   The Division does sponsor conferences and workshops such as In-Service Training for Instructors of Adults, Institute of Marine Biology, In-Service Workshop, Health Education in Public Schools, Industrial Manpower Clinic, Diabetic Workshop, Fashion Show, High School Enrichment Program, Police and Youthful Offenders, etc.   Pay for clinicians varies--many donate time and effort.   For example, the Institute of Marine Biology meets for six consecutive days and the instructor's fee is $720.00.   All available resources and personnel are utilized and some are offered in cooperation with other colleges.   The Division is responsible for the summer session.

IX.   GENERAL

Credit and non-credit courses at off-campus locations are offered for economically deprived populations in four major locations and on a collegiate bus.   Students are appointed to all committees, including the academic policy committee.   The Division of Continuing Education is receiving adequate support from the administration.   The Dean of Continuing Education is responsible to the President.

X.   STUDENT RECRUITMENT

The College uses full-page ads listing courses every semester in the local newspaper.   Scheduled paid announcements are heard on radio and also on CATV.   The College sponsors in-plant training programs for industry and representatives of the college serve on advisory committees for various civic organizations and the Chamber of Commerce. Guest speakers are available for civic clubs.

University of Oregon
Eugene, Oregon
State Division of Continuing Education

Total Enrollment 15,000   Public Institution
Evening Enrollment 9,000   Semester System

I.   ADMISSION POLICIES

There is no deadline for application for admission for

regular and non-degree students.   Students may register for
credit courses before transcripts are submitted and may take
from three to fifteen hours for credit as non-matriculating
students.   If a student is rejected for admission as a regular
student he is advised to apply as an evening student and is
automatically accepted.   Continuing Education students may
obtain registration material at the first class meeting or at
other centers or regional offices.   All cards obtained in the
registration packet are to be completed and returned with a
check to the Division of Continuing Education.   One does not
have to present a transcript of previous high school or college work before registering for the Division of Continuing
Education classes.   The Division cooperates with the University of Oregon on probation and suspension policies, which
apply to both regular and non-degree students.   The evening
degree program for adults does not differ from the day pro-
gram--the evening division does not grant degrees.   Plans
are being formulated to offer a special degree program for
adults.   The State Board of Higher Education formulates the
admission policies for all categories of evening students.
Students may enroll in day and evening classes to a large
extent.   Advantages of this combination are the sharing of
expenses and the intermingling of mature/immature students.
There is no orientation program.   The evening division advisory committee makes suggestions for development and liaison.

II.   TERMINOLOGY

        Title of Division: State Division of Continuing Educa-
tion.   Defined: Oregon has a State system of Higher Education.   The Division of Continuing Education is a branch of
this system.

III.   FEES

        The fee is the same per credit hour for both day and
evening classes.   There is no student body fee, etc.   Refund
policies are based upon a percentage depending upon the date
of withdrawal.

IV.   FACULTY AND FACULTY RECRUITMENT

        The policy regarding the percentage of faculty for eve-
ning classes is that full-time faculty teach no more than one
evening class per term.   The department involved has final
authority for hiring full and/or part-time faculty and the di-

rector may reject a faculty member who has been assigned
to teach evening classes. No full-time faculty members
teach exclusively in the evening and no regular faculty meetings are held. All classes taught in the evening session are
considered overloads. Very little of the budget is spent on
recruitment. Salary range for part-time faculty is $165 per
credit hour which applies also to overloads.

V. SCHEDULING

The Director is responsible for the evening class
schedule which is based largely upon previous offerings.
The Director has the authority to revise the evening schedule.
Three-hour classes are scheduled one night per week. Day
and evening classes in terms of quality are comparable in
every respect. Part-time evening students are not eligible
for the Dean's List. The number of students needed to constitute a class is twelve to fifteen. An instructor's compensation is not reduced when he teaches a class below minimum size.

VI. ORGANIZATIONAL STRUCTURE

The administrative staff consists of four staff members and 50-60 teaching staff. The institution has administrative autonomy but not academic autonomy. The number of
staff members required for an enrollment of 2,000 in non-
credit courses would be four to six.

VII. EDUCATIONAL TELEVISION PROGRAMS

Credit and non-credit courses are offered by educational television through D. C. E. and students earn residence
credit. These credits will count toward a degree. This
program is supervised by the Oregon Educational Broadcasting Co. with part-time faculty teaching under the school district contracts. Faculty members receive additional remuneration for teaching courses on TV. Registration is handled by
Oregon Educational Broadcasting Co. Graduate courses in
educational television are offered and are financed by tuition
with no out-of-state tuition.

VIII. NON-CREDIT PROGRAMS

Non-credit courses are offered in the areas of Business and Management, Arts and Sciences, Engineering, Education and others. These programs do have a budget but are

expected to help pay for the offerings.   Remuneration for
faculty varies per course and depends upon the qualifications
of the instructor.   The Division sponsors conferences and
institutes too numerous to mention.   Conferences sponsored
both by the division and in cooperation with other colleges.
The Division of Continuing Education is not responsible for
the summer session.   Remuneration for clinicians varies.

IX.   GENERAL

Credit and non-credit courses are offered in off-
campus locations.   Students do not participate to any extent
in discussions regarding academic programs.   The evening
program does not receive adequate support as the administration does not recognize the need.   The Director is responsible to the Dean of Faculty and to the Dean of Continuing Education.

The Pennsylvania State University
University Park, Pennsylvania
Division of Continuing Education

Total Enrollment 50, 000   Public Institution
Evening Enrollment 122, 000   Quarter System
   (includes all categories)

I.   ADMISSION POLICIES

The third class session of each quarter is the deadline for admission.   A student may register for credit courses
without transcripts.   Non-matriculating and/or special students may take up to 36 hours of the last 60 credits.   High
school graduation or the equivalent is required for admission.
Students who are rejected as regular students are advised to
enroll as evening students and are automatically accepted if
they are high school graduates.   Mail registration has been
used on an experimental basis only but procedure is under
development.   There are no specific policies regarding probation and suspension.   ACT or CEEB examinations are not
required for adult students in the evening division.   No evening degree program for adults is offered which is different
from the day degree program.   Enrollment during Fall Quarter was 18, 600 part-time--12, 600 undergraduate and 6, 000
graduate students.   An undergraduate degree program is being
considered for adults.   The academic departments formulate

the admission policies for the evening students. Day and
evening students may enroll in the same class at a normal
ratio with no particular advantage either way. There is no
orientation program for evening students.

II. TERMINOLOGY

Title of Division: Continuing Education. Defined:
all forms of university extension and adult education except
Agricultural Extension. Continuing Education defined: the
term "Continuing Education" includes credit and non-credit
courses, conferences, community services, etc. --"a whole
bit of university extension and public services. "

III. FEES

There is no fee differential between day and evening
classes. Refund policy is 50% by course; and 50% refund if
student withdraws during first 50% of total class hours.

IV. FACULTY AND FACULTY RECRUITMENT

There is no policy regarding percentage of faculty to
teach evening classes. Final authority for hiring faculty
members for evening classes lies with the Director of Continuing Education and concurrence with the Academic Dean.
The Director can reject a faculty member who has been assigned to teach evening classes. No full-time faculty is employed to teach exclusively in the evening. Irregular meetings only are held for evening faculty. Faculty members
are allowed to teach two three-credit courses a year or the
equivalent in other non-credit courses, conferences, etc. as
an overload for which they are paid extra. Three to five
percent of the budget is spent on student recruitment and the
amount of budget spent on recruitment of faculty is minimal.
Salary range for part-time faculty is $600 to $800 per three-
credit course. Overloads are paid at the rate of $720 per
three-credit course and up to $100 per day for conferences
by sliding scale.

V. SCHEDULING

The Director of Continuing Education is responsible
for the evening class schedule which is compiled by each of
twenty-two field offices for an overall total of more than 200
class locations. All three-hour classes meet two nights per
week even though studies show no difference in academic per-

formance whether one, two, or three nights per week. A
sizeable number of research projects are underway through
an applied research unit operating under Continuing Education. Day and evening classes are comparable in terms of
quality. Part-time students are not eligible for the Dean's
List. An overall average of fifteen students constitute a
class. Some classes are taught with an enrollment as low
as six and others with enrollments of 35-40. No reduction
of compensation for instructor is involved.

VI. ORGANIZATIONAL STRUCTURE

Administrative staff consists of one hundred plus members including Director, Associate Directors, Assistant Dean,
Assistant Directors, Director of Non-credit Programs, Director of Conferences, and Institutes, Business Manager for
evening, and a large variety of other positions. Teaching
staff consists of 5,100 part-time faculty members and 55
full-time faculty members. The Division does have administrative autonomy but does not have and does not desire academic autonomy.

VII. EDUCATIONAL TELEVISION PROGRAMS

Educational television programs are offered--both
credit and non-credit. Extension credit is earned toward a
degree. Academic department involved supervises the program. Both full and part-time faculty are used for the educational television programs. Faculty members do receive
additional remuneration for teaching courses on TV and/or
receive a reduced teaching load for regular on-campus classes,
depending upon the academic department involved. Registration is handled by Correspondence Instruction or Field Offices
usually by mail or by group registration at specific locations.
Both graduate and undergraduate courses are offered in educational TV and are financed by grants, contracts, fees, and
subsidies. Out-of-state tuition is charged those students who
wish to enroll in the educational television courses (the charge
is much higher for out-of-state enrollees.) Courses are
scheduled from 3 to 3:30, 4 to 5, 6:30 to 8 p. m.

VIII. NON-CREDIT PROGRAMS

The Division offers non-credit courses in the areas of
Business and Management, Arts and Sciences, Engineering,
and other areas. The program is expected to partially pay
for itself but there is a budget for the programs. Remuner-

ation for faculty is a scale depending upon hours/days and total time/travel, etc. Over 300 conferences and institutes were conducted during the past year in cooperation with academic departments. The Division is not responsible for any summer session as such.

IX. GENERAL

There is very little student participation regarding academic program discussion. The Institution does participate in "store front" off-campus credit and non-credit courses for the economically deprived. Currently in operation is a computer-assisted instruction mobile van (computer plus 14 student stations in a 40' x 40' van.) Graduate programs for part-time students are administered mostly in Education. The Director is responsible to the President of the University. The Division does receive adequate support. Audiovisual instructional aids are available.

X. STUDENT RECRUITMENT

Newspaper, radio and television are used for student recruitment. Special motivational appeals are developed for industry and local civic organizations.

Pensacola Junior College
Pensacola, Florida
Evening College

Total Enrollment 12, 000+   Public Institution
Evening Enrollment 5, 000   Semester System
   (including 2000 credit, 1000 enrichment
   and approximately 2000 in voc-tech. programs)

I. ADMISSION POLICIES

There is no deadline for admission to evening classes. Students may register for credit courses before transcripts are submitted. Special or non-matriculating students may not take courses for credit. Regular students must be graduates of a regionally accredited high school, hold an equivalency diploma or USAFI diploma, or transfer from recognized college or university. Students who are rejected as regular students are not advised to apply as evening students.

Mail registration is not used.   Evening students may pre-
reserve classes by mail but must complete registration in
person at the College.   ACT and CEEB are not required but
when available are used for placement and advisement.   Two
undergraduate degrees, Associate of Arts and Associate of
Science, are offered.   The enrollment for the Fall was 45
full-time and 1817 part-time students.   A special, undergraduate degree program in Public Administration is to be offered in
the near future.   The Director of Admissions and Director
of the Evening College formulate the admission policies for
the regular degree students enrolling in the Evening College.
Except in problem cases, day students enroll after evening
registration is complete (i. e. , they are allowed to fill any
remaining vacancy).   There is no real advantage to combined
classes.   An orientation course which evening students may
take (1 semester hour credit) is offered but it is not required
for graduation.   Students are allowed to audit and some selected non-high school graduates may enroll in credit courses.
In the latter case, decision is made on the basis of need for
special information or skills to use in present employment.

II.   TERMINOLOGY

Title of Division: Evening Division.   Defined: College
courses taught in the evening.   This is a pure extension of
the day school although entrance requirements are less stringent.   In addition, no physical education is required for evening students.   Definition of Continuing Education: Any education, credit, non-credit, vocational-technical that adds to
existing education.

III.   FEES

There is no fee differential between day and evening
classes.   The refund policies are the same as day--60% refund if drop is made before deadline date which is approximately ten days after classes begin.

IV.   FACULTY AND FACULTY RECRUITMENT

All full-time faculty teach in the evening or have 13%
of salary subtracted.   Approximately 88% are full-time faculty.   The Academic Dean has the final authority for hiring
full and/or part-time faculty for evening classes and the Director may reject a faculty member who has been assigned
to teach evening classes.   No full-time Instructor is employed
to teach exclusively in the evening.   The Director may en-

gage an instructor without the approval of the department
head. Regular faculty meetings are not held. Regular faculty members are allowed to teach non-credit courses, etc.
but are paid at the established non-credit pay rate of $8.00
per hour. With approval of their department and the Academic Dean, faculty members may teach credit courses at
the University of West Florida (another Pensacola institution).
The Evening College does not recruit faculty. Salary range
for part-time faculty is B.A., $10.00 per semester hour;
M.A., $12.50; Ph.D., $15.00.

V. SCHEDULING

The Director is responsible for the evening class
schedule. Departments submit their recommendations and
the final schedule is prepared based upon need. Courses
are added or subtracted as the Director sees the need.
Three-hour classes are scheduled one night per week. This
is preferable as it allows students to take more than two
courses. There is no research underway at present. The
evening classes are superior in terms of quality as the students are more motivated to study and learning. Part-time
evening students are not eligible for the President's List.
(Full-time students must take twelve hours and have a 3.2
average on a 4.0 scale.) Generally, twelve students constitute a class but an instructor's compensation is not reduced
when he teaches a class with less.

VI. ORGANIZATIONAL STRUCTURE

The administrative staff consists of nine staff members: the Director is responsible for overall administration;
the Assistant Director assumes the Director's tasks in absence of the Director and is responsible for all evening non-
credit programs, seminars, etc.; the Registrar handles evening registration; the Business Manager handles the business
affairs of the Evening College and two Counselors handle all
evening counselling. The teaching staff consists of 175 full-
time instructors and approximately 25 part-time instructors.
For an enrollment of 300, the ideal staff would be two; for
enrollment of 5000, nine staff members.

VII. EDUCATIONAL TELEVISION PROGRAMS

Educational television programs are offered as credit
courses and students earn residence credits which apply toward a degree. The department head and the instructor are

directly responsible for the course. ETV courses are counted
as part of a load and no additional remuneration is paid instructors. The student buys books and materials as for any
other course. ETV courses are undergraduate and are financed through the regular budget. Out-of-state tuition is
charged for the educational TV courses. Classes are scheduled at 8:30 to 10 p. m. and 9 to 10:30 p. m. This program
is successful and is limited only to the extent that courses
are available. All courses offered are produced by the Evening College.

VIII. NON-CREDIT PROGRAMS

Non-credit courses are offered in the areas of Business and Management, Arts and Sciences, Engineering, Education and any area for which there is a demand. There is
a budget for these programs but the programs are expected
to be self-sustaining. Remuneration for full/part-time faculty is $8.00 per clock hour without regard to the length of
the course. This does not depend upon the qualifications of
the instructor or the area of the instruction. The Division
sponsors conferences and institutes such as: Drug Abuse,
Mental Health, National Security Seminar, Travel Seminar,
Pilot's Confab, Rock Hounds, etc. The majority of conferences and seminars are done on a volunteer basis. The evening college sponsors the conferences using qualified faculty
members of the institution. The Summer Session is the responsibility of the Evening College.

IX. GENERAL

Credit and non-credit courses are being offered at
off-campus locations for economically deprived populations.
A student is a voting member of our Curriculum Committee.
Other practices used at the Evening College are audio-tutorial
labs, closed and open circuit TV, directed study, etc. The
Evening College is receiving adequate support. The Director
is responsible to the Vice-President. All known audio visual
aids are being used.

X. STUDENT RECRUITMENT

News articles and public service announcements are
used in student recruitment. Special brochures are liberally
distributed to industry and organizations for the same purpose.

Philadelphia College of Textiles
Philadelphia, Pennsylvania
Evening College

Total Enrollment 2,100   Private Institution
Evening Enrollment 950   Semester System

I. ADMISSION POLICIES

A student may register for credit courses before
transcripts are submitted. "Special" students may take as
many as 60 hours for credit before matriculating. Admission for "special" students includes having the pre-requisites
for the course. Admission requirements for regular students
includes high school graduation with the required subjects,
entrance examinations or an official transcript from the college previously attended. Mail registration is used but represents only 5% of the total registration. A "C" average is
required for retention. No ACT or CEEB scores are required for admission. No special degree program for adults
is available. The Dean or Assistant Dean of the Evening
College formulate the admission policies for evening students.
Day and evening students may enroll in the same classes.
An orientation program is held at the beginning of each semester. The college has been enrolling more transfer students than "new" students the past two or three years. Areas
of concentration: Business, 51 credits; Accounting, 30;
Chemistry, 64; Textiles, 22. Approval of the respective
Dean is required for interchanging day/evening classes for
Fall & Spring terms--not required for summer sessions.
The advantages of a combined class are balance of background, maturity and experience and more economical for
marginal classes.

II. TERMINOLOGY

Title of Division: Evening College. Defined: offering courses, credit and non-credit for both matriculated and
non-matriculated students in the evening for students who are
unable to attend daytime classes. In addition, students can
set "their own pace" in the evening as to the load to be carried. Continuing Education defined: education after and beyond the formal full-time matriculated period, to keep persons abreast of development educationally, technically, professionally, and culturally.

III. FEES

There is a fee differential for day and evening stu-
dents--evening students pay per credit or per course since
most are part-time and loads vary.   Day students pay a flat
fee since they are full-time and carry standard loads.   Refund policies are 70% the first week, 50% during the second
week and none thereafter during the 10 week period.

IV.   FACULTY AND FACULTY RECRUITMENT

Approximately 30-40% of the faculty are full-time.
Evening College does its own hiring of full/part-time faculty,
however, no full-time faculty are hired to teach exclusively
in the evening.   No regular faculty meetings are held.   Approximately 10% of the budget is spent of faculty recruitment.
Salaries range from $550 to $800 for 3-credit courses; $700
to $1200 for 4-hour courses.

V.   SCHEDULING

The Dean is responsible for the evening class schedule which is determined on the basis of available faculty,
student programs, estimated enrollment and frequency of
scheduling previously.   Three-hour classes are scheduled
one night a week in Fall and Spring terms, two nights a
week in the summer (accelerated term.)   Generally speaking,
day classes have better preparation (secondary education) but
less motivation than evening students.   A separate honor list
is maintained for evening students with a minimum of two
courses (6 hours) . . . 1st honors minimum of 3. 50, 2nd
honors minimum of 3. 30.   Normally, 10 to 12 students are
needed to register in order to constitute a class unless the
course is needed by students.

VI.   ORGANIZATIONAL STRUCTURE

Two staff members constitute the administrative staff:
the Dean administering the Evening College and the Assistant
Dean who assists.   Eighty-nine part-time faculty members
constitute the teaching staff.   Three secretaries are employed.

VII.   EDUCATIONAL TELEVISION PROGRAMS

The Evening College does not offer any educational
television programs.

VIII. NON-CREDIT PROGRAMS

Non-credit programs are offered in Engineering, Arts and Sciences, and Education. These programs are expected to pay for themselves. Remuneration for faculty is the same as for teaching credit courses since non-credit courses require the same preparation, time and competency as credit courses. The College does not sponsor conferences, institutes, etc.

IX. GENERAL

Students voice opinions through the Evening Student Council. It is felt that the evening college does not receive adequate support in comparison with the day program. The Dean of the Evening College is responsible to the Dean of the Faculty. Closed circuit TV and regular audio visual aids are used by the Evening College.

X. STUDENT RECRUITMENT

Special newspaper ads are prepared three times per year as well as spot announcements on the radio. Brochures are sent to business and industrial concerns on special courses offered for business and industry.

PMC Colleges
Chester, Pennsylvania
Evening Division

Total Enrollment 2, 897   Private Institution
Evening Enrollment 1, 147   Semester System

I. ADMISSION POLICIES

The deadline for application for admission to Evening classes for all students is: Fall Semester, August 20; Spring Semester, January 5; Summer session, May 20 and June 20. A student may not register for credit courses before transcripts are submitted. Non-matriculating or "special" students may take as many as 30 semester hours of work for credit. The admission requirements for all students are: high school or previous college transcripts and entrance examination (the latter is required unless CEEB's have been taken previously with satisfactory scores). A strict majority of students who are rejected for admission as regular students may be advised to apply as evening students but they are not automatically accepted.   Mail registration is not used as it is felt to be too impersonal.   New enrollees and those previously enrolled attend registration session.   Course roster cards must be signed by the counselor.   The policies regarding probation and dismissal of all students are: all records are evaluated annually (June).   Students are informed of their status by mail, including those disqualified for further attendance.   The ACT or CEEB examination and other tests are required for adults in the evening division and these tests are used as a basis for admission and for placement and advisement.   The evening degree program for adults is the same as the regular day degree program for undergraduates, but there is a special degree for graduates. The degrees for undergraduates are the B. A. , and the B. S. and for the graduates the M. B. A.   The enrollment for the Fall semester was: full-time, 1430; part-time, 1189, undergraduates, 1430 and graduate, 320.   The distribution requirements (language, laboratory science, etc.) for undergraduate degrees depend on major curriculum.   There is a special degree for graduate students, offered by the Division of Economics and Management.   The degree for undergraduates requires 120 semester hours to 137 semester hours and the graduate degree requires 36 semester hours; the areas of concentration together with the credit requirements are: B. A. in Liberal Arts, 120 semester hours; B. S. in Business Administration, 125 semester hours; B. S. in Chemistry, 130 semester hours; B. S. in Engineering, 137 semester hours.   There are plans made to offer a special undergraduate degree program for adults in the near future.   The Evening College Administration formulates the admission policies for all evening students, except for graduate students which is formulated by the Division of Economics and Management. The extent that day and evening students may enroll in the same class is a reciprocal situation.   The advantages and/or disadvantages of the combined class with day and evening students express liking and preference for evening classes-- stress mature environment.   There is an orientation program for evening students during pre-registration counseling. Plans are being made for an Evening Division Advisory Committee.

II.   TERMINOLOGY

The title of the Division: Evening Division.   Defined: general purpose of the Division is to provide college-level opportunity for qualified adults who must attend on part-time basis. Continuing Education defined: Continuing education includes all further learning by the individual adult; credit, non-credit (undergraduate and graduate) and informal programs of various types.

III.   FEES

There is no fee differential for day and evening classes. The refund policies for evening students who drop one or more classes but remain in schools are: refunds made up to and including fifth week of semester according to schedule published in annual bulletin.

IV.   FACULTY AND FACULTY RECRUITMENT

25% of the faculty for evening classes are full-time faculty members. The Dean of the Evening Division in coordination with department head, has the final authority for hiring full and/or part-time faculty members for evening classes. No full-time faculty members who teach exclusively in the evening are employed. The evening director can engage an instructor without the consent of the department head if this person refuses to staff these classes. Regular faculty meetings with the evening faculty are held periodically. The policies regarding regular faculty members teaching credit or non-credit courses or participating in institutes, seminars and conferences as an overload, requires consultation with the department head. One mail point is that the full-time faculty member (day college) must be cleared by his department head to teach the evening course. About five percent of the budget is spent for recruitment. The salary range for part-time faculty is $600 to $900 per course. The salary paid faculty for overloads is based on a semester hour basis according to faculty rank of the individual.

V.   SCHEDULING

The Dean is responsible for the evening class schedule in the institution. The procedure for compiling the evening class schedule is an analysis of sequential and other needs by evening staff followed by coordination with departmental heads. The Dean has the authority to revise or make additions to the evening class schedule. It is preferable to have 3-hour classes two nights per week. The comparison of day and evening classes in terms of quality are: evening courses are at least as good in quality as those of day college.   A high percentage of day faculty who have taught evening courses speak well of their students.   Part-time evening students are eligible for the Dean's List; two courses are required for eligibility.   Ten students must register to constitute a class.   The instructor's compensation is not reduced when he teaches a class below the minimum size.

VI.   ORGANIZATIONAL STRUCTURE

The size of the administrative staff in the evening division is two staff members plus a teaching staff of 20 full-time and 52 part-time members.   The two staff members are: 1) Dean, who has the overall responsibility for the evening operation; 2) the Associate Dean who is responsible for scheduling, classroom assignment, assists with publicity and promotion, adviser to the student council, assists in admissions work, etc.   In our estimation, it is felt that an administrative staff of four (minimum) plus three (minimum) staff members would be required for administering an evening credit program with an evening enrollment of 1000.

VII.   EDUCATIONAL TELEVISION PROGRAMS

The institution does not offer any courses using Educational Television.

VIII.   NON-CREDIT PROGRAMS

The division offers non-credit courses in Remedial English and Mathematics.   This program is expected to pay for itself.   The remuneration to faculty (full or part-time) for teaching a non-credit course is the same as credit-level courses, depending upon the qualifications of the instructor. The division sponsored a seminar this past year--Labor-Management Seminar.   The division sponsors its own conference as its own operation.

IX.   GENERAL

Student at the institution participate in discussions regarding the academic program through direct communication in the Dean's Council and Student Council.   The innovative practices used at the institution are: Law Enforcement Program for police officers and others; coordination with Greater Chester movement for preparation and enrollment of economically deprived; neighborhood club for poor black children; racial attitudes; school study assistance, personal regimes,

health habits, etc.   In general, it is felt that the evening
division is not receiving adequate support (in terms of adequate stress and financial support) in comparison with the
day program.   The administration does not recognize the
need for and the importance of adult educational programs.   The
Dean of the evening division is responsible to the Vice-President in charge of Academic Affairs.   Projectors, films,
language laboratory, and other tapes, are used as audio-
visual and other technical instructional aids in the evening
division.   The Division has an active Chapter of Alpha Sigma
Lambda, the Evening Honor Society.

X.   STUDENT RECRUITMENT

Publicity by newspaper and radio is used for student
recruitment.   Special motivational appeals are developed for
industry--mailings for industry, conferences with representatives of industry and for civic organizations.

<u>Post Junior College</u>
Waterbury, Connecticut
Division of Continuing Education

Total Enrollment 548   Private Institution
Evening Enrollment 119   Semester System

I.   ADMISSION POLICIES

The deadline for application for admission to evening
classes is the time of the first class session.   A student may
register for credit courses before transcripts are submitted.
Students may take up to twelve hours as non-matriculating or
"special" students.   Admission requirements: for regular
degree students, a high school diploma or the equivalent; for
non-matriculating students, adults employed on a full-time
basis or are housewives.   Students who are rejected as day
students are not encouraged to enroll as evening students.
Mail registration is used.   Each bulletin has an application
which may be mailed up to two weeks prior to the first class;
after that time, registration must be in person.   Probation
and dismissal regulations: degree students are placed on
probation if grade point average is less than 2. 0; non-degree
or "special" students have no special policy.   ACT scores
will be required for admission of adult evening students beginning in 1971-72, but the results will be used for placement

and advisement purposes only--not for admission. No special degree program is offered for adults. The number of students enrolled for the A. A. , A. S. and A. A. S. degrees is 548 full-time and 119 part-time students. The distribution requirements: 45 core (liberal arts), 15-18 in concentration, e. g. , accounting, physical education, secretarial science, etc. The Admission Committee of the faculty formulate the admission policies for evening students. Day and evening students may enroll in the same class only "in special student or scheduling circumstances. " No orientation program is held for evening students. There is no Evening Division advisory committee. According to the Director any adult will be admitted, after an interview, "but admission procedures, or matriculation, does not begin until completion of twelve hours. "

II. TERMINOLOGY

Title of Division: Division of Continuing Education. Defined: the continuation of formal education for adults engaged in career - also seminars and institutes for business and industry.

III. FEES

Evening students pay less tuition ($33 per semester hour) with a limit of nine hours for degree students and six hours for non-matriculated students. Justification is that very few of the day school services are available for evening students except academic counseling. Refund policy states that no refund will be made after the first meeting of the class.

IV. FACULTY AND FACULTY RECRUITMENT

There is a policy regarding the percentage of faculty members who are full-time teaching members in the evening. Approximately 80% of the evening faculty are full-time faculty members. The Director of Continuing Education has the final authority for hiring full and/or part-time faculty members for evening classes. The Director of Continuing Education can reject a faculty member for evening classes. No full-time faculty members teach exclusively in the evening. The Director can engage an instructor without the consent of the department head if this person refuses to staff these classes. No regular faculty meetings are held for evening faculty. Faculty members generally teach evening classes as part of

their regular teaching load; if not, they receive extra remuneration according to the regular part-time salary scale.
No budget is spent on faculty recruiting. The salary range
for part-time faculty is: Assistant Instructor - $200 per
semester hour, Instructor - $225 per semester hour, As-
sistant Professor - $250 per semester hour, Associate Pro-
fessor - $275 per semester hour, Professor - $300 per
semester hour.

V. SCHEDULING

The Director of Continuing Education is responsible
for the evening class schedule. Procedures for compiling
the evening class schedule include courses required for all
programs offered each year and summer as well as other
or special curricular requirements every two years and
summer. Three-hour classes are offered one night per
week. Research in adult education is in progress--Perform-
ance Objectives in Business Administration Curriculum. Day
classes are of high quality but the evening graduates do very
well in senior college. Part-time students (evening) are
eligible for the Dean's List with a twelve hour minimum of
3.0 minimum average. A minimum of six students is required to constitute a class. An instructor's compensation
is reduced when he teaches a class below minimum size; he
receives 80% of his normal salary.

VI. ORGANIZATIONAL STRUCTURE

The Division of Continuing Education has an administrative staff of two, including the secretary. The Director
is in charge of the overall operation and is assisted by the
secretary. Recommended size of administrative staff for
300 students would be one staff member; 500 students would
be two staff members; 2000 students would be four staff
members.

VII. EDUCATIONAL TELEVISION PROGRAMS

The Division does not offer any educational television
programs.

VIII. NON-CREDIT PROGRAMS

The Division of Continuing Education offers no non-
credit courses but does offer conferences and institutes.
Typical programs are: Connecticut Conference on Environ-

ment (state-wide), and Management Seminar (one week). Clinicians receive varied fees depending upon the individual and content of the program. The Division of Continuing Education is responsible for the summer session.

IX. GENERAL

Students do have an opportunity to participate in discussions regarding the academic program--especially the evening students. Students may "walk in off the street" as no formal admission requirements are necessary. The Division is receiving adequate financial support. The Director of Continuing Education is responsible to the Dean of Academic Affairs. Audio-visual aids and other equipment is available for evening students. Video tapes will be used this fall.

X. STUDENT RECRUITMENT

Newspaper and radio publicity is used for recruiting. Special motivational appeals are developed for industry and civic organizations.

Pratt Institute
Brooklyn, New York
School of Continuing Professional Studies

Total Enrollment 4, 500   Private Institution
Evening Enrollment 600+   Semester System

I. ADMISSION POLICIES

The deadline for applications for admission to evening classes coincides with the registration date. Students may register for credit courses before transcripts are submitted because all students are non-matriculated until eighteen semester hours of work are completed at Pratt. Special students may take a maximum of eighteen semester hours of work. Admission requirements include the ability to meet standards of the particular course. Regular students must have a high school diploma or its equivalent. No ACT or CEEB scores are required for admission. Mail registration is used for upper class or returning students only. Retention policy requires maintenance of satisfactory academic point average. The overall Institute Policy for admission is determined by the Academic Council. Day and evening students do not normally enroll in the same classes. An orientation program is planned for evening students. The Institute strongly believes in a procedure of using a validation process requiring stated number of hours to be completed, meeting a stated standard before degree candidacy is established.

II. TERMINOLOGY

Title of Division: Division of Building Science and Division of Continuing Education - both Divisions within the School of Continuing Professional Studies. Defined: Applies to formal credit programs for adults (students working at full-time day positions) and non-credit professional programs unrestricted to age or background. Continuing Education defined: Basically, programs, either credit or non-credit, which seek to provide additional education to meet existing need of the individual being served and at no specified age level.

III. FEES

There is no fee differential between day and evening classes. Refund policies are standard based upon a percentage through fifth week of class.

IV. FACULTY AND FACULTY RECRUITMENT

No more than ten percent of the faculty teaching evening classes are full-time faculty members. No full-time faculty members teach exclusively in the evening. The Dean of the School has the final authority for hiring faculty. Faculty in the fall and in the spring. Faculty members may carry an overload if desired. Five percent of the budget is spent on recruiting. Salaries range from $250 to $400 based upon contact hours.

V. SCHEDULING

The Divisional Director is responsible for the evening class schedule subject to the approval of the Dean of the School. Three-hour classes are held once a week. Day and evening classes are comparable "to the extent that factors of age and experience are weighted into the analysis." Part-time evening students are eligible for the Dean's List by taking eight hours with a GPA of 3.0.

VI.   ORGANIZATIONAL STRUCTURE

The Dean, academic and administrative director of the school, is responsible to the Academic Vice-President; the Director is responsible to the Dean, the Director of Non-Credit Programs is responsible for the organization and direction of the non-credit programs and reports to the Dean; evening admissions is handled through the Director of Admissions until sixteen hours of work is completed at which time the student is turned over to the Institute Admissions Office.

VII.   EDUCATIONAL TELEVISION PROGRAMS

No educational television programs are offered.

VIII.   NON-CREDIT PROGRAMS

Non-credit programs are offered in Business and Management.   A budget is provided for these courses.   Remuneration to faculty varies according to length of program and individual involved.   The Division sponsors conferences and workshops--one recently conducted was on Construction Management.

IX.   GENERAL

Students have an opportunity to participate in discussions regarding the academic program through elected student representation serving on the Curriculum Committee and on the Planning Committee.   The evening program is receiving adequate support from the administration.   The Divisional Directors report to the Dean of the School of Continuing Professional Studies.   The Dean reports directly to the Vice-President for Academic Affairs.

X.   STUDENT RECRUITMENT

The School uses the newspaper for publicity purposes, but does not use radio or television.   Special contacts are made with business and industry concerning programs of interest to their personnel.

Prince George's Community College
Largo, Maryland
Evening Division

Total Enrollment 6, 223   Public Institution
Evening Enrollment 1, 763   Semester System

I. ADMISSION POLICIES

Mail registration is not used. The evening program does not differ from the day program. The deadline for application for admission to evening classes for regular and non-degree students is August 1 and January 2. A student may register for credit courses before transcripts are submitted with an academic restriction status. Non-matriculating students may take nine hours credit work. Admission requirements for non-matriculating students are high school graduate and eighteen years of age; regular student must submit high school transcripts and complete the SAT and Achievement test. Students who are rejected for admission as regular students are not advised to apply as evening students-- and are not automatically accepted. A student is on probation when his cumulative grade-point average falls below the minimum standards set by the college. If he fails to raise his average above the minimum standards at the end of the semester he is academically dismissed. This applies only to degree students. Since the evening division is a continuation of the day program, the same tests are required. There are 3, 367 full-time and 2, 856 part-time students enrolled fall quarter (6, 223 undergraduates). The degree, Associate in Arts, requires a total number of sixty hours, with one year of resident work--30 semester hours. No requirements are in force in the undergraduate special degree program. There is no limitation to the extent students may enroll in the same class, which gives the student the opportunity to choose his course scheduling to his advantage. The orientation program for day and evening students is scheduled one week before registration. There is no Evening Division Advisory Committee.

II. TERMINOLOGY

Title of Division: Evening Division. Defined: A continuation of day classes for students who can only attend in the evening. Definition of Continuing Education: Non-credit courses completed with a satisfactory grade and a certificate of completion awarded.

III.   FEES

There is no fee differential between day and evening classes.   After the first five class days there is a refund of 75%; the succeeding five class days a refund of 50%; after the first ten class days there is no refund.

IV.   FACULTY AND FACULTY RECRUITMENT

There is no policy regarding the percentage of full-time faculty members--approximately 73% are full-time. The Dean of Academic Affairs and the Dean of the Evening Division have authority for hiring full and/or part-time faculty and the Dean of the Evening Division may reject a faculty member.   Full-time faculty members are employed to teach exclusively in the evening and they are responsible to the Dean of the Evening Division as well as the Dean of Academic Affairs.   Authority to engage an instructor without the consent of the department head is not given to the Dean. Regular faculty meetings are not held.   An instructor can earn 20% of his annual salary for teaching an overload and there is no limit on non-credit courses, etc.   Salary range for part-time faculty is $200 per contact hour, M. A. degree; $225 with M. A. plus 15-30; $250 with M. A. plus 60; $275 for Ph. D.   Overloads are paid on the part-time scale.

V.   SCHEDULING

The Registrar and Department Chairmen are responsible for the evening class schedule.   The Dean of the Evening Division is allowed to make revisions as necessary.   Three-hour classes are scheduled two and three nights per week-- there is no preference.   There is no research in progress. Day and evening classes are equal in terms of quality.   Part-time evening students are eligible for the Dean's List if they are taking twelve hours and have a cumulative average of 3. 25.   Classes of less than ten students are cancelled.

VI.   ORGANIZATIONAL STRUCTURE

There are 188 full-time and 69 part-time teachers on the teaching staff.

VII.   EDUCATIONAL TELEVISION PROGRAMS

The Evening Division does not offer educational television programs.

VIII. NON-CREDIT PROGRAMS

Non-credit courses are offered in the areas of Community Services, Arts and Sciences and other areas. This program is expected to pay for itself. Remuneration for faculty is part-time rate plus contact hours and is dependent upon the qualifications of the instructor. The Evening Division does not sponsor conferences and institutes. The Division is responsible for the summer session.

IX. GENERAL

There is student representation at the College Senate meetings. No graduate programs are administered by the Evening Division. The Dean is responsible to the President. Audio-visual aids are not used.

X. STUDENT RECRUITMENT

Newspapers, radio and television are employed as means of student recruitment as well as special appeals through the citizens of Prince George's County.

Purdue University
Calumet Campus
Hammond, Indiana
Evening Classes

Total Enrollment 5, 240   Public Institution
Evening Enrollment 3, 305   Semester System

I. ADMISSION POLICIES

Students may apply for admission through the late registration period. Students may register for credit courses before transcripts are submitted. Non-matriculating and/or special students may take up to eleven hours for credit before matriculating. Admission requirements for "special" students include the ability to handle the course work; regular students must have graduated in the upper one-half of their class or should be in the upper one-half of the national average of the SAT - out-of-state in the upper one-fourth. There is no mail registration. Degree students are placed on probation on the basis of their failure to meet the minimum graduation or semester index requirements for any giv-

en semester.   (Scale from 3. 2 to 4. 0.)   Non-degree students
are exempt from the above restrictions; however, their records are reviewed on an annual basis with appropriate activity
by a counselor, CEEB is required for regular students; no
examination for non-degree students.   CEEB scores are used
for placement purposes.   School of Humanities requires Purdue Modern Language Placement Exam.   There is no special
degree program for adults; none is planned for the future.
The University Board of Trustees formulates the admission
policies for all students.   Day and evening students may enroll in the same classes.   There is no orientation program
for evening students.   They may attend the day orientation.
The evening program is a continuation and extension of the
regular collegiate activity on campus.

II.   TERMINOLOGY

Title of Division: No distinct and separate division
for the evening college.   Continuing Education defined:
Formal or informal involving credit or non-credit but in any
event it serves the student by providing him with information, knowledge, or cultural values which enhance his ability
to earn a living, his zeal for living, or his role as a member of society.

III   FEES

All fees are charged on a per credit-hour basis.   Refund policies: 100% first week of class, 60% second week
of class, 20% after fourth week and none thereafter.

IV.   FACULTY AND FACULTY RECRUITMENT

Budgetarily, 25% of the evening classes are covered
as a part of the regular teaching load of full-time faculty.
Usually somewhat more are included in the teaching faculty
for evenings.   The Dean and Director of the Calumet Campus
have the final authority for hiring faculty members.   Recruitment of part-time faculty is delegated to the chairmen
of the various departments.   Regular members may receive
compensation for participating in non-credit courses either
in the form of an overload payment or in the form of an
amount of released time--that is, the equivalent to a portion
of the regular academic load.   Plans are currently being
made to hold an initial orientation session with evening faculty in the Fall and develop from there a schedule of evening
faculty meetings.   Less than 1% of the annual budget is spent

for recruitment. The undergraduate courses are paid at the rate of $150 to $200 per weekly class contact hour and from $120 to $130 per weekly hour. The graduate class salary range is from $200 to $285 per weekly class hour. The total stipend is based on the number of classes and weekly contact hours involved. Overloads are based on faculty salaries, contact hours, and a numerical value attached to the overload course.

V. SCHEDULING

The Dean and Director of the Calumet Campus have the final authority for all class schedules. Information is compiled from the various departments for all parts of the schedule both day and evening. This information is assembled and much of the requirements for the schedule are put together by the Assistant Dean for Academic Affairs in cooperation with the Assistant Director for Administration who is in charge of space use and the Assistant Dean for Evening Administration. Upon the recommendation of the Assistant Dean for Evening Administration, the Director may revise the schedule as needed. Day and evening classes are judged on the same standard and taught according to the same standards. Part-time students are highly motivated. Part-time evening students are eligible for the Dean's List by accumulating twelve hours with grades of "B" or above. Projects are currently being planned to assist in the evaluation of the Careers Opportunity Program which we are operating in cooperation with the School City of Gary. Approximately eight students are required to constitute a class.

VI. ORGANIZATIONAL STRUCTURE

Administrative staff in continuing education or evening division consists of three and one-half members. Teaching staff consists of 150 full-time and 100 part-time faculty members. A time action plan has been formulated which may resolve the question of autonomy by 1973. The Dean and Director have overall management of the Calumet Campus - both day and evening. The Assistant Dean for Evening Administration is responsible for the development of all related services needed by part-time students, for all continuing education programs and coordination of all special contract programs eminating from industry. The Coordinator of Continuing Education is responsible for the development and coordination of all programs, both credit and non-credit; one-half time Coordinator for Supervision Programs is responsible for

the development and coordination of non-credit offerings oriented toward industrial supervision and management.

VII.   EDUCATIONAL TELEVISION PROGRAMS

No courses are offered on educational television.

VIII.   NON-CREDIT PROGRAMS

Non-credit courses offered in Business and Management, Arts and Sciences, Education, Engineering and other
personal interest courses such as those connected with the
ground portion of private pilot training.   Non-credit programs
are expected to pay for themselves.   Remuneration for a
non-credit course is the same as overload formula.   Remuneration depends upon the qualifications of the instructor
and the area of instruction, and an assessment of the course.
Conferences and institutes are sponsored.   Current plans
call for the serious initiation of this kind of activity during
the course of the next year.

IX.   GENERAL

Increasingly, students are members of those faculty
committees whose areas of concern directly affect the students.   Student participation in discussion regarding academic
programs is through the faculty and the administration.   The
administration recognizes the importance of adult education
and gives adequate stress and support to the program.   The
Dean and Director of the Calumet Campus are responsible to
the Vice-President of the Regional Campus Administration.

X.   STUDENT RECRUITMENT

The newspaper is used for periodic advertising and
news releases.   Releases are given to the radio and television.   A number of specific bulletins are published by the
University placing particular stress on technical programs
and special cultural events which are distributed as seen fit
to industry, libraries, schools, local organizations, etc.

Queensborough Community College
Bayside, New York
Evening and General Studies Division

Total Enrollment 8, 700   Public Institution
Evening Enrollment 5, 200   Semester System

I. ADMISSION POLICIES

Deadline for application for admission for degree students is about one month prior to registration. Non-degree students have no deadline and may register for credit courses without transcripts. Mail registration is used only for non-credit courses. Regular degree students must maintain 1. 3 after six-eleven credits; 1. 5 with twelve-twenty-seven credits; 1. 7 with twenty-eight-forty-four credits; 2. 0 with sixty-four plus credits. Placement tests are given to adults in the evening division and results are used for advising. A special degree for adults is being considered. Admission policies for evening students are set by the faculty committee, for non-degree students by the Dean of the Evening and General Studies Division. Day and evening students may enroll in the same classes with permission. There is no orientation for evening students.

II. TERMINOLOGY

Title of Division: Evening and General Studies Division. Defined: A Division of the College with the following areas of responsibility: Evening Session, Adult-Continuing Education Program, Community Service Program, Extension Programs, Basic Educational Skills Training Program and an Urban Center (when developed).

III. FEES

Degree students do not pay tuition; non-degree students pay $15 per semester hour. Refunds are made to students on the following basis: before first class 100%, first week 75%, second week 50%, third week 25%, after third week, none.

IV. FACULTY AND FACULTY RECRUITMENT

Approximately 5% of the faculty teaching evening classes is full-time. Final authority to hire evening faculty lies with the President of the College. Some full-time faculty members teach exclusively in the evening. Regular faculty meetings are held in the fall.   If and when it is necessary for a faculty member to teach on an overload basis, he receives extra compensation. The Dean of Faculty is responsible for faculty recruitment. The salary range for part-time faculty is $16-$25/hour, $240-$371/semester hour. The salary paid the faculty for overloads is the same as part-time faculty if they are paid. There is no set figure for number of students required to constitute a class. The instructor's compensation is not reduced when he teaches a class with small enrollment.

V. SCHEDULING

The Dean of the Evening Division is responsible for the evening class schedule. The Dean has the authority to revise the evening schedule. Three-credit-hour classes are scheduled two nights per week. Part-time evening students are eligible for the Dean's List with a 3.0 after completing fifteen semester hours.

VI. ORGANIZATIONAL STRUCTURE

The size of the administrative staff in the Evening Division totals thirty-eight staff members (includes all clerical and secretarial coverage for academic departments during evening hours). The teaching staff consists of eighteen full-time and 395 part-time teachers (does not include supervisors, administrators, counselors, technicians and librarians). The duties and responsibilities of the staff are as follows: Associate or Assistant Dean coordinates scheduling of classes and assignment of rooms, develops off-campus educational centers, assists in development of new courses and programs, handles general student complaints, assists in registration procedures, prepares miscellaneous reports, represents the college at meetings and conventions, follow-up on production of printed material and advertising, promulgate payroll for adjunct faculty; Coordinator of Adult Education develops and supervises non-credit adult education courses, programs, institutes, coordinates advertising literature for aforementioned; Director of Admissions (evening students) processes applications for day students, processes applications for non-matrics to matric status; Registrar (evening) maintains student records, registration of students, processes changes of programs and withdrawals, processes grades, issues transcripts; Business Manager (evening) is the same individual who works with the day session; other Assistant to

Dean acts as liaison to off-campus educational extension centers, completes miscellaneous reports, coordinates class schedules and registration guides, general supervision of evening classes, attends meetings as instructed.

VII. EDUCATIONAL TELEVISION PROGRAMS

The Evening Division does not offer any courses in educational television.

VIII. NON-CREDIT PROGRAMS

The Evening Division offers non-credit courses in Business and Management, Arts and Sciences, and other areas. This program is expected to pay for itself. The remuneration to faculty depends upon the qualifications of the instructor. The Evening Division sponsored conferences and institutes during the past year, namely, Saturday Reading and Writing Institute, Community Leadership Conference, Secretarial Refresher Forum. The Evening Division is not responsible for the summer sessions at the institution.

IX. GENERAL

Students are on most committees and participate in discussions regarding the academic program. In general, all evening divisions are not receiving adequate support. The Dean of the Evening and General Studies Division is responsible to the President. All audio-visual instructional aids are available to evening classes.

X. STUDENT RECRUITMENT

Newspaper advertising is used--via all New York papers. Special motivational appeals are developed for industry and civic organizations.

The University of Richmond
Richmond, Virginia
University College

Total Enrollment 6, 000+
Evening Enrollment 1, 944
  (93 full-time, 1851 part-time)

Private, Church-related
Institution
Semester System

I. ADMISSION POLICIES

There is no deadline for application for admission to
evening classes only registration deadlines. With the Dean's
permission, some students may register for credit courses
without transcripts. There is no special student category.
If a student receives five failing grades, he is dropped from
"credit" work. There is no probation or suspension policy
for part-time students. Admission policies are formulated
by the full-time evening faculty and the Dean. Day students
may register for evening courses with special permission.
There is an orientation program for evening students. A
Bachelor of Arts is offered and a Bachelor of Commerce degree for evening students only is offered. The undergraduate distribution requirements are: B. C. , 60 hrs. of liberal
arts work, 12 hrs. of English, 6 hrs. of Math, 6 hrs. of
History plus electives; B. A. 42-48 hours in field of concentration. The graduate degrees offered are Master of Commerce and Master of Humanities, which are administered by
the University College with a degree granted by the Graduate
School. A total of 124 hours are required to complete an
undergraduate degree and 36 hours required to complete a
graduate degree. Areas of concentration are: B. A. , 24-48
hours in concentration in English, Economics or History;
B. C. , 18 hours in Accounting, Banking, Economics, Finance,
Management, Marketing Personnel. Admission requirements
are high school diploma, acceptable CEEB scores for the
special degree program; for graduate students a "B" average
in junior and senior years. A new graduate degree is in
the planning stage.

II. TERMINOLOGY

Title of Division: University College. Defined: A
University within a University (not a college) and are oriented toward the community.

III. FEES

Day students pay $140 per three-hour undergraduate
course; evening students pay $54 per three-hour undergrad-
uate course. Refunds are made to students only for reason
of draft or illness.

IV. FACULTY AND FACULTY RECRUITMENT

Approximately 25% of the faculty teaching evening

classes are full-time.   Final authority to hire full-time faculty members lies with the President; part-time members
with the Dean.   The Dean of University College can reject
a faculty member assigned to teach evening classes.   The
full-time evening faculty members who teach exclusively in
the evening are responsible to the Dean of University College.   Regular faculty meetings are held with evening faculty
twice a month.   Faculty members may teach one three-hour
course on an overload basis, with permission.   Salaries
range from $700 to $775.   Overloads are paid at a rate of
$500 per course.

V.   SCHEDULING

The Dean of University College is responsible for the
evening class schedule and has the authority to revise it as
needed.   Three-hour classes are scheduled one night a week.
Day and evening classes are equal in terms of quality.   Part-
time evening students are not eligible for the Dean's List.
Generally, twelve students constitute a class.   Instructor's
fee is not reduced for teaching a class below minimum size.

VI.   ORGANIZATIONAL STRUCTURE

The teaching staff includes 28 full-time and 108 part-
time for day and evening classes in the College.   Being a
branch of the parent university, there is considerable academic and administrative autonomy.   The Dean has charge
of the overall operation and direct administrative responsibility for 350 students in the Day Division.   Two Associate
Deans have charge of the evening program and the non-credit
institute for Business and Community Development with Management, Urban and Research centers.   The Registrar for
day and evening is also the Director of Admissions.

VII.   EDUCATIONAL TELEVISION PROGRAMS

No educational television programs are offered.

VIII.   NON-CREDIT PROGRAMS

Non-credit programs are offered in Business and
Management.   A budget is provided for this program but the
courses are expected to pay for themselves.   Remuneration
to faculty varies--for full-time faculty it is a part of the
regular load.   Approximately 150 conferences were sponsored
during the past year.   Visiting lecturers provide about 90%

of the conferences.   The University College is responsible
for the Evening Summer Session.

IX.   GENERAL

The Evening Division is receiving adequate support.
The Dean of University College is responsible to the President.   Complete audio-visual instructional aids are available
for evening classes.

X.   STUDENT RECRUITMENT

Newspaper publicity is used.

Rider College
Trenton, New Jersey
Evening School

Total Enrollment 6, 291   Private Institution
Evening Enrollment 2, 591   Semester System

I.   ADMISSION POLICIES

All students must register and be in class for the
second meeting.   Students may not register for credit courses
before transcripts are submitted except when a student's report card is present.   Non-matriculating students may take
twelve semester hours of work for credit.   Admission requirements for non-matriculating students are high school
graduate - or GED equivalency - or twenty-one years of age
or GI status.   The same is true for regular student plus
satisfactory matriculation scores on SAT or Ohio test.   Students who are rejected as regular students are not advised
to enroll as evening students - nor are they automatically
accepted.   No mail registration is employed.   Students are
put on probation when their grade point averages fall below
2. 0.   They are eligible for the dismissal list after the second
probation or when they fall below published staggered point
scale.   This applies to all students.   An evening degree program, different from the day program, is offered: Bachelor
of Arts in Liberal Studies for undergraduate students.   Number of students enrolled in the Fall were: 3, 700 full-time,
2, 192 undergraduate, 399 graduate, and 2, 591 part-time.
For the degree, B. S. in Business Administration, sixty-eight
hours of core, sixty hours of professional are required; B. A.

in Liberal Arts, sixty hours core (general), eighteen in one
area, twelve in each of two other areas plus free electives.
The special degree for graduate students is administered by
the graduate school.   The hours required to complete the
degree total 128 for undergraduate and 32 for graduate (M. A.
or M. B. A.).   Areas of concentration with credit requirements are: B. S. in Business Administration, B. S. in Secretarial Science, B. S. in Chemistry, B. A. in Liberal Studies:
128 hrs. 6 AA degrees - 64 hrs.   The admission requirements for the special degree program for undergraduates are
high school graduation or equivalency, 21 years of age or
GI status plus SAT scores.   The evening school admissions
committee formulate the admission policies for the non-matriculating students; the respective schools formulate the admission policies for the regular, graduate and undergraduate
students.   Day students are permitted to enter evening classes
with the Dean's permission.   The combined classes are advantageous in that the heterogeneous students learn more
from peers.   Administratively the evening school is big
enough to be separate.   An orientation program is held the
first week of each semester.   The Evening Division Advisory
Committee's function is purely advisory.   A very important
aspect of any admissions policy is a rejection and/or dismissal policy.

II.   TERMINOLOGY

Title of Division: Evening School, a separate semi-
autonomous, degree-granting part of the College.   Defined:
"The Evening School borrows faculty, courses, and subject
specialists but we have our own management, quality control
and we consider ourselves a vital and unique part of our
College and the future of our national intelligence. "   Continuing Education defined: Education is "e-duco" the leading
of people--outward and upward, continuing is "recurring in-
definitely. "   It is generally institutionalized but need not be.

III.   FEES

Day tuition is approximately $50/hr. ; Evening School
tuition is $38/hr.   Justification is that many more services
are given day students.   Refunds are made at the rate of
80, 60, 40 and 20% during the first four weeks of class.

IV.   FACULTY AND FACULTY RECRUITMENT

There is an unwritten belief that 33 to 50% of the fac-

ulty should be full-time; at the present time the ratio is
50-50. The Dean of the Evening School, in consultation with
the department chairmen, has the final authority for hiring
full/part-time faculty members for evening classes. A policy regarding full-time faculty members who teach exclusively in the evening has been approved but not yet implemented.
The subject matter supervision comes from the department
chairmen. An annual dinner meeting is held in October--the
only general faculty meeting that is held. A regular load
for faculty is twelve semester hours; overloads of four semester hours are permitted. Professional participation in
short conferences is encouraged. Evening School's recruiting expense is negligible. Salary range for part-time faculty
is per contact hour (semester) and ranges: $200, Instructor;
$225, Assistant Professor; $240 Associate Professor; $260,
Full Professor--overloads are paid the same.

V.   SCHEDULING

The Dean is responsible for the evening class schedule. Each spring a full year's schedule is completed. The
Dean issues a note--"What changes, additions or deletions
do you suggest for Fall, Spring, Summer?"--to department
heads. The Dean has the authority to revise the schedule
as needed. Three-hour classes are scheduled one night per
week. Two nights are preferred professionally, but rejected
by most faculty and most students. Many minor research
projects are being undertaken. Generally speaking, the day
and evening classes are equal in terms of quality. In some
cases, the day is better. Part-time students who are carrying eight or more semester hours and who attain a semester
average of 3. 0 or better are eligible for the Dean's List.
Five students must register to constitute a class. An instructor's compensation is reduced if teaching a class below
the minimum size--an instructor may volunteer to teach for
tuition collected.

VI.   ORGANIZATIONAL STRUCTURE

The administrative staff consists of six staff members, four professionals and two clerical. The Dean has
full responsibility for all phases of the Evening School; the
Associate Dean is second in command and is Director of
Guidance and chief of all records; the Assistant to the Dean
gives general aid such as, faculty files, schedules, off-campus records; Director of Off-Campus Centers; Director of
Special Programs; Director of Student Services. The size of

the administrative staff really depends upon supporting secretarial staff and how capable each member is at their job.

VII. EDUCATIONAL TELEVISION PROGRAMS

No educational television programs are offered.

VIII. NON-CREDIT PROGRAMS

Non-credit programs are offered in the areas of Business and Management and Arts and Sciences.   There is no
budget--each program is expected to be self-supporting.   Remuneration to faculty ranges from $200 to $260 per semester
hour or $25-$30 per hour depending upon the qualifications
of the instructor.   The Division is responsible for the conferences and institutes which are sponsored and operated with
qualified faculty and community professionals.   The Division
is responsible for the summer evening classes only.

IX. GENERAL

Student members serve on almost all academic committees.   Remedial programs are offered in Math, English
and Reading.   The Division does not receive adequate sup-
port--actual support is well-believed verbal support.   The
Director is responsible to the Academic Vice-President.
Audio-visual aids are available.   There is an active chapter
of Alpha Sigma Lambda on campus.

X. STUDENT RECRUITMENT

There is $7,500 a year budgeted for newspaper ad-
vertisement; $2,200 per year is budgeted for radio adver-
tisement and no television is used.

Roanoke College
Salem, Virginia
Evening Program and Continuing Education

Total Enrollment 1,180   Private Church-related
   (164 in special courses)   Institution
Evening Enrollment 240 (plus 164)   Semester System

I. ADMISSION POLICIES

Deadline for application for admission to evening
classes is prior to the second week of classes. Deadline
dates: September 18 - Fall, February 5 - Spring. Students
may register in credit courses for non-credit without transcripts. "Special" students may take a maximum of twenty-
one hours before matriculating as degree students. Admission requirements for "special" students include a high school
or college transcript or "Certificate." Regular students are
required to submit a $15 application fee, picture, and tran-
scripts. No CEEB scores are required for evening students.
Day students have to have a score of 500 on the verbal and
500 on mathematics tests. Mail registration is used for returning students. Retention policies: C-first year; C aver-
age-second year; C plus average-third year and fourth year.
Placement tests in mathematics and english are required.
The Dean, Director of Admissions and the Director of Continuing Education formulate the admission policies for the
evening students. Day and evening students may enroll in
the same classes. No orientation program is offered for
evening students. There is no probation--suspension is for
one year and student may reapply for admission. This applies to non-degree students also. Distribution requirements
for undergraduate degrees: 12 hours language, 12 hours humanities, 8 hours sciences, 6 hours mathematics, 6 hours
social studies and 6 hours english. No graduate degrees are
offered. No plans made for offering special degree program
for adults. The Admission Committee formulates the admission policies for all categories of evening students.

II. TERMINOLOGY

Title of Division: Evening Program and Continuing
Education. Defined: This office takes care of evening
classes. The Continuing Education program was added to
take care of non-credit educational activities, seminars, conferences, institutes, business and industrial education. Continuing Education defined: credit and non-credit courses offered by business and industry, high schools, colleges, correspondence education which is beyond high school education
and the normal college age group of 18-22 years of age.

III. FEES

There is a fee differential for day and evening students. Day students pay $211 and evening students pay $100

for three credits per semester. Refund policy: 80% refund during the first week of classes and no refund after that time.

IV. FACULTY AND FACULTY RECRUITMENT

Forty percent of the faculty teaching evening classes are full-time. No full-time faculty members teach exclusively in the evening. The Dean of the College has the final authority for hiring full and part-time faculty. Faculty meetings are held for evening faculty on the first night of class each evening during the first week. Faculty members are paid extra for teaching an overload but they cannot go beyond 15 total hours. The regular teaching load is twelve hours. Salary range for part-time faculty is $233 per credit hour and overloads are paid the same. Ten students must register in order to have a class taught. An instructor's compensation is reduced when he teaches a class below the minimum size. He may elect to teach for fees collected.

V. SCHEDULING

The Director of the Evening Program and Continuing Education is responsible for the evening class schedule. The needs of the students earning degrees and the special needs of the community are attempted to be met. Ninety-five percent of the evening classes meet one night a week. Classes in language, sciences, freshman English and mathematics meet two nights a week. Evening classes are considered superior to day classes. Part-time evening students are not eligible for the Dean's List.

VI. ORGANIZATIONAL STRUCTURE

There are two administrative staff members; eighteen full-time and twelve part-time teaching staff. With evening enrollment of 300-1000 the suggested size of the administrative staff for credit programs would be one administrator; for enrollment of 5000 - 3 administrators.

VII. EDUCATIONAL TELEVISION PROGRAMS

No courses are offered on educational television.

VIII. NON-CREDIT PROGRAMS

Non-credit programs are offered in the areas of Business and Management, Arts & Sciences, Education and Women's Programs.   There is a budget assigned to these programs.   Full and part-time faculty receive $20.00 per clock hour and the remuneration does not depend on qualifications of instructor or area of instruction.   This division sponsors conferences and institutes.   Clinicians are paid $100 to $250 per day for conducting conferences.   Conferences are sponsored with other colleges and also by the Division.

IX.   GENERAL

More stress and support could be given to the evening program.   The Director of the Evening Program is responsible to the Dean and the President.

X.   STUDENT RECRUITMENT

Newspaper stories and announcements are used for publicity purposes as well as radio and television in public service programming.   Business and industry are contacted directly and special mailings are sent.

University of Rochester
Rochester, New York
University School of Liberal and Applied Studies

Total Enrollment 8,438   Private Institution
Evening Enrollment 2,693   Semester System

I.   ADMISSION POLICIES

There are no deadlines for application for admission as there is no formal admission.   Students may register for credit courses before transcripts are submitted.   Non-matriculating students may take sixteen hours for credit.   Regular students are required to submit high school records and transcripts of work taken elsewhere.   Sometimes students who are rejected as regular students are advised to apply as evening students and are automatically accepted.   Mail registration is used--materials are sent upon request and/or to all students registered the preceeding semester.   A student is not placed on any sort of academic probation.   He is advised by a counselor or instructor if his work is poor but he would not be placed on probation or 'separated.'   Tests of any description are not required for adults in the evening

division. A B. S. in General Studies is offered to undergraduates and an M. S. in General Studies is offered graduate students. The number of students enrolled in the fall
quarter totalled 226 full-time, 1088 part-time undergraduates
and 14 full-time, 1365 part-time graduates. Distribution requirements are English III, one literature course, two additional humanities courses, three courses from the Social Sciences group, two courses in Natural Science required to
complete the degree. The graduate degree distribution requirements vary with different programs. The special degree for graduate students is administered by the evening
division with 30 hours required to complete; the undergraduate degree requires 128 hours for completion. Areas of
concentration with credit requirements are: Social Studies,
Humanities, Natural Sciences with 56 hours required. For
admission to candidacy for the degree, a student must have
completed half of his total program with eight courses at
this University; the undergraduate and graduate requirements
are stated specifically for all disciplines. In so far as they
exist, the Dean, with the consent of the Faculty Senate formulate the admission policies (open admission). The Director
of Graduate Studies formulates the admission policies for the
special adult degree program. Students enroll in both day
and evening classes whenever necessary, for reasons of conflict in schedule, or because a course is offered in one division and not in another. The process of exchange seems to
work very well--day school students become aware of differences in people who attend part-time (maturity, experience,
professional training) and evening students are stimulated and
interested by contacts with full-time undergraduates. No orientation program is employed. There is no Evening Division Advisory Committee--the faculty senate approves candidacy for degrees and votes on policies and procedures.

II. TERMINOLOGY

Title of Division: University School of Liberal and
Applied Studies. Defined: It is essentially the evening
counterpart of the College of Arts and Sciences. It combines with the professional schools to comprise the Evening
Session. Definition of Continuing Education: It means that
provision is made for people to study part-time (or full-time
in some cases) at hours which will not infringe on employment. They can work toward a degree, graduate or undergraduate. Conferences and institutes are supplementary.

III. FEES

Evening students pay per course.   Full-time students
attending in the daytime pay a flat fee.   Justification of difference in fees is that day school students benefit from special services and opportunities not available to evening students.   The amount of tuition refunded is reduced at the following rates: 1st week of classes, 10%; 20% second week;
30% third week; 40% fourth week; 60% fifth week and no refund after the eighth week.   If withdrawal is made before
class meeting, tuition is refunded in full.

IV.   FACULTY AND FACULTY RECRUITMENT

There is no policy regarding the percentage of full-
time faculty members.   Approximately 43% are presently
full-time instructors.   Final authority for hiring faculty members for evening classes rests with the Dean.   All appointments are made on the recommendation of the appropriate
department chairman.   The Director has the authority to reject a faculty member and to engage a faculty member without the consent of the department head.   Four meetings are
held each year by the Faculty Senate.   This does not include
faculty members from the professional schools who teach in
the evening.   We encourage regular faculty members to conduct sessions as an overload.   None of the budget is spent
for faculty recruitment.   Salary range for part-time faculty
is from $1060 to $1200 per course determined by rank.
Overloads are paid the same fee.   Salary paid by the course
is: Instructors, $1,060; Assistant Professors, $1,120; Associate Professors, $1,160; Professors, $1,200.

V.   SCHEDULING

The Director is responsible for the evening class
schedule and it is compiled by soliciting course offerings
from the department chairmen.   The Director has the authority to revise the schedule.   Two and a half hour classes are
scheduled two nights per week.   No research is in progress
at the present time.   In terms of quality, day school students
are more homogeneous, probably progress at a more even
pace.   Night school students range widely in age, experience
and ability.   The Evening Session has its own Dean's List
for which part-time students are eligible if they take eight
hours per semester and maintain a 3.5 average.   Ten students must register for a class in order to have it taught--
exceptions are made, however.   An instructor's compensation

is not reduced when he teaches a class below minimum size.

VI.   ORGANIZATIONAL STRUCTURE

The administrative staff consists of two part-time staff members and 133 part-time instructors.   Positions of the staff are: Dean, Associate Dean, Director who is also the Dean of the University School and the Director of Summer and Evening Session, Assistant Director is also the Assistant Dean who is Assistant Director of the Special Sessions, Director of Graduate Studies (part-time), Registrar is on the Registrar staff but is especially appointed to work with evening session, Public Relations is a special assignment.   With an enrollment of 2000 the present staff seems adequate.

VII.   EDUCATIONAL TELEVISION PROGRAMS

There are no educational television programs offered by the University School.

VIII.   NON-CREDIT PROGRAMS

University School offers non-credit courses in reading and study skills and English as a Second Language.   A part of the total budget is used for the non-credit program but it is expected to pay for itself.   Remuneration for teaching a non-credit course varies--depending on the course and the qualifications of the instructor.   University School offers a Consortium Summer Program on Southeast Asia, a workshop in programming Self-Instructional Materials, Individualized Reading Instruction, Teaching about Foreign Culture, Systems Application for School Principals.   Clinicians pay depends on the nature of the institute or workshop.   We use qualified faculty members and visiting lecturers.   The Division is responsible for the summer session.

IX.   GENERAL

There are no off-campus locations for economically deprived populations but in-plant courses are given for the benefit of local industry.   Students participate in discussions informally on a one to one basis frequently.   Graduate programs for part-time students in the evening are offered but are "too lengthy to describe."   The Dean or Director is responsible to the Associate Provost.   The Evening Division receives adequate support in comparison with the day program and the administration does recognize a need for adult

education. There is an Audio-Visual Department whose resources are available to evening classes.

X. STUDENT RECRUITMENT

This is carried on through newspapers, radio, television, industry and organizations.

Rochester Institute of Technology
Rochester, New York
College of Continuing Education

Total Enrollment 15, 000 +   Private Institution
Evening Enrollment 10, 500 +   Semester System

I. ADMISSION POLICIES

The deadline for application for admission to evening
classes is one week after the beginning of classes.   Students
may register for credit courses before transcripts are submitted.   "Special" students may take twelve hours before
matriculation is permitted.   Admission requirements for
"special" students include interest in the course and posses-
sion of pre-requisites stated in the catalog.   Regular students
are required to have a high school diploma (except for non-
degree credit.)   Mail registration is used--Rochester Institute was one of the first institutions to use mail registration.
ACT or CEEB scores are not required for admission (do not
believe scores are valid).   Students do take a mathematics
placement test where appropriate.   The Associate in Arts
degree is offered for adults, with an enrollment of 150 students working toward the degree.   Admission requirements
for this degree are twenty-five years or older.   The program will be enlarged to include a broad emphasis on Fine
Arts as well as General Education.   Day students may enroll in evening classes for make-up, to avoid schedule conflicts and for enrichment.   Evening students, transferred to
night work, may enroll in day classes for not more than two
years.   No Orientation program is offered for evening students.   Additional comments: "We have an open door policy
which results in an attrition no greater than the restrictive
admissions of the day programs.   However, many students
at night take several courses before they decide on matriculation which would invalidate this claim. "   A student is placed
on probation anytime his semester GPA is under 1. 8 (on a

4. 0 system) for the first four semesters or 2. 0 for the fifth and subsequent semesters. A student is eligible for suspension who has been on probation twice, non-consecutively, the next time his GPA falls below the required GPA. Distribution requirements for undergraduate B. S. degree are: 25% Math/Science, 25% General Education and 50% Professional; for graduate degree: distribution requirements are determined by individual student qualifications. A total of 126 hours are required to complete the undergraduate work and 30 semester hours for the graduate work. The Faculty of the College of Continuing Education - day college - formulates the admission policies.

II. TERMINOLOGY

Title of Division: College of Continuing Education. Defined: Any program not part of the day program except where NSF grant is involved. Includes day programs in the Summer Session. Continuing Education defined: Includes any educational activity which follows the point at which the individual had considered his education terminal and which he pursues when an adult. An adult may be defined as anyone over sixteen or who has completed high school.

III. FEES

There is no fee differential between day and evening classes. Refund policy is on a graduated basis.

IV. FACULTY AND FACULTY RECRUITMENT

About 12% of the faculty teaching evening classes are full-time. Some full-time faculty members teach exclusively in the evening. The Dean delegates authority for hiring full and part-time faculty to the Assistant Dean. Faculty meetings for the evening faculty are held in the Fall and the Spring. Full-time faculty members receive extra compensation for teaching evening classes as an overload. Less than 1% of the budget is spent on recruitment. Salaries for 1971-72 will be changed to quarter credits, that is, 2/3 of the amount now stated plus increments averaging 6 1/2%. Present salary range is B. S. - $249- $306; M. S. - $309- $363; Ph. D. - $366- $429.

V. SCHEDULING

The Dean has the responsibility for the evening class

schedule, but most of the work is done by the Assistant Dean
and the Registrar.   The class schedule has evolved over
many years and is revised only insofar as necessary to make
it possible for degree students to schedule their classes on
the most convenient nights.   Most three-hour classes are
scheduled two nights a week.   In comparing day and evening
classes, the following remarks were made by the Dean of
the College of Continuing Education: "The graduate record
examination is administered to all graduates in Mechanical
and Electrical Engineering.   While there has been no significant difference, evening student grades have been higher
although the range is greater.   In accounting we participate
in the national Accounting tests and equal, or better, the day
student scores.   Part-time evening students are eligible for
the Dean's List by accumulating twelve hours per year with
a 3. 2 average.   Twelve students constitute a class except in
cases where the course is needed for graduation.

VI.   ORGANIZATIONAL STRUCTURE

        Eighteen staff members constitute the administrative
staff: the Dean, Associate Dean (at present an unfilled position), the Directors who are in charge of academic area-de-
velopment and direction of programs, curricula, courses,
hires and supervises faculty, advises and counsels students,
inducts proper relations with business and industry, Assistant Director who assists the Directors, Director of Adult
Education Metropolitan Center who administers physical plant,
solicits business and creates with proper academic administrators programs to use facilities, Director of Extended
Services who is responsible for all non-credit programs,
workshops, etc. , Assistant to the Director of Extended Services who has a specific area of academic responsibility with
urban problems, engineering graphic arts, etc. , Registrar is
joint appointment with the day program, Bursar is joint appointment with day program, and Director of Summer Session
with sole responsibility for all non-fourth quarter courses.
Non-credit programs require more "new" additional administration each year - credit programs being repetitive re-
laxes the need for "new" administration.   The teaching staff
consists of seventeen full-time and 435 part-time faculty
members.

VII.   EDUCATIONAL TELEVISION PROGRAMS

        Courses are offered via educational television - both
credit and non-credit with regular degree course credit.   The

Director of the appropriate academic division supervises the program. Instructor time is considered part of the teaching load or paid as an overload basis if appropriate. Both full and part-time faculty are used. Registration is handled via regular procedure. Courses offered are on an undergraduate level--graduate level courses have been considered but the expense is too great. A budget, the TV Center Budget, is expected to be balanced by income. Programs are scheduled at noon and in the evenings. The costs are so high that it appears educational television should be looked upon as "independent" study and techniques developed as such.

VIII. NON-CREDIT PROGRAMS

Non-credit programs are offered in Business and Management, Arts and Sciences, Education, Engineering and other areas. There is a budget provided for this program but classes are expected to pay for themselves. Faculty receive various remuneration for teaching non-credit courses; normally, $15 per hour for each hour of class session, depending upon instruction and qualifications. The Division does sponsor conferences and institutes. Ordinarily, conferences are sponsored in conjunction with an industrial or governmental organization or institute, departments or colleges. The Division is responsible for the summer session.

IX. GENERAL

The Student President (day) sits on the Policy Committee and the Student President (evening) sits on the Central Committee to voice student opinion on the academic programs. The Institute is just beginning to use closed circuit TV both day and evening. "We have an IBM 1500 computer available to all, but specifically for students of the National Technical Institute for the Deaf." The evening program generally receives adequate stress and financial support. The Dean of the College of Continuing Education is responsible to the Vice-President for Academic Administration.

X. STUDENT RECRUITMENT

Newspaper ads and special announcements are used for publicity purposes, but radio and television are not used. Special announcements are made to business and industry and to like organizations, concerning programs of interest to industry and special groups.

Rockford College
Rockford, Illinois
Evening College

Total Enrollment 1, 498   Private Institution
Evening Enrollment 879   Semester System

I. ADMISSION POLICIES

The deadline for application for admission to evening
classes is the opening of the semester.   Students may register for credit courses before transcripts are submitted.
Special students may take up to sixty semester hours for
credit before matriculation.   Admission requirements for
special students include certification of high school graduation (special form).   Regular students must submit a high
school transcript.   No ACT or CEEB scores are required
for admission.   Students must maintain a "C" average.   Averages are checked at sixteen semester hours and probation
assigned if below 2. 0.   Non-degree or special students
dropped at the end of sixteen hours if the 2. 0 average has
not been maintained.   The evening degree program is the
same as the day program.   The Admissions Committee of
the Day College formulates the admission policies for evening
students upon recommendation of the evening staff.   Day students may enroll for one evening class with no restrictions
on how many day students are in each class.   No orientation
program is held for evening students.

II. TERMINOLOGY

Title of Division: Evening College.   Defined: Adult
program for part-time students.   Definition of Continuing Education: Any formal education taken by persons over twenty-
one - seminars, short courses, regular courses for credit
or for non-credit.

III. FEES

There is a fee differential for day and evening students: day - $40 per credit hour; evening - $25 per credit
hour.   No special services are provided for evening students
who come to the campus for one evening class a week.   Refund policy: A graduated percentage during the first three
weeks of a semester.

IV.   FACULTY AND FACULTY RECRUITMENT

Approximately 30% of the faculty teaching evening classes are full-time.   The departmental chairmen have the final authority for hiring full/part-time faculty members. Some full-time faculty members teach exclusively in the evening.   Faculty meetings are held for evening faculty at the beginning of each semester.   Overloads are permissible for faculty members with permission given by the chairman of the department.   Extra remuneration is given for overloads. Twenty percent of the budget is spent for recruitment.

V.   SCHEDULING

The Dean of the Evening College is responsible for the evening class schedule.   The Dean confers with the departmental chairmen in compiling the evening schedule. Three-hour classes are scheduled one night per week.   According to the Dean, the evening classes are excellent and are sometimes superior to day classes.   No Dean's List is used at the College.   The salary range for part-time faculty is $600 to $800 for a three-hour class.   The same salary scale applies to overloads.   Twelve students are required to constitute a class.

VI.   ORGANIZATIONAL STRUCTURE

There are five and one-half staff members in the evening college.   There are twenty full-time and thirty part-time faculty members.   The Dean has full responsibility for administration of the programs with the use of the regular college committees and faculty chairmen.

VII.   EDUCATIONAL TELEVISION PROGRAMS

No information available.

VIII.   NON-CREDIT PROGRAMS

Non-credit programs are offered in the areas of Business and Management and Arts and Sciences.   There is a budget for non-credit programs although they are expected to pay for themselves.   The remuneration for faculty teaching non-credit courses is $35 per class session.   The Evening College is responsible for the summer session.

IX. GENERAL

Once a year, forty students are selected at random
from those anticipating graduation in the next twelve to eighteen months to discuss the academic program at the college.
More adequate stress and financial support could be given
the Evening College, although the administration recognizes
the need and the importance of the adult educational program. The Dean of the Evening College is responsible to
the President.

X. STUDENT RECRUITMENT

The College places several special advertisements
and announcements in the newspaper for publicity purposes
and spot announcements are prepared for radio. Very little
use is made of television. Special posters are distributed
to business and industry.

<u>Rockhurst College</u>
Kansas City, Missouri
Rockhurst College Evening Division

Total Enrollment 2, 476   Private Church-related
Evening Enrollment 1, 331   Institution
                                             Semester System

I. ADMISSION POLICIES

The deadline for application for admission for evening
students, for all categories of students, is September 25,
1970 and February 12, 1971. Students may register for
credit courses before transcripts are submitted and may take
a varied number of hours for credit. Special students do not
need to submit transcripts; regular students must submit
transcripts from all previous colleges and high schools. If
a student is rejected as a regular student, he is not advised
nor accepted automatically to enter the evening division.
Mail registration is not employed. Policies regarding probation and suspension are: below 1. 75 for probation and
below 1. 5 for dismissal; there is no probation policy for
non-degree students. No ACT or CEEB tests are required
for evening students. A degree program, Associate Degree
(80 hours) is offered to adults in the evening division. There
are 1331 full-time students and all are undergraduates. No

language and no science is required. To complete the evening degree program one must complete eighty hours for the A. B. A. and 128 for the B. S. B. A. No plans are being made to offer a special degree program. The Director formulates the admission policies for evening students - all categories. Students may enroll in both day and evening classes, but the students (day-time) are not counted in the evening enrollment. The advantage of this is that it helps both day and evening students to get along better with each other. No orientation program is conducted. The Evening Division Advisory Committee advises and helps the Director of the Evening Division.

II.   TERMINOLOGY

Title of Division: Rockhurst College Evening Division. Defined: A special division run in the evening. According to the Director there is no "Continuing Education"--"all courses are credit courses. "

III.   FEES

The fee for evening classes is lower in order to compete with several evening community colleges. Refunds are made in these amounts: first two weeks, 100%; up to the quarter, 50%; after the quarter, no refund.

IV.   FACULTY AND FACULTY RECRUITMENT

There is no policy regarding the percentage of full-time faculty for the evening classes; approximately 20% are full-time. The Director has the authority to hire full and/or part-time faculty members for evening classes. There are no full-time faculty members who teach exclusively in the evening. The Director can reject faculty members who have been assigned to teach evening classes. No regular faculty meetings are held. Regular faculty members who teach in institutes, seminars, etc. are paid an overload amount. Salary range for part-time faculty is $17, $22 to $35 for one ninety-five minute session--this rate is the same for overloads. If paid by the course, they receive $17 to $34 depending upon number of courses.

V.   SCHEDULING

The Director is responsible for the evening class schedule and compiles it by consulting with the departments before making final decision. This responsibility includes re-

visions to the schedule.   Two-hour classes are scheduled
one night, four-hour classes scheduled two nights.   No research is being attempted at this time.   In quality, evening
classes are rated lower than the day classes.   Part-time
students are not eligible for the Dean's List each semester,
but are eligible at graduation with a grade point average of
3. 0.   Ten students constitute a class.

VI.   ORGANIZATIONAL STRUCTURE

This Division is composed of three staff members
and a teaching staff of nineteen full-time and fifty-nine part-
time faculty members.   The Director controls the evening
division, the Registrar handles the registration and one secretary handles the secretarial and clerical duties.   Three
staff members are required for an enrollment of 1000 students.

VII.   EDUCATIONAL TELEVISION PROGRAMS

No educational television programs are offered by the
Evening Division.

VIII.   NON-CREDIT PROGRAMS

No non-credit programs are offered by the Evening
Division and no conferences are sponsored.

IX.   GENERAL

No off-campus locations are used for classes.   No
graduate programs for part-time students are offered by the
Evening Division.   The Director is responsible to the Academic Dean and the President.   The Evening Division receives equal support as compared to the Day Division.   A
number of audio-visual aids are employed.

X.   STUDENT RECRUITMENT

Newspaper and radio are used for student recruitment.
Contacts are made through industry, organizations, etc.

Rollins College
Winter Park, Florida
School of Continuing Education

Total Enrollment 5, 000   Private Institution
Evening Enrollment 1, 000   Semester System

I. ADMISSION POLICIES

The deadline for applications for admission is September 15 and January 22 -- June 11 for summer.   A student may register - provisionally - before transcripts are
submitted.   Students may take work for credit as non-matriculating or "special" students on a case-by-case basis.
There are no admission requirements for non-matriculating
or "special" students except they must have reason and purpose; regular students must be high school graduates or the
equivalent.   Students rejected as regular students are not
advised to apply for evening classes.   Mail registration is
used for students who have registered for previous semesters.   Probation occurs if the grade average falls below
"C"--failure to raise the "C" in the next twelve hours results in suspension.   No ACT or CEEB examinations are required.   A Bachelor of General Studies is offered for adults
in the evening with an enrollment of 130 full-time and 770
part-time students.   Distribution requirements are: English
6, Humanities 12, Social Science 12, Math 12, (and/or Science) 30 major, 48 electives, with a total of 120 semester
hours to complete.   Areas of concentration are Humanities,
Social Science, Math and/or Science, Prep for Teaching,
Business, Criminal Justice (30 semester hours).   A B. A.
and a B. S. are being considered as special degree programs
for adults.   The College Senate formulates the admission
policies for regular students and the Director of Evening
Programs formulates admission policies for non-matriculating,
non-degree or special students.   Day students may enroll in
evening classes with the permission of the advisor.   Day /
evening combination classes have flexibility and resolve many
class schedule problems but the day classes are not on a
semester basis and some courses are not equivalent.   An
Evening Division Advisory Committee advises and makes policy.

II. TERMINOLOGY

Title of Division: Central Florida School of Continuing Studies.   Defined: College program primarily for adults

who wish to continue their education.   Continuing Education
defined: Education primarily for persons who wish to continue study usually after a period of interruption.

III.   FEES

Evening students pay $25 per semester hour and day
students pay $2400 per year.   Refunds are made at the rate
of 100% up to the final registration date, 75% through second
week and 50% through fifth week.

IV.   FACULTY AND FACULTY RECRUITMENT

College regular faculty have priority to teach evening
classes wherever possible.   Presently, about 30% of the evening staff are full-time faculty members.   The Director of
Continuing Studies has the final authority for hiring faculty
members to teach evening classes.   No full-time faculty,
however, is employed to teach exclusively in the evening.
Regular faculty meetings are held at the beginning of each
term.   Overloads are paid extra at the rate of $1000 per
course.   Salary range is from $700 to $750 per course.

V.   SCHEDULING

The Director is responsible for the evening class
schedule.   Student surveys, past schedules, past student response, course sequencing, instructor availability, facilities
available are all taken into consideration when preparing the
class schedule.   The Director can make revisions, additions,
and/or deletions as deemed necessary.   Three hour classes
are scheduled one night per week.   Day and evening classes
are comparable.   Part-time students are eligible for the
Dean's List at the time of graduation with a grade point average of B+.   Fifteen students constitute a class but exceptions are made.   Regular faculty receive tuition collected
when teaching classes of less than fifteen students; part-time
faculty receive compensation reduced at one-half each student's tuition under fifteen.

VI.   ORGANIZATIONAL STRUCTURE

Six staff members constitute the administrative staff:
the Director supervises the program, directs administrative
staff, formulates, contacts, advises and counsels students,
prepares budget, serves on college committees; five administrative assistants advise, counsel, register students, collect

fees, compile statistics, keep records, evaluate transcripts, check degree programs, etc.

VII. EDUCATIONAL TELEVISION PROGRAMS

No educational television programs are offered.

VIII. NON-CREDIT PROGRAMS

No non-credit programs are offered. A student may audit a class for non-credit. No conferences or institutes are offered by the Division. The first conference is scheduled for April 1971 and will be the Florida Association of Criminal Justice Educators. The Division is responsible for the summer session.

IX. GENERAL

Students are member representatives on the College Senate. Lectures are taped for use by absentees. Adequate support is received from the administration. The Director is responsible to the Dean of the College. Audio-visual aids are available for evening classes.

X. STUDENT RECRUITMENT

Marquee advertising is used along with spot radio announcements and newspaper publicity. Motivational appeals are developed for industry.

Roosevelt University
Chicago, Illinois
College of Continuing Education

Total Enrollment 7, 000   Private Institution
Evening Enrollment 3, 000   Semester System

I. ADMISSION POLICIES

Deadlines for application for admission to evening classes: October 1 (fall), February 10 (spring) and June 23 (summer). A student may register for credit courses before transcripts are submitted on a tentative basis. "Special" students may take a maximum of thirty semester hours for credit. Admission requirements for "special" students in-

clude a 2. 0 average for transfer students, upper-half of
class ACT, SAT or entrance examination and high school
diploma. Regular students must have a high school diploma
and ACT, SAT or Roosevelt University Entrance Examination. Evening students are not required to take the ACT or
CEEB but do take the Roosevelt University Entrance Examinations. No mail registration is used. A special degree
program for adults is available - Bachelor of General Studies
with an enrollment of 500 students. The same admission requirements apply, with different requirements for each area
of concentration. The Director of Admissions and Administrative Council formulate the admission policies for evening
students. The Bachelor of General Studies degree program
is divided into four sections: The Pro-seminar, the required
classes in the area of concentration, the BGS Seminars in
the Humanities, the Social Sciences and the Natural Sciences,
and the supervised internship in community service. Day and
evening students may enroll in the same classes. No orientation program is held for evening students.

II. TERMINOLOGY

Title of Division: College of Continuing Education.
Defined: The College has charge of extension programs and
the adult degree program together with the non-credit vocational programs in the evening.

III. FEES

There is no fee differential for day and evening students. Refund policies: 80% - 1st week; 60% - 2nd week;
40% - 3rd week; 20% - 4th week. Beyond the 4th week -
no refund.

IV. FACULTY AND FACULTY RECRUITMENT

The Dean of Arts and Sciences has the final authority
for hiring full and part-time faculty. No full-time faculty
teach exclusively in the evenings. Faculty meetings are held
for evening faculty periodically. No overloads are permitted.
There is no budget for recruitment. Salary for part-time
faculty is $600 per class.

V. SCHEDULING

The Dean of Arts and Sciences and department heads
are responsible for the evening class schedule. Three-hour

classes are scheduled either one or two nights a week depending upon the subject.   Part-time evening students are eligible for the Dean's List after completing fifteen hours. Fifteen students constitute a class.

VI.   ORGANIZATIONAL STRUCTURE

The administrative staff consists of: the Dean who administers the College together with an Associate and an Assistant Dean, a Director of the Reading Institute, a Director of the Upward Bound Project together with an Administrative Secretary and two additional secretaries.

VII.   EDUCATIONAL TELEVISION PROGRAMS

No educational television programs are offered.

VIII.   NON-CREDIT PROGRAMS

Non-credit programs are offered in Business and Management.   A budget is provided for such programs.   The remuneration for faculty teaching non-credit courses is $600 per course for sixteen class sessions and is dependent upon the area of instruction.   The College of Continuing Education is not currently responsible for conferences, institutes or summer sessions.

IX.   GENERAL

Faculty - student evaluation forms are used.   BGS students have representatives on the Advisory Council to the college.   The Dean of the College of Continuing Education is responsible to the Dean of Faculty.

X.   STUDENT RECRUITMENT

Newspaper articles and advertisements are used for publicity purposes.   Contacts are made with business and industry and with civic organizations.

Russell Sage College
Albany, New York
Russell Sage College Evening Division

Total Enrollment 4, 000   Private Institution
Evening Enrollment 2, 000   Semester System

I. ADMISSION POLICIES

There is no deadline for application for admission for
regular or non-degree students.   Students may take credit
courses before transcripts are submitted.   "Special" students
may take twelve hours of work for credit.   There are no admission requirements for special students; regular students
must submit a high school diploma or the equivalent.   Students who are rejected as regular students are not advised
to apply as evening students.   Mail registration is not ordinarily used but students who live great distances from the
college may register by mail.   Policies regarding probation
and suspension are: less than "C", one semester probation;
next strict probation followed by dismissal; this is true for
all categories of students.   The ACT or CEEB are not required but are suggested as a basis for placement and advisement.   There are no different programs offered to evening
degree students.   Enrollment is: 1500 undergraduates, 400
graduates.   The special degree program for graduate students is administered by the Evening Division of the College.
The total number of hours required to complete an undergraduate degree is 120; graduate requires 30 hours.   Areas
of concentration are listed in the catalog.   The Dean formulates the admission policies for evening students and non-
matriculating students; the Dean for the graduate students.
Day and evening students may enroll in the same class with
appropriate permission.   The advantages of a combined class
are life styles, attitudes, age, and experience mix.   There
is no orientation program and no evening division advisory
committee.

II. TERMINOLOGY

Title of Division: Russell Sage College Evening Division.   Defined: most of the classes meet after 5 p. m.
Continuing Education defined: A varied program to meet various people's needs.

III. FEES

The evening fee is a charge per credit; the day charge is a total charge.

IV.   FACULTY AND FACULTY RECRUITMENT

There is no policy regarding the percentage of faculty for evening classes that are full-time; no full-time faculty is employed to teach exclusively in the evenings.   The Dean has the final authority for hiring full and/or part-time faculty members.   Faculty members are responsible to the Dean.   No regular faculty meetings are held.   The salary range for part-time faculty is $300 to $350 per credit hour and the same for overloads.

V.   SCHEDULING

The Dean is responsible for the evening class schedule which is compiled by reviewing past programs, submitted required courses and complying with student requests.   The Dean has the authority to revise the schedule.   Three-hour classes are scheduled for one and two nights per week.   The two night schedule is preferred.   In terms of quality, day and evening classes are the same--same standards are used and many of the same faculty are used.   Part-time evening students taking six hours and maintaining a 3.0 grade point are eligible for the Dean's List.   Seven or eight students constitute a class.   An instructor's compensation is reduced when teaching a class below the seven or eight minimum. (adjustment made on payment of fees).

VI.   ORGANIZATIONAL STRUCTURE

The administrative staff consists of six staff members: the Dean has the overall administration of the Evening Division, program planning, teacher selection and staff supervision; the Associate Dean is the Director of the Summer Session, catalog preparation, advisement and general administration; clerical assistance.   The teaching staff consists of 135 part-time instructors.   For an enrollment of 200, a staff of eight is required.

VII.   EDUCATIONAL TELEVISION PROGRAMS

No educational television programs are offered at the institution.

VIII. NON-CREDIT PROGRAMS

Non-credit courses are offered in real estate. The program is expected to pay for itself as there is no budget. Faculty remuneration is $300 to $350 per credit hour depending upon the qualifications of the instructor and the area of instruction. The Division does not sponsor conferences and institutes. The Evening Division is responsible for the summer session.

IX. GENERAL

No courses are offered at off-campus locations for the economically deprived populations. The Dean meets with the Student Senate to discuss academic programs. An MS in Nursing and an MS in Education (elementary) are offered as graduate programs for part-time students. The evening program does not get the support and recognition that it deserves. The Dean is responsible to the Academic Vice-President. Audio-visual aids are available for evening classes. There is no active chapter of Alpha Sigma Lambda.

X. STUDENT RECRUITMENT

Student recruitment is accomplished through newspaper publicity.

<u>Sacred Heart University</u>
Bridgeport, Connecticut
Division of Continuing Education

Total Enrollment 1, 800   Private Institution
Evening Enrollment 306   Semester System

I. ADMISSION POLICIES

There is no deadline for application for admission for evening classes and students may register for credit courses before transcripts are submitted. No limit has been set on the number of credit hours a non-matriculating student may take. Admission requirements for non-matriculating students are a high school diploma or the equivalent; for regular students, a high school diploma or equivalent and college board scores in acceptable range. Students who are rejected as regular students are not advised to apply for evening classes

and are not automatically accepted into evening classes.
Students may register by mail by completing the forms, and
after review by the University, completing class admittance
cards and mailing in the proper fee. Policies regarding probation and suspension are: 1. 5, freshmen; 1. 6, sophomore;
1. 8, junior; 2. 0, senior, for degree students, but there is
no specific formula, except an overall review of performance,
for non-degree students. The ACT is required for degree
students; no other kind of tests are required and the one
score is not used as a basis for admission. A degree program differing from the day degrees is offered for adults--
Associate in Arts. Part-time students enrolled total 307 undergraduates. The distribution requirements (language, science, etc.) for undergraduate degrees is sixty-four hours.
The special degree for graduate students in the evening division is administered by the Division requiring 128 hours for
completion. Areas of concentration: Associate - business
64, accounting 64, liberal studies 64; Bachelor - business,
history, psychology, sociology, English (all with 64 credit
requirements). The admission requirements are the same
as for other degrees. The Director of Admissions formulates the admission policies for the regular and the special
adult degree students. There is no limit to the extent students may enroll in day and evening classes. The advantages
of combined classes is the help it offers to improve the diversity of the class. No orientation program is employed.
The Evening Division Advisory Committee gives feedback and
ideas as to changes needed.

II. TERMINOLOGY

Title of Division: Continuing Education. Defined:
Adult education or part-time education. Definition of Continuing Education: Offerings in vocational and liberal arts;
credit and non-credit, degree and special.

III. FEES

The difference of $35 for one credit hour in the eve-
ning and $40 for the same in the day is justified by the level
of services provided. Refund policies are scaled withdrawals,
i. e. , 100%, 80%, etc.

IV. FACULTY AND FACULTY RECRUITMENT

There is no policy regarding the percentage of faculty
for evening classes that are full-time faculty members. The

Dean of the Faculty has authority for hiring faculty members
for this Division. The Director does not have the authority
to reject or employ faculty members. No regular faculty
meetings are held with evening faculty. Faculty members
are not paid more than 25% for overloads. Thirty-three percent of the budget is spent for recruitment. The salary
range for part-time faculty is $540-$600 for a three-hour
credit course; same for overloads.

V.   SCHEDULING

The Director is responsible for the evening class
schedule which is compiled by working in conjunction with
the day school schedule, except for special courses. The
Director has the authority to revise the schedule. Three-
hour classes are scheduled for one and two nights per week,
but one night is preferred. No research is in progress.
The quality of the evening classes is somewhat lower than
the day program. Part-time evening students are not eligible
for the Dean's List which requires twelve hours. Six students constitute a class. An instructor's compensation is
reduced below the breakeven point when he teaches a class
below the minimum size.

VI.   ORGANIZATIONAL STRUCTURE

The administration staff consists of two staff members
and 46 part-time instructors. The Director is in charge of
the Division which includes development and recruiting. The
Assistant Director is on hand during the evening sessions.
For an enrollment of 300 for credit programs one staff member is necessary.

VII.   EDUCATIONAL TELEVISION PROGRAMS

The Division of Continuing Education offers no educational television programs.

VIII.   NON-CREDIT PROGRAMS

The Division offers non-credit courses in Business
and Management and Theology. There is no budget for these
programs and it is expected to pay for itself. Faculty members receive $600 per course. Salary does not depend upon
qualifications of instructor or upon area of remuneration.
Conferences in Theology are sponsored by the Division using
qualified faculty members of the institution.

IX.   GENERAL

No off-campus courses are offered.   The Student Advisory Committee participates in discussions regarding the academic program.   The Evening Division does not receive equal support even though the administration does recognize the need and importance of adult education.   The Director is responsible to the Dean of the College.   Audio-visual aids are available for evening students.   Summer sessions are not the responsibility of the Division.

X.   STUDENT RECRUITMENT

Recruitment of students is accomplished through newspapers and radio.   The activity of recruitment in industry is being developed.

San Diego Evening College
San Diego, California
Evening College

Total Enrollment 22, 000   Public Community College
Evening Enrollment 12, 000   Semester System

L   ADMISSION POLICIES

The deadline date for application for admission to evening classes for all students is Sept. 4, Jan. 27, and June 9. A student may register for credit courses before transcripts are submitted.   The number of hours that may be taken for credit as non-matriculating or "special" students depends on the goals.   Admission requirements for non-matriculating or "special" students is 18 years of age or over and profit from instruction; for regular students, high school graduation.   Students who are rejected for admission as regular students are not advised to apply as evening students.   Only TV courses may be registered by mail.   Policy regarding probation and dismissal for degree students is less than a C=probation, down 10 grade points=disqualification.   It is the same for non-degree or "special" students.   The ACT or CEEB examination is required for all matriculating students.   Other tests are required depending upon the major.   They are used as a basis for admission in certain areas or for placement and advisement.   The evening degree program for adults is the same as the day degree program with expanded majors.

Degrees are A. A. and A. S.   There are 85 full-time students,
12, 000 part-time, 12, 085 undergraduate.   Requirements are
English (3-6 units), Amer. Insts. (3-6 units), Psychology
(3 units), Health Education (2 units), Natural Sciences (6-9
units), Math (3 units), Fine Arts & Humanities (2-3 units),
P. E. each semester (1/2-1), Major (16-20 units). Admissions
and Guidance Committee formulates the admission policies
for the evening students and for regular degree, non-matriculating, non-degree or "special", and special adult degree
students.   Day and evening students may enroll in the same
class according to need.   Combined classes with day and
evening students assists students with split work schedules,
meets needs of housewives and others who wish a degree or
certificate of proficiency.   There is an orientation program
for evening students preceding the Fall Semester.   There is
a President's Advisory Committee which advises on policy.

II.   TERMINOLOGY

Title of Division: Evening College (Adult Education
Division provides training for high school diplomas, short-
term vocational courses and special basic education for the
disadvantaged Americanization.) Defined: District-wide responsibility for all on and off-campus degree and certificate
classes after 4:00 p. m.   Meets varied and unique needs of
the metropolitan S. D. C. C. D.   Continuing Education defined:
Provides educational opportunities consistent with community
needs: 1. Preparation for advanced degrees, 2. Training
and retraining in a variety of business and technical areas
in which obsolescence can be predicted within a period of
two to five years.

III.   FEES

No tuition for day and evening classes.

IV.   FACULTY AND FACULTY RECRUITMENT

There is no policy regarding the percentage of faculty
for evening classes that are full-time faculty members.   1/16
are full-time.   The President has the final authority for hiring full and/or part-time members for evening classes.   The
Director of the Evening Division can reject a faculty member
who has been assigned to teach evening classes.   Some full-
time faculty members teach exclusively in the evening.   They
are responsible to the Director of the Evening Division.
The Evening Director can engage an instructor without the

consent of the department head if this person refuses to staff these classes. A regular faculty meeting with the evening faculty is held once each semester. Policy regarding regular faculty members teaching credit or non-credit courses or participating in institutes, seminars and conferences as an overload as funds are available for seminars or conferences @ $15 per full-time faculty member. 1/20 of budget is spent for recruitment. Salary range for part-time faculty is: Step 1-$156, Step 2-$162, Step 3-$169, Step 4-$176. No overloads are allowed for faculty. Faculty members are paid by the course, the same as part-time faculty.

V. SCHEDULING

Deans and coordinators are responsible for the evening class schedule. The Dean or Director has the authority to revise the schedule as needed. Three-hour classes are scheduled one night per week; two nights are preferred but there are insufficient classrooms. There are research projects in progress which will be available in March. Day and evening classes are equal in terms of quality. Part-time evening students are eligible for the Dean's List after completing six units with a 3.6 grade point average. In order to have a class taught there must be a 28-1 ratio. The instructor's compensation is not reduced when he teaches a class below minimum size.

VI. ORGANIZATIONAL STRUCTURE

No information received.

VII. EDUCATIONAL TELEVISION PROGRAMS

Courses in educational television are offered for credit and non-credit. Students earn residence credit. These credits count toward a degree. The TV coordinator supervises educational television courses. The program is handled (registration) through the Admissions Office. Faculty members receive additional remuneration for teaching courses on TV. Both full-time and part-time faculty members are used. Undergraduate courses in educational TV are offered, and financed by TV station plus some district monies. Out-of-state tuition charge is the same as that for on-campus residents. Courses are scheduled 6 to 7 a.m.

VIII.   NON-CREDIT PROGRAMS

Non-credit courses are offered in the areas of Business and Management and technical areas.   No special budget is set up for the program.   Courses, however, are not necessarily expected to pay for themselves.   Salary for non-credit courses is $9.68 per hour.   Remuneration depends upon the qualifications of the instructor.   College sponsors conferences and institutes including such programs as Seminar in Electronics and Criminal Justice.   A conference may be of 3 or 4 week duration.   Conferences are frequently locally sponsored or given by California State Agencies.

IX.   GENERAL

The institution offers credit and non-credit courses in "store front" locations for economically deprived populations.   Students have an opportunity to participate in discussions regarding the academic program through membership in the Academic Senate.   Multi-media practices are used at the College.   No graduate programs are offered for part-time students which are administered by the Evening Division. The Evening Division is not receiving adequate support in comparison with the day program.   The Director or Dean of the Evening Division is responsible to the Associate Superintendent.   All instructional aids are obtained through the Library.

X.   STUDENT RECRUITMENT

Publicity for student recruitment is through the newspaper.

<u>Seminole Jr. College</u>
Sanford, Florida
Division of Evening Studies

Total Enrollment 2, 200   Public Institution
Evening Enrollment 664   Quarter System

I.   ADMISSION POLICIES

The deadline for application for admission to the evening classes is the first night of the class.   Students may register before transcripts are submitted.   Non-matriculating

and/or "special" students may not take work for credit.
Regular students must have a high school education but there
are no requirements for non-matriculating or "special" students. Students rejected as regular students are not advised
to apply as evening students. No mail registration is used.
Degree students with a GPA of 1.5 are placed on probation
and suspended the next term if GPA is not 1.7. No ACT or
CEEB examinations are required. No evening degree program for adults is offered. Evening student enrollment was
71 full-time and 593 part-time during the Fall quarter. Undergraduate distribution requirements are: Communication,
5 hours, Social Science, 8 hours; Science, 9 hours; Mathematics, 3 hours; Humanities, 7 hours; Physical Education,
4 hours. The admission policies are formulated by the faculty and trustees. Combined classes provide a better program. No orientation program is conducted for evening students. An open-door policy allows any high school graduate
to attend.

II. TERMINOLOGY

Title of Division: Division of Evening Studies. Continuing Education defined: both credit and non-credit courses
given to persons who have completed their formal education.

III. FEES

There is no fee differential for day and evening classes. No refunds are allowed except for students withdrawing
within the first ten days.

IV. FACULTY AND FACULTY RECRUITMENT

Approximately 46% of the faculty are full-time faculty
members but none teach exclusively in the evening. One
course may be carried as an overload. The salary range
for part-time faculty is $8.50 to $12.50 per hour of class;
overloads range the same. Final authority for hiring full
and/or part-time faculty members for evening classes lies
with the trustees. The Director cannot reject an evening
faculty member or cannot employ a full-time faculty member
for evening classes. Regular faculty meetings are held for
evening faculty at the beginning of each term. No budget is
set aside for faculty recruiting.

V.   SCHEDULING

The Director is responsible for the evening class
schedule which is coordinated by the coordinator and department chairman prior to the Dean of Instruction's approval.
The Director does not have the authority to revise class
schedules.   All three-hour classes are scheduled one night
per week.   Day and evening classes are equal in quality.
Part-time students are eligible for the Dean's List if they
carry six hours of 3. 0 or better GPA.   Minimum size of
the class depends upon the individual class but is usually dependent upon ten students.   The instructor's compensation is
not reduced if he teaches a class with less than ten students.

VI.   ORGANIZATIONAL STRUCTURE

Administrative staff consists of two staff members:
the Director and one other.   The teaching staff consists of
29 full-time and 34 part-time faculty members.   The ideal
administrative staff size would be eight for every 5000 students.

VII.   EDUCATIONAL TELEVISION PROGRAMS

No educational television programs are offered.

VIII.   NON-CREDIT PROGRAMS

Non-credit programs are offered through the Division
of Extended Services and include courses in Arts and Sciences, Business and Management as well as vocational and
occupational courses.   A budget is provided for these courses.
Remuneration for full or part-time faculty teaching non-credit courses is $7. 50 per contact hour.   The Division of Ex-
tended Services also sponsor conferences and institutes such
as: Drug Seminar, Counseling Seminar, Quality Control
Seminar.   Clinicians' salaries range from $25 to $100 per
day.   Summer sessions are the responsibility of the Division
of Extended Services.

IX.   GENERAL

The Evening Studies Division does receive adequate
support and the administration recognizes the need and the
importance of adult education programs.   Video-tape, movies,
overhead projectors, slide projectors, tape recorders, etc. ,
are available for use by the Division.   The Director of the

Division of Evening Studies is responsible to the Dean of Instruction.

X. STUDENT RECRUITMENT

Newspaper, radio and television publicity is used for student recruitment. Special motivational appeals are made to industry and to local organizations.

Sir George Williams University
Montreal, Canada
Evening Division

Total Enrollment 18, 000   Private Institution
Evening Enrollment 12, 000   Year System

I. ADMISSION POLICIES

Deadline for application for admission to evening classes is about two months prior to registration. Students may not register for credit courses without submitting transcripts. Admission requirements are the same as for day students unless a person wants to enter under "mature matriculation" status. Students enrolled in evening classes must maintain the same academic standards as all day students. There is no special degree for adults. Admission policies for all students are set by the University Council. Day students are allowed to enroll in evening classes after evening students have registered and vice-versa. There is no orientation program for evening students. Students failing two-fifths are placed on probation.

II. TERMINOLOGY

Title of Division: Evening Division. Defined: Includes all classes scheduled after 6 p. m. and Saturday mornings. All education is, or ought to be, life-long continuing education, i. e. , related to what has gone in the past and oriented toward the possibilities of the future.

III. FEES

There is no fee differential between day and evening classes. Refunds are made at the rate of 25% if drops are within the first two weeks of class and no refunds thereafter.

IV.   FACULTY AND FACULTY RECRUITMENT

Final authority to hire faculty lies with the Board of Governors with recommendations from the Vice Principal Academic and the Dean along with department chairmen and faculty concerned.   Salaries range from $1000 for two-hour courses to $1650 for four-hour courses.   There is no over-load pay.

V.   SCHEDULING

The Registrar is responsible for the class schedules in consultation with the academic deans.   Three credit hour courses are scheduled one night a week.   There is no sig-nificant difference in grade distribution between day and eve-ning classes.   Part-time evening students are eligible for the Dean's List after completing thirty semester hours with a 3. 0 grade point average.   Ten students constitute a class.

VI.   ORGANIZATIONAL STRUCTURE

"Although the University has a day, evening and a graduate division, it is more correct to say that we run a University operation from 8:30 a. m. to 11:00 p. m.   Our full-time faculty are scheduled to teach day, evening and gradu-ate work.   Our part-time faculty likewise.   It would be more correct to say we have a university with full and part-time students rather than a day/evening program. "

VII.   EDUCATIONAL TELEVISION PROGRAMS

The Evening Division does not offer any TV courses.

VIII.   NON-CREDIT PROGRAMS

The Evening Division does not offer any non-credit programs.

IX.   GENERAL

Students participate in discussion regarding academic program by holding membership on all important councils and boards, including the University Council and Academic Plan-ning Committee.   The evening division is receiving adequate support.   Complete audio-visual instructional aids are avail-able for use in evening classes.

X. STUDENT RECRUITMENT

Newspapers are used for publicity.

<u>University of South Carolina</u>
Columbia, South Carolina
Evening Division: College of General Studies

Total Enrollment 14, 000   Public Institution
Evening Enrollment 1, 200   Semester System

I. ADMISSION POLICIES

Deadline for application for admission to evening classes is the first scheduled day of classes. A student is not allowed to register before his transcripts have been submitted. Fifteen hours of credit work can be taken as non-matriculating or "special" student if a satisfactory SAT score is achieved and special application submitted. Regular students must meet all admission requirements of the University. Rejected students are not accepted as evening students on an automatic basis. Degree students are placed on academic probation if the GPA is below 2. 00 at the end of any semester or summer session. The ACT or CEEB examination is required for adults in the evening division and is used as a basis for admission. Fall enrollment included 750 full-time and 450 part-time students (850 undergraduate and 350 graduate). A special degree program for adults is under consideration, both undergraduate and graduate. The faculty is responsible for formulating the admission policies for evening students. Evening students may enroll in day classes depending upon class size and availability. The advantage of a combined day/evening class is that working students are able to carry a full academic load. An orientation is conducted at registration for evening students. An admission advisory committee is being considered.

II. TERMINOLOGY

Title of Division: Evening Division: College of General Studies. Defined: Created to meet the cultural and professional needs of men and women who are employed during the day. Definition of Continuing Education: Formal or informal, credit or non-credit offerings designed to meet the educational needs of individuals over their entire life span.

III.   FEES

There is no fee differential for day and evening classes.
The refund policy is a declining rate over a five-week period.

IV.   FACULTY AND FACULTY RECRUITMENT

Approximately 90% of the evening faculty are full-
time faculty members.   The Dean of the College of General
Studies has the final authority for hiring full and/or part-
time faculty for evening classes.   The Director can reject
a faculty member who has been assigned to teach evening
classes.   There are full-time faculty employed who teach
exclusively in the evening and who are responsible to the
Director of the Evening Division.   The Director can engage
an instructor without the permission of the department head
if necessary.   Regular faculty meetings are conducted once
each semester and as needed throughout the year.   Faculty
members are paid for any overload.   Part-time faculty salaries range from $600 to $1000.

V.   SCHEDULING

The Dean is responsible for the evening class schedule and has the authority to make revisions as necessary.
Demand and faculty availability dictate course offerings.
Three-hour classes meeting two nights per week are generally highly motivated.   Part-time students attending evening classes are eligible for the Dean's List; they must carry
12 hours with a GPA of 3. 50.   Ordinarily fifteen students
are required to constitute a class.   The instructor's compensation is not reduced when he teaches a class below minimum size.

VI.   ORGANIZATIONAL STRUCTURE

The Evening Division consists of ten staff members
including the Dean who is responsible for the total program,
the Assistant Dean who assists in the total program, the
Director of Non-credit Programs who organizes, plans and
supervises non-credit programs, and the Director of Conferences and Institutes who is responsible for planning, organizing and supervising conferences and institutes.   The teaching staff consists of 85 full-time and 15 part-time faculty
members.   Being a branch of a state university, the institution has academic and administrative autonomy which is
shared in some instances with other colleges.   The ideal

size of administrative staff to administer evening credit programs with an enrollment of 2000 would be 10; with 5000 enrollment - 15 staff members.

VII.   EDUCATIONAL TELEVISION PROGRAMS

Both credit and non-credit courses are offered by
educational television.   Students earn resident credit and the
credit does count toward a degree - either undergraduate or
graduate.   The College or department offering the course and
instructor supervise that course.   Teachers may enroll if
the course is required for State Certification or for general
interest.   Both full and part-time faculty are used.   Faculty
members carry a reduced teaching load for regular on-campus classes when teaching courses on TV.   The teaching
load is reduced by the number of courses taught.   Office of
Registration handles all registration for the Educational Television courses using standard registration procedures.   TV
courses are scheduled in the afternoons, 1:30 to 4:30, and in
the evening, 6:30 to 9:30.   The program is increasing as
funds and needs increase.

VIII.   NON-CREDIT PROGRAMS

Non-credit courses are offered in Business and Management, Arts and Sciences, Engineering, Education and
special interest areas.   These programs are expected to be
self-supporting.   Remuneration for faculty (full or part-time)
is $200 for 16 class sessions, depending upon the qualifica-
tion of the instructor and the area of instruction.   The Division does sponsor workshops, conferences and institutes such
as Advanced Cosmetology Institute, Drug Interactions Seminar, Legal Secretaries Conference, Business and Professional
Women's Conference.   There are no fixed rates of pay for
clinicians for these conferences and institutes.   The Evening
Division is responsible for the evening portion of the summer session.

IX.   GENERAL

Students participate in discussions regarding the academic program through Student-Faculty Committees.   Students must be in good standing in the Graduate School in
order to attend evening graduate programs.   The Evening
Division does receive adequate support in comparison with
the day programs.   The Dean of the Evening Division is responsible to the University Provost.   The College has a com-

plete Audio-Visual Department.

X. STUDENT RECRUITMENT

Newspaper articles, radio and television are used for publicity purposes in student recruiting.

University of South Florida
Tampa, Florida
Center of Continuing Education

Total Enrollment 17, 000+ (overall)   Public Institution
Evening Enrollment - No separate   Quarter System
   evening division

I. ADMISSION POLICIES

The deadline date for all categories of students is: Fall, August 5; Spring, February 17; Winter, November 25; Summer, May 12. A student may not register for credit courses before transcripts are submitted. Non-matriculating students may take forty-five undergraduate hours or twelve graduate hours for credit. Admission requirements for non-matriculating students are a secondary school record indicating overall "C" average (if no previous college work has been taken) and proof of graduation. Students with previous college must submit a statement of good standing or satisfactory transcripts. If the latest college attended was out of the state of Florida, a confidential personal student questionnaire must be completed before admission. Admission requirements for regular students are: official transcripts sent directly from secondary school indicating graduation, favorable character recommendation from secondary school and an overall "C" average in academic subjects and a minimum score of 300 on the Florida Twelfth Grade Test. The University of South Florida offers a special Bachelor of Independent Studies degree program for adults through the College of Liberal Arts which is administered by the Center for Continuing Education. Admission requirements for the degree program are: twenty-five years of age or older, must meet the same general requirements to the University as regular degree applicants, must provide sufficient reasons for being unable to dedicate a block of time as a resident to complete a regular degree program. The Director of Admissions rules on the admission of an applicant to the Uni-

versity.   Authority to accept or reject BIS degree program
rests with the BIS screening committee.   The BIS degree
program does not involve credit hours, specific courses, and
semester or quarters.   There is no one enrollment or admissions date.   Orientation conferences are scheduled from
time-to-time on the basis of need.   The first three areas,
Humanities, Natural Sciences and Social Sciences, come in
no necessary order.   After completing these areas, a student undertakes inter-area studies which is comprised of
integrated study involving cross disciplinary issues or problems.   After successfully completing the area comprehensive
examination, a student is admitted to an appropriate area
seminar.   The comparison seminar (following the period of
independent study) for the first three areas is three weeks
in duration with the fourth area seminar of four weeks.   The
admission requirements and achievement levels in the day
and evening courses are the same.   Any student accepted to
the University may enroll in courses offered in the evening
which are appropriate to his program.   Mail registration is
not used for on-campus classes, but is used for continuing
education off-campus credit courses.   Probation for degree
and non-degree students is below 1.5 for 45 hours attempted;
1.7 between 45 and 89 hours attempted; below 2.0 over 89
hours attempted.   A student who fails to have a 2.0 cumulative grade point ratio after attempting 135 quarter hours
is automatically disqualified.   All freshmen students must
have completed the Florida Twelfth Grade Test; other freshmen students must have a total score of 900 on the Scholastic
Aptitude Test with no less than 450 on the Verbal.   Graduate students, degree seeking, must have scores from GRE
which are satisfactory to the program.   There is no orientation program for evening students.

II.   TERMINOLOGY

Title of Division: Center for Continuing Education.
Defined: Coordination of off-campus credit courses, non-
credit activities, community service and special adult degree
program.   Continuing Education defined: The administrative
unit charged with the responsibility of extending to the community (local, state and national) those relevant and unique
resources possessed by the University.

III.   FEES

There is no fee differential for day and evening
classes.   A full refund will be made for a full-time or part-

time student making a complete withdrawal from the University during the Drop and Add period of any quarter.   De-
ductions from authorized refunds will be made for unpaid accounts due the University.

IV.   FACULTY AND FACULTY RECRUITMENT

The policy regarding the percentage of faculty for
evening classes that are full-time faculty members is an
academic area consideration since Continuing Education does
not staff courses.   Recruitment is the responsibility of the
appropriate academic area.   Policies regarding regular faculty members teaching credit and/or non-credit courses as
overloads: Participation with permission of the Dean to the
extent of 20% of their annual salary.   Compensation for each
activity is established by the Center for Continuing Education.
Compensation for faculty is negotiated within limits established by University policy--paid by the course on a variable
scale.   No overload for credit courses is paid when course
is taught on-campus.

V.   SCHEDULING

Each academic area head is responsible for the evening class schedule.   There is no separate schedule for evening classes.   All classes are submitted by academic areas.
Twenty percent of total classes must be scheduled after 5
p. m.   Three-hour classes are scheduled one night per week.
There is no research in progress.   Funding is being sought
for study of need by adults for special degree programs.
Part-time students are not eligible for the Dean's List.   Number of students required to constitute a class is flexible, depending upon overall productivity by academic unit.

VI.   ORGANIZATIONAL STRUCTURE

There are four professional staff members for the
Center for Continuing Education.   Responsibilities of staff:
Dean - responsible for all supervision of Continuing Educa-
tion; Directors - one for the BIS Adult Degree Program, one
for off-campus; Assistant to the Dean and Coordinator of
Off-Campus credit courses and assigned non-credit programs.

VII.   EDUCATIONAL TELEVISION PROGRAMS

The Center for Continuing Education offers no educational television programs.

VIII   NON-CREDIT PROGRAMS

Non-credit courses are offered in the following areas: Business and Management, Arts and Sciences, Engineering, Education and other areas.   These programs pay for themselves since there is no budget.   Remuneration for faculty teaching a non-credit course is negotiated and depends upon the qualifications of the instructor and upon the area of instruction.   The Center sponsors conferences and institutes such as: Speed Reading Development, Creative Dramatics for Children and an Investment Seminar for Florida Trust Investment Officers.   Conferences are sponsored by the institution and also in cooperation with other colleges.   The Center is not responsible for the summer session.

IX.   GENERAL

No off-campus courses are offered for the economically deprived populations.   Student participation in discussions regarding the academic program is through membership on various university and academic area committees.   No graduate programs are offered for part-time students.   All masters level programs are open to part-time students.   The Center uses standard audio-visual materials.   There is no active chapter of Alpha Sigma Lambda.

X.   STUDENT RECRUITMENT

Usual means are used for student recruitment - newspapers, radio, etc.

South Texas Junior College
Houston, Texas
Evening College

Total Enrollment 4, 378   Private Institution
Evening Enrollment 1, 967   Semester System

I.   ADMISSION POLICIES

There are no deadlines for application for admission. Students may register for credit courses before transcripts are submitted on a provisional basis.   No student can take work for credit as non-matriculating or "special" student. All students must be high school graduates.   Rejected stu-

dents (regular) are not advised to apply as evening students
and are not automatically accepted.   On a 4. 0 system, a
1. 5 is required; failure to maintain a 1. 5 results in probation for one semester followed by suspension.   The ACT or
CEEB examinations are not required for admission.   Other
test results are used for placement and advising only.   Associate in Arts degree is offered.   The fall quarter enrollment for full-time students was 1, 930; part-time 2, 448.   Undergraduate degree requirements are: 12 hours English,
6-8 hours Science, 3 hours Math, 8 hours Language, 17-19
hours electives.   The Dean formulates all admission policies.

II.   TERMINOLOGY

Title of Division: Evening College.   Defined: Day
classes offered as night classes.

III.   FEES

There is no fee differential for day and evening
classes.   There is a sliding percentage of refund for both
day and evening students.

IV.   FACULTY AND FACULTY RECRUITMENT

Seventy-five percent of the faculty are full-time.   The
department chairmen have the final authority for hiring full
and/or part-time faculty.   The Director can reject a faculty
member who has been assigned to teach an evening class or
can engage an instructor without the consent of the department head if necessary.   Regular faculty meetings are not
held for the evening faculty.   Faculty are allowed to teach
a one-course overload for extra pay at the rate of $510 per
course; part-time faculty rate is $480-$510 per course.

V.   SCHEDULING

The Dean is responsible for the evening class schedule which is based upon the previous year's schedule with
additions or deletions in keeping with the enrollment.   All
three-hour classes are scheduled two nights per week.   Students with nine hours or more who have a 3. 5 average are
eligible for the Dean's List.   At least ten students constitute
a class.

VI. ORGANIZATIONAL STRUCTURE

Not applicable since the evening program is a continuation of the day program.

VII. EDUCATIONAL TELEVISION PROGRAMS

There are no educational television programs offered by the Evening College.

VIII. NON-CREDIT PROGRAMS

Non-credit programs are offered in the areas of Business and Management. These are self-supporting programs with no budget allocations. The remuneration for full or part-time faculty teaching non-credit courses is $480 to $510 per course for forty-eight one-hour class sessions or an equivalent thereof, and is based upon the area of instruction.

IX. GENERAL

The administration does recognize the importance and the need for adult education programs. The Dean is responsible to the President.

X. STUDENT RECRUITMENT

Student recruitment is publicized via newspaper, radio and television. Special motivational appeals are made for industry and for organizations.

University of Southern Mississippi
Hattiesburg, Mississippi
Division of Continuing Education

Total Enrollment 8, 000   Public Institution
Evening Enrollment 1, 500   Quarter System

I. ADMISSION POLICIES

The deadline for application for admission for regular students is three weeks prior to registration. There is no deadline for non-degree students. Students may take up to sixteen quarter hours as non-matriculating students. Admission requirements are high school graduation or recom-

mendation from the last college attended. The ACT is required for adults in the evening division and is used as a
basis for admission as well as for advisement. There is no
system for mail registration. Students on probation and under suspension are eligible to admit to non-credit or non-
degree courses. There is no special degree program for
adults. Admission policies are set by the Admissions Office
and the academic deans for regular degree students. The
school or department offering special programs sets the admission requirements for non-matriculating and/or non-degree students. Day and evening students may enroll in the
same classes. Orientation for evening students is combined
with the day students' orientation.

II. TERMINOLOGY

Title of Division: Division of Continuing Education.
Defined: The Administrative unit responsible for all credit
and non-credit programs over and above those administered
by day deans of the University.

III. FEES

Refunds are made to students on a graduating percentage basis.

IV. FACULTY AND FACULTY RECRUITMENT

A ratio of 50-50 is maintained regarding the percentage of faculty (full-time) who teach evening classes. Final authority to hire evening faculty lies with the Board of
Trustees of Institutions of Higher Learning of the State of
Mississippi. The Dean of the Division of Continuing Education can reject a faculty member assigned to teach evening
classes. Some full-time faculty members teach exclusively
in the evening and are responsible to the Dean of the Division.
Regular faculty meetings are held the second week of the
quarter. Faculty members are not allowed to teach on an
overload basis. Less than one percent of the budget for the
division is spent on faculty recruiting.

V. SCHEDULING

The Dean of the Division of Continuing Education is
not responsible for the evening class schedule. The Academic Deans have this responsibility. The Dean of the Division cannot make revisions to the evening class schedule.

Three-hour classes are scheduled one night per week. Day
and evening classes are equal in terms of quality.   Part-
time students are eligible for the Dean's List with a grade
point average of 3. 25 after completing fifteen quarter hours.

VI. ORGANIZATIONAL STRUCTURE

The Division of Continuing Education has an administrative staff of fifteen members and a teaching staff of twenty-one full-time and 150 part-time faculty members.   The
Division is headed by a Dean and includes three directors -
Director of Adult Education, Director of Non-Credit Programs
and Director of Conferences, Institutes and Extension.

VII. EDUCATIONAL TELEVISION PROGRAMS

The Division of Continuing Education does not sponsor
educational television programs.

VIII. NON-CREDIT PROGRAMS

Non-credit programs are offered in Business and Management, Arts and Sciences, Education and Home Economics
through the Division of Continuing Education.   Faculty members are paid at the rate of $15 per contact hour or $246
per course for eight two-hour sessions.   Clinicians are paid
$50 a day or $200 for a week's conference.   Conferences
and workshops are sponsored in cooperation with other colleges and divisions primarily--however, the Division serves
as a sponsoring agent for these activities frequently.   The
Division is not responsible for the summer session.   In 1970,
a total of 9033 individuals attended institutes, conferences
and workshops at the University of Southern Mississippi which
included eleven credit activities, fifty-seven non-credit activities and sixty-four activities either for credit or non-credit.
Typical activities included Children's Book Festival, Aero-
space Education Workshop, School Health Institute, Mississippi
School Counselor Workshop, Land Owners Conference and the
14th Annual Instrumental Conductors Conference.

IX. GENERAL

Students participate very little in discussions regarding academic programs.   In general, all evening divisions
are not receiving enough support.   The Dean of the Division
of Continuing Education is responsible to the Dean of the University.   Audio-visual instructional aids are available for eve-

ning classes.

X. STUDENT RECRUITMENT

Newspaper and radio publicity is used. Sometimes guest speakers are included in programs for the Chamber of Commerce and other civic organizations.

Southwestern Michigan College
Dowagiac, Michigan
Division of Continuing Education

Total Enrollment 1, 200   Public Community College
Evening Enrollment 400   Semester System

I. ADMISSION POLICIES

There is no deadline for application for admission. Students may register for credit courses before transcripts are submitted on a conditional basis.   Non-matriculating and / or special students may take up to eleven hours of work.   A high school diploma or GED equivalent is required for admission of regular students; there is no requirement for non-matriculating or special students.   As a two year community college, Southwestern Michigan College has an open-door policy and students are automatically accepted in the evening program if they are rejected as regular students.   No mail registration is used.   A student who falls below the following levels will be placed on probation: 1. 5 CGPA for 12 to 23 hours; 1. 7 for 24 to 35 hours; 1. 8 CGPA for 36 to 47 hours; 1. 9 for 48 to 61 hours and 2. 0 CGPA at 62 hours.   A student who falls below these standards on two successive levels, will be academically dismissed for the period of one semester not including Summer session.   If a student is dismissed at the end of a Spring semester, he may enroll in the Summer session and bring his CGPA up to standard for readmittance in the Fall.   No ACT or CEEB examinations are required for admission.   An A. A. , A. S. , and A. A. S. are offered - the evening degree program has same content with slightly different emphasis.   Fall enrollments totalled 800 full-time, and 400 part-time students.   Distribution requirements are divided into four groups: Communications and Humanities, 20 hours, Social Sciences, 9 hours, Natural Sciences and /or Mathematics, 8 hours, Physical Education, 2 hours.   Sixty-two hours are required to complete the degree program.   The

Administrative Cabinet formulates the admission policies.
There are no policies regarding day/evening class enrollment. Varying experience is difficult for the instructor but
enriching for the day students. No orientation program is
held.

II. TERMINOLOGY

Title of Division: Division of Continuing Education.
Defined: All activities that encompass learning. Continuing
Education defined: Much broader... to include outreach activities, consultative services to the community, resource
and coordinative services.

III. FEES

There is no fee differential between day and evening
classes. Refund policies are based on 90% to end of the
first week, 80% of the second week, 60% of the third and
fourth week and no refund after the fourth week.

IV. FACULTY AND FACULTY RECRUITMENT

The percentage of full-time faculty teaching evening
classes is 50% but there is no policy regarding the percentage. The Director of Continuing Education has the final
authority for hiring faculty. No full-time faculty is employed
to teach exclusively in the evenings. No regular faculty
meetings are held for evening faculty. Policies regarding
regular faculty members teaching credit or non-credit
courses as overloads state one credit course and one community service certificate course maximum concurrently in
one semester. Five percent of the budget is spent on recruitment. Salaries range $7 to $10 for each contact hour
on community service programs, $175 per credit hour per
semester. There are no overloads in the evening since the
Continuing Education program is separate from that of the
daytime.

V. SCHEDULING

The Director is responsible for the evening class
schedule which is coordinated with department chairmen using
student surveys and historical records. Three-hour classes
are scheduled one night per week. In the rural situation,
one night per week is preferred. Evening classes have a
slight edge over day classes in terms of quality. Students

must have a twelve hour load to qualify for the Dean's List and in most cases part-time students are not eligible. Twelve students constitute a class generally.

VI. ORGANIZATIONAL STRUCTURE

One administrative officer, the Director, administers the program in the Division of Continuing Education with a teaching staff of 26 part-time faculty members. His responsibilities include the following: 1) participates in the formation of academic and administrative policy, 2) plans and directs the Continuing Education program through the consulting with Department Heads and Dean of Arts and Sciences and applied sciences, 3) works with individuals and advisory committees to develop non-credit vocational and special interest continuing education courses, recruits and evaluates continuing education faculty, organizes a speaker's bureau and publishes an appropriate brochure for this service, etc., etc.

VII. EDUCATIONAL TELEVISION PROGRAMS

No educational television programs are offered.

VIII. NON-CREDIT PROGRAMS

Non-credit programs are offered in the areas of Business and Management, Arts and Sciences, Education and other areas. There is a budget set up to cover the programs. Remuneration to faculty is $7 to $10 per contact hour, depending upon qualifications of instructor. The Division does sponsor workshops and conferences such as: Art Education Workshop, Drug Institute, Management Seminars and Para-prof Workshop. There is no set policy regarding salary for clinicians. The Division is responsible for the Summer session.

IX. GENERAL

Off-campus courses for the economically deprived populations are in the planning stage. Students are members of the administrative council and standing committees. The institution is organizing packaged independent study courses. No graduate courses are offered for part-time students. The Division does receive adequate support from the administration. The Director is responsible to the President. Audiovisual aids are available to the evening classes.

X. STUDENT RECRUITMENT

Seventy percent of the publicity for student recruitment is through the newspaper, 10% through radio and 20% through television. Special motivational appeals are made to industry and to civic organizations.

Springfield College
Springfield, Massachusetts
Division of Continuing Education

Total Enrollment 1, 900   Private Institution
Evening Enrollment 400   Semester System

I. ADMISSION POLICIES

The deadline for application for admission to evening classes for freshmen is February 15; for non-degree students there is no deadline. Students may register for credit courses before transcripts are submitted. "Special" or non-degree students may take as many as thirty semester hours' work for credit. The admission requirements for "special" students include a high school diploma; for regular students, a Scholastic Aptitude Test is required, together with an English Composition Achievement Test with no cutoff point plus all regular credentials - transcripts, medical examination and recommendations. Mail registration will go into effect by the summer. Retention policies require: 1.70 for freshmen, 1.85 for sophomores, 1.95 for juniors, 2.0 for seniors. No special retention policy for "special" students. The Director of Continuing Education in conjunction with the Committee on Admissions formulates the admission policies for evening students. The Director of the Division formulates the policies for "special" students. Day and evening students may enroll in the same class if day students have class conflicts or schedule problems. There is no special degree for graduate students (which is administered by the Graduate School). The area of concentration together with the credit requirements is: All majors in Arts and Sciences, and Community Education. The admission requirements for the special degree programs are the same as day program. There is no consideration to offer a special degree program for adults in the near future.

II.   TERMINOLOGY

Title of Division: Division of Continuing Education.
Defined: Continuing Education basically represents the opportunity for adults to earn their undergraduate degree on a
part-time basis and includes non-credit institutes, conferences, workshops and extension courses.

III.   FEES

There is no fee differential for day and evening
classes.   Refund policies provide for a full reimbursement
up to the end of the third week of class.   After the beginning
of the fourth week, there is no reimbursement.

IV.   FACULTY AND FACULTY RECRUITMENT

Approximately 75% of the faculty teaching evening
classes are full-time and have priority for teaching in the
evening.   The Director of the Division of Continuing Education has the final authority for hiring full/part-time faculty
members for evening classes.   No regular faculty meetings
are held for evening faculty.   Full-time faculty can teach
one course each ten-week term as an overload.   Total participation for additional responsibilities including non-credit
institutes should not exceed 120%.   No percentage of the
budget is spent for recruitment.   The salary for part-time
faculty is $607 to $847 depending upon rank.   The same
salary schedule applies to overloads taught by regular faculty.

V.   SCHEDULING

The Director of the Division of Continuing Education
is responsible for the evening class schedule.   Recommendations are made by the Division Heads with the final scheduling made by the Committee on Continuing Education with
the approval of the Director.   Three-hour classes are held
one or two nights per week.   Many four-hour classes are
now scheduled for two evenings.   Day and evening classes
are comparable in terms of quality.   Part-time students are
not eligible for the Dean's List.   The minimum number of
students required to constitute a class is ten.   Salaries are
adjusted for smaller classes - 10% of the base salary and
the number of students registered figure in the adjusted salary.

VI. ORGANIZATIONAL STRUCTURE

The administrative staff consists of five staff members. The teaching staff consists of forty full-time and twenty part-time members. The Director is responsible for the overall administration of the evening division. The Assistant Director is responsible for budgets, counseling, advising and special interest programs.

VII. EDUCATIONAL TELEVISION PROGRAMS

The Division of Continuing Education does not offer educational television programs.

VIII. NON-CREDIT PROGRAMS

The Division offers non-credit courses in Business and Management and other courses. There is no budget for the non-credit program as it is expected to pay for itself. The remuneration to faculty (full or part-time) for teaching a non-credit course varies. The Division sponsored conferences and institutes this past year: Library Institute, Massachusetts Government. Clinicians are paid $100 to $150 per day for conferences. Both qualified faculty members of the institution and visiting lecturers are used for conferences. The Division is not responsible for the summer session.

IX. GENERAL

Students participate on the Student Advisory Board and have representation on the Committee on Continuing Education . . . the decision and policy-making committee for Continuing Education. Open House Workshops are held for library administrators. Some day classes are designed for adults. More stress and financial support are needed for evening programs. The Director of Continuing Education is responsible to the Academic Dean.

X. STUDENT RECRUITMENT

Newspaper advertisements and newsstories are used for publicity purposes together with spot announcements on the radio. Little use is made of television. Non-credit management seminars are held for business and industry.

St. Francis College
Brooklyn, New York
Evening Session

Total Enrollment 2, 353   Church-related Institution
Evening Enrollment 643   Semester System

I.   ADMISSION POLICIES

There is no admission deadline to evening classes.
Students may not register for credit courses before transcripts are submitted.   There is no "special" student category.   Admission requirement for regular students is a high
school diploma with sixteen units.   No ACT or CEEB scores
are required for admission.   Mail registration is used.   Students pre-register with an advisor and mail in their registration.   At the time of registration only course changes are
made--changes must be approved by the advisor.   Retention
policy: a student may be continued on probation one time
and if a 1. 8 GPA for a sophomore or a 2. 0 average is not
obtained the student is dropped.   St. Francis College is offering a special degree program for adults--Life Experience.
The Faculty Committee on Admissions formulates the admission policies for evening students.   Students may enroll in
both day and evening classes.   An orientation program for
evening students is held during registration.   After 32 hours,
a student must matriculate or leave.   There are 126 hours
required to complete the BBA.

II.   TERMINOLOGY

Title of Division: Evening Sessions.   Defined: As
opposed to Day Sessions.   Continuing Education defined: Education beyond the secondary level without degree designation.

III.   FEES

There is no fee differential between day and evening
classes in tuition.   However, students in the Evening Session
pay $10 college fee; day students pay a $35 college fee.
Refunds are made at the rate of 100% before the end of the
first week and after that time there is no refund.

IV.   FACULTY AND FACULTY RECRUITMENT

Approximately 75% of the faculty teaching evening
classes are full-time.   No full-time faculty members teach

exclusively in the evening.   The Board of Trustees has the
final authority for hiring full and part-time faculty.   No faculty meetings are held for evening faculty.   Overloads for
faculty members are discouraged.

V. SCHEDULING

The Director of Evening Sessions has the responsibility for the evening class schedule.   Three-hour classes are
held two nights a week.   Day and evening classes are equal
in quality.   Part-time evening students are eligible for the
Dean's List by taking eight or more hours with a 3. 0 average.

VI. ORGANIZATIONAL STRUCTURE

Two staff members comprise the administrative staff:
the Dean and Assistant Director.   Teaching staff consists of
forty-seven full-time and eleven part-time faculty members.

VII. EDUCATIONAL TELEVISION PROGRAMS

A Method of Instructional Techniques is offered on
educational television, earning credit toward a degree.   Specialists in the field are responsible for supervising the program using part-time faculty.   Continuing Education Division
handles the registration.   Student tuition sponsors the programs which are scheduled in the late afternoon.

VIII. NON-CREDIT PROGRAMS

Non-credit courses are offered in the areas of Business and Management, Arts and Sciences.   There is a budget
but the courses are expected to pay for themselves.   Remuneration for faculty is $15 per hour or $250 per course
for six class sessions.   The Division does not sponsor conferences or institutes and is not responsible for the summer
session.

IX. GENERAL

Students participate in discussions regarding the academic program through their Student Government which is an
Academic Affairs Committee.   The Academic Dean meets
with student leaders four times a year.   Adequate support
and financial assistance are given to the Evening Session.
The Director is responsible to the Academic Dean.

X. STUDENT RECRUITMENT

Newspaper stories and advertisements are used for publicity purposes.

St. Joseph's College
Philadelphia, Pennsylvania
Evening College

Total Enrollment 6, 600   Private, Church-related
Evening Enrollment 4, 800   Institution
                                         Semester System

I. ADMISSION POLICIES

Deadline for application is thirty days prior to the beginning of the term.   Non-degree students are accepted up to registration.   Students may register for credit courses without transcripts.   "Isolated Credit" status permits students to take courses on a non-degree basis but matriculation is encouraged.   There is no stated limit on the amount of work a non-matriculating student may take for credit. Admission requirement for non-matriculating students is high school graduation; for regular students must be a high school graduate with eighty (or coll. cert.) grade in fifteen Carnegie units (twelve of which must be academic).   Students must maintain a 1. 5 for eighteen credits; 1. 7 for thirty credits; 1. 9 for sixty credits; 2. 0 is required for graduation. No special degree programs are offered and none are considered.   Students who are rejected for admission as regular students are advised to apply as evening students.   This happens twenty or thirty times each fall or spring; late applicants or border-line applicants (day college) are referred to the Evening College with a specified program.   We "automatically" accept these students.   Experience has shown that these students should be treated and regarded as evening college students.   Mail registration is employed and is successful with 60% of students using mail registration.   A month is designated (ending two weeks or so before "regular" registration) for mail pre-registration.   Students may pick up (or be mailed) registration "packets" which include four-part registration form, data identification card--then library card, return envelope, class schedule.   To pre-register, a student must include his adviser's approval roster cards.   After new students are accepted and have scheduling interview they are

permitted to pre-register. Admission policies are set by
the Dean and his staff. Day and evening students may enroll in the same class with permission of their Deans. The
ACT or CEEB is not required for adults in the evening.
They are helpful for advisement--as is CLEP. There is no
special degree for adults but there are three majors that the
day session does not have: BA in Social Studies, BA in Business Administration, MA in Education (General Ed.). The
number of students enrolled during the Fall was 341 regular,
1165 part-time, graduate part-time 191. Distribution requirements are the same as for the liberal arts degree--
eighteen credits. There is no graduate school per se. The
total number of hours required to complete the degree is 120
for undergraduates and 30 for graduate students. Admission
requirements for the special degree is the same for all baccalaureate degrees for undergraduates and graduates -- must
have a C+ or better and acceptable grades on GRE. The admission policies for the evening regular degree students are
formulated by the Dean of the Evening College and for graduates, the grad committee, Ed. Pol. Committee, Council and
the President. The Dean is responsible for the non-matriculating and special adult degree students. The advantages of
the combined class with day and evening students are that any
combination has very heavy/very light enrollment, conse-
quently, no problems. There is an orientation program for
evening students one Sunday afternoon before the term.

II. TERMINOLOGY

Title of Division: St. Joseph's Evening College. Defined: Although 85% descriptive, it is a misnomer--after-
noon, Saturday morning and summer day and evening sessions
are directed through this division. Definition of Continuing
Education: Post baccalaureate, re-tooling or cultural courses.

III. FEES

The charge for evening classes is by the course; day
charges are a flat semester fee (hardly any part-time students). To equate day and evening tuitions, the day session
is charging $50 a credit and evening is charging $35. For
1971-72, the day session will charge $60 a credit for extra
courses and evening charge will be $38. Day students have
many services and extras not available or not desired by the
part-time students attending evening classes. Refunds for
full or partial withdrawals are paid at the rate of 80% for
the first and second week, 60% for third week and so on until

sixth week at which time no refund is paid.

IV.   FACULTY AND FACULTY RECRUITMENT

There is no policy regarding the percentage of faculty
for evening classes that are full-time faculty members.   Approximately 5% are full-time evening college teachers and
approximately 31% are full-time day teachers teaching at
night.   The Executive Vice-President has the final authority
for hiring faculty for evening classes.   The Dean of the Evening Division may reject a faculty member who has been assigned to teach evening classes and the full-time faculty who
teach exclusively in the evening are responsible to the Dean.
The department chairmen engage instructors.   Regular faculty meetings are not held.   The evening faculty members
are invited to departmental meetings.   Regular faculty members may participate in institutes, etc. with the approval of
the Executive Vice-President and the present policy is to
allow it.   None of the budget is spent on faculty recruitment.
Salary range for part-time faculty is $720-$1070 for a three
semester hour course.   The same rate is applied to overloads.

V.   SCHEDULING

The Dean is responsible for the evening class schedule.   The schedule is based upon the needs of the students.
The departments choose the courses and the Division schedules the times.   The Dean has the authority to revise but the
faculty receive more requests than the Dean does for changes.
The Division prefers to have a year schedule made six
months in advance and no alterations made.   Three-hour
classes are scheduled, by preference, two nights per week.
A study has been made on the academic progress of evening
students of the first, second, third, fourth and fifth quintile
in high school; students admitted in 1963-1964-1965.   The
open door policy in the Evening Division means the average
student is lower in quality.   This may affect teaching and
grading.   The Administration is aware of this and there is
a high percentage of failure and dropouts.   Part-time students (evening) are eligible for the Evening Division's own
Dean's List.   Since there are so many students with under
thirty credits, freshmen are not classified, but sophomores,
juniors, seniors qualify for Dean's List with a 3.0 average.
Ten students constitute a class.   There is no reduction of
compensation for an instructor who teaches a class below
minimum size.

VI.   ORGANIZATIONAL STRUCTURE

The administrative staff consists of twenty-three members (five "exempt" administrators and two "hourly" department supervisors; sixteen clerical, two student aids.) The teaching staff consists of eleven full-time and 191 part-time. The Dean has administrative responsibility overall; the Assistant Dean assists the Dean in his duties; the Executive Vice-President oversees the evening college operations, curriculum and the faculty - indirectly; the Director of Academic Advising is in charge of Admissions; the Evening College has its own Registrar.   Other staff members are a Director of Student Affairs who is part-time coordinator with extra curriculars and also student academic advisor; one cashier who reports to the Evening College Dean but works with the College Treasurer; Recorder who works with the data office on admissions, applications, permanent records, storing, grading, etc.   There is no administrative staff required for conferences, etc. as they are absorbed in the credit program. For an enrollment of 5000 credit program students the ideal staff would be twenty-four.   The Evening College has eight part-time faculty academic advisers each working six hours for two evenings per week.

VII.   EDUCATIONAL TELEVISION PROGRAMS

No educational television programs are offered at St. Joseph's Evening College.

VIII.   NON-CREDIT PROGRAMS

A few non-credit courses are offered in the areas of English and Math as well as Industrial Chemistry.   There is no budget for non-credit programs--they are expected to pay for themselves.   Faculty members receive the same remuneration for non-credit courses as they do for credit courses.   This remuneration depends upon qualifications of the instructor.   The College is responsible for the Summer Session.

IX.   GENERAL

There are no off-campus offerings.   Three evening college students sit on the "College Council", our supreme soviet subject only to the President and the Board.   Ten evening students sit on "College Assembly" and have a vote. They hold voting memberships in college standing committees.

The Evening College students have their own student council.
Canvases are made by direct questionnaire through the student council on curricula changes, calendar, etc.   Many
recommendations have come from the student body, sifted by
the committee and some get to the council floor.   An MA in
General Education is offered part-time students in the evening.   The Evening College receives adequate support in
comparison with the day program.   The Dean is responsible
to the Executive Vice-President.   All of the usual, but un-
complicated audio-visual and technical aids are used: slide
projectors, overheads, opaques, etc.   There is an active
chapter of Alpha Sigma Lambda.

X.   STUDENT RECRUITMENT

Student recruitment is carried out by quarter page
ads before each session in the newspapers.   Brochures,
flyers, letters are mailed to industries, schools and school
systems.

St. Louis University
St. Louis, Missouri
Metropolitan College

Total Enrollment 10, 000   Private Institution
Evening Enrollment 2, 000   (church-related)
                                             Semester System

I.   ADMISSION POLICIES

The deadline for application for admission to evening
classes is the day of registration.   Students may register
for credit courses before transcripts are submitted.   Non-
matriculating or "special" students may take an unlimited
number of courses for credit.   Scores on ACT or CEEB are
not necessarily required for admission but may be used if
necessary for advisement.   Mail registration is used for
Metropolitan College non-degree credit courses only.   The
various colleges formulate the admission policies for evening
students.   Day and evening students may enroll in the same
area.   An orientation program is held for evening students
at the beginning of each semester.

II. TERMINOLOGY

Title of Division: Metropolitan College. (Degree programs are administered by the Evening Division of the College of Arts and the School of Commerce and Finance). Metropolitan College offers a continuing, non-degree education for adults. Continuing Education defined: The learning needed for a satisfying life, that can be accomplished only after completion of each individual's formal education.

III. FEES

There is a fee differential for students attending day or evening classes. Day students pay $58 per semester hour; evening students pay $40 per semester hour. This is due to fewer services offered evening students. Students receive refunds for courses dropped on a percentage scale through one-half of the semester.

IV. FACULTY AND FACULTY RECRUITMENT

Approximately 85% of the faculty teaching evening classes in Metropolitan College are full-time faculty members. No faculty members in the evening division of Arts and Sciences are full-time. The Deans of the various schools are responsible for hiring full- and part-time faculty members for evening classes. Faculty members are paid for teaching overloads in the evening.

V. SCHEDULING

The Dean of Metropolitan College is responsible for the evening class schedule in his own college. The Dean of Arts and Sciences and Commerce and Finance are responsible for their programs. The Registrar collects and publishes information regarding the evening class schedule. The evening classes in Metropolitan College compare favorably with day classes. Part-time evening students are eligible for the Dean's List.

VI. ORGANIZATIONAL STRUCTURE

The administrative staff of Metropolitan College consists of two administrative officers and four clerical staff members. The teaching staff consists of 53 part-time faculty members. The Dean has the overall responsibility for the administration of the college plus all certificate pro-

grams; all programs in the areas of Engineering, Business,
Arts and Humanities, Law, Social and Physical Science,
Social Work, Divinity and TV programs. A coordinator of
the Medical Center Programs is responsible for the continuing education programs in Nursing and Dentistry. Recommended administrative staff size for an evening student body
of 2000 would be three staff members (for credit courses
only).

VII. EDUCATIONAL TELEVISION PROGRAMS

The Metropolitan College offers non-credit courses
on educational television. No residence credit may be earned
since these are non-credit courses. The Dean of Metropolitan College supervises the educational courses. Instructors receive extra remuneration as an overload for teaching
these courses. No registrations are held. The educational
television courses are financed partly by an administrative
fund and partly by station funds. No out-of-state tuition is
charged. Courses are scheduled from 6:30 to 7:00 a. m.

VIII. NON-CREDIT PROGRAMS

Metropolitan College offers non-credit courses in the
areas of Business and Management, Arts and Sciences, Education, Engineering and other areas. A budget is provided
for administering this program, but the program is expected
to pay for itself. Faculty members are paid $250 per course
for ten class sessions. Metropolitan College sponsored
twenty-four conferences and institutes during the past year.
Clinicians are paid $150 per day, $300 per two days, or
$750 per week. Conferences are sponsored by the College
using qualified faculty and/or visiting lecturers. The College is not responsible for the summer session.

IX. GENERAL

Evening students do not have an opportunity to participate in discussions regarding the academic program. The
need and importance of adult education are not given equal
support with the day program. The Dean is responsible to
the Academic Vice-President.

X. STUDENT RECRUITMENT

Publicity includes ads and news releases in the newspaper and spot announcements on radio and television. Spe-

cial motivational appeals are developed for industry and for civic organizations.

St. Mary's Dominican College
New Orleans, Louisiana
Division of Continuing Education

Total Enrollment 755   Church-related
Evening Enrollment 340   Institution
(275 cr. & 65 non-cr.)   Semester System

I. ADMISSION POLICIES

The deadline for application for admission is September 1, February 5, and June 9. Transcripts must be submitted before registration. There is no limit on the amount of work that can be taken for credit by non-matriculating students. For non-credit students, no formal application or previous academic record is required. For credit students, the application falls in one of the following categories: admission of high school graduates, admission by examination, or admission of transfer students. Students are not advised to apply to, nor automatically accepted in, the Division of Continuing Education if rejected as regular students. After being admitted to the college, students may mail admission card to the Division along with the required fee and upon receipt of this the Continuing Education office requests the financial office to bill student for remaining fees and tuition. In order that the student maintain the required academic standing and continue in the course, the following minimum standards must be met: a quality point average of 1.5 after the first semester of the freshman year; a quality point average of 1.7 after the second semester of the freshman year; a quality point average of 2.0 after the first semester of the sophomore year and after every subsequent semester. Students failing to meet these specified requirements will be placed on probation for one semester and subject to dismissal from the College if they are unable to attain an average of 2.0 in the work scheduled for the probation period. These policies apply to all students. The CEEB is required and used as a basis for admission and advisement. An undergraduate, two-year program leading to a Certification in Corrections is offered exclusively in the evening for adult students. During the Fall Quarter, there were 36 part-time students enrolled in the program. Students in the Corrections Program are encouraged to enroll in courses in the areas of Psychology, Social Welfare and Sociology. No graduate programs are offered. A total of sixty-seven semester hours are necessary to complete the Certificate Program. Admission requirements are the same as for other programs. A special degree program, B. S. in Corrections, will be offered in the near future. The Dean of the College, Director of Admissions and the Faculty Admissions Committee formulate the admission policies for all students. Day and evening students may cross-register, the advantage being a broadening of educational horizons of different age groups. No orientation program is held. The Evening Division Advisory Committee alerts the Director to the possibilities of new programs.

II. TERMINOLOGY

Title of Division: Division of Continuing Education. Defined: The offerings of a quality education at reasonable rates to members of the adult community. Definition of Continuing Education: a never-ending process with no necessary relationship to degrees held. Credit courses are an integral part of Continuing Education.

III. FEES

Fees are: $12.00 in-service teachers; $22 regular continuing education students; $50 part-time day students. It is the duty of the individual to apply to the treasurer in writing for refund in the case of withdrawal. Refunds on tuition are made at the rate of 80% within the first week of the semester, 60% within one to three weeks and no refund after the fifth week.

IV. FACULTY AND FACULTY RECRUITMENT

No full-time faculty are employed to teach evening classes. The President assumes final authority for hiring faculty members for the evening classes. The Director can recommend that an instructor be rejected. Informal person-to-person meetings are held. Faculty members may teach one non-credit course as an overload with the permission of the President. None of the budget is spent on recruitment. Salary range for part-time faculty is $175 per semester hour.

V. SCHEDULING

The Director of the evening session is responsible
for the evening class schedule.   He makes the schedule and
has it approved by the department chairmen.   The Director
has the authority to revise the schedule.   Three-hour classes
are scheduled one and two nights per week; the preference
is dependent upon the course.   Research in the form of a
Bachelor of Liberal Studies is underway.   An attempt is
made to keep day and evening classes equal in terms of
quality.   Part-time students are not eligible for the Dean's
List.   Enough students must enroll in a class to pay for the
instructor's salary.   An instructor's salary is reduced when
teaching a class below the minimum size after conference
with the instructor concerned.

VI. ORGANIZATIONAL STRUCTURE

The administrative staff consists of two and twenty-
thirty part-time faculty members.   The Director is in charge
of the entire continuing education program.   The Assistant
Director is responsible to the Director--they share the duties
of the continuing education office.   For an enrollment of 300,
three staff members would be required.

VII. EDUCATIONAL TELEVISION PROGRAMS

The Division of Continuing Education does not offer
educational television programs.

VIII. NON-CREDIT PROGRAMS

Non-credit courses are offered in the areas of Business and Management and other areas.   The programs are
expected to pay for themselves.   The remuneration to faculty
depends upon the course and the qualifications of the instructor.   The Evening Division does not sponsor conferences,
etc. and is partially responsible for the summer session.

IX. GENERAL

No courses are offered in off-campus locations.   Students participate in discussions regarding academic programs
by being members of the Curriculum Committee.   Courses
are being offered that are of definite service to the com-
munity--our Corrections Program, for instance.   The Evening Division receives adequate support in comparison to the

day program.   The Director is responsible to the Dean of
the College.   Movie projectors, slide and film projectors,
tape recorders, etc. are used as audio-visual aids.

X.   STUDENT RECRUITMENT

The student recruiting is accomplished through newspapers, radio and television.

St. Peter's College
Jersey City, New Jersey
Evening Session

Total Enrollment 4, 800   Church-related Institution
Evening Enrollment 2, 300   Trimester System

I.   ADMISSION POLICIES

The deadline for application for admission for regular
and non-degree students is one week before the first class.
Students may register for credit classes before transcripts
are submitted, by way of exception.   Non-matriculating students may take up to thirty-six hours for credit; admission
requirements being a high school diploma or equivalent with
a 75% average in high school; the same is true for regular
students.   Rejected students are advised to apply as evening
students but are not automatically accepted.   Mail registration is not used.   Policies regarding probation and suspension
for degree and non-degree students are: up to thirty-six
credits yearly average and cumulative average below 1. 6
means probation; up to seventy-two credits below 1. 8 means
probation; up to 129 credits below 2. 0 means probation.   No
tests are required.   No special degree program is offered
in the evening and there are no plans for one in the near
future.   The Admission Policy Committee, the Dean and the
Director of Administration formulate the admission policies
for all categories.   Day and evening students may enroll in
the same class with the approval of the Deans.   An orientation program is held in early fall.   There is no Evening
Division Advisory Committee.

II.   TERMINOLOGY

Title of Division: Evening Session.   Defined: To
indicate that the evening session is not a separate division

of the College. Definition of Continuing Education: Education of part-time students through credit and non-credit programs.

III. FEES

The college fee is $2.00 per credit in the evening session and in the day session it is a flat rate of $53.00 per term. The tuition is the same - $48 per credit hour as of July, 1971. The justification for the difference is that there are less services in the evening. Refunds are made in the following manner: 80% the first week, 60% the second week, 40% the third week.

IV. FACULTY AND FACULTY RECRUITMENT

Approximately 35% of the evening faculty members are full-time--there is no policy regarding the percentage. The Dean of the Evening Session has final authority for hiring part-time faculty members and the Dean has the authority to reject a faculty member. Full-time faculty members are employed by the Dean to whom they are responsible. Regular faculty meetings are not held. Regular faculty may teach one course (3 credits) per trimester. The salary range for part-time faculty is $165-$290 per credit hour, based upon rank. The salary for overloads is the same.

V. SCHEDULING

The Registrar is responsible for the evening class schedule. He requests schedules from chairmen after he determines the number of class sections needed. The Dean has the authority to revise the schedule. Three-hour classes are scheduled one night per week. Day and evening classes are equal in quality though there is some variability--depending upon teacher and subject. Part-time students who carry eighteen hours and maintain a 3.5 average are eligible for the Dean's List. Twelve students must register for a class before the class will be taught. An instructor's compensation is reduced when he teaches a class below minimum size.

VI. ORGANIZATIONAL STRUCTURE

The administrative staff consists of three staff members: the Dean who is in charge of academic procedures, advisement of students and faculty in so far as they partici-

pate in the evening session; a full-time Director who is in
charge of admission three times a year, program advisement and recruiting; a part-time Registrar who handles registration for the evening sessions three times a year, accepts
transcripts and processes VA applications.   The teaching
staff consists of forty-two full-time and 101 part-time faculty
members.

VII.   EDUCATIONAL TELEVISION PROGRAMS

The Evening Session does not offer any educational
television programs.

VIII.   NON-CREDIT PROGRAMS

The Evening Session does not offer non-credit programs but is responsible for the summer session.

IX.   GENERAL

No courses are offered on off-campus locations.   Students are respresented on college committees.   No graduate
programs for part-time students are offered by the evening
sessions.   The evening session is not receiving adequate
support in comparison with the day program but the administration does recognize the need for adult education.   The
Dean is responsible to the day academic Dean of the College.
TV and projection equipment are used as audio-visual aids.

X.   STUDENT RECRUITMENT

The newspaper is used for student recruitment purposes.

Suffolk University
Boston, Massachusetts
Evening Division

Total Enrollment 5, 231   Private Institution
Evening Enrollment 1, 495   Semester System

I.   ADMISSION POLICIES

Deadlines for applications for admission for regular
students: August 20, January 7 and June 16.   Deadlines for

"special" students: September 17, January 28 and June 19.
Students may register for credit courses before transcripts
are submitted if they are "special" students or if credit is
to be transferred to another college.   At least 30 hours may
be taken for credit as a "special" student, with some additional hours allowed with special permission.   Admission requirements for "special" students includes high school graduation with no SAT - CEEB required for "older" students.
Admission requirements for regular students include high
school graduation, SAT-CEEB (waived for mature students).
Transfer students must have a 2. 0 (C) average.   Mail registration is used for day and evening Summer students.   Students submit course selections and check to the Accounting
Office.   The Accounting Office refers the form to the Registrar who mails registration forms and class slips to the
student.   Retention policies: 1. 8-freshmen; 1. 9-sophomores,
2. 0-juniors and seniors.   Sometimes C. L. E. P. or reading
tests are required.   The Bachelor of Sciences in General
Studies is offered as a special degree for adults--with 40
students enrolled in the program.   The distribution for this
degree is: Humanities, 12 semester hours; Social Science,
12, Biology and Physical Science 14, English 12, History 6,
Language 12.   Total number of hours required to complete
the degree is 122.   The areas of concentration together with
the credit requirements are: Humanities 42 semester hours,
Social Science 42, Science 42.   The admission requirement
for the special degree programs is a High School diploma.
The Evening Division is considering offering a special degree graduate program for adults in the near future.   The
Admissions Committee formulates the admission policies for
the evening students; for non-matriculating, non-degree or
"special" students (with credit) the Director of Admissions
and Dean; and for special adult degree students, the Admissions Committee for undergraduate students and the Graduate
Committee for Graduate Students.   A Master of Liberal Arts
program is being developed.   Day and evening classes are
interchangeable, but first year evening students may not normally take day courses.   No Orientation program for evening students is held.

II.   TERMINOLOGY

Title of Division: Evening Division.   Defined: It is
responsible for graduate and undergraduate evening courses
(with the exception of Law which is a separate unit), and for
extension courses.   We offer no non-credit courses at present, but could if we had the staff and space.   Definition of

Continuing Education: "I tend to associate Adult Education
with non-credit courses, and Continuing Education with credit
courses. "

III. FEES

Tuition is $40 per semester hour for both full-time
day students and evening with the exception that full-time day
students pay $1400 per year.   There is a fee differential
with day and evening classes: the evening rate is kept lower
to remain competitive with State colleges.   Refund policies:
80% within the 1st week; 60% within the 2nd week; 40% within the 3rd week; 20% within the 4th week; thereafter - none.

IV.   FACULTY AND FACULTY RECRUITMENT

51% of the faculty teaching evening classes are full-
time.   All full-time faculty are required to teach evening
courses as part of their full teaching load when they are
needed.   The President and the Board of Trustees have the
final authority for hiring full and part-time faculty.   No faculty meetings are held for evening faculty.   Faculty members may teach extension courses or institutes for extra
salary and regular courses as an overload.   They may also
teach a course at another college for extra salary.   The
salary range for part-time faculty is $700 for a three se-
mester hour course.   There is no salary paid the faculty for
overloads, but a proposal to pay $700 is under consideration.
In the Summer, the compensation paid by the course to the
faculty is as follows: (Part-time) Lecturer, $700; Instructor,
$700; Assistant Professor, $800; Associate Professor, $900;
Professor, $1000.   There must be eight students registered
to constitute a class.   Although the instructor's compensation
is ordinarily reduced when he teaches a class below the minimum size, there is authorization to offer six courses that do
not meet minimum enrollment and pay faculty their full salary.   This assumes these courses are essential to the program.   In rare instances, a teacher may teach at reduced
salary equal to tuition receipts.

V.   SCHEDULING

The Associate Dean of the Evening Division has the
responsibility for the evening class schedule together with
the day deans and department chairmen.   The registrar as-
signs classrooms.   Department chairmen recommend course
offerings and teaching assignments.   These are modified in

order to provide a balanced schedule and to minimize course
conflicts.   Three-hour courses are scheduled one or two
nights a week.   Day and evening classes are equal in quality.
Part-time evening students are eligible for the Dean's List
by taking nine semester hours with a 3. 0 (B) average.

VI.   ORGANIZATIONAL STRUCTURE

The administrative staff consists of one staff member
and 56 full-time and 53 part-time teachers.   The administrative responsibilities of the Associate Dean include the development and supervision of the evening program; advising,
preparation of advertising and promotional material; development of curriculum; preparation of course schedules; directing
the Summer session and teaching one course.   It is estimated
that the recommended size of an administrative staff required
for administering an evening credit program would be as follows: with an enrollment of 300 students, one staff member
and one for organizing and administering non-credit courses,
conferences and institutes; 500-one staff member plus one;
800-two staff members plus one; 1000-three staff members
plus 1; 5000-five staff members plus three.   The number depends on whether the evening program is autonomous or re-
lies on the services of day Deans and other administrators.

VII.   EDUCATIONAL TELEVISION PROGRAMS

The Evening Division does not offer any courses in
Educational Television.

VIII.   NON-CREDIT PROGRAMS

The Evening Division does not offer any non-credit
courses.   The division is responsible for the Summer session
at the institution.

IX.   GENERAL

Scholarship assistance is available to economically deprived individuals who are qualified to take college work.
Students participate in discussions regarding the academic
program through a Joint Student-Faculty Committee.   Recommendations are made by student government.   Suffolk University has an Interdisciplinary Senior Honors Program; also
students are placed in Social Work Agencies as part of their
Field Experience course.   Adequate stress and financial support are given to the evening program.   The Dean is respon-

sible directly to the Vice-President and Dean of the College of Liberal Arts and Sciences.

X. STUDENT RECRUITMENT

Newspaper stories and ads are used for publicity. No use of radio and television is made for publicity purposes. Special announcements are prepared for business and industry and for civic organizations.

University of Tampa
Tampa, Florida
Continuing Education

Total Enrollment 1, 978   Private Institution
Evening Enrollment 400   Semester System

I. ADMISSION POLICIES

The deadline for application for admission to evening classes is the starting date for each semester. Students may register without transcripts with permission from the Director of Admissions. Non-matriculated students may take twelve hours work which is validated by performance. Admission requirements for regular degree students are high school graduate or GED equivalency and scores on CEEB tests. Students must maintain a minimum grade point average on a sliding scale from 1. 75 for under 45 hours to 2. 0 for 90 hours or more. No special degree program is offered for adults. The Faculty Admissions Committee, the Faculty Dean and the Director of Admissions formulate the admission policies for evening students. Day and evening students may enroll in the same classes. There is no orientation program for evening students.

II. TERMINOLOGY

Title of Division: Continuing Education. Defined: Offers courses for credit or non-credit (as the student qualifies or if the material is of college level). Courses are open with above restrictions to all the community.

III. FEES

There is no fee differential between day and evening

classes.   Students are charged a drop fee of $3. 00 and ob-
tain full refund if the change is made before classes start.
Otherwise a sliding scale prevails.

IV.   FACULTY AND FACULTY RECRUITMENT

Approximately 25% of the faculty teaching evening
classes are full-time faculty members.   Final authority to
hire faculty lies with the Vice-President for Academic Affairs.   The Director of Continuing Education can reject a
faculty member assigned to teach evening classes.   No regular faculty meetings are held.   Faculty members are paid
extra when they teach overloads.   No budget is used for recruitment.   Salary for part-time faculty is $500 for Masters
Degree per three-hour course; $600 for Ph. D per three-hour
course; the same for full-time faculty.

V.   SCHEDULING

The Director of Continuing Education is responsible
for the evening class schedule in consultation with the Registrar and Department Heads.   Three-hour classes are scheduled both one and two nights a week depending upon the
course.   Day and evening classes are equal in terms of quality.   Sometimes the evening courses suffer due to part-time
faculty.   Part-time evening students are not eligible for the
Dean's List.   Normally ten students must be registered to
constitute a class.

VI.   ORGANIZATIONAL STRUCTURE

The program in Continuing Education is administered
by one staff member who is the Director.   The teaching
staff consists of 35 part-time faculty members.   The Director is responsible for all administration and direction in
Adult Education, non-credit programs, conferences, institutes, and extension.

VII.   EDUCATIONAL TELEVISION PROGRAMS

No educational television programs are sponsored by
Continuing Education at the University.

VIII.   NON-CREDIT PROGRAMS

The program in continuing education includes non-
credit courses in the areas of Business Management, Arts

and Sciences and other areas.   The non-credit program is
expected to pay for itself.   Faculty members receive $300
to $500 per course for 8 to 10 class sessions.   The pro-
gram also includes conferences and institutes including the
following: American Institute of Real Estate Appraisers,
Police Community Relations Institute, Real Estate Course
and Fire and Casualty Insurance.   Conferences are sponsored
not only by the university but in cooperation with local Junior
Colleges on several programs.   The Director of Continuing
Education is not responsible for the summer session.

IX.   GENERAL

Students are members of many committees and participate in discussions regarding academic programs through
them.   Committee participation is being expanded, with weekly meetings with the President, Vice-President and Department Chairmen.   The Director of Continuing Education is
responsible to the Vice-President of Academic Affairs.

X.   STUDENT RECRUITMENT

Newspaper, radio and television publicity is used.
Special motivational appeals are made through industry and
civic organizations such as the Chamber of Commerce.

Temple University
Philadelphia, Pennsylvania
School of Business Administration

Total Enrollment Approx. 40, 000   Semi-public Institution
Evening Enrollment 1, 700+   (State-related but re-
   (School of Bus. Adm. Only)   tains private status)
                                           Semester System

NOTE: The evening programs are decentralized at the Uni-
        versity and administered by each school.   Temple
        has an off-campus division and a Division of Busi-
        ness and Government Services who handle non-credit
        courses in management development, technical areas
        of administration, specialized courses, etc.   This
        survey was answered by the School of Business Ad-
        ministration and applies only to that School.

I.   ADMISSION POLICIES

The deadline for application for admission is the first
week of class each semester.   Students may not normally
register without transcripts.   Non-matriculating and special
students may take not more than sixty semester hours as
non-matriculating and/or special students.   Admission requirements for non-matriculating or special students are high
school graduation; regular students must have high school
diploma, SAT scores, and be in upper 3/5 of high school
class.   No mail registration is used.   Students must maintain a 2. 0 average in order to avoid probation; dismissal
results when record indicates inability to do college work.
SAT scores are used as basis for admission as well as placement and advisement.   Bachelor of Science is offered as an
evening degree program for undergraduates and a M. B. A.
for graduates.   There were 755 full-time and 1682 part-time
students enrolled as undergraduates in the fall; 127 full-time
and 763 part-time in the graduate program.   Distribution requirements are at least 40% in Liberal Arts, and no lab science is required in the evening.   Total number of hours to
complete the undergraduate degree is 128; graduate requires
30 hours.   No additional special degree programs are being
considered.   The Administrative Office of the University
formulates the admission policies.   Evening students may
not normally register for day classes.   Day students, however, may register for evening classes.   Advantages are
social and cultural with flexibility from the student's point of
view.   There is no orientation for evening students.   An
Evening Division Advisory Committee keeps overall surveil-
lance on the evening program and advises accordingly.

II.   TERMINOLOGY

Title of Division: School of Business Administration -
undergraduate evening division.   Defined: The Division of
the School of Business Administration which administers the
evening undergraduate adult higher education including degree
and non-degree/credit and non-credit courses for adults with
programs operating at one or more levels by various schools.

III.   FEES

There is no fee differential between day and evening
classes.   All pay same fees for matriculation.   Refunds are
made on a declining basis: 80% first week, 60% second week,
and so on; no refund after fifth week.

IV.   FACULTY AND FACULTY RECRUITMENT

The percentage of full-time is kept at 50%; it is intended that evening classes should be staffed by full-time faculty in the future.   The Dean of the School has final authority in hiring full-time and part-time faculty.   No overloads are allowed.   No faculty meetings are held for evening faculty members.   Approximately 5% of the budget is spent on recruitment.   The salary range for part-time faculty is $300 to $600 per semester hour.

V.   SCHEDULING

The Director in cooperation with the department chairmen is responsible for the evening class schedule which is finally approved by the Dean.   There are no three-hour classes; all four-hour classes are conducted one and two nights.   "A Comparative Study of Day and Evening Undergraduate Students in Temple University," a dissertation by John S. Schultz in May 1966 is completed research.   Day and evening classes are comparable in terms of quality. Part-time evening students are not eligible for the Dean's List.   Ten to fifteen students constitute a class.

VI.   ORGANIZATIONAL STRUCTURE

Two staff members and ten department chairmen comprise the administrative staff.   The Associate Dean plans, develops, and administers the undergraduate evening program in the School of Business Administration.   The teaching staff consists of 122 full-time (day and evening classes) and 51 part-time for evening classes only.   Staff requirements depend upon many factors associated with how the university or college is structured and organized and how the individual programs are administered.

VII.   EDUCATIONAL TELEVISION PROGRAMS

No educational television programs are offered.

VIII.   NON-CREDIT PROGRAMS

Non-credit courses are not offered.

IX.   GENERAL

The off-campus Division offers many courses in a

variety of locations. Students are members of committees and college councils. Day students have participated in Course-Faculty Evaluation Program. No graduate program is offered for part-time students by the School of Business Administration; the Graduate Division of the School is a separate division. The Associate Dean is responsible to the Dean of the School of Business Administration. Audio-visual aids are available for evening classes.

X. STUDENT RECRUITMENT

Newspapers, radio and television are used for student recruitment. Special motivational appeals are made to industry.

The University of Tennessee at Chattanooga
Chattanooga, Tennessee
Division of Continuing Education

Total Enrollment 4, 350   State Institution
Evening Enrollment 1, 597   Semester System
  (includes day students enrolled
  in evening classes)

I. ADMISSION POLICIES

Deadline for application for admission is two weeks prior to registration. Students may register for regular credit courses without transcripts only with approval by the Director of Admissions. Students desiring regular college credit must meet the same standards for admission as those entering day classes. As an entrance examination, evening students may take SCAT in lieu of ACT or CEEB. Students who have attained the age of 21 and have sufficient educational background and experience to profit from courses desired may register as Adult Specials for non-degree credit without meeting regular admission standards. Students must maintain at least the following grade point average: 1. 50 after 24 hours; cumulative average of at least 2. 00 after 56 hours. Students on probation must maintain a 2. 0 average. There is no special degree program for adults. Admission policies for undergraduates are set by the Admission Committee and approved by faculty. After a student has attempted from 12 to 23 hours he will be suspended or dismissed if he has failed all academic courses. From 24 to 35 hours, stu-

dents are expected to have cumulative average of 1. 50; from
56 hours, cumulative average of at least 2. 0.   The same
applies to "special" students.   There is no program difference from the day degree program offered evening degree
adults.   No special degree program is being considered in
the near future.   The admissions committee formulates the
admission policies for undergraduate, regular, non-degree
and special adult degree students.   The graduate council
formulates the policies for graduate students.

II.   TERMINOLOGY

Title of Division: Division of Continuing Education.
Defined: A division with the responsibility for coordinating
evening classes, administering off-campus classes, and directing the program of institutes, seminars and non-credit
courses.

III.   FEES

Tuition: undergraduate, in-state, $22. 50 per se-
mester hour; out-of-state, $40. 50 per semester hour; grad-
uate, in-state, $31. 50 per semester hour, out-of-state,
$52. 50 per semester hour.   Day students have some services
not available to evening students.

IV.   FACULTY AND FACULTY RECRUITMENT

77% teaching evening classes are full-time faculty
members.   Final authority to hire part-time evening faculty
lies with the day Deans.   Overloads for regular faculty members are not usually permitted in credit courses, but limited
participation in seminars with additional compensation is approved.   None of the budget is spent for recruitment.

V.   SCHEDULING

The Dean is responsible for recommending the evening class schedule: it is compiled in the Dean's office.
Three credit hour classes are scheduled two nights a week.
A self-study project was undertaken by the Chattanooga College Committee in 1967.   Part-time students are not eligible
for the Dean's List.

VI.   ORGANIZATIONAL STRUCTURE

The administrative staff consists of three staff members, 73 full-time and 21 part-time faculty members. As a major campus in the University of Tennessee system, we have autonomy. Of course, we must comply with Systems Regulations. The Director acts as coordinator for evening programs, administers extension or off-campus programs, administers program of non-credit courses, institutes and seminars, serves as liason officer for institutional research, serves as liason officer to Office of Federal Programs, American Association of State Colleges and Universities. It is difficult to estimate the size of administrative staff without knowledge of the program and activities.

VII.   EDUCATIONAL TELEVISION PROGRAMS

Educational TV programs have been offered but not at the present time. They were credit courses and students could earn residence credit. These credits will count toward a degree. A regular faculty member from the appropriate department supervised the educational television courses. Full-time faculty members are used to teach the courses. The Division of Continuing Education has not offered courses through TV since becoming a state university.

VIII.   NON-CREDIT COURSES

Non-credit programs are offered in the areas of business and management, arts and sciences, education and engineering. This program is expected to be self-sustaining. Faculty remuneration is $20 per hour and remuneration does not depend on qualifications of instructor. The Division sponsors conferences such as Pre-Retirement Planning, Management Development, Estate Planning, Consumer Education. Clinicians are paid $100-$300 for one-day conferences. Conferences are sponsored both by the Division of Continuing Education and in cooperation with another college. The Division of Continuing Education is responsible for the Summer session.

IX.   GENERAL

Complete audio-visual instructional aids are available for evening classes. The Director of Continuing Education is responsible to the Vice Chancellor for Academic Affairs.

X.   STUDENT RECRUITMENT

Newspaper articles as well as radio and television

publicity are used. Special motivational appeals have been developed for business and industry in the form of brochures for special programs for employees. The Chamber of Commerce, The Society for the Advancement of Management and other organizations in the area assist in promoting community service programs.

The University of Tennessee
Knoxville, Tennessee
Division of Continuing Education

Total Statewide Enrollment: Public Institution
      38087   Quarter System
Total Enrollment (Knoxville) 23, 696
Evening Enrollment 2, 716

I. ADMISSION POLICIES

There is no deadline for application for admission to evening classes. A student may register for credit courses before transcripts are submitted. Non-matriculating or "special" students may take up to 90 quarter hours for credit before matriculation. Admission requirements for regular students: graduate of an accredited high school of GED, ACT of 17 or 2. 25 GPA for fall quarter only. Admission requirements for "special" students: 21 years of age. Students who are rejected for admission as regular students are not advised to apply as evening students. Mail registration is used. Students receive a pre-printed registration form, a self-addressed, stamped envelope, and a copy of both the credit course offerings and the non-credit course offerings for the next quarter. Students enter the department name, course number, section number, hours credit, and hour and days for which they desire to register on the registration form and return the form to the university together with a check or money order. The student then receives a class card for each course in which he is enrolled and a receipt for payment of fees. The class card is the student's admission to class. Parking permits are not purchased by mail. Probation and suspension regulations: 0-35. 9 hours, 1. 00; 36-83. 9 hours, 1. 50; 85-150 hours, 2. 00 and over 150 hours, students will be checked for graduation requirement averages only. Students who do not reach the required average will be placed on academic probation, and will be dropped from the university after one quarter if they do not attain the required cumulative grade point average. The ACT or CEEB examination is required for admission to the Fall quarter only. No special degree program is offered for adults. The enrollment includes 55 full-time and 2661 part-time students with 1912 undergraduate and 804 graduate students. The Faculty Senate formulates the admission requirements for evening students. Advantages - more courses may be offered; disadvantages - larger classes. No Orientation Program is offered for evening students. There is no Evening Division Advisory Committee.

II. TERMINOLOGY

Title of Division: Continuing Education. Defined: Includes Departments of Conferences and Evening School under the Dean of Continuing Education. Definition of Continuing Education: Includes formal and informal classes regardless of the length of the course or program.

III. FEES

There is no fee differential for day and evening classes. Refund policies: 100% through 20%; none after four weeks of the quarter.

IV. FACULTY AND FACULTY RECRUITMENT

The final authority for hiring full and/or part-time faculty members is shared between the Evening School Director and the academic department head. The Director may reject a faculty member who has been assigned to teach evening classes. No full-time faculty members teach exclusively in the evening. The Director may not engage an instructor without the consent of the department head. No regular faculty meetings are held for evening faculty. The departmental and college policy varies regarding the teaching of credit courses in the evening. The University policy is one credit course overload. There is no limit on non-credit courses and conferences. No budget is used for recruitment. The salary range for part-time faculty members: $166. 66 - $200 per credit hour. The same salary range applies for overloads.

V. SCHEDULING

The Director is responsible for the evening class schedule. The Associate Director plans and coordinates the

evening class schedule with the various departments.   The
Associate Director has the authority to revise or make additions to the evening class schedule.   Three-hour classes are
scheduled one or two nights per week depending upon the
particular course.   The Division conducts a student survey
of evening students.   Part-time students are eligible for the
Dean's List.   Requirement: 12 hours with a 3. 00 point average.   The minimum size of evening classes is 6 or 7 students.   An instructor's compensation is not reduced for teaching classes below the minimum size.

VI.   ORGANIZATIONAL STRUCTURE

The administrative staff consists of 8 staff members
with a teaching faculty of 372 full-time and 88 part-time faculty members.   The Division is headed by a Dean, who administers all the programs in Continuing Education including
evening classes and conferences.   He is assisted by 4 assistant directors who administer off-campus programs, programming of evening courses, student records, and non-
credit programs.   A Director of conferences and institutes
together with two coordinators plan all short term non-credit
offerings.   In addition, a cashier handles all receipts and
expenditures, and a Project Director heads the Head Start
Supplementary Training - a funded program.   The suggested
size of an administrative staff for various-sized student
bodies: 300-1 administrator; 500-800-2 administrators; 1000-
3 administrators; 2000-5000-4 administrators.   For non-
credit courses, conferences and institutes: 300-1 adminis-
trator; 500-2000-2 administrators; 5000-3 administrators.
Additional comment: "in all cases, add one more person
who is responsible for both programs. "

VII.   EDUCATIONAL TELEVISION PROGRAMS

The Division of Continuing Education offers no Educational Television courses.

VIII.   NON-CREDIT PROGRAMS

The Division of Continuing Education offers non-credit
courses and conferences in Business and Management, Engineering, Arts and Sciences, Home Economics, Agriculture
and Communications.   No separate budget is supplied for
these programs.   The program is expected to pay for itself
but does not.   Faculty members are paid approximately $20
per hour or $400 per course involving 20 class sessions.

The remuneration depends upon the qualifications of the instructor and upon the area of instruction. The division sponsors conferences and institutes including such conferences as the following: Applied Work Measurement and Methods Engineering, Quality Control Seminar, Production Planning and Control Seminar, Basic Management Analyst Training Program, Tennessee High School Journalism Institute I and II, Conference on Legal Services for the Appalachian Area, Small Business Management Institute, several Inventory Management Seminars, Fourth Annual Tennessee Industries Week, Tax Forum, Flight Instructor Instrument Seminar, Microfilm and Its Applications, Southern Conference on Slavic Studies, Southern Appalachian Science Fair, Engineering Economy, Labor-Management Relations Clinic, Sex Education Workshop, High School Choral Camps, etc. Clinicians are paid up to $500 for one day; up to $1000 for two days, and up to $1200 for one week. The Division is not responsible for the Summer session.

IX. GENERAL

Students are requested to suggest courses to be offered in the evening. No graduate programs are administered by the Division of Continuing Education. The evening program is not receiving adequate financial support. The Dean is responsible to the Vice-Chancellor of Academic Affairs. Video-tapes, an electro-writer, etc. are available for evening classes.

X. STUDENT RECRUITMENT

The newspaper, radio and television are used for publicity purposes. Plant papers are used for publicity with industry. Special motivation appeals are developed for the Real Estate Board, Garden Clubs, CLU Chapters, etc.

Texas Christian University
Fort Worth, Texas
Evening College

Total Enrollment: Approx. 6, 500   Church-related
Evening Enrollment: Approx. 1, 500   Institution
                                            Semester System

I. ADMISSION POLICIES

If admission procedures are not completed at the time
of registration, students are admitted provisionally.   There
is no limit to the amount of work a student may take as a
non-matriculate.   Mail registration is used.   Students request mail packets, complete, the staff processes the registration before regular registration.   Students must maintain
a "C" average.   A special degree program for adults is offered: Bachelor of Arts degree with divisional concentration
in Humanities, Natural Sciences (including Math) or Social
Sciences.   Admission policies are set by the Admissions Office in consultation with Evening College and University Council.   Day and evening students may enroll in the same
classes.

II. TERMINOLOGY

Title of Division: The Evening College.   Defined:
An extension of the College facilities into the evening hours
in order to make university education available to those unable to attend day classes and especially to fix responsibility
for seeing that the needs of adults are met.

III. FEES

Tuition is charged until the date of official withdrawal
according to a set table: one week or less, 10%; two weeks,
20%; three weeks, 30%; four weeks, 50%; five weeks, 70%;
six weeks, 90%; over six weeks, 100%.

IV. FACULTY AND FACULTY RECRUITMENT

The policy regarding the percentage of faculty for
evening classes that are full-time faculty members is a minimum of 25%; approximately 40% are full-time.   Final authority for hiring faculty lies with the Dean and department
chairmen jointly.   Some full-time faculty members teach exclusively in the evening.   Regular faculty meetings are held
annually for entire faculty--periodically for special groups as
necessary.   Faculty may teach only non-credit courses on an
overload basis.   Salaries for part-time faculty range from
$400 to $750.   Part-time faculty are not permitted to teach
overloads.

V. SCHEDULING

The Assistant Dean formulates the evening class schedule. Three-hour classes are scheduled either one or two evenings per week. Part-time students are not eligible for the Dean's List. Normally, ten students constitute a class; any instructor teaching a class with less than the minimum gets a percentage of the normal salary.

VI. ORGANIZATIONAL STRUCTURE

The administrative staff consists of the Dean, an Assistant Dean, a Director of Special Courses, and a Director of Civic Affairs. The Assistant Dean is in charge of admissions and counseling.

VII. EDUCATIONAL TELEVISION PROGRAMS

Educational television is offered through TAGER-TV with credit courses earning residence credit toward a degree. Both full and part-time faculty members are used. Teachers enroll for educational TV courses on campus. Instructors carry a reduced teaching load of regular on-campus classes. Registration is handled through the Graduate School.

VIII. NON-CREDIT PROGRAMS

Non-credit courses are offered in Business and Management, Arts and Sciences, Engineering and other recreational areas. The program does pay for itself. Remuneration to faculty depends upon qualifications of the instructor and the area of instruction; usually runs $100 per course for one class session. The Evening College does offer conferences and institutes such as the Chamber of Commerce Institute, Civil Affairs Institute, the Management Seminar, etc. Clinicians are paid $1000 [sic] for each day of a conference. The Evening College is not responsible for the summer session.

IX. GENERAL

The students participate in discussions regarding the academic programs through the Student Council. Special seminars are held for faculty members in order to increase teaching effectiveness. The Dean is responsible to the Vice-Chancellor.

X. STUDENT RECRUITMENT

Newspaper, radio and television publicity is used.
Public relations is handled through special motivational appeals developed for industry and organizations. A joint effort with SMU and the University of Dallas is being made to
offer courses to six industrial plants via television.

Thomas More College
Covington, Kentucky
Evening and Saturday Division

Total Enrollment 3, 000   Church-related
Evening Enrollment 956 credit   Institution
                    774 non-credit   Semester System

I. ADMISSION POLICIES

Deadline for application for admission to evening
classes is two weeks after classes begin. Students may register for credit courses without transcripts. There is no
limit to the number of hours of credit work a non-matriculated student may take. Admission requirements are high
school graduation or the equivalent. Students must maintain
a 2. 0 cumulative average after twenty hours if they did not
meet admission standards of the Day Division and 2. 0 after
thirty hours if they did meet the admission standards of the
Day Division. Admission policies are set by the Admissions
Committee. Day and evening students may register in the
same class. There is no orientation program for evening
students other than pre-registration counseling. Probation
after twenty hours if GPA is lower than 2. 0; dismissal after
thirty hours if 2. 0 has not been attained. There are no automatic dismissals; each individual case is studied in committee. Degrees offered for adults through the Evening and
Saturday Division include: the Bachelor of Arts and the Associate of Arts. Associate degree programs are offered in
Accounting, Art, Business Administration, Chemical Technology, Computer Science, Economics, English, History,
Philosophy, Psychology and Sociology. Two special sequences
in Bachelor's Program in Sociology are Corrections and Child
Welfare. Distribution requirements for bachelor's degree:
English, 12; Fine Arts, 4; Foreign Language, 6-9; Philos-
ophy, 12; Theology, 12; Mathematics, 6; Natural Science, 8;
Social Science, 9; Associate Degree: English, 6; Philosophy,

6; Theology, 6; Mathematics, 6; Social Science, 3-6 for a total of 64 hours to complete. The Associate Degree in Electronics Technology and in Law Enforcement will be offered, beginning in the fall of 1971.

II. TERMINOLOGY

Title of Division: Evening and Saturday Division. Defined: All work taken for self-improvement or cultural development.

III. FEES

Day and evening students pay $32 a credit hour tuition. Refunds are scaled at the rate of 100% first week, 80% second week, on to fifth week at which time no refunds are made. (Tuition is $29.00 per hour as of June 1, 1971.)

IV. FACULTY AND FACULTY RECRUITMENT

Final authority to hire faculty lies with the President. The Dean of the Evening and Saturday Division may reject a faculty member who has been assigned to teach evening classes. Full-time faculty teaching evening classes is 23%. Overloads for faculty members are permitted if the Academic Dean approves them. The Evening and Saturday Division Faculty Association meets regularly. Salaries for part-time faculty are: $160 per semester hour with an AB degree; $175 per semester hour with a M.A. degree and $185 for an instructor with a Ph.D. degree or equivalent. The salary scale for overloads for regular faculty members: Instructor - $180; Assistant Professor - $185; Associate Professor - $190; Professor - $195.

V. SCHEDULING

The Dean of Evening and Saturday Classes is responsible for the evening class schedule and has the authority to revise the schedule. Three-hour classes are scheduled one night per week. Day and evening classes are equal in terms of quality with slight departmental variations. Part-time evening students are eligible for the Dean's List with a minimum of eight hours credit and a GPA of 3.5.

VI. ORGANIZATIONAL STRUCTURE

The administrative staff consists of two full-time

members and one half-time staff member with a teaching
staff of 19 full-time teachers taking part of the load in the
Evening and Saturday Division, and 63 part-time faculty
members.   The Division is headed by a Dean who is responsible for the credit programs and course offerings as
well as academic standards.   He works closely with Department Chairmen in scheduling evening courses.   Assistant to
the Dean supervises non-credit programs and is responsible
for academic counseling and student affairs.   The Director
of Conferences and Institutes plans programs of a remedial
nature for special interest groups and also is in charge of
institutes and special programs.

VII.   EDUCATIONAL TELEVISION PROGRAMS

The Evening and Saturday Division does not offer educational television programs.

VIII.   NON-CREDIT PROGRAMS

Non-credit courses are offered in Business and Management, Arts and Sciences, Education, College Preparatory
(remedial), Fine Arts, Theology, Computer Technology, Real
Estate, Hobby, and self-improvement courses.   An advertising budget is provided but the courses are expected to pay
for themselves.   Remuneration for faculty is $175 per course
for eight class sessions.   Conferences and institutes offered
during the past year were Institute on Religious Life, Institute on "What's Happening in the Church?", Institute on In-
troduction to Direct Supervision, Operation Access (for admission to college), Operation Second Chance (for on-going
college or readmission).   Clinicians receive up to $50 per
day for conferences and institutes.   Non-credit students are
surveyed for possible interest in various courses.

IX.   GENERAL

Non-credit courses are being offered in converted
buildings in an urban area.   Students discuss academic programs through extensive counseling.   Non-credit students are
surveyed for courses of possible interest.   The Evening and
Saturday Division is receiving adequate support but the faculty does not completely recognize the importance of continuing education.   The Dean is responsible to the Vice-President for Academic Affairs.   Audio-visual instructional aids
are available for evening classes.

X. STUDENT RECRUITMENT

Newspaper publicity is used. Special motivational appeals have been developed for industry in the form of individual letters to Personnel Directors each semester. Letters are also sent to Directors of civic organizations each semester and various clubs on the mailing lists.

University of Toledo
Toledo, Ohio
Division of Adult Continuing Education

Total Enrollment 13, 000   Public Institution
Evening Enrollment 4, 000   Quarter System

I. ADMISSION POLICIES

Deadline for application for admission to evening classes is one month prior to the registration date. Students may not register for credit courses before transcripts are submitted. Students do not register as "special" students. Admission requirements for regular students require submission of high school and/or college transcripts. Beginning students are expected to submit scores on the CEEB. Mail registration is used. Students obtain approved programs for registration and registrar handles registration. Bills are sent out and must be paid before quarter ends. Three-fourths of the students register by mail. There is no retention policy for evening students. No special degree program is offered for adults. The Faculty Admissions Committee in cooperation with the Admissions Office formulates the admission policies for evening students. Day and evening students may enroll in the same classes. No orientation program is scheduled for evening students. Students whose average falls below 2. 0 are automatically placed on probation; below 1. 0 represents suspension for at least two consecutive quarters.

II. TERMINOLOGY

Title of Division: Division of Adult Continuing Education. Defined: The Division of Adult and Continuing Education operates as a part of the year-round service of the University, providing degree work through the various colleges as well as instruction for groups interested in non-credit spe-

cial programs.   Responsibility for coordination of this program rests with the Division but credit courses, whether
offered during the day or evening are the responsibility of
the Dean of the College insofar as content, faculty, academic
regulations and standards are concerned.   Continuing Education is all phases of study - credit, non-credit, conferences,
institutes for remedial retreading, updating, etc.

III.   FEES

There is no fee differential between day and evening
classes.   Refund policy dictates that refunds will be made
at the rate of 100% on the first eight calendar days, 90% on
the fourteenth calendar day, 60% thereafter.   In non-credit
courses there is no refund after the class convenes.

IV.   FACULTY AND FACULTY RECRUITMENT

Nearly all of the faculty members teaching evening
classes are full-time.   No full-time faculty teach exclusively
in the evening.   The academic deans have the final authority
for hiring full and/or part-time faculty.   Department heads
must staff classes.   Regular faculty members receive additional remuneration for teaching non-credit institutes as an
overload.   Salary ranges from $10 to $25 per hour for part-
time faculty.   Faculty are paid $750-$1000 per course for
overloads.

V.   SCHEDULING

The academic deans are responsible for the evening
class schedule and submit to the Registrar.   Three-hour
classes are scheduled two evenings per week.   Day and evening classes are equal in quality.   Part-time evening students are not eligible for the Dean's List.   Twelve to fifteen
students constitute a class.

VI.   ORGANIZATIONAL STRUCTURE

The administrative staff consists of five staff members with a teaching staff of fifteen full-time and twenty-five
part-time faculty members.

VII.   EDUCATIONAL TELEVISION PROGRAMS

Non-credit courses are offered on educational television.   Students receive certificate of completion.   Division

of Adult and Continuing Education supervises the program
which is handled as an in-service/in-plant type program,
using in-plant discussion leaders.   Courses are financed by
participating industry and scheduled at 8 a. m. , 12:30 p. m.
and 3:30 p. m.

VIII.   NON-CREDIT PROGRAMS

Non-credit programs are offered in the areas of Business and Management, Arts and Sciences, and Engineering.
A budget is set aside for the program but courses are expected to pay for themselves.   Remuneration for faculty averages $15. 00/credit hour depending upon area of instruction
and qualifications of instructor.   The Division does not sponsor the conferences, workshops, and institutes without the
cooperation of other colleges.

IX.   GENERAL

Student participation in discussions regarding the academic program is through student government.   Honor students may participate in non-credit courses for enrichment.
Adequate stress and financial support are given to the evening
program.   The Dean is responsible to the President.

X.   STUDENT RECRUITMENT

The Sunday supplement is used for publicity purposes
together with spot announcements on the radio.   The local
educational television station will be used for publicity stories
and announcements throughout the year.   The institution mails
200, 000 pieces of promotional literature each year to business and industry, provides brochures and Sunday supplements to the Chamber of Commerce.

University of Toronto
Toronto, Canada
Division of University Extension

Total Enrollment 24, 772   Public Institution
Evening Enrollment 5, 734   Quarter System

I.   ADMISSION POLICIES

The deadline for application for admission to evening

classes: August 15 (fall and winter) and April 1 for summer
evening classes, May 15 for summer day classes.   Students
may not register for credit courses before transcripts are
submitted.   There are no "special" students.   Evening students must meet the same admission requirements as day
students but are not obligated to take the ACT or CEEB examinations for admission.   An English Language Facility
Test is administered when indicated.   Mail registration is
used--application and registration form is mailed to undergraduate and as requested from new students.   Before beginning classes, a student is required to consult a counselor.
The following degrees are available to full-time students:
B. A. , B. Sc. , and B. Sc. N.   The Committee on Admissions
formulates the admission policies for evening students.   Day
students may enroll in evening classes by permission and as
quota allows in different classes.   Evening students receive
counselling, library orientation, and enroll in a writing laboratory.   Any failure to meet the course requirements incur
the penalty of refused registration in the Faculty.   A student
whose attendance at lectures or labs, or whose work is
deemed by the Council of the Faculty to be unsatisfactory,
may have his registration cancelled at any time by the Council.   A mature student on probation must obtain standing on
the initial attempt in at least three of his first five subjects
in order to have his probationary status removed.   If the
student fails more than two of his first five subjects, he
will not be allowed to re-register in any degree course.   Total number of hours required to complete a three-year degree is fifteen full courses; four-year degree is twenty full
courses.

II.   TERMINOLOGY

Title of Division: The Division of University Extension.   Defined: Divisions are units of the University as are
Colleges, Faculties, schools and centers.   Continuing Education includes any systematic course of study, credit or non-
credit at any level.

III.   FEES

There is no fee differential between day and evening
classes.   A pro-rate refund on each course from which the
student withdraws before February 15.

IV.   FACULTY AND FACULTY RECRUITMENT

Most of the evening faculty members are full-time but some are cross-appointed with other faculties or departments; approximately 90% are full-time.   No full-time faculty members teach exclusively in the evening.   All the teaching staff are appointed or recommended by the appropriate teaching department.   Faculty meetings are held for evening faculty in the late afternoons.   Instead of overloads, the institution prefers cross-appointments so that extension programs are part of the faculty members normal work load.   Recruitment of suitable faculty members is the chief obstacle of cross-appointments.   Salaries are shared 50/50 with A & S generally.

V.   SCHEDULING

The Director is responsible for the evening class schedule.   The schedule is compiled by the estimated need based on experience.   Schedules are announced six years [sic] in advance.   Three-hour classes are scheduled one or two evenings a week.   There is no Dean's List.   There are no minimum class sizes.

VI.   ORGANIZATIONAL STRUCTURE

Eighteen staff members comprise the administrative staff: the Director with responsibility for both credit and non-credit areas, summer and winter programs, executive committee member of those Faculty Councils participating in part-time programme; Assistant Directors with responsibility for credit programmes, planning, liaison with the Faculties, hiring teaching staff upon recommendations of the department chairmen, administration of programme, coordinate independent study, control, evaluate and general administration; Course Coordinator, with responsibility for creating, developing, evaluating and administering non-credit programme, maintains liaison with University Faculties and community organizations and hires staff; Division Administrator with principal responsibility of budgeting for the Division; Secretary of the Division is responsible for certain statutory reports to the Senate, organizing University Certificate Programme; Supervisors of Publicity and Advertising (part-time) organize schedules, preparation and distribution of materials; Counsellors with responsibility for academic counseling and various administrative duties; Administrative Assistants who make physical arrangements for classes, implement regulations, etc.

VII.   EDUCATIONAL TELEVISION PROGRAMS

No programs are offered in educational television.

VIII.   NON-CREDIT PROGRAMS

The Division offers non-credit programs in the area of Business and Management, Arts and Sciences, Education, Engineering and Public Affairs, Transportation and Hygiene. The program is expected to pay for itself.   Professors receive $51. 50 per hour, Associate Professors $36. 00 per hour, Assistant Professors $29. 00 per hour, Lecturers $23. 50 per hour.   Non-faculty instructors recommended by department heads receive $23. 50 per hour for first year of teaching, $25. 00 per hour for second year, etc.   No conferences or institutes are offered by the Division.   Summer sessions are the responsibility of the Division but there are also other summer sessions in other divisions slightly different in nature.

IX.   GENERAL

Students participate in discussions regarding the academic program for student members of the curriculum committee--a relatively new feature of the University.   More stress and financial support could be given to the evening program.   The Director is responsible to the Provost.

X.   STUDENT RECRUITMENT

Newspaper ads and special news stories are used for publicity purposes together with radio and television.   Special motivational appeals are made to business and industry.   According to the Director, "the chief appeal is to the individual" to meet his needs as he sees them.

<u>Towson State College</u>
Towson,   Maryland
Evening and Summer Programs

Total Enrollment 8, 861   Public Institution
Evening Enrollment 4, 226   Semester System

I. ADMISSION POLICIES

There is a deadline for application for admission to Evening classes, namely, September 12, January 23 and June 18. Students may register for credit courses before transcripts are submitted. Non-matriculating or "special" students may take twelve to thirty hours of work for credit. There are no admission requirements for non-matriculating and/or "special" students. Regular student admission requirements are: twelve credits of "C", transcripts for transfer students. Students who are rejected for admission as regular students are automatically accepted. The procedure for registration is: (after receipt of course application) fee assessment and registration materials mailed to student; after receipt of tuition, class admit cards, fee receipt, I. D. sticker, parking permit, etc. are mailed to student. The policies regarding probation and dismissal for degree students are based upon class level--after 64 credits, 2+ QPA; non-degree or "special" students, none and advised of inability to achieve degree after sixty-four credits. The ACT or CEEB examination for adults in the evening division is not required. Other tests are used as a basis for admission and for placement and advisement. The evening degree program for adults is the same as the day degree program. Distribution requirements for undergraduate degrees are: fifteen courses in four groups--Art, Science, Social Science and Physical Education; graduate degrees: Education - eighteen, Psychology plus one field related to teaching area. The special degree program for graduate students is administered by the evening division of the college course scheduling registration and payroll or by the graduate school admission. The total number of hours to complete the degree is 128 for undergraduate and 30 for graduate. Areas of concentration are: Major requirements - 30-60 credits. Main areas are Art, Education, Business Administration, Math, Sociology, Psychology, History and Social Studies. The Standards Committee formulates the admission policies for the evening students. Enrollment totals 281 day students enrolled in evening classes and 180 evening students in the day classes. Advantages of combined classes include scheduling advantages but disadvantages include budgeting and encroachment for Evening College. There is no orientation program for evening students. The Evening Division Advisory Committee reviews policy, recommends to the academic council. Degree candidates are admitted by the Admissions Office with the same requirements as day students.

II. TERMINOLOGY

Title of Division: Evening and Summer Division.
Defined: Division responsible for part-time students which
is self-supporting. In a broader sense, education pursued
by adults whether or not related to a degree program--ar-
bitrarily excludes full-time day students.

III. FEES

Evening classes are on a per-credit basis; however,
evening students may take day classes on evening rates.
The State subsidy support full-time, two semester college
only. The refund policies for evening students who drop
one or more classes but remain in college are: refunded
90% - 50% or nothing on per-course basis depending upon
equivalent time span.

IV. FACULTY AND FACULTY RECRUITMENT

Approximately 85% of the faculty teaching evening
classes are full-time faculty members. The Evening College Dean, with departmental consent, has the final authority
for hiring full and/or part-time faculty members for evening classes. The Director of the Evening Division can reject a faculty member who has been assigned to teach evening classes. There are no regular faculty meetings with
evening faculty. The policies regarding regular faculty
teaching credit or non-credit courses or participating in institutes, etc. as an overload require a limit of one three-credit
course per semester, six credits per term in the summer.
No percentage of the budget is spent on faculty recruiting.
Salary range for part-time faculty is: 15% of base salary
for six credits in the summer session. The compensation
paid for each course is as follows: for three credits by
rank - Instructor, $604, Assistant, $683, Associate, $761,
Professor, $840 (evening semesters). The number of stu-
dents needed to constitute a class is explained "variable
parameters arranged--based on salaries plus costs. " The
instructor's compensation is not reduced when teaching a
class below minimum size, for example: Independent Study
courses--instructor receives tuition, undergraduate $22 per
credit and $30 per credit for graduate.

V. SCHEDULING

The Director is responsible for the evening class

schedule. The procedure for compiling the evening class schedule is negotiation with departments. The Director has the authority to revise or make additions to the evening class schedule. Three-hour classes are scheduled two nights per week. There are research projects completed or in progress at the inner college and community surveys. The comparison of day and evening classes in terms of quality is "theoretically equal." Part-time evening students are eligible for the Dean's List.

VL ORGANIZATIONAL STRUCTURE

The administrative staff consists of four administrators and six staff members. The teaching staff consists of 170 regular day faculty and 85 part-time faculty members. The duties and responsibilities of the Dean include overall program administration; Associate Director is responsible for the finance and general administrative assistance; two other academic coordinators are responsible for student advisement and various other duties listed above. It is estimated that the ideal staff size required to administering an evening credit program would be two staff members for an enrollment of 300; eight staff for 2000; twelve to twenty staff for 5000 not including clerical staff.

VIL EDUCATIONAL TELEVISION PROGRAMS

The Evening College offers credit courses in educational television which count toward a degree. (Students earn residence credit, no distinction, courses taught on TV are not taught as a subject.) The Dean of the Evening College with departmental consent supervises educational television courses. The university policy in handling the program for teachers is the same as on-campus courses. TV station is reimbursed separately. Faculty receive additional remuneration for teaching courses on TV. The Evening College office (for students desiring credit) handles the registration.

VIIL NON-CREDIT PROGRAMS

The College does not offer non-credit courses in "store front" locations for economically deprived populations.

IX. GENERAL

Students do not participate in any discussions regarding the academic program except through questionnaires.

The Evening College offers graduate programs for part-time
students which are administered by the Evening College.
The entire Graduate Program is administered by the Evening
College except for admissions and faculty certifications.	In
general, the Evening College is not receiving adequate sup-
port in comparison with the day program.	The Administra-
tion partially recognizes the need and the importance of adult
education programs.	The Director of the Evening College is
responsible to the Dean of the College.	The audio-visual
aids and other technical instructional aids that are used in
the Evening College are the Services of Institutional A. V.
organization plus academic courses in the field.

## X.	STUDENT RECRUITMENT

Students for educational television courses are contacted by the College departments who are involved in the
courses.

Trenton State College
Trenton, New Jersey
Division of Field Service

Total Enrollment 9, 500					Public Institution
Evening Enrollment 3, 750					Semester System
	(350 full-time; 3, 400 part-time)

## I.	ADMISSION POLICIES

There is no deadline for application for admission to
evening classes.	A student may register for credit courses
before transcripts are submitted.	"Special" students may
register for credit courses and may take an unlimited num-
ber of courses.	Admission requirement for all students in-
cludes high school graduation.	ACT or CEEB scores are
not required.	Students may register for undergraduate
courses by mail.	The students send in registration card and
check.	In turn, the school sends back the class admit cards
and bursar's receipt.	Retention policies: 1. 6 after 30 hours
attempted, 1. 8 after 60 hours attempted, and 2. 0 after 90
hours attempted.	The Dean of Instruction formulates the ad-
mission policies in cooperation with the evening director.
Day students rarely enroll in the same classes with evening
students.	No orientation program is held for evening stu-
dents.	An "Open Admission Policy" is used.	All degree

and non-degree students are placed on a "warning" status when their cumulative average falls below 2.0 (C). There is no probation status as such for students in the division. Completion of a degree requires 124 hours. The Division of Continuing Education formulates the admission policies for the evening undergraduate students.

II. TERMINOLOGY

Title of Division: Division of Field Services. Defined: The title in no way reflects the function of the division and a title change is forthcoming. Definition of Continuing Education: That work which is undertaken during adult life and may include credit work, non-credit work and study toward an undergraduate or graduate degree.

III. FEES

Full-time day students pay a flat tuition of $175 per term. Evening undergraduates pay $20 per credit; graduates $25. Refund policies: 100% before classes begin, 60% during first third of term; 30% between first third and first half of term, nothing after the first half of the semester.

IV. FACULTY AND FACULTY RECRUITMENT

Approximately 35% of the faculty for undergraduate courses and 90% of the faculty for graduate courses are full-time faculty members teaching during the evening. No full-time faculty members teach exclusively in the evening. All full-time and part-time faculty members are hired upon the recommendation of department chairmen to the Dean of Instruction. Faculty meetings are held for evening faculty the beginning of each term. Full-time faculty members are permitted to teach six credit hours overload during an academic year.

V. SCHEDULING

The Director of Field Services is responsible for the evening class schedule. The graduate office gives Field Services the graduate offerings to schedule; the Field Services office determines the undergraduate courses to be offered. Three-hour classes are scheduled one evening a week. Day classes are somewhat better in quality than evening classes due to more full-time faculty members. Part-time evening students are not eligible for the Dean's List.

VI. ORGANIZATIONAL STRUCTURE

The administrative staff consists of seven staff members with five secretaries and a teaching staff of 145 full-time and 207 part-time faculty members. The Board of Higher Education passes on degrees and on courses. The Director is responsible for the administration of the Division and the summer program. The Assistant Directors, four in number, are responsible for personnel planning, recruiting, catalog materials, registration, counseling, etc. The Counselors assist the Assistant Directors.

VII. EDUCATIONAL TELEVISION PROGRAMS

The Division of Field Services does not sponsor educational television courses.

VIII. NON-CREDIT PROGRAMS

The Division of Field Services does not sponsor any non-credit programs.

IX. GENERAL

The Division is responsible for the summer session. Most evening programs in this area are fund raisers for the day school program. Students have no opportunity to participate in any discussion regarding academic programs. More stress and financial support could be given to the evening program--more emphasis is placed on the day program. The Director of Field Services is responsible to the Dean of Instruction.

X. STUDENT RECRUITMENT

The institution places advertisements in three local newspapers periodically to publicize special programs.

Tulane University
New Orleans, Louisiana
University College

Total Enrollment 10, 456   Private Institution
Evening Enrollment 2, 002   Semester System

I. ADMISSION POLICIES

The deadline for application for admission is ten days prior to registration. However, late applicants are accepted. Students may register for credit courses before transcripts are submitted on a provisional basis. Students may not register for credit courses as non-matriculating or special students. Secondary school graduates, students with some college background, and mature students are admissible to credit courses upon presentation of a satisfactory secondary or college transcript and satisfactory scores on the SCAT, ACT or CEEB college entrance examinations. Students who are rejected for admission as regular students are not usually advised to take evening classes but sometimes a part-time load is recommended. No mail registration is used; however, the University now has a pre-billing service. Regarding probation and suspension, freshman students must pass four units with a QPA of 1. 2, after eight units a student must have a 1. 6 QPA or be placed on probation. Probation must be removed by the end of two additional units of work. No special evening degree program is available for adults. The Administrative Faculty formulates the admission policies for evening students. Students may cross-register for day/evening classes with the approval of their advisor. One disadvantage - the diversity of backgrounds of the students. No orientation program is held for evening students. There is an Evening Division Advisory Committee whose responsibility it is to consider the academic performance of the students.

II. TERMINOLOGY

Title of Division: University College. Defined: University College derives its name from the fact that it offers courses selected from the various fields of the arts, sciences, and business administration as represented in various colleges and schools of the University. Continuing Education defined: Education beyond the terminal degree of education of the student.

III. FEES

The fee differential between day and evening students is as follows: $260 per unit per semester during the day; $105 per unit per semester for evening and $1, 050 for full-time enrollment - day or night. Justification is that full-time students are charged on a package basis - one day course is determined proportionately. Refund policies: first

week is full refund, second week is one-half through one-
fourth to fourth week.

IV.   FACULTY AND FACULTY RECRUITMENT

The University has no official policy regarding the
percentage of faculty members teaching evening classes who
are full-time.   However, approximately 44% of the evening
faculty are full-time faculty members.   The Dean of University College has the final authority for hiring full/part-time
faculty members for evening classes.   No full-time faculty
members teach exclusively in the evening.   The Department
Heads are consulted regarding faculty appointments.   Regular
faculty meetings are held with evening faculty once each semester.   No part of the budget is spent for recruitment.
The salary for part-time faculty members ranges from $500
to $725 per course; for overloads from $700 to $975 per
course.

V.   SCHEDULING

The Dean of University College has the responsibility
for scheduling evening classes.   The departments set up the
schedule with instructors and then submit it to the Dean who
may revise the schedule or make additions to the schedule
if the need arises.   Three-hour classes are taught one or
two nights per week depending upon the course.   Some
courses, such as Computer Systems, can be taught more
efficiently for a double period.   Classes are also taught on
Saturday mornings for a double period.   Day and evening
classes are equal in quality.   A Dean's List is prepared for
University College students - four units are required with a
grade point average of 3. 4.   The minimum class size is ten
students; the instructor's compensation is not reduced if the
class does not reach the minimum size.

VI.   ORGANIZATIONAL STRUCTURE

The University College has an administrative staff of
nine members with a teaching staff of seventy full-time and
94 part-time faculty members.   University College is headed
by a Dean with the following additional staff members: Assistant Dean who is responsible for the non-credit program,
a Director of Conferences and Institutes, and two assistants -
one responsible for office management and student counseling,
and one responsible for the Bulletin, schedule and faculty appointments.   Three secretaries and a Record Secretary are

listed with the administrative staff.

VII. EDUCATIONAL TELEVISION PROGRAMS

The University College does not sponsor educational television programs.

VIII. NON-CREDIT PROGRAMS

The University College offers non-credit courses in Business and Management and Arts and Sciences.   A budget is provided for the program but the courses are expected to pay for themselves.   Faculty members receive $30 to $50 per class.   The remuneration depends upon the qualifications of the instructor, the area of instruction and the class size. The College does sponsor conferences and institutes such as the ASHRAE, Symposium on Air Conditioning, IAHU-DITC Disability Insurance Research Seminar, American Institute of Real Estate Appraisers and the National Association of Real Estate Brokers.   Clinicians for conferences are paid at the rate of $100 per day or $500 per week.   Some conferences and institutes are sponsored with other colleges.   The University College is not responsible for the summer school program.

IX. GENERAL

No report was made in the survey as to student participation in discussions regarding the academic program. No graduate programs are offered for part-time students which are administered by the University College.   There is an active chapter of Alpha Sigma Lambda on campus.

X. STUDENT RECRUITMENT

Newspaper, radio and television programs are used for publicity.

Union College
Schenectady, New York
Special Programs

Total Enrollment 1, 800   Private Institution
Evening Enrollment 1, 500   Quarter System

I.   ADMISSION POLICIES

There is no deadline for application for admission to evening classes.   A student may register for credit courses before transcripts are submitted.   Non-matriculating/special students may take 10 hours for credit.   Admission requirements for non-matriculating students are a high school diploma, satisfactory prerequisites for the courses; for regular students, a high school diploma and completion of 8-10 credits as special student satisfactorily.   Students who are rejected for admission as regular students are not advised to apply as evening students.   Mail packets are sent on request if registration is desired in this manner.   There is no probation status; a student is advised that he is not proceeding toward a degree and asked not to re-register; this applies to regular and non-degree students.   ACT or CEEB examination for adults is not required.   There is no special degree program for adults in the evening session.   There were 60 full-time, 1450 part-time, 550 undergraduates and 900 graduate degree students enrolled in the college during the Fall quarter.   No plans are being made to offer a special degree program for adults in the near future.   The Director of the Special Programs formulates the admission policies for all categories of students.   Enrollment in both day and evening classes is open to any student.   The evening students are more mature and stable; the day students are better prepared academically, so it is a good mixture.   There is no orientation program and no Evening Division Advisory Committee.

II.   TERMINOLOGY

Title of division: Special Programs.   Continuing Education represents the 10% of a person's time needed to keep up personally, socially and professionally with the world today.

III.   FEES

The tuition for the day program is $270 per course; for the evening program, $117 per course.   Justification is incremental accounting.   Refund policies are: first week 80%, second week 60%, no refunds thereafter.

IV.   FACULTY AND FACULTY RECRUITMENT

There is no policy regarding the percentage of faculty

for evening classes that are full-time faculty members.   Approximately 60% are full-time in the applied fields, 90% in all others.   The department chairmen have final authority for hiring full and/or part-time faculty members for evening classes.   With great difficulty, the director can reject a faculty member who has been assigned to teach evening classes. The director may engage an instructor if the department head refuses to do so.   No full-time faculty members are employed to teach exclusively in the evening.   Regular faculty meetings are not held.   The college approves overloads, but for graduate faculty, no overloads are permitted.   None of the budget is spent for recruitment of faculty, but much publicity is used.   The salary range for part-time faculty is $250 per credit for Union College; $300-$400 for graduate faculty.   The same is paid for overloads.

V.   SCHEDULING

The Director is responsible for the evening class schedule which is compiled in cooperation with the department chairmen.   The Director has the authority to revise / make additions to the class schedule.   Three-hour classes are scheduled both one night and two nights, depending on material.   There are presently no research projects.   Comparison of day and evening classes in terms of quality is difficult to make because of the differences in students and their goals and the difference in methods.   Part-time evening students are eligible for the Dean's List if they have a "B" average.   Normally ten students are required to enroll to constitute a class.   An instructor's compensation is not reduced when he teaches a class below minimum size.

VI.   ORGANIZATIONAL STRUCTURE

The administrative staff consists of eight staff members and 60 part-time teaching staff.   The Director administers the duties of the registrar, advisors, development, finances, advertising, publications, scheduling, faculty relations, institutes, public relations, community service.   For an enrollment of 1500 in credit programs three staff members and seven secretaries are required.

VII.   EDUCATIONAL TELEVISION PROGRAMS

Credit courses are offered in Educational Television, through which students may earn resident credit, and credit toward a degree.   The Director supervises these courses.

There is no policy for employing teachers; both full-time and part-time faculty are used. Faculty members do not receive additional remuneration for teaching educational television courses, but have a reduced teaching load for regular on-campus classes, course for course. The Special Programs handles registration for the TV courses, just as regular registration. Both undergraduate and graduate courses are offered in these courses, which are financed by Foundation Grants. These courses are scheduled for evening times.

VIII. NON-CREDIT PROGRAMS

Non-credit courses are offered in the areas of business and management and engineering. There is no budget and the program is expected to pay for itself. The remuneration varies for teaching, and depends upon the area of instruction. Seven conferences and institutes are sponsored. Clinicians receive up to $250 per day. The Special Programs sponsors the conferences, and is also responsible for the Summer session.

IX. GENERAL

No courses are offered in off-campus locations for economically deprived populations. Students do not participate in discussions regarding the academic program. The entire graduate program of 900 students, 10 masters and two doctors degrees are administered by the Evening Division. The evening division does not receive adequate support, nor does the administration recognize the need and importance of adult education programs. The director is responsible to the President. All kinds of audio-visual and technical instructional aids are used. There is no chapter of Alpha Sigma Lambda.

X. STUDENT RECRUITMENT

This is done through newspaper and radio publicity as well as through contact with industries.

Upsala College
East Orange, New Jersey
Division of General Studies

Total Enrollment 1, 500   Private, Church-related
Evening Enrollment 450-500   Semester System

I. ADMISSION POLICIES

The deadlines for application for admission to evening classes are August 15, January 15, and June 1. A student may register for credit courses before transcripts are submitted. Non-matriculating or special students may take an unlimited amount of work for credit. The admission requirements for non-matriculating or special students are a high school diploma or GED plus course pre-requisites; for regular students the SAT score is also required. Students who are rejected as regular students are advised to apply for evening classes and are automatically accepted most of the time. Students may register for credit courses by mail by completing registration form indicating course desired and returning with check to cover tuition and fees. Class cards are then mailed to the student. The policies regarding probation and suspension require degree students to maintain an average of 1. 75 or over; non-degree or special students must maintain the same average as a degree student but they are dismissed if three courses are failed consecutively. No ACT or CEEB or other test scores are required for adults in the evening division. The evening degree program for adults is different from the day program. The undergraduate programs offered in the evening include the B. A. and B. S. degrees. Fall enrollment was 23 full-time and 427 part-time students. General requirements for the undergraduate degree are: English, one semester, Natural Sciences, two semesters, Social Sciences, three semester hours, Humanities, three semester and twelve courses in the area of concentration. Total number of hours required to complete the degree is 128 which includes 32 four-hour courses. The areas of concentration include: 12 courses in the area; eight above 100 level of which four are at the 300 level or more. Four of the eight must be in a single academic department. The Faculty Council formulates the admission policies for all evening students. Day students are discouraged from taking evening study. It is presumed that the evening students usually raise the level of the class because of life experiences. There is no orientation program for evening students. The Institution believes admission policies are

flexible yet individual; that the general intent is to encourage
continuing education in credit and non-credit areas.

II. TERMINOLOGY

Title of Division: Division of General Studies. Defined: Academic activities not covered by the regular day
college. Continuing Education defined: Any process by
which persons try to improve their skills through credit or
non-credit courses, i. e. , continued pursuit of knowledge.

III. FEES

There is a fee differential between day and evening
classes. The part-time evening tuition is about 83% of the
part-time day tuition. The justification for this is financial.
The refund policy for evening drops: one or more classes
dropped but remaining in school allows from 80% to 0% refund depending upon the time class is dropped.

IV.   FACULTY AND FACULTY RECRUITMENT

There is no policy regarding the percentage of faculty
for evening classes that are full-time faculty members; approximately 1. 08% are full-time. The department chairmen
and the Dean of the College have final authority for hiring
full/part-time faculty members for evening classes. No
full-time faculty members teach exclusively in the evening.
No regular faculty meetings are held with the evening faculty.
Regular faculty members teaching credit and non-credit
courses or participating in conferences etc. as an overload
are limited to one course per session in the evening and two
courses in the summer session. There is an indeterminate
percentage of the budget spent on the recruiting - since departments do their own recruiting. The salary range for
part-time faculty is $600 to $800 per course per semester.
The same salary is paid the faculty for overloads, although
full-time faculty are permitted to carry no more than one
course per semester as an overload. If the faculty is paid
by the course, their compensation for each course depends
upon number of contact hours per week. All classes with
fewer than ten registrants are reviewed but there is no specified number of students required to constitute a class. Compensation reduction is not a normal practice, however, occasionally when the faculty member prefers a course that
otherwise should or would be cancelled he receives virtually
the entire tuition income from the course. This is done only

as a service to the faculty member and reduces the inconvenience that would arise from no remuneration for an overload.

V. SCHEDULING

The Director is responsible for the evening class schedule. The procedure for compiling the schedule is that department chairmen submit proposed offerings which are edited by the Director who eliminates conflicts and approves final schedule to be published. The Director has the authority to revise as necessary. Three-hour classes are scheduled two nights per week. Some classes lend themselves to one night per week but others do not. There are no research projects in progress at present. The day and evening classes compare favorably. Part-time evening students are not eligible for the Dean's List but the possibility is being considered.

VI. ORGANIZATIONAL STRUCTURE

The size of the administrative staff is three with a teaching staff of 64 part-time faculty members. The Dean is responsible for the academic program for both day and evening; the Assistant Dean is responsible for academic counseling and the Director is responsible for the evening and summer programs.

VII. EDUCATIONAL TELEVISION PROGRAMS

No courses are offered on educational television.

VIII. NON-CREDIT PROGRAMS

The Evening Division offers non-credit courses in Business and Management and Arts and Sciences. There is a budget although the courses are expected to pay for themselves. The remuneration for faculty is $400-$500 per course for each class session. The rate depends upon the qualifications of the instructor. The Evening Division does sponsor conferences and institutes. The past year included such conferences as Institute for Insurance Education. Both qualified faculty members and visiting lecturers are used. The Evening Division is responsible for the summer session.

IX. GENERAL

The extent to which students at the institution participate in any discussion regarding academic programs is limited to suggestions regarding the offerings.   Internship programs combining class study with field work is one of the
innovative practices used at the institution.   It is felt that
the evening division is not receiving adequate support in
comparison with the day program.   The administration does
recognize the need and the importance of adult education.
The Director is responsible to the Dean of the College.   The
usual audio-visual aids are available.

X. STUDENT RECRUITMENT

Newspaper publicity and radio are used for student
recruitment.

Utah State University
Logan, Utah
University Extension

Total Enrollment 9, 000   Public Institution (closely
Evening Enrollment 500   related to church)
                                            Quarter System

I. ADMISSION POLICIES

There is no deadline for admission applications.   A
student may register for credit courses before transcripts
are submitted.   Non-matriculating students (or special students) may take a fifteen hour (quarter hour) limit but it is
hoped that the fifteen hour limitation can be increased.   Satisfactory evidence of high school completion is the only admission requirement.   Students who are rejected as regular
students are not advised to apply as evening students.   No
mail registration is used.   A 2. 0 average is required - probation and suspension policies are university-wide.   No ACT
or CEEB scores are required for adults.   Degree candidates
must apply for admission and this process does include ACT.
Fall quarter enrollment totalled forty-four full-time and 898
part-time (390 undergraduates and 552 graduates).   A special
degree program for adults is being considered.   The Provost-Continuing Education along with the administration and
the Admissions Committee is responsible for the admission

policies. An unlimited enrollment of day/evening students is encouraged due to the small enrollment in some classes and so that students can find a better selection of courses. There is no orientation for evening students and no evening advisory committee. A study is being made on admission standards for minority groups holding positions in Head Start, WIN, CAP, etc.

II. TERMINOLOGY

Title of Division: University Extension. Defined: A combined unit, co-op and continuing education, offered by a land grant school is dominated by co-op extension.

III. FEES

Self-support is demanded for evening classes. Refund policies on a graduated basis are three-fourths of fee after first class, one-half after three classes, etc.

IV. FACULTY AND FACULTY RECRUITMENT

Approximately 90% of the faculty is full-time. Final authority for hiring faculty members lies with the related department. The Director does have authority to reject a faculty member assigned to teach evening classes. Full-time faculty are employed to teach exclusively in the evenings. These faculty are responsible to the Extension Division and to the English Department. No faculty meetings are conducted for evening faculty. Regular faculty members are allowed to teach a maximum of one class per quarter over and above the normal routine. Less teaching is encouraged. Two percent of the budget is spent on faculty recruiting. Salary for part-time faculty ranges from $140 to $180/qtr. hr. with distance of travel being a factor.

V. SCHEDULING

The Director is responsible for scheduling evening classes with the cooperation of the departments. Needs are assessed and demands are considered followed by an appeal to the departments for qualified professors to teach. Sometimes adjunct professors are recruited to assist. The Director has the authority to revise the class schedule. A Maryland study supports scheduling three-hour classes on one night but for all purposes, two nights are preferred. A study has just been completed entitled USU Educational Services on

the Uintah and Ouray Indian Reservations.   This was a historical study.   Day/evening classes are equally qualified.
Part-time students are not eligible for the Dean's List.   Ten
students are required to constitute a class.   There is no reduction in instructor compensation if the class is taught with
less than the minimum number of students.

VI. ORGANIZATIONAL STRUCTURE

The administrative staff consists of 113 staff members and the teaching staff consists of one full-time teacher
and 100 part-time teachers.   The Vice-President is designated as Director of Cooperative Extension and is responsible
for the total program.   Assistant Directors, totalling eleven,
are responsible for four of the geographical areas in Utah.
The Director of Non-Credit Programs is responsible for on-off campus programs, conferences, and institutes.   The ideal
staff size depends upon local conditions but seemingly three
staff members for every 5,000 students would be agreeable.

VII. EDUCATIONAL TELEVISION PROGRAMS

Educational television programs are offered.   Students
earn residence credit and can work toward a degree.   The
new IMLS (Instructional Media and Library Sciences) Department and the related academic department are responsible for
supervising the program.   Full-time faculty are used and additional remuneration is given.   The Extension Class Division
handles registration for the educational television courses.
Mail registration is used along with personal registration.
The educational TV courses are financed through registration
fees and a small grant.   Programs are scheduled at 7:00
p. m. on closed circuit.   The program is very limited as
resources are not adequate.

VIII. NON-CREDIT PROGRAMS

Non-credit programs are offered in Business Management, Arts and Sciences, Education and Engineering.   There
is a budget but the programs are expected to pay for themselves.   Proximity to population is a serious problem.   The
remuneration for full or part-time faculty teaching non-credit
classes is $120 per course for 10 one-hour class sessions.
Conferences and institutes are sponsored by the Division involving Cooperative Extension subject matter - youth programs for the L. D. S. church.   Clinicians are paid at a rate
of $25-$50 per day.   All conferences sponsored by the Divi-

sion are offered in cooperation with the departments. The Division is not responsible for the summer session.

IX. GENERAL

Students are invited to comment. Courses are offered in response to requests. Tele-lectures are used for off-campus courses. Quality faculty are flown to two off-campus centers. Selected graduate courses are offered with residence requirements for graduate students. There is not adequate support given to the evening division. The Director is responsible to the Vice-President for Extension. The tele-lecture, ETV, two way conference phones and films are used through the Audio-visual Area. A tele-writer is soon to be added.

X. STUDENT RECRUITMENT

Advertising is carried by newspaper, radio spot announcements plus public service, TV special features and spot announcements periodically. Invitations are sent to (closely allied programs) civic organizations.

University of Utah
Salt Lake City, Utah
Division of Continuing Education
Department of Evening Classes

Total Enrollment 24, 000   Public Institution
Evening Enrollment 5, 000-6, 000   Quarter System

I. ADMISSION POLICIES

There is no deadline for application for admission to evening classes. A student may register for credit courses before transcripts are submitted. Non-matriculating students may take 45 hours of work for credit. Admission requirements for both regular and non-matriculating students: must be 21 years of age, a high school graduate and not have been dismissed from another university. Students who apply for day school and are rejected are advised to apply as evening students if they are recommended by the Admissions Office. Mail registration is employed. The application is included in the quarterly class schedule which is mailed to all students. Students turn this in and the necessary forms are

sent to them. First quarter freshmen must achieve a GPA
of 1. 5, second and third quarters-1. 75, fourth and subsequent
quarters-2. 0. ACT and CEEB examinations are not required
for adults but other tests are used for placement. The Faculty Senate formulates the admission policies for the evening
students of all categories. Day students may enroll in the
evening classes. The advantages lie mostly for the day student. There is no orientation program. The Evening Division Advisory Committee acts in an advisory capacity only.

II. TERMINOLOGY

Title of division: Division of Continuing Education,
Department of Evening Classes. Definition: The term "Evening Classes" connotates classes set up primarily for the
adult evening student but are available to the day student as
his schedule demands. Continuing Education defined: The
educational experience beyond that normally received by the
participant, regardless of age.

III. FEES

There is very little fee differential between day and
evening classes. A full load is the same. The justification
for a smaller fee is fewer services being offered. 75% will
be refunded if a withdrawal form is presented to the Division
of Continuing Education before the 1st class of the second
week and after the 1st class has been held; 50% will be refunded if a withdrawal form is presented after the 1st class
of the second week but before the 1st class of the third
week; 25% will be refunded if form is presented after the 1st
class of the third week, but before the 1st class of the 4th
week. No refund will be made after the 1st class of the
4th week has been held.

IV. FACULTY AND FACULTY RECRUITMENT

Approximately 92% of evening faculty are full-time.
The department chairmen have the final authority for hiring
full and/or part-time faculty members. The director may,
under certain conditions, reject a faculty member who has
been assigned to teach. Very few full-time faculty members
are employed who teach exclusively in the evenings. They
are responsible to the director of the evening division. The
director cannot engage an instructor without the consent of
the department head if he refuses to staff the classes. Regular faculty meetings are not held. Faculty members may

teach as many institutes, etc. as they desire so long as they
do not surpass the overload policy of the University, i. e. ,
15 credit hours per quarter.   2 1/2 percent of the budget is
spent for recruitment.   Salary range for part-time faculty is
$120-$239 per credit hour.   Overload salary range is: 1/63
times their annual salary per credit hour, maximum $239
per credit hour.

V. SCHEDULING

The Director is responsible for the evening class
schedule, which is compiled with the cooperation of the department heads.   The Director has the authority to revise
the schedule.   Three hour classes are scheduled one night
per week, which is preferable.   There is no research in
progress.   Day and evening classes compare equally in terms
of quality.   The University of Utah does not have a Dean's
List.   The number of students registering to constitute a
class varies, according to the demands of the graduate and
undergraduate programs.   The instructor's compensation is
not reduced when he teaches a class below the minimum size.

VI. ORGANIZATIONAL STRUCTURE

The administrative staff consists of 17 staff members
(9 part-time); six full-time and 494 part-time teaching staff.
The Division of Continuing Education falls under the administrative structure of the University.   The following are positions held by the staff: Dean, Associate Dean, Director of
Adult Education, Director of Non-Credit Programs, Director
of Conferences and Institutes, Registrar (evening), Business
Manager and other positions.   For an enrollment of 5, 000
for credit program 17 full and 9 part-time staff members
are required.

VII. EDUCATIONAL TELEVISION PROGRAMS

Both credit and non-credit educational television programs are offered; students may earn residence credit for
credit courses and the work will count toward a degree.   The
Director of Evening Classes supervises these courses.   Faculty members are paid the same as teaching an on-campus
class.   Both full-time and part-time faculty members are
used, and they are paid additional remuneration for the educational television courses, which may be done either by
mail or in person.   Graduate and undergraduate courses are
offered, which are self-financed from the income.   These

courses are scheduled Monday through Thursday, 4:10 to
5:10 p. m.

VIII.   NON-CREDIT PROGRAMS

Non-credit courses are offered in the areas of Business and Management, Engineering, Education and in Remedial Areas.   This program is expected to pay for itself.
Faculty receive the same remuneration as they do for credit
courses.   The Division of Continuing Education sponsors conferences and institutes; the Department of Evening Classes
does not.   Conferences are sponsored both by the evening
division and in cooperation with another college.   The Division of Continuing Education is not responsible for the Summer session.

IX.   GENERAL

Off-campus locations are used for course offerings
for the economically deprived.   Students do not participate
in discussions regarding academic programs.   Graduate programs in Business, Engineering and Education are offered
for part-time students.   The evening program does not receive the support it should in comparison with the day program.   The Dean is responsible to the Dean of the Division
of Continuing Education.   All the usual types of media are
available to students.   There is no chapter of Alpha Sigma
Lambda.

X.   STUDENT RECRUITMENT

Recruitment is carried out through newspaper, radio
and television publicity.   Special publicity is aimed at industry and organizations.

Utica College
Syracuse University
Utica, New York
Continuing Education

Total Enrollment 1, 750   Private Institution
Evening Enrollment 1, 400   Semester System

I. ADMISSION POLICIES

The deadline for application for admission applies to regular students and is June 1 and January 5.   There is no deadline for special or non-degree students.   Students may register for credit courses prior to submission of transcripts and may take up to ninety hours for credit as non-matriculating or special students.   Students must be high school graduates or the equivalent.   Students who are rejected as regular students are advised to enroll as evening students and are automatically accepted on a non-matriculated basis. Registration packets are mailed to all students registered the preceding term.   Mail registration is held for two weeks and starts two or three weeks prior to in-person registration.   Probation is on a sliding scale with 1.67 for freshmen and 1.97 for seniors as a standard.   If the student is under twenty-five years of age, the ACT and/or CEEB examination is required and used as a basis for admission.   A proposal draft has been submitted for a flexible degree program for adults but as yet no special degree for adults is offered. The Continuing Education office and the Admissions Office formulate the admission policies.   Day students are allowed to register for evening classes up to 10% of the evening registration.   There are mixed feelings regarding the day/evening combination--however, an advantage seems to be that of exposing both to differing viewpoints and permitting certain courses to be offered which would otherwise have too low of an enrollment.   There is no orientation program for evening students.

II. TERMINOLOGY

Title of Division: Division of Continuing Education. Defined: "Although most people in the College consider this to be just an evening program, we have tried to view it in a broader sense as any type of program (credit or non-credit) offered to adults on a part-time basis.   We see Continuing Education encompassing both courses, seminars, institutes, etc. offered either in the day or in the evening.   We try to think of it in the sense of a program which attempts to provide and encourage life long learning for a wide variety of people and achieved through a variety of means. "

III. FEES

Evening students taking fewer than ten credit hours pay $41.50 per credit hour.   Those taking more than ten and

day students pay $1, 040.   Lesser evening rates because of
fewer services and to encourage enrollment--the ten or more
hours is applied to discourage students from switching from
day to evening status.   Refunds are based upon 80% within
the first week, 60% the second week and no refund after the
fifth week.

IV.   FACULTY AND FACULTY RECRUITMENT

There is no policy regarding the percentage of regular faculty who teach evening classes.   However, regular
faculty are encouraged to teach in the evening as much as
possible.   Approximately 50% of the faculty are full-time.
Final authority for hiring full and/or part-time faculty for
evening classes lies with the area--sometimes the Continuing
Education Office and sometimes with the department that is
offering the course.   The Director can reject a faculty member who has been assigned to teach evening classes and has
used this authority in the past.   No full-time faculty is employed to teach exclusively in the evening but this has not
always been the case--in the past faculty members have
been employed to teach exclusively on a very limited scale.
There are no faculty meetings held for evening faculty.   Because of local conditions, regular faculty are encouraged to
teach credit, non-credit, etc. as an overload.   Salary ranges
from $570 to $780 for three-hour credit courses for part-
time faculty.   Overloads range from $225 per credit hour
for instructors to $300 per credit hour for full professors.

V.   SCHEDULING

The Director is responsible for the evening class
schedule in cooperation with the division chairmen.   Three-
hour classes are scheduled one and two nights per week--
core courses generally meet two evenings per week and other
courses meet once.   In a survey made in the Fall of 1970,
71% of the students favored one night classes.   Within the
last couple of years a very interesting "turnabout" has taken
place.   Traditionally students, faculty, etc. felt that the evening program was inferior to the day program.   Now the
regular faculty feels the evening students are much better
than the day students and they enjoy teaching in the evening.
In short, it would appear that the evening students today seem
to fit the image of what a college student should be.   Part-
time evening students are eligible for the new Dean's List
which was established in the Fall 1970 for evening students.
Students must carry six hours with a 3. 2 average.   Normally

ten students constitute a class but classes have run with less due to special circumstances.

VI.   ORGANIZATIONAL STRUCTURE

Three staff members make up the administrative staff--the Director with overall responsibility, Assistant Director with responsibility for all phases of credit programs, and a counselor with responsibility for all activities relating directly to students.   The teaching staff consists of 55 full-time and 55 part-time faculty members (varying from term to term).

VII.   EDUCATIONAL TELEVISION PROGRAMS

No educational television programs are offered.

VIII.   NON-CREDIT PROGRAMS

Non-credit programs are offered in the areas of Business and Management, Engineering, Arts and Sciences, and Reading Programs for Children and College Preparatory Program.   No budget is set up for non-credit programs--they are expected to pay for themselves.   The Division is responsible for the summer session.   Remuneration to faculty depends upon the nature of the overall course: no blanket policy is established.

IX.   GENERAL

Day students are represented on the College Council and all committees; evening students do not participate in discussions regarding the academic program.   Innovative practices are being seriously explored for the first time. About sixty graduate education courses and twenty graduate courses in other areas are offered in cooperation with Syracuse University.   Graduate courses are for residence credit. The Director is responsible to the President.   Audio-visual equipment is available to evening classes.   Traditionally, the evening program has been thought of as an "endowment" for the college but the college has failed to provide the necessary support for the program.   The President is sympathetic to the evening program and there is general concern because of the threat of competition from new state universities.

X.   STUDENT RECRUITMENT

Newspaper, radio, television are all used for student recruitment.

Virginia Commonwealth University
Richmond, Virginia
The Evening College

Total Enrollment 10, 600   Public Institution
Evening Enrollment 4, 500   Semester System
(4, 500 day combination)

I.   ADMISSION POLICIES

Students may make application for admission to evening classes through late registration during the first week
of classes.   A student may register for credit classes before transcripts are submitted.   "Special" students may take
a maximum of twenty hours of credit before matriculating.
Admission requirements for "special" students include high
school graduation and/or good standing.   This statement is
certified by the former institution.   Admission requirements
for regular students includes being accepted as a degree-
seeking student after matriculation through the Admissions
Office and acceptance by the specific school involved.   Mail
registration is used during the month of August for the fall
semester and from December through January for the spring
semester and the month of May for summer school.   ACT or
CEEB scores are required for admission.   The Dean of the
various colleges formulates the admission policies for the
evening students.   Day and evening students may enroll in
the same classes.   No orientation program is held for evening students.   Policies regarding probation and suspension
are the same as day school.   This applies to non-degree or
"special" students also.   No different evening degree program
is offered.   No special degree is offered for adults.   Evening College at VCU is an integral part of the total university.   Same degrees are available for adults via admissions.
No plans are being made to offer a special degree program
for adults in the near future.   Admission policies are the
same for all categories of students.

II. TERMINOLOGY

Title of Division: The Evening College and the Summer School, with the Director carrying titles of Director of each and the Dean of Continuing Education. Defined: a separate administration operating much as a second shift would do in industry. Continuing Education defined: Study by adults, either credit or non-credit, in the late afternoon, the evening and on Saturday mornings.

III. FEES

Day and evening students pay the same tuition, but Evening College students do not pay activity fees. Refund policies: prior to beginning of classes - 100%; within two weeks (due to illness) 50%; no refunds after second week.

IV. FACULTY AND FACULTY RECRUITMENT

Approximately 45% of the faculty teaching classes in the evening are full-time faculty members but none teach exclusively in the evening. The Deans of the various colleges have the authority to hire full or part-time faculty members. Written contracts for adjunct faculty teaching in the Evening College are prepared and signed by the Director. Faculty meetings are held at the beginning of each semester. Faculty members teach evening classes as part of their regular load but occasionally they are paid for teaching non-credit courses. Salary range for faculty: full-time $705-3 credit course per semester; $785 for 2 nights a week meeting. Part-time, $235 per credit for undergraduate study meeting one night per week; $60 extra for pure graduate instruction; $80 extra for three credit course meeting twice a week. No payment for overloads. There are 180 faculty members teaching one or more Evening College courses as a part of their regular day time load; 235 adjunct faculty teach at the above-mentioned rates. Less than 5% of the budget is spent for recruitment.

V. SCHEDULING

The Director of the Evening College has the responsibility for scheduling evening classes. The Dean originates the first suggested schedule for the catalog in cooperation with the department heads. Most three-hour classes meet one evening per week with a few classes meeting two evenings. Day and evening classes are equal in terms of qual-

ity.   Part-time students (evening) are eligible for the Dean's
List on the same basis as day students.   For a class to be
taught the general number of enrollees are: five for graduate; eight for junior-senior level; twelve for freshman-soph-
omore--there is flexibility in this, however.

VI.   ORGANIZATIONAL STRUCTURE

The size of the administrative staff in the evening
division is fifteen staff members with heavy use of part-time
employees and students.   The size of the teaching staff is
180 full-time and 235 part-time.   The duties and responsibilities of each staff member: The Dean who is administratively responsible for the program of continuing education;
The Director of Evening College and Summer Sessions; five
Assistant Directors who are assistants to the Director; one
secretary to the Evening College.   For an enrollment of
5, 000 fifteen staff members are needed for credit programs
and five staff members for non-credit courses, etc.   Evening College and Summer School administration is one and
the same.

VII.   EDUCATIONAL TELEVISION PROGRAMS

Two credit courses are offered in Educational Television.   Residence credit is given for these courses.   Students come to campus on five Saturday mornings every semester for two hours and forty minute classes with the instructor of the TV course.   These credits will count toward
a degree.   The Evening College handles registration for the
TV courses which is conducted during regular registration
and at the first semester meeting.   There is limited supervision for these two courses from the School of Education
and Arts and Sciences along with the Evening College.   Full-
time faculty are employed.   These two undergraduate courses
are financed through the total budget.   "We do not charge
out-of-state fees for Evening College students since they are
presumed to be state residents. "   These courses are scheduled on Tuesdays and Thursdays, 3:30-4:00 p. m. and Mondays and Wednesdays, 4:00-4:30 p. m.   VCU Health Sciences
Division makes considerable use of television in its normal
instructional program.   At the Academic Division we still
think educational television will play a larger role in adult
education in the years ahead.

VIII.   NON-CREDIT PROGRAMS

Non-credit programs are offered but are limited to
the area of Business and Management. Management Center
reports directly to School of Business for immediate supervision and budgeting.   They are offered in other areas.   The
program is expected to pay for itself.   Remuneration for
faculty teaching a non-credit course varies.   Courses vary
from six to fourteen weeks in length and remuneration varies
from $12 to $20 an hour.   This remuneration depends upon
qualifications of both instructor and area of instruction.
There is flexibility to cooperate with conferences and institutes via the Management Center and directly out of a limited
Center for Continuing Education.   VCU is able to get considerable teaching and leadership talent free for the asking
and the arranging.   Occasionally the pay for clinicians is as
high as $100 per day plus expenses.   Conference sponsor-
ship is limited in comparison to many large state universities.   The total program planning, admissions, registration and all Summer School operations--6231 students in
1971--handled by the same Summer School-Evening College
office.

IX.   GENERAL

Students have little opportunity to participate in discussions regarding academic programs.   Innovative practices
used are five classes taught by educational television, 500-
600 adult students attend classes on Saturday mornings.   Adequate support is given to the evening program.   The Director
of Continuing Education is responsible to the Vice-President
of Academic Affairs and the Provost.

X.   STUDENT RECRUITMENT

The Evening College catalog is published as a 28-page
tabloid size insert annually.   Radio and television publicity
are used.   Occasional letters are sent to business and industry and to various civic organizations concerning programs.

Washburn University of Topeka
Topeka, Kansas
Department of Continuing Education

Total Enrollment 4, 500   Public Institution
Evening Enrollment 1, 000   Semester System

L   ADMISSION POLICIES

The deadline for application for admission to evening classes is three weeks before registration. A student may register conditionally for credit courses before transcripts are submitted. Special students may take a maximum of eighteen semester hours for credit before matriculation. Admission requirements for special students include good standing at previous institution or out of college at least one year. For regular students the requirements are high school graduation, ACT scores, and a physical examination for those taking over six hours. No mail registration is used. Retention policies: one to ten hours - no GPA; eleven to thirty-two hours - 1. 5; thirty-three to fifty-four hours - 1. 8; over fifty-four, 2. 0. The Academic Policy Committee formulates the admission policies for evening students. The Director of Admissions sets policies for special students. Day and evening students enroll in the same classes. No orientation program is planned for evening students. Undergraduate degrees require five hours in eight or nine general education groups including composition; 124 hours are required to complete the degree and thirty-three hours required for graduate programs.

II.   TERMINOLOGY

Title of Division: Department of Continuing Education. Defined: Community services as opposed to classical degree seeking concept applied to other students.

III.   FEES

There is no fee differential for day and evening classes. Refund policies: Graduated refunds over the first five weeks for withdrawals - partial or total.

IV.   FACULTY AND FACULTY RECRUITMENT

Approximately 50% of the faculty teaching evening classes are full-time but no full-time faculty teach exclusive-

ly in the evening. The Director has the final authority for
hiring faculty members for evening classes. A maximum
of three credit hours of overload are permitted each semester for faculty members. Only 1% of the budget is spent on
recruiting. Salary for part-time faculty is $160 per; the
same for overload.

V. SCHEDULING

The Director is responsible for the evening class
schedule with recommendations made by the various departments. Most three-hour classes are scheduled two nights a
week; a few meet one night a week. Day and evening classes
are approximately equal in quality. Students range of performance is greater than in day classes. Part-time evening
students are eligible for the Dean's List after accumulating
twelve hours. Normally, fifteen students constitute a class.

VI. ORGANIZATIONAL STRUCTURE

Administrative staff consists of nine staff members
and the teaching staff consists of 100 part-time faculty members. The Director, Assistant Director administer the evening college and Forley AFB program along with other special programming. The ideal staff for specific enrollments
is difficult to estimate where administrative responsibilities
are decentralized.

VII. EDUCATIONAL TELEVISION PROGRAMS

Educational television courses are offered both for
credit and non-credit. All courses offered at the institution
are for residence credit. Department chairmen are responsible for supervising their own courses. Both full and part-
time faculty are used for television and are credited with
three hours for each credit hour taught. Registration is
handled by the Department of Continuing Education either by
mail or in person. Financing is covered by a general fund
and tuition is the same as for on-campus students. Classes
are scheduled in the afternoon and evening, i. e. , 3 p. m. and
10 p. m. The program is in the process of being expanded.

VIII. NON-CREDIT PROGRAMS

Non-credit programs are offered in the areas of Business and Management, Arts and Sciences, and in Education,
Engineering and other areas. Courses are expected to pay

for themselves.   Remuneration for faculty is $10 per hour.
Secretarial Seminars, Arts Council Seminars, Conferences
of Aging, Urban Policy Conferences, etc. are sponsored by
the Department.   Pay scale for clinicians varies.   Sponsorship
is usually in cooperation with one of the academic departments.   The Department of Continuing Education is responsible for the summer session.

IX.   GENERAL

Students have little opportunity to participate in discussions regarding the academic program.   Adequate stress
and financial support is given to the evening program.   The
Director of Continuing Education is responsible to the Vice-
President of Academic Affairs.

X.   STUDENT RECRUITMENT

News stories and special announcements are used for
publicity purposes.   Special contacts are made to business
and industry and to various clubs and organizations.

Washington University
St. Louis, Missouri
School of Continuing Education

Total Enrollment 11,597   Private Institution
Evening Enrollment 4,363   Semester System

I.   ADMISSION POLICIES

Deadline for application for admission is prior to the
beginning of the second week of courses.   Students may register for credit courses without transcripts on a provisional
basis.   Non-degree students may take a maximum of sixty
semester hours.   Admission requirements are high school
graduation, GED or special examination.   Mail registration
is used--registrations are accepted up to one week prior to
the opening of the semester.   Students must maintain a "C"
average after completion of thirty hours.   There is no special degree for adults.   Admission policies are set by the
administrative board of the School of Continuing Education
and the summer school.   Day and evening students may register for the same classes with the Dean's approval.   Suspension and probation occur with a grade point below 1.0.

Financial and disciplinary reasons may give rise to either. Special degree programs for adults offered in the evening are: Bachelor of Technology, B. S. in Systems and Data Processing, Industrial Management and Urban Affairs. During the fall quarter the enrollment was forty-three full-time and 3505 part-time students. The distribution requirements are: Composition and Rhetoric - 6, Humanities - 12, Social Sciences - 12, Science-Math - 12, Arts and Science electives - 12, with a total of 120 hours for completion. Areas of concentration are: Accounting, Business Administration, Chemistry, Economics, English, History, Industrial Management, Sociology, Systems and Data Processing (computer applications, computer electronics, electrical power, mechanical design, structural design, thermo-mech energy). Credit requirements vary from 36 to 60 units. Admission requirements for the special degree programs are high school graduation or the equivalent.

II. TERMINOLOGY

Title of Division: School of Continuing Education. Defined: Including general evening degree and certificate work; also conferences, lectures, and other continuing activities including some professional education.

III. FEES

Day students pay $80 per semester hour, evening students pay $40 per semester hour. This is justified because the cost of instruction for the day is greater.

IV. FACULTY AND FACULTY RECRUITMENT

Approximately 21% of the faculty teaching evening classes are full-time. Final authority to hire evening faculty lies with the Dean of the School of Continuing Education. The Dean also has the authority to reject a faculty member if he is unsatisfactory. A faculty member who participates in courses on an overload basis can do so only when the amount received does not exceed 20% of his regular salary. Salary ranges from $185 to $285 per unit for part-time faculty.

V. SCHEDULING

The Dean of the School of Continuing Education is responsible for the evening class schedule. Three credit hour courses are scheduled one night a week, except when labora-

tories are involved. There is no Dean's List at Washington
University. Twelve students constitute a class. The instructor is paid 75% of tuition collected when the class is
less than twelve.

VI. ORGANIZATIONAL STRUCTURE

Twenty-one staff members are included in the administrative staff. The Dean is responsible for the development and implementation of policies regarding the administration of the School of Continuing Education; the Assistant
Dean and Director is responsible for the implementation of
policies regarding the conduct of credit and non-credit programs in University College; the Director of Summer School
and Assistant Dean is responsible, as the planner and executive of summer courses for both the day and evening divisions; Director of Residential Adult Education Center is responsible for the overall upkeep of the facilities, staff and
food service and for the scheduling of all conferences and
short courses; the Director of Conferences and Institutes administers the policies regarding the planning and/or development of all conferences, workshops, institutes associated
with Washington University and its resources both on and
off campus; the Director of Admissions and Adult Counseling
Service administers policies regarding the administration and
retention of all students in University College and is responsible for the conduct of the Adult Counseling Service; the Business Manager maintains financial records as appropriate
dealing with income and expenditures of the School of Continuing Education.

VII. EDUCATIONAL TELEVISION PROGRAMS

No educational television programs are offered.

VIII. NON-CREDIT PROGRAMS

Non-credit programs are offered in the areas of Business and Management, Arts and Sciences, Education, Engineering and Urban Affairs. There is a budget for non-
credit programs but the programs are expected to pay for
themselves. Remuneration is determined by faculty rank and
area of instruction. Clinicians receive from $50 to $500
per day for conferences and institutes sponsored by the School
of Continuing Education. The School is responsible for the
summer session.

IX. GENERAL

Students participation in discussions regarding the academic program with day faculty and evening administrators in the Committee on Academic Policy.   In general, all evening divisions are not receiving adequate support.   The Dean is responsible to the Vice Chancellor and Associate Provost.   Audio-visual instructional aids are available for evening classes.

X. STUDENT RECRUITMENT

Newspaper, radio and television publicity is used. Brochures and special contacts are made by some departments.

University of Washington
Seattle, Washington
Evening Classes

Total Enrollment 32, 500   Public Institution
Evening Enrollment 993   Quarter System
Day /Evening 4, 024

I. ADMISSION POLICIES

The deadline for application for admission for all categories of students is June 1, July 15, February 1, November 1 and May 5.   Students may not register for credit courses before transcripts are submitted.   Non-matriculating students may take any amount of work for credit.   Students, rejected for regular admission, are not advised to enroll in evening classes.   Mail registration is not used.   Policies regarding suspension and probation are the same as for the day school and the evening classes have been integrated into the day curriculum for all students.   Examinations such as the ACT and CEEB are required for matriculated, adult students and are used as a basis for admission.   No different degree program is offered in Evening Classes for adults.   A study is being conducted on a special degree program for adults.   The administration and faculty formulate the admission policies for all students.   In all cases, matriculated students have a priority over non-matriculated students in enrolling for day and evening classes.   This allows adults to mingle with regular students and vice versa.   An orienta-

tion program is held for matriculating students at the same
time as the regular university program.   There is no evening advisory committee.   The admission to Evening Classes
is limited by the enrollment limitations of the University and
the fact that they are integrated with the day classes.

II.   TERMINOLOGY

Title of Division: Evening Classes.   Defined: All
classes held on campus from 5:30 p. m. and after.   Continuing Education defined: Learning experiences organized on a
systematic basis for persons over 21 years of age who cannot for their own reasons be full-time regular students.

III.   FEES

There is no fee differential between day and evening
classes.   The refund policies for evening students are the
same as for the day program.

IV.   FACULTY AND FACULTY RECRUITMENT

There is no policy regarding the percentage of faculty
for evening classes that are full-time faculty members.   The
related academic departments, with the approval of the Director of Evening Classes, has the final authority for hiring
full/part-time faculty members.   The Director has veto
power in regard to assigned faculty.   No full-time faculty
members are employed to teach exclusively in the evening.
The Director cannot engage an instructor without the consent
of the department head.   Regular faculty meetings are not
held.   Faculty members are encouraged to participate in all
types of courses as well as seminars and conferences.   No
budget is spent on recruitment.   Salaries range from $16 to
$20 per contact hour for part-time faculty.

V.   SCHEDULING

The Director is mutually responsible for the evening
class schedule with the academic departments.   Departments
make forecasts which are compiled into a schedule.   Three-
hour classes are scheduled one night a week--one night preferred.   There is no research project in print.   Day and
evening classes are equal in terms of quality.   Part-time
students are eligible for the Dean's List.   Evening classes
are supported entirely by State funds.   Cancellation of a
class depends upon the instructor.

VI. ORGANIZATIONAL STRUCTURE

The administrative staff consists of six staff members and 177 part-time faculty members. The positions of the staff are: the Director who is responsible for the administration of all credit classes after 5:30 p. m. which are offered at the University. The Division of Evening Studies is one of five divisions within Continuing Education which includes: Division of Evening Classes, Division of Continuing Studies, Division of Independent Studies, Division of Extension Services and Division of Community Development. The Division of Continuing Studies is responsible for residential seminars, lecture-discussion series, non-credit courses, women's studies, Title I, HEA Programs, State Technical Service Program and Young People's Program. The Division of Extension Services is responsible for short lectures and concerts, radio broadcast services, short courses and conferences, statewide art extension, telecourses and Civil Defense Training.

VII. EDUCATIONAL TELEVISION PROGRAMS

Non-credit educational television programs are offered. Students do not receive residence or extension credit. An attempt is being made to set up a program offering telecourses for credit which will count toward a degree. The television coordinator and manager of the telecourses supervises the program. Professors are paid on a per program basis and paid to produce a viewer's guide. Full-time faculty members receive additional remuneration for teaching courses on TV. At the present time, there are no registration procedures. A proposal has been made that registration for courses for credit be handled by the Division of Independent Study. Primarily, the educational television programs are financed through State funds. There is a small return from the sale of guides and other services. Telecourses presently run on educational channel at 7 p. m. Mondays, 9:30 p. m. Thursdays, 4 p. m. Monday, Wednesday and Fridays; 12:30 p. m. Tuesdays and Thursdays. The series also run on commercial TV stations throughout the State at various times--usually early morning.

VIII. NON-CREDIT PROGRAMS

Non-credit courses are offered in areas of Business and Management, Arts and Sciences, Engineering, Education and others. A budget is set up but the programs are partially self-sustaining. The compensation to instructors varies greatly depending upon the character and length of the course. Generally speaking, however, the instruction is at a rate of $12 to $18 per contact hour. Evening Classes sponsored 103 conferences and institutes during the past year on a great variety of subjects. Conferences are sponsored by the Division in cooperation with other academic departments, colleges and schools.

IX. GENERAL

Many students participate as members of committees in an advisory capacity. The Evening Classes operate under an enrollment limitation of 32,000 for the University. A recent innovation was to permit adults to register on a space available basis in all credit classes if they can obtain the permission of the instructor, by paying a regular fee through a highly simplified registration process. Evening Classes receives adequate support as it is an integrated program and the administration does recognize the need for adult education. The Director is responsible to the President of the University. Substantial audio-visual and technical instructional aids are available.

X. STUDENT RECRUITMENT

Student recruiting is done through newspapers, radio and television with appeals made to industry and organizations.

Wayne State University
Detroit, Michigan
Division of Urban Extension

Total Enrollment 33,000   Public Institution
Evening Enrollment 12,000   Trimester System

I. ADMISSION POLICIES

No deadline is set for application for admission to evening classes. A student may register for credit classes before transcripts are submitted. "Special" students may take an unlimited number of credit hours before matriculation. Admission requirements for "special" students: undergraduate - none; baccalaureate degree for graduate course offerings; regular students admission requirements vary according to the various schools within the University. No ACT or CEEB scores are required. Mail registration is used. Complete packets are returned to the Extension office for pre-processing and then sent on to the Registrar's Office. No orientation program is held for evening students. Probation and suspension policies: A "C" average or better is required for undergraduates; a "B" average for graduate students. Those on probation who do not improve their grades are required to withdraw. No special degree program is offered for adults. Admission policies for extension students are formulated by the Division of Urban Extension in concert with the schools and colleges of the University.

II. TERMINOLOGY

Title of Division: Division of Urban Extension. Defined: The extension of programming of the University to an urban setting.

III. FEES

There is some difference between courses taught on campus and extended campus courses. A graduated refund policy is used.

IV. FACULTY AND FACULTY RECRUITMENT

Approximately 70-80% of the faculty teaching evening classes are full-time but no full-time faculty members teach exclusively in the evening. The department chairmen and the Director of the Division of Urban Extension have the authority to hire full/part-time faculty. No more than one course per term may be taught on an overload basis. The salary range for part-time faculty is $10 - $25 per contact class hour. Overloads are paid at the rate of $525 for Assistant Professor; $625, Associate Professor; $750, Professor. An instructor's salary is not reduced for teaching a class below the minimum size. A minimum of twelve to fifteen students constitute a class.

V. SCHEDULING

The Director of Urban Extension is responsible for the evening class schedule which is based upon the "interest and goals of the students and the availability of the faculty." Three-hour classes meet one night per week. Day and eve-

ning classes are comparable in terms of quality.   Part-time
extension students are not eligible for the Dean's List.

VI.   ORGANIZATIONAL STRUCTURE

The Division of Urban Extension is headed by a Dean;
the administrative staff consists of twenty-eight professional
staff members with twenty-four clerical and technical employees.   The teaching staff consists of 495 part-time teachers for credit and non-credit courses.   The Dean is responsible for the overall administrative policies, including the
budget.   He also acts as Executive Director of Detroit Ad-
venture--a cultural unit.   The Assistant Dean has the normal
responsibilities for this office and directs the credit programs'
unit.   Each unit has a Director who is responsible for the
credit and non-credit courses, conferences and institutes in
his area.   He assumes responsibility and overall supervision
and works with the budget.   The Assistant to the Dean is
responsible for the overall fiscal matters, approves all expenditures and is responsible for many administrative functions within the Office of the Dean.   The Director of Non-
credit Programs is responsible for the University Center for
Adult Education and the Applied Management and Technology
Center.   The Director of Conferences and Institutes Center
is responsible for programs offered at the Center.   The Assistant Director of Detroit Adventure is responsible for the
cultural activities sponsored by twenty-two member institutions comprising this group.   The Director of the Scientific
and Technical Information Center publishes digests on air
and water quality control for subscriptions.   He prepares
scientific information.   The Associate Director of the Credit
Programs Office is responsible for the administration and
coordination of the program and the program budget.   The
Program Coordinators (one each for Education, Liberal Arts,
Business Management and Engineering) work with college
units on courses and teaching staff.

VII.   EDUCATIONAL TELEVISION PROGRAMS

Credit courses are offered by the Division of Urban
Extension on educational television.   Students may earn residence credit.   On the cumulative record, however, they are
identified as having been taken "off-campus. "   These courses
do count toward a degree.   Usually television courses are
taught by members of the regular professional staff.   The
Program Coordinator is the liaison with the various departments.   Teachers may enroll for "certificate" credits in the

Extension Division prior to formal admission to a higher degree program. The registration office handles registration for educational TV. Instructor salaries are paid on the overload basis for TV courses; the commercial TV station absorbs other costs as a public service. No out-of-state tuition is charged. Courses are scheduled from 6:30 to 7 a. m. or 7:00 to 7:30 a. m. daily.

VIII. NON-CREDIT PROGRAMS

The Division of Urban Extension does offer non-credit courses in Business and Management, Arts and Sciences, Education and Engineering. One unit (UCAE) is in cooperation with the University of Michigan. There is a budget for several administrators which pays only a fraction of the program costs. Practically 90% of the program is self-sustaining. The salary rate for teaching non-credit programs depends upon the qualifications of the instructor and the length of the course. For example, the salary stipend for teaching a two-hour course meeting sixteen weeks is as follows: Associate Professor and UCAE Lecturer $512, Professor $576. The stipend also varies for off-campus teaching within and beyond a 30-mile radius. The Division sponsors conferences and institutes. Typical programs include: Treatment of Rheumatic Arthritis, Michigan Concern for Children and Youth, Behavior Modifications, Successful Programs, Industrial Toxicology, etc. The stipend for clinicians for conferences varies depending upon the topic, qualifications of the lecturer and other variables. The Division is responsible for the summer session.

IX. GENERAL

Students have little opportunity to discuss the academic programs except by informal discussion. Adequate stress and financial support are given to the evening program. The Director of Urban Extension is responsible to the Dean and the Vice-President for Academic Affairs.

X. STUDENT RECRUITMENT

Newspaper ads and news stories are used for publicity as well as radio and television. Contacts are made with business and industry and also with various civic organizations to publicize the special programs offered by the Division.

University of West Florida
Pensacola, Florida
Office of Continuing Education

Total Enrollment 3, 500   Public Institution
Evening Enrollment 715   Jr. , Sr. , and Grad.
(Winter Quarter)   level courses - only
                                             Quarter System

I.   ADMISSION POLICIES

Registration by mail is used for off-campus credit
courses offered through continuing education. The student
may register at either the first or second class meeting and
mail in his registration materials with fees before a particular deadline date each quarter. No application for admission is required. Before completing fifteen hours, a student
may apply for admission to a degree program and if approved, apply his off-campus work toward a degree.

II.   TERMINOLOGY

Title of Division: Continuing Education. Defined:
The function of continuing education at the University of West
Florida is to administer off-campus credit courses and both
on and off campus non-credit courses. It is that service
that allows opportunities for individuals who are unable to
pursue full-time programs to fulfill both degree studies and
personal educational goals.

III.   FEES

Off-campus courses are $3. 00 per quarter credit
hour more than an individual course on-campus. Extra expense is involved in setting up off-campus courses which
justifies the increase in the cost.

IV.   FACULTY AND FACULTY RECRUITMENT

Off-campus courses are taught primarily by regular
faculty members and in some cases by qualified adjunct instructors. Approximately 90% of the faculty is full-time.
Department chairmen have the final authority for hiring faculty members for evening classes. Compensation for participation in institutes, conferences and seminars cannot exceed 20% of an instructor's annual salary. Part-time faculty
are paid $750 to $1, 250 per credit course according to faculty rank; 9% of instructor's base pay for overloads.

V. SCHEDULING

The Director is responsible for the evening class
schedule which is compiled according to availability of instructors and off-campus sites. Most classes are five-hour
courses and are scheduled twice weekly in 2 1/2 hour segments. Fifteen students must register for a class in order
to have the class taught.

VL ORGANIZATIONAL STRUCTURE

The administrative staff consists of the Director who
administers off-campus credit programs and non-credit programs both on and off campus and who is responsible to the
Assistant Vice-President for Education, a Director of Adult
Education Center who administers off-campus university
center and is responsible to the Director of Continuing Education, a Director of Non-Credit Programs who administers
in-service training programs on a half-time basis and teaches
on a half-time basis and is responsible to the Assistant Vice-
President for Education. All academic and administrative
decisions are subject to the Board of Regents criteria.

VII. EDUCATIONAL TELEVISION PROGRAMS

The Division of Continuing Education does not offer
any educational television courses.

VIII. NON-CREDIT PROGRAMS

Non-credit programs are offered in Business and
Management, Arts and Sciences, Education and general sub-
jects. Such programs are expected to pay for themselves.
Faculty receives remuneration of $100 per day for daily
sessions, $25 per hour for nightly sessions. The Division
does sponsor conferences, workshops and institutes such as:
Florida Association of Science Teachers, Second Annual
Management Conference (SAM), Case Studies in Industrial
Management, Effective Communication for Managers, etc.

IX. GENERAL

Student representatives attend University Council and
relevant meetings. Students are free to discuss any problems relating to the academic program. Graduate courses
for part-time students are offered both off and on campus
during the evening and can lead to degrees upon approval of

students program for adults.   The Evening Division lacks
sufficient staff in some areas.   Support is dependent upon
legislative apportionment.   The Director is responsible to
the Assistant Vice-President for Education.   Audio-visual
aids are available through the Audio-Visual Department.   The
Office of Continuing Education is responsible for two off-
campus university centers, at Eglin AFB and at Panama
City.

X.   STUDENT RECRUITMENT

Courses are publicized through all available media.

Western New England College
Springfield, Massachusetts
Evening Division

Total Enrollment 3, 000   Private Institution
Evening Enrollment 2, 003   Semester System

I.   ADMISSION POLICIES

There is no deadline for application for admission to
evening classes.   A student may register for credit courses
before transcripts are submitted.   Special students may take
a maximum of thirty-six hours before matriculation.   Admission requirements for special students include the ability
to handle the course offered.   Regular students must have
sixteen acceptable units of high school credit (each degree
has particular demands).   No ACT or CEEB scores are required for admission.   No mail registration is used.   Retention policies: Two years on probation followed by separation from the college.   A second separation is permanent.
The institution is considering offering a special degree program for adults which will be an Associate Degree in General Education after sixty - sixty-six hours of three/four
years of evening work.   The Director of Admissions formulates the admission policies for evening students with the
advice and consent of the Academic Deans.   Day and evening
students may enroll in the same classes.   No orientation
program is held for evening students.

II.   TERMINOLOGY

Title of Division: Evening Division of WNEC.   Defined: "It's college with the sun set. "

III. FEES

Fees for day and evening students are about the same with the exception that day students pay a "lump" sum and evening students pay $40 per semester hour.   Refund policy: A refund schedule varying from 100% to 0% after five weeks of class but only to those with doctor's excuses or those who move away by company order.

IV.   FACULTY AND FACULTY RECRUITMENT

Every day faculty member, with few exceptions, is expected to teach one and only one evening class at extra pay.   Approximately 40% of the faculty teaching evening classes are full-time but no full-time faculty members teach exclusively in the evening.   The Dean of the subject matter field has the final authority for hiring faculty members for the evening classes - with the advice and consent of the Evening Director.

V.   SCHEDULING

The Director of the Evening Division is responsible for the evening class schedule.   Students tentatively select courses for next year in March.   The results dictate next year's schedule.   Three-hour classes meet two evenings per week.   According to the Director, twice a week is preferred by 96% of the students.   Comparison of day and evening classes: "Evening classes are better - students are more serious minded. "   Part-time evening students are eligible for the Dean's List by accumulating eighteen credit hours with a GPA of 3. 0.

SECTIONS VI. -VII. -VIII.

No information received.

IX.   GENERAL

Students have very little opportunity to participate in any discussions regarding the academic program.   Innovative practices: Calculus and Physics are studied together for half a night each, twice a week.   In this college, the evening college "supports the day division. "   The Director of the Evening Division is responsible to the Academic Vice-President.

X. STUDENT RECRUITMENT

News releases are used for publicity as well as radio
and television and various mailings to business and industry.

Wichita State University
Wichita, Kansas
Division of Continuing Education

Total Enrollment 12, 500   State Institution
Evening Enrollment 3, 200   Semester System

I. ADMISSION POLICIES

The deadline for application for admission for all students is two weeks prior to registration. Students may register before transcripts are submitted, provisionally, after
all others have enrolled. All students must be admitted to
the University before enrolling in Credit Courses. Unless
they are degree-bound there is no limit on the number of
hours they may accumulate in Continuing Education. Admission requirements for all students are graduation from Kansas High School or upper-half of high school class if out-of-
state. Students who are rejected for admission as regular
students are not advised to enroll as evening students, nor
are they automatically accepted. Mail registration is used
provided the student has pre-registered. Packets are mailed
out one month in advance of registration with a cut-off for
return one week preceding opening of registration. A student
will be placed on probation for the next term in which he en-
rolls if his cumulative grade point index falls below the requirements of the college in which he is enrolled. Probation
is removed when the cumulative grade point index reaches
the required level. This applies to all students. ACT and
CEEB examinations are not required of adults. A degree
program, different from the day program, is not offered for
adults enrolled in the evening session. No plans are being
made to offer a special degree program for adults. The Admissions Committee formulates the admission policies for
all categories of undergraduate students and the Graduate Admissions Committee formulates the policies for graduate students. Day and evening students may enroll in the same
class 100%. The advantages of this is flexibility for students; better utilization of faculty and a healthier educational
climate for all. An orientation program is held during reg-

istration. The Continuing Education Committee functions in a technical and advisory capacity and is not concerned with policy.

II. TERMINOLOGY

Title of Division: Division of Continuing Education. Defined: Non-degree bound at the institution. Students begin where they are and continue their education on both the Credit-Non-Credit and formal-informal bases.

III. FEES

There is no fee differential between day and evening classes; refunds are made on a graduated scale for complete withdrawal but no refund is permitted for partial withdrawal.

IV. FACULTY AND FACULTY RECRUITMENT

There is no rigid policy regarding the percentage of full-time faculty for evening classes; approximately 75% are full-time. The Department Chairmen have final authority for hiring full and/or part-time faculty members and the director may reject a faculty member only by persuasion. No full-time faculty members are employed who teach exclusively in the evening. The director may not engage an instructor without the consent of the department head unless this person refuses to staff the classes. There are no overloads for credit. Payment may be made on non-credit if it does not exceed one credit hour equivalent per semester. There is no restriction on one-time speakers for conferences, etc. 5% of the budget is spent on recruitment. The salary range for part-time faculty is $135 per credit hour. Salary is not allowed for overloads except in emergencies; then it is negotiated.

V. SCHEDULING

The director is not responsible for the evening class schedule except by request and persuasion; the department heads arrange this schedule. This is developed by the Department Chairmen and modified, sometimes, by Continuing Education Committee request. The director may revise/make additions to the schedule only with the consent of the chairmen of the departments. Three hour classes are scheduled two nights per week for undergraduates, especially in the lower division courses. A research project, Continuing Education for Women, is in progress. Comparison of day and evening classes in terms of quality is done only informally by faculty teaching day and night concurrently. Part-time evening students are eligible for the Dean's List if they carry a 12-hour load and maintain a 3. 250 grade point. Although it varies usually 10 students in a lower division course must register for a class in order to have it taught. The instructor's compensation is not reduced when he teaches a class below the minimum size.

VI. ORGANIZATIONAL STRUCTURE

The administrative staff consists of seven staff members and 10 part-time (all non-credit) teaching staff. The positions of the staff are the Director, the Director of Non-Credit Programs, a Counsellor and a Coordinator of special programs.

VII. EDUCATIONAL TELEVISION PROGRAMS

No educational television programs are offered.

VIII. NON-CREDIT PROGRAMS

Non-credit courses are offered in the areas of business and management, arts and sciences and fine arts. The non-credit courses are expected to be self-supporting except for administrative staff expenses and facilities. Remuneration for all faculty teaching non-credit courses varies with each course. The following conferences are sponsored: Community Improvement, Secretarial Seminar; Media and the Humanities; Opportunities for Women (2) and Extra Dimension. Clinicians receive $100 per day. Conferences are usually sponsored with another department or college but are not required. The evening program is not responsible for the Summer session.

IX. GENERAL

Courses, credit and/or non-credit, are offered in locations off-campus for the economically deprived populations. Students participate in discussion regarding the academic program by broad representation on committees. No graduate programs for part-time students are offered by the Evening Division. Adequate support is not given to the evening division because of failure to increase the staff and an insufficient budget. The Director of the Division of Continuing Education is responsible to the Vice-President of Academic Affairs. All audio-visual and technical instructional aids on campus are available to the evening program. There is no active Chapter of Alpha Sigma Lambda.

X. STUDENT RECRUITMENT

Student recruitment is carried on through publicity in newspapers, radio, T. V. and appeals to industry and organizations.

<u>College of William and Mary</u>
Williamsburg, Virginia
School of Continuing Studies

Total Enrollment 4, 200   Public Institution
Evening Enrollment 1, 250   Semester System
Fall Quarter Enrollment 1, 085

I. ADMISSION POLICIES

There is no deadline for application for admission to evening classes. Students may enroll provisionally for credit courses before transcripts are submitted. Degree students adhere to regular college policies. "Special" students may take a maximum of 18 semester hours for credit before matriculation. Admission requirements for non-degree or "special" students include "evidence of good standing in the institution previously attended." For regular students, the regular college admission requirements for the program in which the student is enrolled apply, including the ACT or CEEB scores. Mail registration is used. Students previously admitted and in good standing submit a "Request for Mail Registration" form from the bulletin with tuition check. The office staff types necessary registration forms from the request. There are no retention policies for the non-matriculated students--"they are self-eliminating." Non-degree or "Special" students who cannot perform adequately eliminate themselves. The evening degree program for adults is the same as the day degree program. The Director of the Evening College with the approval of the Admissions Committee formulates the admission policies for evening students, with the School offering the degree for regular degree students and the Faculty of the School of Continuing Studies formulates the policies of the non-matriculating, non-degree or "Special" students. Day students must have special permission from their Dean to enroll in the evening classes. No orientation program is held for evening students.

II. TERMINOLOGY

Title of Division: School of Continuing Studies (Evening College is a unit of Continuing Studies). Defined: Programs primarily for mature adults who find it necessary or desirable to continue their formal education on a part-time basis.

III. FEES

Day and evening students pay the same fees. Refund policies: 1) mail registrants who withdraw prior to regular registration receive full refund minus $5.00 processing fee; 2) withdrawal prior to deadline (2nd week) 75% refund. No refunds are given after the second week.

IV. FACULTY AND FACULTY RECRUITMENT

Approximately 90% of the faculty teaching evening classes are full-time and no full-time faculty members teach exclusively in the evening. The Dean of Continuing Studies with the cooperation of department heads has the final authority for hiring full and part-time faculty members. No faculty meetings are held for evening faculty. Most faculty members are allowed one class as an overload for which they receive additional compensation. The salary range for part-time faculty is three credit courses $675-$825; for overloads, depending upon rank, $750-$825 for three credit hour courses. A minimum of 10 required for a class to be taught. The instructor's compensation is not reduced when he teaches the class below the minimum size.

V. SCHEDULING

The Dean is responsible for the evening class schedule which is based upon the estimated needs of the students, available faculty, etc. Three-hour classes are scheduled one night per week. Day and evening classes compare favorably in quality. Part-time evening students are not eligible for the Dean's List.

VI. ORGANIZATIONAL STRUCTURE

The administrative staff of Continuing Studies consists of one staff member and 1 1/2 clerical staff members. The teaching staff varies by the semester. The Dean is responsible for the entire continuing education program at the policy level. The Assistant Dean is responsible for directing operation of Evening College and Division of Extension. The Assistant Director/Directors work in the field, largely administering off-campus program for a specific area. Conferences and Institutes are presently coordinated by the Associate Dean. The Director of Extension is also the Associate Dean. There is also a director of the Summer session--responsible for planning and administering the entire Summer program.

VII. EDUCATIONAL TELEVISION PROGRAMS

Credit courses are offered in Educational Television but the College does not generate any. Students only earn extension credit. These courses count toward a degree, subject to the approval of the Academic Dean. The Continuing Studies staff supervises the educational television courses. The program for teachers is a program of the School of Education and the Faculty of Arts and Sciences and is administered by the School of Continuing Studies in the evening, summer and in the field. The Continuing Studies staff supervise these courses, and also the registration. These courses are financed by tuition and are scheduled at times convenient to public school teachers (evenings or Saturdays).

VIII. NON-CREDIT PROGRAMS

There are non-credit courses offered occasionally upon request. There is no budget as this program is expected to pay for itself. The School of Continuing Studies sponsors conferences and institutes. Two such conferences were: "Instrumentation Short Course" and "A Title VIII Conference" offered in June of 1970. The stipend for clinicians varies. Both qualified faculty members of the institution and visiting lecturers are used for these conferences. The School of Continuing Studies is responsible for the Summer session at the institution.

IX. GENERAL

Students have little opportunity to participate in any

discussion regarding the academic program. More stress
and financial support could be given to the evening program.
The administration generally recognizes the importance and
the need of the adult evening program.

X. STUDENT RECRUITMENT

News stories are placed in the newspapers, and given
to radio and television, but the institution allows no advertising.

University of Windsor
Windsor, Ontario, Canada
Division of Extension

Total Enrollment 4, 200   Public Institution
Evening Enrollment 1, 973   Canadian System

I. ADMISSION POLICIES

The deadline for application for admission to evening
classes is August 15 (fall) and June 15 (summer). Students
may register for credit courses before transcripts are submitted only under exceptional circumstances. "Special" students may take six full courses for credit before matriculating. Non-matriculated or "special" students must be over
21 years of age and out of Grade 13 for two years or Grade
12 for three years in order to be admitted. Regular students are admitted after completing Grade 13 with 60% on
at least seven papers. Mail registration is used. The student clips the section from the brochure requesting materials
for registration by mail. If the course is approved, materials are sent and the student is registered by returning
them with a check for tuition. Retention policy is that a
student must pass four out of six and have a 50% average.
The Senate formulates the admission policies for evening
students. Day and evening students may enroll in the same
classes. Additional comments on admission: "We do demand
rather close counseling in the selection of each subject, insuring that it helps to fulfill degree requirements. "

II. TERMINOLOGY

Title of Division: Division of Extension. Defined:
An extension of the day program to those unable to attend in

the daytime.

III. FEES

Day and evening students pay the same fees. Refund policy: "Diminishing by certain percentage according to weekly segments. "

IV. FACULTY AND FACULTY RECRUITMENT

Approximately 98% of the faculty teaching evening classes are full-time but no full-time faculty members teach exclusively in the evening. The Dean of the Faculty has the final authority for hiring full and part-time faculty members for evening classes. No faculty meetings are held for evening faculty. The salary range for part-time faculty is the same as for full-time faculty. One sixth of the base salary for the rank is paid for faculty for overloads. There is no specific number of students required to constitute a class. The instructor's compensation is not reduced when he teaches a small class.

V. SCHEDULING

The Director of Extension is responsible for the evening class schedule. According to the Director, "We try to avoid difficult combinations, and keep courses and their prerequisites on the same evening. " Three hour classes meet one night per week. Day and evening classes are equal in quality. No Dean's List is published.

VI. ORGANIZATIONAL STRUCTURE

The Division of Continuing Education is one of the functions of the Extension Division. The major part of the work of the Division of Extension is devoted to credit work but it also handles a few non-credit courses which it considers under the heading of Continuing Education. It is not a separate structure and the details of the programs are part of the general duties of the regular Extension staff. In our estimation, the administrative staff required for the administration of an evening credit program with an evening enrollment of 300 to 500 would be two staff members; 800 to 2, 000 would be three staff members. It must be kept in mind that these figures are relative to the other services this operation would receive from such offices as Registrar and Treasurer.

VII.   EDUCATIONAL TELEVISION PROGRAMS

There are no courses offered using educational television.

VIII.   NON-CREDIT PROGRAMS

The Division offers non-credit courses in Business
and Management and Arts and Sciences.   This program is
expected to pay for itself.   The faculty, full or part-time,
receives one-sixth of the base salary depending upon the
lecturer's rank for teaching a non-credit course.   Non-faculty
receive two-thirds of this figure.   The remuneration depends
upon the qualification of the instructor.

IX.   GENERAL

Students have no opportunity to participate in any discussions regarding the academic program.   Adequate stress
and financial support are given to the evening program.   The
Director of Extension is responsible to the Academic Vice-
President.   Closed circuit television is used for some instruction.   The Division is responsible for the summer session.

X.   STUDENT RECRUITMENT

News stories and special ads are used for publicity.
No radio and television publicity are used.   No contact is
made with business or industry.

Xavier University
Cincinnati, Ohio
Evening College

Total Enrollment 6, 100   Church-related Institution
Evening Enrollment 1, 400   Semester System

I.   ADMISSION POLICIES

Deadline for application for admission to evening
classes is the official registration date.   If all credentials
are not in order at the time of registration, students are
allowed to register as special students only - pending receipt of transcripts.   A "Special" or non-matriculating student

may take up to six (6) hours credit unless he intends to be a full-time student but is awaiting arrival of transcripts. Admission requirements for special or non-matriculating students are high school graduation or over 21 years of age and high school graduation equivalency; for regular students the requirement is 50th percentile on tests or equivalent on high school testing program plus "C" average in high school. Students who are rejected for admission as regular day students are advised to apply as evening students but are not automatically accepted. It should be noted that 197 full-time students are enrolled in 12 or more semester hours and do not work at a full-time job. Mail registration is used for currently enrolled students who are counseled in advance and for others wishing to register for certain core courses. Probation relates to below 2.0 QPA with dismissal after two or more semesters without improvement. ACT or CEEB scores are not required but accepted in lieu of other tests. A BSBA in General Business and various associate degrees are offered as evening degree programs for adults. Total number of hours required to complete undergraduate degree is 120 (graduate 30) with majors in Elementary Education, Chemistry, Commercial Art, Economics, English, History, Political Science, Mathematics, Modern Languages, Philosophy, Sociology, Psychology, plus seven areas of concentration in the Bachelor of Science in Business Administration. A special degree program for adults is being considered but not yet formulated. The Dean is totally responsible for formulating admission policies for the evening college. The combined day/evening class situation provides a better cross section of age and experience. An orientation is conducted for evening students as well as a yearly convocation.

II. TERMINOLOGY

Title of Division: Evening College (which includes both credit and non-credit courses). Defined: An accredited four-year college granting bachelor and associate degrees but also offering special non-credit courses for adults. Continuing Education defined: A process through which a motivated individual may expand his education either on a credit or non-credit basis--or both--according to his own schedule.

III. FEES

There is a fee differential of $50 a semester for students not attending full-time. This is an activity fee-- not a tuition. Refunds are prorated by course according to a set schedule.

IV. FACULTY AND FACULTY RECRUITMENT

Approximately 60-70% of the faculty for evening classes is full-time. The Dean has full authority for hiring full/part-time faculty members for evening classes with the assistance of the department chairmen. The Dean can reject a faculty member who has been assigned. No full-time faculty teach exclusively in the evenings. A faculty meeting is held only once a year with evening faculty. Salary range for part-time faculty is $500-$560 for three hour courses.

V. SCHEDULING

The Dean is responsible for the evening class schedule with the cooperation and assistance of the department chairmen. The Dean does have authority to revise, add or delete, the schedule. Three-hour classes scheduled one night a week is preferred. An experiment of "Friday Night Adult Education Center" is now in progress. Using QPA and teacher appraisal there is a favorable comparison between day and evening classes in terms of quality. Part-time evening students are eligible for the Dean's List--Evening College Dean's List only--with 6. 0 semester hours at 3. 25. A minimum of eight registrants are required to teach a class. An instructor's compensation is reduced when he teaches a class below minimum size. If he is a part-time teacher or a full-time teacher on an overload he is paid $60. 00 per student when below eight if he agrees to teach the class.

VI. ORGANIZATIONAL STRUCTURE

The Dean is totally responsible for the administration of the Evening College. He is a member of fifteen university committees and teaches one graduate course per semester; the Assistant Dean runs the Summer school, teaches 1/2 load and assists in the evening college administration. Three full-time clerical assistants and the equivalent of one full-time counselor. Teaching staff consists of 100-120 full-time and 60-80 part-time (a variable of about 60-70% full-time--enough to staff 190-200 classes). The desired staff size would be five staff members for 300 students; six staff members for 1000 students, assuming that counseling is part of a staff job.

VII.   EDUCATIONAL TELEVISION PROGRAMS

Courses in "How to Teach" are offered on TV but others are seldom offered. Students do earn resident credit for the offering. The College of Education is responsible for supervising the course with normal registration procedures used.

VIII.   NON-CREDIT PROGRAMS

Non-credit programs are offered in Arts and Sciences, Business and Management, Education and Remedial. Programs are expected to pay for themselves. Remuneration for faculty is $200 per 16 clock hours. Appalachian Problems in Community was offered last year under the program of conferences and institutes. The Evening College is responsible for the Summer session.

IX.   GENERAL

Students participate in discussions regarding academic programs at their request or as members of committees. Graduate programs for part-time students are administered through the Graduate School with 3,000 registrants. Stress and financial support are adequate but not comparable with the day program. The Dean is responsible to the Academic Vice-President. Audio-visual instructional aids are complete and available.

X.   STUDENT RECRUITMENT

Publicity is used together with announcements on radio and television. All free media are used.